CREEDS, CONFESSIONS,
AND CATECHISMS

CREEDS, CONFESSIONS, AND CATECHISMS

A Reader's Edition

Edited by Chad Van Dixhoorn

WHEATON, ILLINOIS

Creeds, Confessions, and Catechisms: A Reader's Edition

Copyright © 2022 by Crossway

Published by Crossway
    1300 Crescent Street
    Wheaton, Illinois 60187

All rights reserved. No part of this publication may be reproduced, stored in a retrieval system, or transmitted in any form by any means, electronic, mechanical, photocopy, recording, or otherwise, without the prior permission of the publisher, except as provided for by USA copyright law. Crossway® is a registered trademark in the United States of America.

Supplemental material: Introductions to creeds, confessions, and catechisms copyright © 2019 by Crossway. Creeds, confessions, and catechisms were selected and introductions were prepared by Rev. Dr. Chad Van Dixhoorn. Special thanks to the Trinity Psalter Hymnal Joint Venture board for granting Crossway permission to use the creeds and confessional material found in the *Trinity Psalter Hymnal*. Chalcedonian Definition © Norman P. Tanner, ed., 2005, *Decrees of the Ecumenical Councils*, vol. 1, Burns & Oates, an imprint of Bloomsbury Publishing Plc. Used by permission. All rights reserved. Augsburg Confession adapted from *Concordia: The Lutheran Confessions—A Reader's Edition of the Book of Concord*, 2nd ed. © 2005, 2006 Concordia Publishing House. Used by permission. All rights reserved. Belgic Confession, Heidelberg Catechism, and Canons of Dort adapted from Doctrinal Standards as found in *Psalter Hymnal* (© 1987, 1988, Faith Alive Christian Resources / Christian Reformed Church in North America; Doctrinal Standards translations © 1985, 1986, 1988). Used by permission. All rights reserved. London Baptist Confession adapted from James M. Renihan, *Faith and Life for Baptists: The Documents of the London Particular Baptist Assemblies, 1689–1695* (RBAP, 2016).

Cover design: Jordan Singer

First printing 2022

Printed in China

All Scripture quotations in the book introduction are from the ESV® Bible (The Holy Bible, English Standard Version®), copyright © 2001 by Crossway, a publishing ministry of Good News Publishers. Used by permission. All rights reserved.

Hardcover ISBN: 978-1-4335-7987-5
ePub ISBN: 978-1-4335-8260-8
PDF ISBN: 978-1-4335-8258-5
Mobipocket ISBN: 978-1-4335-8259-2

Library of Congress Cataloging-in-Publication Data

Names: Van Dixhoorn, Chad B. editor.
Title: Creeds, confessions, and catechisms : a readers's edition / edited by Chad Van Dixhoorn.
Description: Wheaton, Illinois : Crossway, 2022. | Includes bibliographical references and index.
Identifiers: LCCN 2021033670 (print) | LCCN 2021033671 (ebook) | ISBN 9781433579875 (hardcover) | ISBN 9781433582585 (pdf) | ISBN 9781433582592 (mobipocket) | ISBN 9781433582608 (epub)
Subjects: LCSH: Creeds. | Catechisms.
Classification: LCC BT990 .C653 2022 (print) | LCC BT990 (ebook) | DDC 238—dc23
LC record available at https://lccn.loc.gov/2021033670
LC ebook record available at https://lccn.loc.gov/2021033671

Crossway is a publishing ministry of Good News Publishers.

RRDS			33	32	31	30	29	28	27	26	25	24	23
16	15	14	13	12	11	10	9	8	7	6	5	4	

CONTENTS

INTRODUCTION

Brief statements of key doctrines have been with us since the beginning of biblical history. They often focus on God and the way of salvation. Old Testament readers encounter in the capstone of the books of Moses, "Hear, O Israel: The LORD our God, the LORD is one" (Deut. 6:4). New Testament readers overhear Paul summarizing to the Corinthians his own teaching: "I delivered to you as of first importance what I also received: that Christ died for our sins in accordance with the Scriptures, that he was buried, that he was raised on the third day in accordance with the Scriptures, and that he appeared to Cephas, then to the twelve" (1 Cor. 15:3–5).

The desire to state truth openly is a basic Christian instinct. Cults hide things. Christ's disciples share what they have learned. Unsurprisingly, historians have found dozens of summaries of scriptural teaching from the centuries following the ascension of Christ and the deaths of his apostles. It was not unusual for such statements to begin with the Latin word *credo*, meaning, "I believe." These early creeds, like those in the Scriptures, often focused on what the church understood to be true about God; on what is and is not true about the person of Christ; or on what we must believe about the work of Christ as Savior.

As it happens, later creeds tended to be longer than earlier ones. By the time of the Protestant Reformation of the 1500s, so much had been learned—and so many doctrines were being disputed between the Reformers and Rome—that creeds were supplemented by longer lists of doctrines that Christians confessed. Creeds were still in use, most often in worship, but now confessions were written to explain what Lutheran and Reformed Christians believed. These documents carefully explained what doctrines were held in common with the old faith of Rome while also stating clearly where the Reformers were forced to disagree with Rome in their recovery of the teachings of the early church and, most basically, of the Bible. They also explained where the Reformers disagreed with one another.

Naturally, because confessions say more, more confessions were needed. Here we find a contrast with creeds. Creeds have a wide circulation among Christian churches. One creed can serve Baptists, Presbyterians, Anglicans, and Lutherans alike. But these communions needed something more precise than a creed if they were to possess working documents that united like-minded missionaries and church members, if they were to train teachers of the word successfully, or if they wished to advance clear communication between preachers and parishioners, with the one seeking a place to serve and the other seeking a pastor.

While not typically *used* in worship, these confessions were *useful* for worship. Careful distinctions provided richer material for praise than did broad generalizations. Saying more about the character of God and the grace of the gospel encouraged more confidence in prayer. Confessions also paid careful attention to precise terminology, a kind of labeling that promoted learning. Such a technique has proved useful in studies of the natural world and of language; it is useful in the study of the Bible, too.

Concerning justification, for example, the Scriptures speak of a righteousness of Christ credited to those who do not deserve it. They also speak of a free gift of forgiveness purchased by Christ for sinners. Sometimes the Bible tethers this righteousness to justification. And sometimes it ties forgiveness to justification. The authors of Reformation confessions noted these associations of words and ideas. They did not see tension or confusion. On the contrary, they concluded that *justification* must be the Bible's umbrella term for a credited righteousness, on the one hand, and divine forgiveness, on the other—two distinct but united aspects of the one doctrine of justification.

In light of such detail, discovered after careful study of the Scriptures, it is hardly possible for an attentive Christian to be content with only and always speaking of "salvation" in general. Once alert to fuller teaching, Christians ought to explain and then celebrate justification. And then one discovers adoption, then the blessing of sanctification, then perseverance, and so on. The Reformation-era confessions identify, explain, and celebrate these gifts with gratitude: through such statements we confess our faith to God and before the world.

Creeds, confessions, and catechisms most obviously serve a doctrinal purpose. Nonetheless, if they have sufficient gravitas, they enjoy an ecumenical purpose as well. These historic statements remind us that the content of the Christian faith does not continually change; they bring Christians of the present into conversation with Christians of the past. Classic creeds, confessions, and catechisms also remind us that we do not read the Bible only as individuals; we read it as one body, experiencing significant unity as we do so. These are things that a list of bullet points on a church website cannot do. Such lists may have the *form* of a creed, but they will never have the full *function* of a creed.

Four of the better-known creeds of the early church, two of which were written by ecumenical councils, are printed here for the use of individuals and churches. The confessions and catechisms that follow are particularly significant texts in Protestant history. These are defining documents for Lutherans, Anglicans, the Dutch Reformed, Presbyterians, and Baptists. Sometimes with slight adjustments, they have been used by many millions of Christians.

These creeds, confessions, and catechisms do not possess equal standing with Scripture—nothing could rise to the level of this library of sixty-six books from God. Creeds, confessions, and catechisms are useful only to the extent that they reproduce faithfully the teaching of Scripture itself. But they serve Christians well in their attempt to understand one another better; they help us to listen quietly when we too often talk noisily.

This book also may be a helpful teaching tool for churches, perhaps offering paragraphs that can be incorporated into worship in order to help God's people state what they believe, confess their sin, and profess faith in Christ, all by the power of his Spirit. And it may enable readers to benefit from a paragraph or a set of questions and answers that summarizes Christian truth in profoundly helpful ways.

Chad Van Dixhoorn
Editor

The Apostles' Creed

INTRODUCTION

The Apostles' Creed is both the best known and the least known of all postbiblical creeds. Its doctrine is apostolic, as it proclaims the high points of New Testament teaching. Elements of the Apostles' Creed are found in summaries of the faith by early Christian writers, with some lines matching word for word. Christians employ this creed in worship more than any other creed. Nonetheless, its origins are shrouded in mystery. We do not know who wrote this first-person statement of faith, even if we are sure that it was not written by any of the apostles themselves.

In this summary of the faith we find a basic call to believe in a God who is Father, Son, and Holy Spirit—the three headings organizing the creed. Here we confess a God who is both Father and Creator; a Savior who is God's Son and Mary's son; and a redeeming work that begins with humiliation and ends with exaltation. Here too we see a compressed account of the Holy Spirit's work in gathering the church—bringing Christians into communion with God and each other.

Perhaps the most useful feature of the creed is its balanced picture of Christ. This creed reminds us that the Lord who came first to rescue us will come a second time to judge us. This is what the church confesses in the Apostles' Creed: that we are saved by Jesus, from Jesus. It is on this basis alone that believers are now forgiven, will one day be raised, and will forever live with Christ.

THE APOSTLES' CREED

I believe in God the Father Almighty,
    Maker of heaven and earth.

I believe in Jesus Christ, his only-begotten Son, our Lord;
    who was conceived by the Holy Spirit, born of the Virgin Mary;
    suffered under Pontius Pilate;
    was crucified, dead, and buried;
    he descended into hell;
    the third day he rose again from the dead;
    he ascended into heaven,
    and sits at the right hand of God the Father Almighty;
    from there he shall come to judge the living and the dead.

I believe in the Holy Spirit;
    the holy catholic[1] church;
    the communion of saints;
    the forgiveness of sins;
    the resurrection of the body;
    and the life everlasting. Amen.

---

1   "Catholic" means universal; that is, there is one church across all times, places, and peoples.

The Nicene Creed

INTRODUCTION

The text customarily called the Nicene Creed has a three-part history in the Western church. The creed was issued as a brief statement at the Council of Nicaea (AD 325), while the First Council of Constantinople (381) later provided a substantial addition concerning the Holy Spirit. Thus historians term this creed the Niceno-Constantinopolitan Creed. Even later, a line in the creed was changed (in the Western church only) to capture the significant teaching that the Holy Spirit proceeds not only from the Father but from the Son as well. It is this fuller document in its Western form that is provided here.

The Nicene Creed contains many of the lines found in the Apostles' Creed, but it was written chiefly in response to minimizations and even denials of the divinity of Christ. Thus the creed asserts that Jesus is of the same (not similar) essence or substance as the Father. It states that he is begotten and not "made," unlike every other thing visible or invisible. Even the rhythmic phrases often translated "God of God, Light of Light, very God of very God" are connectional, equalizing phrases. They underline three times that the Son is "of" (in the sense of "from") the Father. These lines, taken with those about the Holy Spirit, are best read as reflections on the equality and closeness of the Three who are One. Together these lines form the most closely held and widely confessed statement about our triune God in the Christian church.

THE NICENE CREED

I believe in one God, the Father Almighty,
  Maker of heaven and earth, and of all things visible and
    invisible.

And in one Lord Jesus Christ, the only-begotten Son of God,
  begotten of the Father before all worlds;
  God of God, Light of Light, very God of very God;
  begotten, not made, being of one substance with the Father,
    by whom all things were made.
  Who, for us men and for our salvation,
    came down from heaven
    and was incarnate by the Holy Spirit of the Virgin Mary,
    and was made man;
  and was crucified also for us under Pontius Pilate;
  he suffered and was buried;
  and the third day he rose again, according to the Scriptures;
  and ascended into heaven, and sits on the right hand of the
    Father;
  and he shall come again, with glory, to judge the living and the
    dead;
    whose kingdom shall have no end.

And I believe in the Holy Spirit, the Lord and Giver of life;
  who proceeds from the Father and the Son;

who with the Father and the Son together is worshiped and
   glorified;
who spoke by the prophets.
And I believe in one holy catholic[1] and apostolic church.
I acknowledge one baptism for the remission of sins;
and I look for the resurrection of the dead,
   and the life of the world to come. Amen.

1   "Catholic" means universal; that is, there is one church across all times, places, and peoples.

The Athanasian Creed

INTRODUCTION

This account of the catholic or universal faith of the church further clarifies the doctrine of the Trinity. It also offers what is recognized as a classic statement on Christology. Dire warnings are attached for anyone who fails to hold unswervingly to the whole of the creed. As jarring as these notes sound to modern ears, they remind us that rightly knowing God has always been a matter of utmost importance to the church.

The main emphasis of the first part of the Athanasian Creed is the unity, distinctness, and equality of the divine persons. These traits are set out in nearly a dozen triads of assertions about the Father, Son, and Holy Spirit, sometimes in abstractions (they share the same "qualities") and sometimes in particulars (each is almighty, each is Lord). The painstaking care shown in the setting out of these points makes for clarity of presentation with minimal technical language.

The second part of the creed proclaims Jesus Christ as God and man equally, insisting on both the unity and also the distinctness of Christ's divinity and humanity. Without naming any particular heresy, the creed addresses those errors that supercharge Christ's humanity and those that allege that at the incarnation Christ became some new hybrid creation that was neither properly human nor fully divine.

Also called "The Exposition of the Catholic Faith" or "Quicumque Vult" (from its opening Latin words), the Athanasian Creed was thought in the Middle Ages to have been penned by Athanasius of Alexandria. The text first appeared about a century after his death, and, since attempts to identify its true author(s) have not yet been successful, many Christian communities have chosen to retain the name of Athanasius in connection to this creed.

THE ATHANASIAN CREED

[1] Whoever desires to be saved should above all hold to the catholic[1] faith. [2] Anyone who does not keep it whole and unbroken will doubtless perish eternally.

[3] Now this is the catholic faith: that we worship one God in Trinity and the Trinity in unity, [4] neither confounding their persons nor dividing the essence. [5] For the person of the Father is a distinct person, the person of the Son is another, and that of the Holy Spirit still another. [6] But the divinity of the Father, Son, and Holy Spirit is one, the glory equal, the majesty coeternal. [7] Such as the Father is, such is the Son and such is the Holy Spirit. [8] The Father is uncreated, the Son is uncreated, the Holy Spirit is uncreated. [9] The Father is immeasurable, the Son is immeasurable, the Holy Spirit is immeasurable. [10] The Father is eternal, the Son is eternal, the Holy Spirit is eternal. [11] And yet there are not three eternal beings; there is but one eternal being. [12] So too there are not three uncreated or immeasurable beings; there is but one uncreated and immeasurable being. [13] Similarly, the Father is almighty, the Son is almighty, the Holy Spirit is almighty. [14] Yet there are not three almighty beings; there is but one almighty being. [15] Thus, the Father is God, the Son is God, the Holy Spirit is God. [16] Yet there are not three gods; there is but one God. [17] Thus, the Father is Lord, the Son is Lord, the Holy Spirit is Lord. [18] Yet there are not three lords; there is but one Lord. [19] Just as Christian

---

1   "Catholic" means universal; that is, there is one church across all times, places, and peoples.

truth compels us to confess each person individually as both God and Lord, [20] so catholic religion forbids us to say that there are three gods or lords. [21] The Father was neither made nor created nor begotten from anyone. [22] The Son was neither made nor created; he was begotten from the Father alone. [23] The Holy Spirit was neither made nor created nor begotten; he proceeds from the Father and the Son. [24] Accordingly, there is one Father, not three fathers; there is one Son, not three sons; there is one Holy Spirit, not three holy spirits. [25] None in this Trinity is before or after, none is greater or smaller; [26] in their entirety the three persons are coeternal and coequal with each other. [27] So in everything, as was said earlier, the unity in Trinity, and the Trinity in unity, is to be worshiped. [28] Anyone then who desires to be saved should think thus about the Trinity.

[29] But it is necessary for eternal salvation that one also believe in the incarnation of our Lord Jesus Christ faithfully. [30] Now this is the true faith: that we believe and confess that our Lord Jesus Christ, God's Son, is both God and man, equally. [31] He is God from the essence of the Father, begotten before time; and he is man from the essence of his mother, born in time; [32] completely God, completely man, with a rational soul and human flesh; [33] equal to the Father as regards divinity, less than the Father as regards humanity. [34] Although he is God and man, yet Christ is not two, but one. [35] He is one, however, not by his divinity being turned into flesh, but by God's taking humanity to himself. [36] He is one, certainly not by the blending of his essence, but by the unity of his person. [37] For just as one man is both rational soul and flesh, so too the one Christ is both God and man. [38] He suffered for our salvation; he descended to hell; he arose from the dead on the third day; [39] he ascended to heaven; he is seated at the Father's right hand; [40] from there he will come to judge the living and the dead. [41] At his coming all people

will arise bodily [42] and give an accounting of their own deeds. [43] Those who have done good will enter eternal life, and those who have done evil will enter eternal fire.

[44] This is the catholic faith: that one cannot be saved without believing it firmly and faithfully.

The Chalcedonian Definition

INTRODUCTION

The Council of Ephesus in AD 431 forbade the making of any new creed. The Council of Chalcedon, which met in 451 to confront new errors, chose to issue a decree to affirm earlier versions of the Nicene Creed (both the 325 and the 381 versions) and also to offer a concise clarification regarding the church's teaching about the person of Christ. The council then promptly banned anyone else from making a new creed, no matter how good his or her intentions.

This clarification, formula, or definition was the clearest statement to date on the person of the Lord Jesus Christ. It confesses who Christ is now: God and man, one person in two natures (hence its language of both natures coming together in one person). Unlike earlier creeds, it does not emphasize the actual event of the incarnation, the person of the Son taking to himself humanity. Famously, it also offers a series of denials about Christ when it teaches that the natures of Christ "undergo no confusion, no change, no division, no separation." This "negative," or *apophatic*, theology reflects a belief among many Greek-speaking Christians that much of what we say about God—perhaps the best of what we say about God—involves saying what he is *not*.

The level of detail offered in the creed, including the use of the term "natures," eventually alienated those who preferred earlier statements of faith. Thus, while this creed is held by Western Christians and the Eastern Orthodox Church, the Oriental Orthodox, including various Coptic churches, do not subscribe to the Chalcedonian Definition.

THE CHALCEDONIAN DEFINITION

Following the saintly fathers, we all with one voice teach the confession of one and the same Son, our Lord Jesus Christ: the same perfect in divinity and perfect in humanity, the same truly God and truly man, of a rational soul and a body; consubstantial with the Father as regards his divinity, and the same consubstantial with us as regards his humanity; like us in all respects except for sin; begotten before the ages from the Father as regards his divinity, and in the last days the same for us and for our salvation from Mary, the virgin God-bearer, as regards his humanity; one and the same Christ, Son, Lord, only-begotten, acknowledged in two natures which undergo no confusion, no change, no division, no separation; at no point was the difference between the natures taken away through the union, but rather the property of both natures is preserved and comes together into a single person and a single subsistent being; he is not parted or divided into two persons, but is one and the same only-begotten Son, God, Word, Lord Jesus Christ, just as the prophets taught from the beginning about him, and as the Lord Jesus Christ himself instructed us, and as the creed of the fathers handed it down to us.

The Augsburg Confession

INTRODUCTION

The Augsburg Confession is the most significant confession of the early Reformation period. As early as 1527, theologians associated with the University of Wittenberg, including Martin Luther and his colleague Philip Melanchthon, had written statements of faith for educational and apologetical purposes. Three further sets of articles of the faith with overlapping content were written for German leaders with Lutheran sympathies in the year prior to the writing of the Augsburg Confession (1530). This confession drew on the full range of these prior positive efforts while at the same time responding to the hundreds of criticisms of Lutheranism that had been published and then submitted to the reigning Holy Roman Emperor, Charles V.

The imperial council at Augsburg, at which the Lutheran princes and their supporters presented their confession, offered a second chance for the Protestant movement to gain imperial approval. Assembled chiefly by Melanchthon, with editorial input from princes and scholars, the document contains three parts: a prefatory address to Charles V, articles of faith covering key doctrines, and a further cluster of articles refuting errors of the Roman church.

The preface and confession are designed in part to show that the developing Reformation was not a threat to civil authorities. Multiple opportunities are taken to affirm the importance of magistrates, and it is no accident that at strategic points the confession mentions loyalty to Germany and opposition to Islam—matters of heightened interest in the northern reaches of the empire.

The articles themselves begin as concise paragraphs but turn into short sermons when the topics of free will and good works are discussed. Wherever possible, continuity with the past is emphasized. Some matters of disagreement—for example, purgatory and the pope as antichrist—are silently passed over (contrary to Luther's wishes). Throughout the first twenty-one articles the general order of the Apostles' Creed is followed, and key statements, such as that on the doctrine of God, contain no surprises. Throughout, Luther's main emphases are maintained. Typical of the Reformation period, not only are errors described but groups of opponents are named and denounced as well.

The final section, Articles 22–28, deals chiefly with the practices and disciplines of the Lutheran churches in Germany. Cataloguing a history of abuses related to priestly marriage, monks, the mass, and rules about meats and other foods, the Augsburg Confession also details the problems with Roman Catholic church government and rules related to the confession of sin. Here the confession cleverly exploits disagreements within the Roman tradition itself, citing comments by reform-minded popes, contrasts with the teachings of church fathers, and corrective teachings of Scripture.

The Augsburg Confession remains one of the doctrinal standards for confessional Lutherans. An early edition of the work was officially adopted in the Book of Concord (1580), the main repository of eight authoritative Lutheran confessions and catechisms. It is that authoritative edition that is supplied here.

THE AUGSBURG CONFESSION

The Confession of Faith which was submitted to His
Imperial Majesty Charles V at the Diet of Augsburg
in the year 1530 by certain princes and cities

*I will speak of thy testimonies before kings, and
will not be put to shame. Psalm 119:46*

Preface to the Emperor Charles V

[1] Most Invincible Emperor, Caesar Augustus, Most Clement Lord: Inasmuch as Your Imperial Majesty has summoned a Diet of the Empire
here at Augsburg to deliberate concerning measures against the Turk,
that most atrocious, hereditary, and ancient enemy of the Christian
name and religion, in what way, namely, effectually to withstand his
furor and assaults by strong and lasting military provision; [2] and
then also concerning dissensions in the matter of our holy religion
and Christian Faith, that in this matter of religion the opinions and
judgments of the parties might be heard in each other's presence; and
considered and weighed among ourselves in mutual charity, leniency,
and kindness, [3] in order that, after the removal and correction of such
things as have been treated and understood in a different manner in
the writings on either side, these matters may be settled and brought
back to one simple truth and Christian concord, [4] that for the future

one pure and true religion may be embraced and maintained by us, that as we all are under one Christ and do battle under Him, so we may be able also to live in unity and concord in the one Christian Church.

[5] And inasmuch as we, the undersigned Elector and Princes, with others joined with us, have been called to the aforesaid Diet the same as the other Electors, Princes, and Estates, in obedient compliance with the Imperial mandate, we have promptly come to Augsburg, and—what we do not mean to say as boasting—we were among the first to be here.

[6] Accordingly, since even here at Augsburg at the very beginning of the Diet, Your Imperial Majesty caused to be proposed to the Electors, Princes, and other Estates of the Empire, amongst other things, that the several Estates of the Empire, on the strength of the Imperial edict, should set forth and submit their opinions and judgments in the German and the Latin language, [7] and since on the ensuing Wednesday, answer was given to Your Imperial Majesty, after due deliberation, that we would submit the Articles of our Confession for our side on next Wednesday, [8] therefore, in obedience to Your Imperial Majesty's wishes, we offer, in this matter of religion, the Confession of our preachers and of ourselves, showing what manner of doctrine from the Holy Scriptures and the pure Word of God has been up to this time set forth in our lands, dukedoms, dominions, and cities, and taught in our churches.

[9] And if the other Electors, Princes, and Estates of the Empire will, according to the said Imperial proposition, present similar writings, to wit, in Latin and German, giving their opinions in this matter of religion, [10] we, with the Princes and friends aforesaid, here before Your Imperial Majesty, our most clement Lord are prepared to confer amicably concerning all possible ways and means, in order that we may come together, as far as this may be honorably done, and, the matter between us on both sides being peacefully discussed without offensive

strife, the dissension, by God's help, may be done away and brought back to one true accordant religion; [11] for as we all are under one Christ and do battle under Him, we ought to confess the one Christ, after the tenor of Your Imperial Majesty's edict, and everything ought to be conducted according to the truth of God; and this it is what, with most fervent prayers, we entreat of God.

[12] However, as regards the rest of the Electors, Princes, and Estates, who constitute the other part, if no progress should be made, nor some result be attained by this treatment of the cause of religion after the manner in which Your Imperial Majesty has wisely held that it should be dealt with and treated namely, by such mutual presentation of writings and calm conferring together among ourselves, [13] we at least leave with you a clear testimony, that we here in no wise are holding back from anything that could bring about Christian concord—such as could be effected with God and a good conscience— [14] as also Your Imperial Majesty and, next, the other Electors and Estates of the Empire, and all who are moved by sincere love and zeal for religion, and who will give an impartial hearing to this matter, will graciously deign to take notice and to understand this from this Confession of ours and of our associates.

[15] Your Imperial Majesty also, not only once but often, graciously signified to the Electors, Princes, and Estates of the Empire, and at the Diet of Spires held AD 1526, according to the form of Your Imperial instruction and commission given and prescribed, [16] caused it to be stated and publicly proclaimed that Your Majesty, in dealing with this matter of religion, for certain reasons which were alleged in Your Majesty's name, was not willing to decide and could not determine anything, but that Your Majesty would diligently use Your Majesty's office with the Roman Pontiff for the convening of a General Council. [17] The same matter was thus publicly set forth at greater length a year ago at the last Diet which met at Spires.

[18] There Your Imperial Majesty, through His Highness Ferdinand, King of Bohemia and Hungary, our friend and clement Lord, as well as through the Orator and Imperial Commissioners caused this, among other things, to be submitted: that Your Imperial Majesty had taken notice of; and pondered, the resolution of Your Majesty's Representative in the Empire, and of the President and Imperial Counselors, and the Legates from other Estates convened at Ratisbon, [19] concerning the calling of a Council, and that your Imperial Majesty also judged it to be expedient to convene a Council; and that Your Imperial Majesty did not doubt the Roman Pontiff could be induced to hold a General Council, because the matters to be adjusted between Your Imperial Majesty and the Roman Pontiff were nearing agreement and Christian reconciliation; [20] therefore Your Imperial Majesty himself signified that he would endeavor to secure the said Chief Pontiff's consent for convening, together with your Imperial Majesty such General Council, to be published as soon as possible by letters that were to be sent out.

[21] If the outcome, therefore, should be such that the differences between us and the other parties in the matter of religion should not be amicably and in charity settled, then here, before Your Imperial Majesty we make the offer in all obedience, in addition to what we have already done, that we will all appear and defend our cause in such a general, free Christian Council, for the convening of which there has always been accordant action and agreement of votes in all the Imperial Diets held during Your Majesty's reign, on the part of the Electors, Princes, and other Estates of the Empire. [22] To the assembly of this General Council, and at the same time to Your Imperial Majesty, we have, even before this, in due manner and form of law, addressed ourselves and made appeal in this matter, by far the greatest and gravest. [23] To this appeal, both to Your Imperial Majesty and to a Council, we still adhere; neither do we intend nor

would it be possible for us, to relinquish it by this or any other document, unless the matter between us and the other side, according to the tenor of the latest Imperial citation should be amicably and charitably settled, allayed, and brought to Christian concord; [24] and regarding this we even here solemnly and publicly testify.

Chief Articles of Faith

ARTICLE 1
Of God

[1] Our Churches, with common consent, do teach that the decree of the Council of Nicaea concerning the Unity of the Divine Essence and concerning the Three Persons, [2] is true and to be believed without any doubting; that is to say, there is one Divine Essence which is called and which is God: eternal, without body, without parts, of infinite power, wisdom, and goodness, the Maker and Preserver of all things, visible and invisible; [3] and yet there are three Persons, of the same essence and power, who also are coeternal, the Father the Son, and the Holy Ghost. [4] And the term "person" they use as the Fathers have used it, to signify, not a part or quality in another, but that which subsists of itself.

[5] They condemn all heresies which have sprung up against this article, as the Manichaeans, who assumed two principles, one Good and the other Evil: also the Valentinians, Arians, Eunomians, Mohammedans, and all such. [6] They condemn also the Samosatenes, old and new, who, contending that there is but one Person, sophistically and impiously argue that the Word and the Holy Ghost are not distinct Persons, but that "Word" signifies a spoken word, and "Spirit" signifies motion created in things.

ARTICLE 2
Of Original Sin

[1] Also they teach that since the fall of Adam all men begotten in the natural way are born with sin, that is, without the fear of God, without trust in God, and with concupiscence; [2] and that this disease, or vice of origin, is truly sin, even now condemning and bringing eternal death upon those not born again through Baptism and the Holy Ghost.

[3] They condemn the Pelagians and others who deny that original depravity is sin, and who, to obscure the glory of Christ's merit and benefits, argue that man can be justified before God by his own strength and reason.

ARTICLE 3
Of the Son of God

[1] Also they teach that the Word, that is, the Son of God, did assume the human nature in the womb of the blessed Virgin Mary, [2] so that there are two natures, the divine and the human, inseparably enjoined in one Person, one Christ, true God and true man, who was born of the Virgin Mary, truly suffered, was crucified, dead, and buried, [3] that He might reconcile the Father unto us, and be a sacrifice, not only for original guilt, but also for all actual sins of men.

[4] He also descended into hell, and truly rose again the third day; afterward He ascended into heaven that He might sit on the right hand of the Father, and forever reign and have dominion over all creatures, [5] and sanctify them that believe in Him, by sending the Holy Ghost into their hearts, to rule, comfort, and quicken them, and to defend them against the devil and the power of sin.

[6] The same Christ shall openly come again to judge the quick and the dead, etc., according to the Apostles' Creed.

ARTICLE 4
Of Justification

[1] Also they teach that men cannot be justified before God by their own strength, merits, or works, [2] but are freely justified for Christ's sake, through faith, when they believe that they are received into favor, and that their sins are forgiven for Christ's sake, who, by His death, has made satisfaction for our sins. [3] This faith God imputes for righteousness in His sight (Romans 3–4).

ARTICLE 5
Of the Ministry

[1] That we may obtain this faith, the Ministry of Teaching the Gospel and administering the Sacraments was instituted. [2] For through the Word and Sacraments, as through instruments, the Holy Ghost is given, who works faith; where and when it pleases God, in them that hear the Gospel, [3] to wit, that God, not for our own merits, but for Christ's sake, justifies those who believe that they are received into grace for Christ's sake.

[4] They condemn the Anabaptists and others who think that the Holy Ghost comes to men without the external Word, through their own preparations and works.

ARTICLE 6
Of New Obedience

[1] Also they teach that this faith is bound to bring forth good fruits, and that it is necessary to do good works commanded by God, because of God's will, but that we should not rely on those works to merit justification before God. [2] For remission of sins and justification is

apprehended by faith, as also the voice of Christ attests: When ye shall have done all these things, say: We are unprofitable servants (Luke 17:10). [3] The same is also taught by the Fathers. For Ambrose says: It is ordained of God that he who believes in Christ is saved, freely receiving remission of sins, without works, by faith alone.

ARTICLE 7
Of the Church

[1] Also they teach that one holy Church is to continue forever. The Church is the congregation of saints, in which the Gospel is rightly taught and the Sacraments are rightly administered.

[2] And to the true unity of the Church it is enough to agree concerning the doctrine of the Gospel and the administration of the Sacraments. [3] Nor is it necessary that human traditions, that is, rites or ceremonies, instituted by men, should be everywhere alike. [4] As Paul says: One faith, one Baptism, one God and Father of all, etc. (Eph. 4:5–6).

ARTICLE 8
What the Church Is

[1] Although the Church properly is the congregation of saints and true believers, nevertheless, since in this life many hypocrites and evil persons are mingled therewith, it is lawful to use Sacraments administered by evil men, according to the saying of Christ: The Scribes and the Pharisees sit in Moses' seat, etc. (Matt. 23:2). [2] Both the Sacraments and Word are effectual by reason of the institution and commandment of Christ, notwithstanding they be administered by evil men.

[3] They condemn the Donatists, and such like, who denied it to be lawful to use the ministry of evil men in the Church, and who thought the ministry of evil men to be unprofitable and of none effect.

ARTICLE 9
Of Baptism

[1] Of Baptism they teach that it is necessary to salvation, and that through Baptism is offered the grace of God, [2] and that children are to be baptized who, being offered to God through Baptism are received into God's grace.

[3] They condemn the Anabaptists, who reject the baptism of children, and say that children are saved without Baptism.

ARTICLE 10
Of Lord's Supper

[1] Of the Supper of the Lord they teach that the Body and Blood of Christ are truly present, and are distributed to those who eat the Supper of the Lord; [2] and they reject those that teach otherwise.

ARTICLE 11
Of Confession

[1] Of Confession they teach that Private Absolution ought to be retained in the churches, although in confession an enumeration of all sins is not necessary. [2] For it is impossible according to the Psalm: Who can understand his errors? (Ps. 19:12).

ARTICLE 12
Of Repentance

[1] Of Repentance they teach that for those who have fallen after Baptism there is remission of sins whenever they are converted [2] and that the Church ought to impart absolution to those thus returning

to repentance. [3] Now, repentance consists properly of these two parts: [4] One is contrition, that is, terrors smiting the conscience through the knowledge of sin; [5] the other is faith, which is born of the Gospel, or of absolution, and believes that for Christ's sake, sins are forgiven, comforts the conscience, and delivers it from terrors. [6] Then good works are bound to follow, which are the fruits of repentance.

[7] They condemn the Anabaptists, who deny that those once justified can lose the Holy Ghost. [8] Also those who contend that some may attain to such perfection in this life that they cannot sin.

[9] The Novatians also are condemned, who would not absolve such as had fallen after Baptism, though they returned to repentance.

[10] They also are rejected who do not teach that remission of sins comes through faith but command us to merit grace through satisfactions of our own.

ARTICLE 13
Of the Use of the Sacraments

[1] Of the Use of the Sacraments they teach that the Sacraments were ordained, not only to be marks of profession among men, but rather to be signs and testimonies of the will of God toward us, [2] instituted to awaken and confirm faith in those who use them. Wherefore we must so use the Sacraments that faith be added to believe the promises which are offered and set forth through the Sacraments.

[3] They therefore condemn those who teach that the Sacraments justify by the outward act, and who do not teach that, in the use of the Sacraments, faith which believes that sins are forgiven, is required.

ARTICLE 14
Of Ecclesiastical Order

Of Ecclesiastical Order they teach that no one should publicly teach in the Church or administer the Sacraments unless he be regularly called.

ARTICLE 15
Of Ecclesiastical Usages

[1] Of Usages in the Church they teach that those ought to be observed which may be observed without sin, and which are profitable unto tranquility and good order in the Church, as particular holy days, festivals, and the like.

[2] Nevertheless, concerning such things men are admonished that consciences are not to be burdened, as though such observance was necessary to salvation.

[3] They are admonished also that human traditions instituted to propitiate God, to merit grace, and to make satisfaction for sins, are opposed to the Gospel and the doctrine of faith. [4] Wherefore vows and traditions concerning meats and days, etc., instituted to merit grace and to make satisfaction for sins, are useless and contrary to the Gospel.

ARTICLE 16
Of Civil Affairs

[1] Of Civil Affairs they teach that lawful civil ordinances are good works of God, [2] and that it is right for Christians to bear civil office, to sit as judges, to judge matters by the Imperial and other existing laws, to award just punishments, to engage in just wars, to serve as soldiers, to make legal contracts, to hold property, to make oath when required by the magistrates, to marry a wife, to be given in marriage.

[3] They condemn the Anabaptists who forbid these civil offices to Christians.

[4] They condemn also those who do not place evangelical perfection in the fear of God and in faith, but in forsaking civil offices, [5] for the Gospel teaches an eternal righteousness of the heart. Meanwhile, it does not destroy the State or the family, but very much requires that they be preserved as ordinances of God, and that charity be practiced in such ordinances. [6] Therefore, Christians are necessarily bound to obey their own magistrates and laws [7] save only when commanded to sin; for then they ought to obey God rather than men (Acts 5:29).

ARTICLE 17
Of Christ's Return to Judgment

[1] Also they teach that at the Consummation of the World Christ will appear for judgment, and will raise up all the dead; [2] He will give to the godly and elect eternal life and everlasting joys, [3] but ungodly men and the devils He will condemn to be tormented without end.

[4] They condemn the Anabaptists, who think that there will be an end to the punishments of condemned men and devils.

[5] They condemn also others who are now spreading certain Jewish opinions, that before the resurrection of the dead the godly shall take possession of the kingdom of the world, the ungodly being everywhere suppressed.

ARTICLE 18
Of Free Will

[1] Of Free Will they teach that man's will has some liberty to choose civil righteousness, and to work things subject to reason. [2] But it has no power, without the Holy Ghost, to work the righteousness of God,

that is, spiritual righteousness; since the natural man receiveth not the things of the Spirit of God (1 Cor. 2:14); [3] but this righteousness is wrought in the heart when the Holy Ghost is received through the Word. [4] These things are said in as many words by Augustine in his *Hypognosticon*, Book III:

> We grant that all men have a free will, free, inasmuch as it has the judgment of reason; not that it is thereby capable, without God, either to begin, or, at least, to complete aught in things pertaining to God, but only in works of this life, whether good or evil. [5] "Good" I call those works which spring from the good in nature, such as, willing to labor in the field, to eat and drink, to have a friend, to clothe oneself, to build a house, to marry a wife, to raise cattle, to learn divers useful arts, or whatsoever good pertains to this life. [6] For all of these things are not without dependence on the providence of God; yea, of Him and through Him they are and have their being. [7] "Evil" I call such works as willing to worship an idol, to commit murder, etc.

[8] They condemn the Pelagians and others, who teach that without the Holy Ghost, by the power of nature alone, we are able to love God above all things; also to do the commandments of God as touching "the substance of the act." [9] For, although nature is able in a manner to do the outward work (for it is able to keep the hands from theft and murder), yet it cannot produce the inward motions, such as the fear of God, trust in God, chastity, patience, etc.

ARTICLE 19
Of the Cause of Sin

Of the Cause of Sin they teach that, although God does create and preserve nature, yet the cause of sin is the will of the wicked, that is, of the devil and ungodly men; which will, unaided of God, turns itself from God, as Christ says in John 8:44: When he speaketh a lie, he speaketh of his own.

Of Good Works

[1] Our teachers are falsely accused of forbidding Good Works. [2] For their published writings on the Ten Commandments, and others of like import, bear witness that they have taught to good purpose concerning all estates and duties of life, as to what estates of life and what works in every calling be pleasing to God. [3] Concerning these things preachers heretofore taught but little, and urged only childish and needless works, as particular holy days, particular fasts, brotherhoods, pilgrimages, services in honor of saints, the use of rosaries, monasticism, and such like. [4] Since our adversaries have been admonished of these things, they are now unlearning them, and do not preach these unprofitable works as heretofore. [5] Besides, they begin to mention faith, of which there was heretofore marvelous silence. [6] They teach that we are justified not by works only, but they conjoin faith and works, and say that we are justified by faith and works. [7] This doctrine is more tolerable than the former one, and can afford more consolation than their old doctrine.

[8] Forasmuch, therefore, as the doctrine concerning faith, which ought to be the chief one in the Church, has lain so long unknown, as all must needs grant that there was the deepest silence in their sermons concerning the righteousness of faith, while only the doctrine of works was treated in the churches, our teachers have instructed the churches concerning faith as follows:

[9] First, that our works cannot reconcile God or merit forgiveness of sins, grace, and justification, but that we obtain this only by faith

when we believe that we are received into favor for Christ's sake, who alone has been set forth the Mediator and Propitiation (1 Tim. 2:5), in order that the Father may be reconciled through Him. [10] Whoever, therefore, trusts that by works he merits grace, despises the merit and grace of Christ, and seeks a way to God without Christ, by human strength, although Christ has said of Himself: I am the Way, the Truth, and the Life (John 14:6).

[11] This doctrine concerning faith is everywhere treated by Paul, e.g., Ephesians 2:8: By grace are ye saved through faith; and that not of yourselves; it is the gift of God, not of works, etc.

[12] And lest anyone should craftily say that a new interpretation of Paul has been devised by us, this entire matter is supported by the testimonies of the Fathers. [13] For Augustine, in many volumes, defends grace and the righteousness of faith, over against the merits of works. [14] And Ambrose, in his *De Vocatione Gentium*, and elsewhere, teaches to like effect. For in his *De Vocatione Gentium* he says as follows:

> Redemption by the blood of Christ would become of little value, neither would the preeminence of man's works be superseded by the mercy of God, if justification, which is wrought through grace, were due to the merits going before, so as to be, not the free gift of a donor, but the reward due to the laborer.

[15] But, although this doctrine is despised by the inexperienced, nevertheless God-fearing and anxious consciences find by experience that it brings the greatest consolation, because consciences cannot be set at rest through any works, but only by faith, when they take the sure ground that for Christ's sake they have a reconciled God. [16] As Paul teaches in Romans 5:1: Being justified by faith, we have peace with God. [17] This whole doctrine is to be referred to that conflict of the terrified conscience, neither can it be understood apart from

that conflict. [18] Therefore inexperienced and profane men judge ill concerning this matter, who dream that Christian righteousness is nothing but civil and philosophical righteousness.

[19] Heretofore consciences were plagued with the doctrine of works, they did not hear the consolation from the Gospel. [20] Some persons were driven by conscience into the desert, into monasteries hoping there to merit grace by a monastic life. [21] Some also devised other works whereby to merit grace and make satisfaction for sins. [22] Hence there was very great need to treat of, and renew, this doctrine of faith in Christ, to the end that anxious consciences should not be without consolation but that they might know that grace and forgiveness of sins and justification are apprehended by faith in Christ.

[23] Men are also admonished that here the term "faith" does not signify merely the knowledge of the history, such as is in the ungodly and in the devil, but signifies a faith which believes, not merely the history, but also the effect of the history—namely, this article: the forgiveness of sins, to wit, that we have grace, righteousness, and forgiveness of sins through Christ.

[24] Now he that knows that he has a Father gracious to him through Christ, truly knows God; he knows also that God cares for him, and calls upon God; in a word, he is not without God, as the heathen. [25] For devils and the ungodly are not able to believe this article: the forgiveness of sins. Hence, they hate God as an enemy, call not upon Him, and expect no good from Him. [26] Augustine also admonishes his readers concerning the word "faith," and teaches that the term "faith" is accepted in the Scriptures not for knowledge such as is in the ungodly but for confidence which consoles and encourages the terrified mind.

[27] Furthermore, it is taught on our part that it is necessary to do good works, not that we should trust to merit grace by them, but because it is the will of God. [28] It is only by faith that forgiveness of sins is apprehended, and that, for nothing. [29] And because through

faith the Holy Ghost is received, hearts are renewed and endowed with new affections, so as to be able to bring forth good works. [30] For Ambrose says: Faith is the mother of a good will and right doing. [31] For man's powers without the Holy Ghost are full of ungodly affections, and are too weak to do works which are good in God's sight. [32] Besides, they are in the power of the devil who impels men to divers sins, to ungodly opinions, to open crimes. [33] This we may see in the philosophers, who, although they endeavored to live an honest life could not succeed, but were defiled with many open crimes. [34] Such is the feebleness of man when he is without faith and without the Holy Ghost, and governs himself only by human strength.

[35] Hence it may be readily seen that this doctrine is not to be charged with prohibiting good works, but rather the more to be commended, because it shows how we are enabled to do good works. [36] For without faith human nature can in no wise do the works of the First or of the Second Commandment. [37] Without faith it does not call upon God, nor expect anything from God, nor bear the cross, but seeks, and trusts in, man's help. [38] And thus, when there is no faith and trust in God all manner of lusts and human devices rule in the heart. [39] Wherefore Christ said in John 15:5: Without Me ye can do nothing; [40] and the Church sings:

Lacking Thy divine favor,
There is nothing found in man,
Naught in him is harmless.

ARTICLE 21
Of the Worship of the Saints

[1] Of the Worship of Saints they teach that the memory of saints may be set before us, that we may follow their faith and good works,

according to our calling, as the Emperor may follow the example of David in making war to drive away the Turk from his country. For both are kings. [2] But the Scripture teaches not the invocation of saints or to ask help of saints, since it sets before us the one Christ as the Mediator, Propitiation, High Priest, and Intercessor. [3] He is to be prayed to, and has promised that He will hear our prayer; and this worship He approves above all, to wit, that in all afflictions He be called upon. [4] 1 John 2:1: If any man sin, we have an Advocate with the Father, etc.

[A Summary Statement]

[5] This is about the Sum of our Doctrine, in which, as can be seen, there is nothing that varies from the Scriptures, or from the Church Catholic, or from the Church of Rome as known from its writers. This being the case, they judge harshly who insist that our teachers be regarded as heretics. [6] There is, however, disagreement on certain Abuses, which have crept into the Church without rightful author-ity. And even in these, if there were some difference, there should be proper lenity on the part of bishops to bear with us by reason of the Confession which we have now reviewed; because even the Canons are not so severe as to demand the same rites everywhere, [7] neither, at any time, have the rites of all churches been the same; [8] although, among us, in large part, the ancient rites are diligently observed. For it is a false and malicious charge that all the ceremonies, all the things instituted of old, are abolished in our churches. [9] But it has been a common complaint that some abuses were connected with the ordinary rites. These, inasmuch as they could not be approved with a good conscience, have been to some extent corrected.

Articles in Which Are Reviewed the Abuses
Which Have Been Corrected

[1] Inasmuch, then, as our churches dissent in no article of the faith from the Church Catholic, but only omit some abuses which are new, and which have been erroneously accepted by the corruption of the times, contrary to the intent of the Canons, we pray that Your Imperial Majesty would graciously hear both what has been changed, and what were the reasons why the people were not compelled to observe those abuses against their conscience. [2] Nor should Your Imperial Majesty believe those who, in order to excite the hatred of men against our part, disseminate strange slanders among the people. [3] Having thus excited the minds of good men, they have first given occasion to this controversy, and now endeavor, by the same arts, to increase the discord. [4] For Your Imperial Majesty will undoubtedly find that the form of doctrine and of ceremonies with us is not so intolerable as these ungodly and malicious men represent. [5] Besides, the truth cannot be gathered from common rumors or the revilings of enemies. [6] But it can readily be judged that nothing would serve better to maintain the dignity of ceremonies, and to nourish reverence and pious devotion among the people than if the ceremonies were observed rightly in the churches.

ARTICLE 22

Of Both Kinds in the Sacrament

[1] To the laity are given Both Kinds in the Sacrament of the Lord's Supper, because this usage has the commandment of the Lord in Matthew 26:27: Drink ye all of it, [2] where Christ has manifestly commanded concerning the cup that all should drink. [3] And lest any man should craftily say that this refers only to priests, Paul in

1 Corinthians 11:27 recites an example from which it appears that the whole congregation did use both kinds. [4] And this usage has long remained in the Church, nor is it known when, or by whose authority, it was changed; although Cardinal Cusanus mentions the time when it was approved. [5] Cyprian in some places testifies that the blood was given to the people. [6] The same is testified by Jerome, who says: The priests administer the Eucharist, and distribute the blood of Christ to the people. [7] Indeed, Pope Gelasius commands that the Sacrament be not divided (dist. II., De Consecratione, cap. Comperimus). [8] Only custom, not so ancient, has it otherwise. [9] But it is evident that any custom introduced against the commandments of God is not to be allowed, as the Canons witness (dist. III., cap. Veritate, and the following chapters). [10] But this custom has been received, not only against the Scripture, but also against the old Canons and the example of the Church. [11] Therefore, if any preferred to use both kinds of the Sacrament, they ought not to have been compelled with offense to their consciences to do otherwise. [12] And because the division of the Sacrament does not agree with the ordinance of Christ, we are accustomed to omit the procession, which hitherto has been in use.

ARTICLE 23
Of the Marriage of Priests

[1] There has been common complaint concerning the examples of priests who were not chaste. [2] For that reason also Pope Pius is reported to have said that there were certain causes why marriage was taken away from priests, but that there were far weightier ones why it ought to be given back; for so Platina writes. [3] Since, therefore, our priests were desirous to avoid these open scandals, they married wives, and taught that it was lawful for them to contract matrimony.

[4] First, because Paul says in 1 Corinthians 7:2, 9: To avoid fornication, let every man have his own wife. Also: It is better to marry than to burn. [5] Secondly Christ says in Matthew 19:11: All men cannot receive this saying, where He teaches that not all men are fit to lead a single life; for God created man for procreation (Gen. 1:28). [6] Nor is it in man's power, without a singular gift and work of God, to alter this creation. [For it is manifest, and many have confessed that no good, honest, chaste life, no Christian, sincere, upright conduct has resulted (from the attempt), but a horrible, fearful unrest and torment of conscience has been felt by many until the end.] [7] Therefore, those who are not fit to lead a single life ought to contract matrimony. [8] For no man's law, no vow, can annul the commandment and ordinance of God. [9] For these reasons the priests teach that it is lawful for them to marry wives.

[10] It is also evident that in the ancient Church priests were married men. [11] For Paul says, in 1 Timothy 3:2, that a bishop should be chosen who is the husband of one wife. [12] And in Germany, four hundred years ago for the first time, the priests were violently compelled to lead a single life, who indeed offered such resistance that the Archbishop of Mayence, when about to publish the Pope's decree concerning this matter, was almost killed in the tumult raised by the enraged priests. [13] And so harsh was the dealing in the matter that not only were marriages forbidden for the future, but also existing marriages were torn asunder, contrary to all laws, divine and human, contrary even to the Canons themselves, made not only by the Popes, but by most celebrated Synods. [Moreover, many God-fearing and intelligent people in high station are known frequently to have expressed misgivings that such enforced celibacy and depriving men of marriage (which God Himself has instituted and left free to men) has never produced any good results, but has brought on many great and evil vices and much iniquity.]

[14] Seeing also that, as the world is aging, man's nature is gradually growing weaker, it is well to guard that no more vices steal into Germany.

[15] Furthermore, God ordained marriage to be a help against human infirmity. [16] The Canons themselves say that the old rigor ought now and then, in the latter times, to be relaxed because of the weakness of men; which it is to be wished were done also in this matter. [17] And it is to be expected that the churches shall at some time lack pastors if marriage is any longer forbidden.

[18] But while the commandment of God is in force, while the custom of the Church is well known, while impure celibacy causes many scandals, adulteries, and other crimes deserving the punishments of just magistrates, yet it is a marvelous thing that in nothing is more cruelty exercised than against the marriage of priests. [19] God has given commandment to honor marriage. [20] By the laws of all well-ordered commonwealths, even among the heathen, marriage is most highly honored. [21] But now men, and that, priests, are cruelly put to death, contrary to the intent of the Canons, for no other cause than marriage. [22] Paul, in 1 Timothy 4:3, calls that a doctrine of devils which forbids marriage. [23] This may now be readily understood when the law against marriage is maintained by such penalties.

[24] But as no law of man can annul the commandment of God, so neither can it be done by any vow. [25] Accordingly, Cyprian also advises that women who do not keep the chastity they have promised should marry. His words are these (Book I, Epistle XI): But if they be unwilling or unable to persevere, it is better for them to marry than to fall into the fire by their lusts; they should certainly give no offense to their brethren and sisters.

[26] And even the Canons show some leniency toward those who have taken vows before the proper age, as heretofore has generally been the case.

ARTICLE 24

Of the Mass

[1] Falsely are our churches accused of abolishing the Mass; for the Mass is retained among us, and celebrated with the highest reverence. [2] Nearly all the usual ceremonies are also preserved, save that the parts sung in Latin are interspersed here and there with German hymns, which have been added to teach the people. [3] For ceremonies are needed to this end alone that the unlearned be taught [what they need to know of Christ]. [4] And not only has Paul commanded to use in the church a language understood by the people (1 Cor. 14:2, 9), but it has also been so ordained by man's law. [5] The people are accustomed to partake of the Sacrament together, if any be fit for it, and this also increases the reverence and devotion of public worship. [6] For none are admitted except they be first examined. [7] The people are also advised concerning the dignity and use of the Sacrament, how great consolation it brings anxious consciences, that they may learn to believe God, and to expect and ask of Him all that is good. [In this connection they are also instructed regarding other and false teachings on the Sacrament.] [8] This worship pleases God; such use of the Sacrament nourishes true devotion toward God. [9] It does not, therefore, appear that the Mass is more devoutly celebrated among our adversaries than among us.

[10] But it is evident that for a long time this also has been the public and most grievous complaint of all good men that Masses have been basely profaned and applied to purposes of lucre. [11] For it is not unknown how far this abuse obtains in all the churches, by what manner of men Masses are said only for fees or stipends, and how many celebrate them contrary to the Canons. [12] But Paul severely threatens those who deal unworthily with the Eucharist when he says in 1 Corinthians 11:27: Whosoever shall eat this bread, and drink this

cup of the Lord, unworthily, shall be guilty of the body and blood of the Lord. [13] When, therefore our priests were admonished concerning this sin, Private Masses were discontinued among us, as scarcely any Private Masses were celebrated except for lucre's sake.

[14] Neither were the bishops ignorant of these abuses, and if they had corrected them in time, there would now be less dissension. [15] Heretofore, by their own connivance, they suffered many corruptions to creep into the Church. [16] Now, when it is too late, they begin to complain of the troubles of the Church, while this disturbance has been occasioned simply by those abuses which were so manifest that they could be borne no longer. [17] There have been great dissensions concerning the Mass, concerning the Sacrament. [18] Perhaps the world is being punished for such long-continued profanations of the Mass as have been tolerated in the churches for so many centuries by the very men who were both able and in duty bound to correct them. [19] For in the Ten Commandments it is written in Exodus 20:7: The Lord will not hold him guiltless that taketh His name in vain. [20] But since the world began, nothing that God ever ordained seems to have been so abused for filthy lucre as the Mass.

[21] There was also added the opinion which infinitely increased Private Masses, namely that Christ, by His passion, had made satisfaction for original sin, and instituted the Mass wherein an offering should be made for daily sins, venial and mortal. [22] From this has arisen the common opinion that the Mass takes away the sins of the living and the dead by the outward act. [23] Then they began to dispute whether one Mass said for many were worth as much as special Masses for individuals, and this brought forth that infinite multitude of Masses. [With this work men wished to obtain from God all that they needed, and in the mean time faith in Christ and the true worship were forgotten.]

[24] Concerning these opinions our teachers have given warning that they depart from the Holy Scriptures and diminish the glory of

the passion of Christ. [25] For Christ's passion was an oblation and satisfaction, not for original guilt only, but also for all other sins, [26] as it is written in Hebrews 10:10: We are sanctified through the offering of Jesus Christ once for all. [27] Also, in 10:14: By one offering He hath perfected forever them that are sanctified. [It is an unheard-of innovation in the Church to teach that Christ by His death made satisfaction only for original sin and not likewise for all other sin. Accordingly it is hoped that everybody will understand that this error has not been reproved without due reason.]

[28] Scripture also teaches that we are justified before God through faith in Christ, when we believe that our sins are forgiven for Christ's sake. [29] Now if the Mass take away the sins of the living and the dead by the outward act justification comes of the work of Masses, and not of faith, which Scripture does not allow.

[30] But Christ commands us in Luke 22:19: This do in remembrance of Me; therefore the Mass was instituted that the faith of those who use the Sacrament should remember what benefits it receives through Christ, and cheer and comfort the anxious conscience. [31] For to remember Christ is to remember His benefits, and to realize that they are truly offered unto us. [32] Nor is it enough only to remember the history; for this also the Jews and the ungodly can remember. [33] Wherefore the Mass is to be used to this end, that there the Sacrament [Communion] may be administered to them that have need of consolation; as Ambrose says: Because I always sin, I am always bound to take the medicine. [Therefore this Sacrament requires faith, and is used in vain without faith.]

[34] Now, forasmuch as the Mass is such a giving of the Sacrament, we hold one communion every holy day, and, if any desire the Sacrament, also on other days, when it is given to such as ask for it. [35] And this custom is not new in the Church; for the Fathers before Gregory make no mention of any private Mass, but of the common Mass [the

Communion] they speak very much. [36] Chrysostom says that the priest stands daily at the altar, inviting some to the Communion and keeping back others. [37] And it appears from the ancient Canons that some one celebrated the Mass from whom all the other presbyters and deacons received the body of the Lord; [38] for thus the words of the Nicene Canon say: Let the deacons, according to their order, receive the Holy Communion after the presbyters, from the bishop or from a presbyter. [39] And Paul, in 1 Corinthians 11:33, commands concerning the Communion: Tarry one for another, so that there may be a common participation.

[40] Forasmuch, therefore, as the Mass with us has the example of the Church, taken from the Scripture and the Fathers, we are confident that it cannot be disapproved, especially since public ceremonies, for the most part like those hitherto in use, are retained; only the number of Masses differs, which, because of very great and manifest abuses doubtless might be profitably reduced. [41] For in olden times, even in churches most frequented, the Mass was not celebrated every day, as the Tripartite History (Book 9, chap. 33) testifies: Again in Alexandria, every Wednesday and Friday the Scriptures are read, and the doctors expound them, and all things are done, except the solemn rite of Communion.

ARTICLE 25
Of Confession

[1] Confession in the churches is not abolished among us; for it is not usual to give the body of the Lord, except to them that have been previously examined and absolved. [2] And the people are most carefully taught concerning faith in the absolution, about which formerly there was profound silence. [3] Our people are taught that they should highly prize the absolution, as being the voice of God, and pronounced by God's command. [4] The power of the Keys is

set forth in its beauty and they are reminded what great consolation it brings to anxious consciences, also, that God requires faith to believe such absolution as a voice sounding from heaven, and that such faith in Christ truly obtains and receives the forgiveness of sins. [5] Aforetime satisfactions were immoderately extolled; of faith and the merit of Christ and the righteousness of faith no mention was made; wherefore, on this point, our churches are by no means to be blamed. [6] For this even our adversaries must needs concede to us that the doctrine concerning repentance has been most diligently treated and laid open by our teachers.

[7] But of Confession they teach that an enumeration of sins is not necessary, and that consciences be not burdened with anxiety to enumerate all sins, for it is impossible to recount all sins, as Psalm 19:12 testifies: Who can understand his errors? [8] Also Jeremiah 17:9: The heart is deceitful; who can know it? [9] But if no sins were forgiven, except those that are recounted, consciences could never find peace; for very many sins they neither see nor can remember. [10] The ancient writers also testify that an enumeration is not necessary. [11] For in the Decrees, Chrysostom is quoted, who says thus:

I say not to you that you should disclose yourself in public, nor that you accuse yourself before others, but I would have you obey the prophet who says: "Disclose thy way before God." Therefore confess your sins before God, the true Judge, with prayer. Tell your errors, not with the tongue, but with the memory of your conscience, etc.

[12] And the Gloss (*Of Repentance*, Distinct. V, *Cap. Consideret*) admits that Confession is of human right only [not commanded by Scripture, but ordained by the Church]. [13] Nevertheless, on account of the great benefit of absolution, and because it is otherwise useful to the conscience, Confession is retained among us.

[1] It has been the general persuasion, not of the people alone, but also of those teaching in the churches, that making Distinctions of Meats, and like traditions of men, are works profitable to merit grace, and able to make satisfactions for sins. [2] And that the world so thought, appears from this, that new ceremonies, new orders, new holy days, and new fastings were daily instituted, and the teachers in the churches did exact these works as a service necessary to merit grace, and did greatly terrify men's consciences, if they should omit any of these things. [3] From this persuasion concerning traditions much detriment has resulted in the Church.

[4] First, the doctrine of grace and of the righteousness of faith has been obscured by it, which is the chief part of the Gospel, and ought to stand out as the most prominent in the Church, in order that the merit of Christ may be well known, and faith, which believes that sins are forgiven for Christ's sake be exalted far above works. [5] Wherefore Paul also lays the greatest stress on this article, putting aside the Law and human traditions, in order to show that Christian righteousness is something else than such works, to wit, the faith which believes that sins are freely forgiven for Christ's sake. [6] But this doctrine of Paul has been almost wholly smothered by traditions, which have produced an opinion that, by making distinctions in meats and like services, we must merit grace and righteousness. [7] In treating of repentance, there was no mention made of faith; only those works of satisfaction were set forth; in these the entire repentance seemed to consist.

[8] Secondly, these traditions have obscured the commandments of God, because traditions were placed far above the commandments of God. Christianity was thought to consist wholly in the observance of certain holy days, rites, fasts, and vestures. [9] These observances had

won for themselves the exalted title of being the spiritual life and the perfect life. [10] Meanwhile the commandments of God, according to each one's calling, were without honor namely, that the father brought up his offspring, that the mother bore children, that the prince governed the commonwealth—these were accounted works that were worldly and imperfect, and far below those glittering observances. [11] And this error greatly tormented devout consciences, which grieved that they were held in an imperfect state of life, as in marriage, in the office of magistrate; or in other civil ministrations; on the other hand, they admired the monks and such like, and falsely imagined that the observances of such men were more acceptable to God.

[12] Thirdly, traditions brought great danger to consciences; for it was impossible to keep all traditions, and yet men judged these observances to be necessary acts of worship. [13] Gerson writes that many fell into despair, and that some even took their own lives, because they felt that they were not able to satisfy the traditions, and they had all the while not heard any consolation of the righteousness of faith and grace. [14] We see that the summists and theologians gather the traditions, and seek mitigations whereby to ease consciences, and yet they do not sufficiently unfetter, but sometimes entangle, consciences even more. [15] And with the gathering of these traditions, the schools and sermons have been so much occupied that they have had no leisure to touch upon Scripture, and to seek the more profitable doctrine of faith, of the cross, of hope, of the dignity of civil affairs, of consolation of sorely tried consciences. [16] Hence Gerson and some other theologians have grievously complained that by these strivings concerning traditions they were prevented from giving attention to a better kind of doctrine. [17] Augustine also forbids that men's consciences should be burdened with such observances, and prudently advises Januarius that he must know that they are to be observed as things indifferent; for such are his words.

[18] Wherefore our teachers must not be looked upon as having taken up this matter rashly or from hatred of the bishops, as some falsely suspect. [19] There was great need to warn the churches of these errors, which had arisen from misunderstanding the traditions. [20] For the Gospel compels us to insist in the churches upon the doctrine of grace, and of the righteousness of faith; which, however, cannot be understood, if men think that they merit grace by observances of their own choice.

[21] Thus, therefore, they have taught that by the observance of human traditions we cannot merit grace or be justified, and hence we must not think such observances necessary acts of worship. [22] They add hereunto testimonies of Scripture. Christ, in Matthew 15:3, defends the Apostles who had not observed the usual tradition, which, however, evidently pertains to a matter not unlawful, but indifferent, and to have a certain affinity with the purifications of the Law, and says in 15:9: In vain do they worship Me with the commandments of men. [23] He, therefore, does not exact an unprofitable service. Shortly after He adds: Not that which goeth into the mouth defileth a man. [24] So also Paul, in Romans 14:17: The kingdom of God is not meat and drink. [25] And in Colossians 2:16: Let no man, therefore, judge you in meat, or in drink, or in respect of an holy day, or of the Sabbath day; [26] also: If ye be dead with Christ from the rudiments of the world, why, as though living in the world, are ye subject to ordinances: Touch not, taste not, handle not! [27] And Peter says in Acts 15:10: Why tempt ye God to put a yoke upon the neck of the disciples, which neither our fathers nor we were able to bear? But we believe that through the grace of the Lord Jesus Christ we shall be saved, even as they. [28] Here Peter forbids to burden the consciences with many rites, either of Moses or of others. [29] And in 1 Timothy 4:1–3 Paul calls the prohibition of meats a doctrine of devils; for it is against the Gospel to institute or to do such works

that by them we may merit grace, or as though Christianity could not exist without such service of God.

[30] Here our adversaries object that our teachers are opposed to discipline and mortification of the flesh, as Jovinian. But the contrary may be learned from the writings of our teachers. [31] For they have always taught concerning the cross that it behooves Christians to bear afflictions. [32] This is the true, earnest, and unfeigned mortification, to wit, to be exercised with divers afflictions, and to be crucified with Christ.

[33] Moreover, they teach that every Christian ought to train and subdue himself with bodily restraints, or bodily exercises and labors that neither satiety nor slothfulness tempt him to sin, but not that we may merit grace or make satisfaction for sins by such exercises. [34] And such external discipline ought to be urged at all times, not only on a few and set days. [35] So Christ commands in Luke 21:34: Take heed lest your hearts be overcharged with surfeiting; [36] also in Matthew 17:21: This kind goeth not out but by prayer and fasting. [37] Paul also says in 1 Corinthians 9:27: I keep under my body and bring it into subjection. [38] Here he clearly shows that he was keeping under his body, not to merit forgiveness of sins by that discipline, but to have his body in subjection and fitted for spiritual things, and for the discharge of duty according to his calling. [39] Therefore, we do not condemn fasting in itself, but the traditions which prescribe certain days and certain meats, with peril of conscience, as though such works were a necessary service.

[40] Nevertheless, very many traditions are kept on our part, which conduce to good order in the Church, as the Order of Lessons in the Mass and the chief holy days. [41] But, at the same time, men are warned that such observances do not justify before God, and that in such things it should not be made sin if they be omitted without offense. [42] Such liberty in human rites was not unknown to the Fathers. [43] For in

the East they kept Easter at another time than at Rome, and when, on account of this diversity, the Romans accused the Eastern Church of schism, they were admonished by others that such usages need not be alike everywhere. [44] And Irenaeus says: Diversity concerning fasting does not destroy the harmony of faith; as also Pope Gregory intimates in Dist. XII, that such diversity does not violate the unity of the Church. [45] And in the *Tripartite History*, Book 9, many examples of dissimilar rites are gathered, and the following statement is made: It was not the mind of the Apostles to enact rules concerning holy days, but to preach godliness and a holy life [to teach faith and love].

ARTICLE 27
Of Monastic Vows

[1] What is taught on our part concerning Monastic Vows, will be better understood if it be remembered what has been the state of the monasteries, and how many things were daily done in those very monasteries, contrary to the Canons. [2] In Augustine's time they were free associations. Afterward, when discipline was corrupted, vows were everywhere added for the purpose of restoring discipline, as in a carefully planned prison. [3] Gradually, many other observances were added besides vows. [4] And these fetters were laid upon many before the lawful age, contrary to the Canons.

[5] Many also entered into this kind of life through ignorance, being unable to judge their own strength, though they were of sufficient age. [6] Being thus ensnared, they were compelled to remain, even though some could have been freed by the kind provision of the Canons. [7] And this was more the case in convents of women than of monks, although more consideration should have been shown the weaker sex. [8] This rigor displeased many good men before this time, who saw that young men and maidens were thrown into convents

for a living. They saw what unfortunate results came of this procedure, and what scandals were created, what snares were cast upon consciences! [9] They were grieved that the authority of the Canons in so momentous a matter was utterly set aside and despised. [10] To these evils was added such a persuasion concerning vows as, it is well known, in former times displeased even those monks who were more considerate. [11] They taught that vows were equal to Baptism; they taught that by this kind of life they merited forgiveness of sins and justification before God. [12] Yea, they added that the monastic life not only merited righteousness before God but even greater things, because it kept not only the precepts, but also the so-called "evangelical counsels."

[13] Thus they made men believe that the profession of monasticism was far better than Baptism, and that the monastic life was more meritorious than that of magistrates, than the life of pastors, and such like, who serve their calling in accordance with God's commands, without any man-made services. [14] None of these things can be denied; for they appear in their own books. [Moreover, a person who has been thus ensnared and has entered a monastery learns little of Christ.]

[15] What, then, came to pass in the monasteries? Aforetime they were schools of theology and other branches, profitable to the Church; and thence pastors and bishops were obtained. Now it is another thing. It is needless to rehearse what is known to all. [16] Aforetime they came together to learn; now they feign that it is a kind of life instituted to merit grace and righteousness; yea, they preach that it is a state of perfection, and they put it far above all other kinds of life ordained of God. [17] These things we have rehearsed without odious exaggeration, to the end that the doctrine of our teachers on this point might be better understood.

[18] First, concerning such as contract matrimony, they teach on our part that it is lawful for all men who are not fitted for single life

to contract matrimony, because vows cannot annul the ordinance and commandment of God. [19] But the commandment of God is in 1 Corinthians 7:2: To avoid fornication, let every man have his own wife. [20] Nor is it the commandment only, but also the creation and ordinance of God, which forces those to marry who are not excepted by a singular work of God, according to the text in Genesis 2:18: It is not good that the man should be alone. [21] Therefore they do not sin who obey this commandment and ordinance of God.

[22] What objection can be raised to this? Let men extol the obligation of a vow as much as they list, yet shall they not bring to pass that the vow annuls the commandment of God. [23] The Canons teach that the right of the superior is excepted in every vow; [that vows are not binding against the decision of the Pope;] much less, therefore, are these vows of force which are against the commandments of God.

[24] Now, if the obligation of vows could not be changed for any cause whatever, the Roman Pontiffs could never have given dispensation for it is not lawful for man to annul an obligation which is simply divine. [25] But the Roman Pontiffs have prudently judged that leniency is to be observed in this obligation, and therefore we read that many times they have dispensed from vows. [26] The case of the King of Aragon who was called back from the monastery is well known, and there are also examples in our own times. [Now, if dispensations have been granted for the sake of securing temporal interests, it is much more proper that they be granted on account of the distress of souls.]

[27] In the second place, why do our adversaries exaggerate the obligation or effect of a vow when, at the same time, they have not a word to say of the nature of the vow itself, that it ought to be in a thing possible, that it ought to be free, and chosen spontaneously and deliberately? [28] But it is not unknown to what extent perpetual chastity is in the power of man. [29] And how few are there who have taken the vow spontaneously and deliberately! Young maidens and

men, before they are able to judge, are persuaded, and sometimes even compelled, to take the vow. [30] Wherefore it is not fair to insist so rigorously on the obligation, since it is granted by all that it is against the nature of a vow to take it without spontaneous and deliberate action.

[31] Most canonical laws rescind vows made before the age of fifteen; for before that age there does not seem sufficient judgment in a person to decide concerning a perpetual life. [32] Another Canon, granting more to the weakness of man, adds a few years; for it forbids a vow to be made before the age of eighteen. [33] But which of these two Canons shall we follow? The most part have an excuse for leaving the monasteries, because most of them have taken the vows before they reached these ages.

[34] Finally, even though the violation of a vow might be censured, yet it seems not forthwith to follow that the marriages of such persons must be dissolved. [35] For Augustine denies that they ought to be dissolved (XXVII. Quaest. I, Cap. *Nuptiarum*), and his authority is not lightly to be esteemed, although other men afterwards thought otherwise.

[36] But although it appears that God's command concerning marriage delivers very many from their vows, yet our teachers introduce also another argument concerning vows to show that they are void. For every service of God, ordained and chosen of men without the commandment of God to merit justification and grace, is wicked, as Christ says in Matthew 15:9: In vain do they worship Me with the commandments of men. [37] And Paul teaches everywhere that righteousness is not to be sought from our own observances and acts of worship, devised by men, but that it comes by faith to those who believe that they are received by God into grace for Christ's sake.

[38] But it is evident that monks have taught that services of man's making satisfy for sins and merit grace and justification. What else is this than to detract from the glory of Christ and to obscure and deny

the righteousness of faith? [39] It follows, therefore, that the vows thus commonly taken have been wicked services, and, consequently, are void. [40] For a wicked vow, taken against the commandment of God, is not valid; for (as the Canon says) no vow ought to bind men to wickedness.

[41] Paul says in Galatians 5:4: Christ is become of no effect unto you, whosoever of you are justified by the Law, ye are fallen from grace. [42] To those, therefore, who want to be justified by their vows Christ is made of no effect, and they fall from grace. [43] For also these who ascribe justification to vows ascribe to their own works that which properly belongs to the glory of Christ.

[44] Nor can it be denied, indeed, that the monks have taught that, by their vows and observances, they were justified, and merited forgiveness of sins, yea, they invented still greater absurdities, saying that they could give others a share in their works. [45] If anyone should be inclined to enlarge on these things with evil intent, how many things could he bring together whereof even the monks are now ashamed! [46] Over and above this, they persuaded men that services of man's making were a state of Christian perfection. [47] And is not this assigning justification to works? [48] It is no light offense in the Church to set forth to the people a service devised by men, without the commandment of God, and to teach that such service justifies men. For the righteousness of faith, which chiefly ought to be taught in the Church, is obscured when these wonderful angelic forms of worship, with their show of poverty, humility, and celibacy, are cast before the eyes of men.

[49] Furthermore, the precepts of God and the true service of God are obscured when men hear that only monks are in a state of perfection. For Christian perfection is to fear God from the heart, and yet to conceive great faith, and to trust that for Christ's sake we have a God who has been reconciled, to ask of God, and assuredly to expect

His aid in all things that, according to our calling, are to be done; and meanwhile, to be diligent in outward good works, and to serve our calling. [50] In these things consist the true perfection and the true service of God. It does not consist in celibacy, or in begging, or in vile apparel. [51] But the people conceive many pernicious opinions from the false commendations of monastic life.

[52] They hear celibacy praised above measure; therefore they lead their married life with offense to their consciences. [53] They hear that only beggars are perfect; therefore they keep their possessions and do business with offense to their consciences. [54] They hear that it is an evangelical counsel not to seek revenge; therefore some in private life are not afraid to take revenge, for they hear that it is but a counsel, and not a commandment. [55] Others judge that the Christian cannot properly hold a civil office or be a magistrate.

[56] There are on record examples of men who, forsaking marriage and the administration of the Commonwealth, have hid themselves in monasteries. [57] This they called fleeing from the world, and seeking a kind of life which would be more pleasing to God. Neither did they see that God ought to be served in those commandments which He Himself has given and not in commandments devised by men. [58] A good and perfect kind of life is that which has for it the commandment of God. [59] It is necessary to admonish men of these things.

[60] And before these times, Gerson rebukes this error of the monks concerning perfection, and testifies that in his day it was a new saying that the monastic life is a state of perfection.

[61] So many wicked opinions are inherent in the vows, namely, that they justify, that they constitute Christian perfection, that they keep the counsels and commandments, that they have works of supererogation. All these things, since they are false and empty, make vows null and void.

ARTICLE 28

Of Ecclesiastical Power

[1] There has been great controversy concerning the Power of Bishops, in which some have awkwardly confounded the power of the Church and the power of the sword. [2] And from this confusion very great wars and tumults have resulted, while the Pontiffs, emboldened by the power of the Keys, not only have instituted new services and burdened consciences with reservation of cases and ruthless excommunications, but have also undertaken to transfer the kingdoms of this world, and to take the Empire from the Emperor. [3] These wrongs have long since been rebuked in the Church by learned and godly men. [4] Therefore our teachers, for the comforting of men's consciences, were constrained to show the difference between the power of the Church and the power of the sword, and taught that both of them, because of God's commandment, are to be held in reverence and honor, as the chief blessings of God on earth.

[5] But this is their opinion, that the power of the Keys, or the power of the bishops, according to the Gospel, is a power or commandment of God, to preach the Gospel, to remit and retain sins, and to administer Sacraments. [6] For with this commandment Christ sends forth His Apostles in John 20:21–22: As My Father hath sent Me, even so send I you. Receive ye the Holy Ghost. Whosesoever sins ye remit, they are remitted unto them; and whosesoever sins ye retain, they are retained. [7] And in Mark 16:15: Go preach the Gospel to every creature.

[8] This power is exercised only by teaching or preaching the Gospel and administering the Sacraments, according to their calling either to many or to individuals. For thereby are granted, not bodily, but eternal things, as eternal righteousness, the Holy Ghost, eternal life. [9] These things cannot come but by the ministry of the Word and the Sacraments, as Paul says in Romans 1:16: The Gospel is the power of

God unto salvation to every one that believeth. [10] Therefore, since the power of the Church grants eternal things, and is exercised only by the ministry of the Word, it does not interfere with civil government; no more than the art of singing interferes with civil government. [11] For civil government deals with other things than does the Gospel. The civil rulers defend not minds, but bodies and bodily things against manifest injuries, and restrain men with the sword and bodily punishments in order to preserve civil justice and peace.

[12] Therefore the power of the Church and the civil power must not be confounded. The power of the Church has its own commission to teach the Gospel and to administer the Sacraments. [13] Let it not break into the office of another; let it not transfer the kingdoms of this world; let it not abrogate the laws of civil rulers; let it not abolish lawful obedience; let it not interfere with judgments concerning civil ordinances or contracts; let it not prescribe laws to civil rulers concerning the form of the Commonwealth. [14] As Christ says in John 18:36: My kingdom is not of this world; [15] also in Luke 12:14: Who made Me a judge or a divider over you? [16] Paul also says in Philippians 3:20: Our citizenship is in heaven; [17] and in 2 Corinthians 10:4: The weapons of our warfare are not carnal, but mighty through God to the casting down of imaginations.

[18] After this manner our teachers discriminate between the duties of both these powers, and command that both be honored and acknowledged as gifts and blessings of God. [19] If bishops have any power of the sword, that power they have, not as bishops, by the commission of the Gospel, but by human law having received it of kings and emperors for the civil administration of what is theirs. This, however, is another office than the ministry of the Gospel.

[20] When, therefore, the question is concerning the jurisdiction of bishops, civil authority must be distinguished from ecclesiastical jurisdiction. [21] Again, according to the Gospel or, as they say,

by divine right, there belongs to the bishops as bishops, that is, to those to whom has been committed the ministry of the Word and the Sacraments, no jurisdiction except to forgive sins, to judge doctrine, to reject doctrines contrary to the Gospel, and to exclude from the communion of the Church wicked men, whose wickedness is known, and this without human force, simply by the Word. [22] Herein the congregations of necessity and by divine right must obey them, according to Luke 10:16: He that heareth you heareth Me. [23] But when they teach or ordain anything against the Gospel, then the congregations have a commandment of God prohibiting obedience. Matthew 7:15: Beware of false prophets; [24] Galatians 1:8: Though an angel from heaven preach any other gospel, let him be accursed; [25] 2 Corinthians 13:8: We can do nothing against the truth, but for the truth. [26] Also: The power which the Lord hath given me to edification, and not to destruction. [27] So, also, the Canonical Laws command (II. Q. VII. Cap., *Sacerdotes*, and Cap. *Oves*). [28] And Augustine (*Contra Petiliani Epistolam*): Neither must we submit to Catholic bishops if they chance to err, or hold anything contrary to the Canonical Scriptures of God.

[29] If they have any other power or jurisdiction, in hearing and judging certain cases, as of matrimony or of tithes, etc., they have it by human right, in which matters princes are bound, even against their will, when the ordinaries fail, to dispense justice to their subjects for the maintenance of peace. [30] Moreover, it is disputed whether bishops or pastors have the right to introduce ceremonies in the Church, and to make laws concerning meats, holy days and grades, that is, orders of ministers, etc. [31] They that give this right to the bishops refer to this testimony in John 16:12–13: I have yet many things to say unto you, but ye cannot bear them now. Howbeit when He, the Spirit of Truth, is come, He will guide you into all truth. [32] They also refer to the example of the Apostles, who commanded to abstain from blood and from things strangled (Acts 15:29). [33] They refer to

the Sabbath day as having been changed into the Lord's Day, contrary to the Decalog, as it seems. Neither is there any example whereof they make more than concerning the changing of the Sabbath day. Great, say they, is the power of the Church, since it has dispensed with one of the Ten Commandments!

[34] But concerning this question it is taught on our part (as has been shown above) that bishops have no power to decree anything against the Gospel. The Canonical Laws teach the same thing (Dist. IX). [35] Now, it is against Scripture to establish or require the observance of any traditions, to the end that by such observance we may make satisfaction for sins, or merit grace and righteousness. [36] For the glory of Christ's merit suffers injury when, by such observances, we undertake to merit justification. [37] But it is manifest that, by such belief, traditions have almost infinitely multiplied in the Church, the doctrine concerning faith and the righteousness of faith being meanwhile suppressed. For gradually more holy days were made, fasts appointed, new ceremonies and services in honor of saints instituted, because the authors of such things thought that by these works they were meriting grace. [38] Thus in times past the Penitential Canons increased, whereof we still see some traces in the satisfactions.

[39] Again, the authors of traditions do contrary to the command of God when they find matters of sin in foods, in days, and like things, and burden the Church with bondage of the law, as if there ought to be among Christians, in order to merit justification a service like the Levitical, the arrangement of which God had committed to the Apostles and bishops. [40] For thus some of them write; and the Pontiffs in some measure seem to be misled by the example of the law of Moses. [41] Hence are such burdens, as that they make it mortal sin, even without offense to others, to do manual labor on holy days, a mortal sin to omit the Canonical Hours, that certain foods defile the conscience that fastings are works which appease God that sin in

a reserved case cannot be forgiven but by the authority of him who reserved it; whereas the Canons themselves speak only of the reserving of the ecclesiastical penalty, and not of the reserving of the guilt.

[42] Whence have the bishops the right to lay these traditions upon the Church for the ensnaring of consciences, when Peter, in Acts 15:10, forbids to put a yoke upon the neck of the disciples, and Paul says, in 2 Corinthians 13:10, that the power given him was to edification not to destruction? Why, therefore, do they increase sins by these traditions?

[43] But there are clear testimonies which prohibit the making of such traditions, as though they merited grace or were necessary to salvation. [44] Paul says in Colossians 2:16–23: Let no man judge you in meat, or in drink, or in respect of an holy day, or of the new moon, or of the Sabbath days. [45] If ye be dead with Christ from the rudiments of the world, why, as though living in the world, are ye subject to ordinances (touch not; taste not; handle not, which all are to perish with the using) after the commandments and doctrines of men! which things have indeed a show of wisdom. [46] Also in Titus 1:14 he openly forbids traditions: Not giving heed to Jewish fables and commandments of men that turn from the truth.

[47] And Christ, in Matthew 15:13–14 says of those who require traditions: Let them alone; they be blind leaders of the blind; [48] and He rejects such services: Every plant which My heavenly Father hath not planted shall be plucked up.

[49] If bishops have the right to burden churches with infinite traditions, and to ensnare consciences, why does Scripture so often prohibit to make, and to listen to, traditions? Why does it call them "doctrines of devils" (1 Tim. 4:1)? Did the Holy Ghost in vain forewarn of these things? [50] Since, therefore, ordinances instituted as things necessary, or with an opinion of meriting grace, are contrary to the Gospel, it follows that it is not lawful for any bishop to institute or exact such services. [51] For it is necessary that the doctrine of Christian

liberty be preserved in the churches, namely, that the bondage of the Law is not necessary to justification, as it is written in the Epistle to the Galatians 5:1: Be not entangled again with the yoke of bondage. [52] It is necessary that the chief article of the Gospel be preserved, to wit, that we obtain grace freely by faith in Christ, and not for certain observances or acts of worship devised by men.

[53] What, then, are we to think of the Sunday and like rites in the house of God? To this we answer that it is lawful for bishops or pastors to make ordinances that things be done orderly in the Church, not that thereby we should merit grace or make satisfaction for sins, or that consciences be bound to judge them necessary services, and to think that it is a sin to break them without offense to others. [54] So Paul ordains, in 1 Corinthians 11:5, that women should cover their heads in the congregation, and in 1 Corinthians 14:30, that interpreters be heard in order in the church, etc.

[55] It is proper that the churches should keep such ordinances for the sake of love and tranquility, so far that one do not offend another, that all things be done in the churches in order, and without confusion (1 Cor. 14:40; cf. Phil. 2:14); [56] but so that consciences be not burdened to think that they are necessary to salvation, or to judge that they sin when they break them without offense to others; as no one will say that a woman sins who goes out in public with her head uncovered provided only that no offense be given.

[57] Of this kind is the observance of the Lord's Day, Easter, Pentecost, and like holy days and rites. [58] For those who judge that by the authority of the Church the observance of the Lord's Day instead of the Sabbath day was ordained as a thing necessary, do greatly err. [59] Scripture has abrogated the Sabbath day; for it teaches that, since the Gospel has been revealed, all the ceremonies of Moses can be omitted. [60] And yet, because it was necessary to appoint a certain day, that the people might know when they ought to come together, it appears that

the Church designated the Lord's Day for this purpose; and this day seems to have been chosen all the more for this additional reason, that men might have an example of Christian liberty, and might know that the keeping neither of the Sabbath nor of any other day is necessary.

[61] There are monstrous disputations concerning the changing of the law, the ceremonies of the new law, the changing of the Sabbath day, which all have sprung from the false belief that there must needs be in the Church a service like to the Levitical, and that Christ had given commission to the Apostles and bishops to devise new ceremonies as necessary to salvation. [62] These errors crept into the Church when the righteousness of faith was not taught clearly enough. [63] Some dispute that the keeping of the Lord's Day is not indeed of divine right, but in a manner so. They prescribe concerning holy days, how far it is lawful to work. [64] What else are such disputations than snares of consciences? For although they endeavor to modify the traditions, yet the mitigation can never be perceived as long as the opinion remains that they are necessary, which must needs remain where the righteousness of faith and Christian liberty are not known.

[65] The Apostles commanded in Acts 15:20 to abstain from blood. Who does now observe it? And yet they that do it not sin not; for not even the Apostles themselves wanted to burden consciences with such bondage; but they forbade it for a time, to avoid offense. [66] For in this decree we must perpetually consider what the aim of the Gospel is.

[67] Scarcely any Canons are kept with exactness, and from day to day many go out of use even among those who are the most zealous advocates of traditions. [68] Neither can due regard be paid to consciences unless this mitigation be observed, that we know that the Canons are kept without holding them to be necessary, and that no harm is done consciences, even though traditions go out of use.

[69] But the bishops might easily retain the lawful obedience of the people if they would not insist upon the observance of such traditions

as cannot be kept with a good conscience. [70] Now they command celibacy; they admit none unless they swear that they will not teach the pure doctrine of the Gospel. [71] The churches do not ask that the bishops should restore concord at the expense of their honor; which, nevertheless, it would be proper for good pastors to do. [72] They ask only that they would release unjust burdens which are new and have been received contrary to the custom of the Church Catholic. [73] It may be that in the beginning there were plausible reasons for some of these ordinances; and yet they are not adapted to later times. [74] It is also evident that some were adopted through erroneous conceptions. Therefore it would be befitting the clemency of the Pontiffs to mitigate them now, because such a modification does not shake the unity of the Church. For many human traditions have been changed in process of time, as the Canons themselves show. [75] But if it be impossible to obtain a mitigation of such observances as cannot be kept without sin, we are bound to follow the apostolic rule, Acts 5:29, which commands us to obey God rather than men.

[76] Peter, in 1 Peter 5:3, forbids bishops to be lords, and to rule over the churches. [77] It is not our design now to wrest the government from the bishops, but this one thing is asked, namely, that they allow the Gospel to be purely taught, and that they relax some few observances which cannot be kept without sin. [78] But if they make no concession, it is for them to see how they shall give account to God for furnishing, by their obstinacy, a cause for schism.

Conclusion

[1] These are the chief articles which seem to be in controversy. For although we might have spoken of more abuses, yet, to avoid undue length, we have set forth the chief points, from which the rest may be readily judged. [2] There have been great complaints concerning

indulgences, pilgrimages, and the abuse of excommunications. The parishes have been vexed in many ways by the dealers in indulgences. There were endless contentions between the pastors and the monks concerning the parochial right, confessions, burials, sermons on extraordinary occasions, and innumerable other things. [3] Issues of this sort we have passed over so that the chief points in this matter, having been briefly set forth, might be the more readily understood. [4] Nor has anything been here said or adduced to the reproach of anyone. [5] Only those things have been recounted whereof we thought that it was necessary to speak, in order that it might be understood that in doctrine and ceremonies nothing has been received on our part against Scripture or the Church Catholic. For it is manifest that we have taken most diligent care that no new and ungodly doctrine should creep into our churches.

[6] The above articles we desire to present in accordance with the edict of Your Imperial Majesty, in order to exhibit our Confession and let men see a summary of the doctrine of our teachers. [7] If there is anything that anyone might desire in this Confession, we are ready, God willing, to present ampler information according to the Scriptures.

[8] Your Imperial Majesty's faithful subjects:
[9] John, Duke of Saxony, Elector.
[10] George, Margrave of Brandenburg.
[11] Ernest, Duke of Lueneberg.
[12] Philip, Landgrave of Hesse.
[13] John Frederick, Duke of Saxony.
[14] Francis, Duke of Lueneburg.
[15] Wolfgang, Prince of Anhalt.
[16] Senate and Magistracy of Nuremburg.
[17] Senate of Reutlingen.

The Belgic Confession

INTRODUCTION

Although first written in French, the Belgic Confession is best known in Dutch and German translation and stands as one of three confessional documents typically used in Reformed denominations originating in northern Europe.

The Belgic Confession was produced in 1561 during an intense time of confession writing—almost fifty Reformed confessions and catechisms in twenty years. The confession stands out for its doctrinal warmth and its author's courage. It was written by Guido de Bres, a pastor who served in what is today called Belgium and was a one-time student of John Calvin. In this confession, de Bres sought to persuade the Spanish king, Philip II—whose forces occupied the Low Countries—that Protestants should not be persecuted for their faith, given that what they believe is thoroughly biblical. Within a few years de Bres paid for his faith with his life.

The thirty-seven articles of the Belgic Confession begin with the doctrine of God and man's knowledge of God, giving considerable attention to the authority and sufficiency of the Scriptures and to the biblical canon. Only with those foundations established do Articles 8–11 offer a lengthy statement and defense of the doctrine of the Trinity and the deity of Christ and the Holy Spirit. Articles on creation and providence are followed by a discussion of man's creation, the fall, and sin.

A robust article on election sets the stage for five articles on the redemption purchased by Christ, leading into articles on justification by faith and the necessity of sanctification. One heading addressing the abolishment of the ceremonial law is paired with another announcing Christ's all-sufficiency as our intercessor. Here readers encounter a standout chapter—and one of the confession's longest—in which believers are led into a dialogue in which each doubt about Christ's willingness and qualification to save us is powerfully answered by the words of Scripture.

The importance of the church, its order, and its sacraments occupy nine further articles. The discussions of both the government of the church and the doctrine of the Lord's Supper are distinctly Reformed in flavor. Instruction about church government advocates rule by minister and elders, with deacons assisting. Treatment of the Supper emphasizes that Christ is present by his Holy Spirit and that this benefit is derived from the Supper only by those who receive it in faith.

Articles on the civil magistrate (along with comments elsewhere) deliberately distinguish the Reformed from Anabaptists. Indeed, while the confession complains about a variety of problems, Anabaptists are cited for the widest range of errors. The fact that the article on the civil magistrate draws attention to the Anabaptists is an ominous reminder that concepts of Christian liberty remained in their infancy during the long Reformation.

THE BELGIC CONFESSION

ARTICLE 1

The Only God

We all believe in our hearts and confess with our mouths that there is a single and simple spiritual being, whom we call God—eternal, incomprehensible, invisible, unchangeable, infinite, almighty; completely wise, just, and good, and the overflowing source of all good.

ARTICLE 2

The Means by Which We Know God

We know him by two means:

First, by the creation, preservation, and government of the universe, since that universe is before our eyes like a beautiful book in which all creatures, great and small, are as letters to make us ponder the invisible things of God: his eternal power and his divinity, as the apostle Paul says in Romans 1:20.

All these things are enough to convict men and to leave them without excuse.

Second, he makes himself known to us more openly by his holy and divine Word, as much as we need in this life, for his glory and for the salvation of his own.

ARTICLE 3

The Written Word of God

We confess that this Word of God was not sent nor delivered by the will of men, but that holy men of God spoke, being moved by the Holy Spirit, as Peter says.[a]

Afterward our God—because of the special care he has for us and our salvation—commanded his servants, the prophets and apostles, to commit this revealed Word to writing. He himself wrote with his own finger the two tables of the law.

Therefore we call such writings holy and divine Scriptures.

a 2 Pet. 1:21

ARTICLE 4

The Canonical Books

We include in the Holy Scripture the two volumes of the Old and New Testaments. They are canonical books with which there can be no quarrel at all.

In the church of God the list is as follows:

In the Old Testament,

> the five books of Moses: Genesis, Exodus, Leviticus, Numbers, Deuteronomy;
> the books of Joshua, Judges, Ruth;
> the two books of Samuel,
> the two books of Kings,
> the two books of Chronicles;
> the books of Ezra, Nehemiah, Esther;
> the book of Job,

the Psalms,

the three books of Solomon: Proverbs, Ecclesiastes, the Song of
Songs;

the five books of the four major prophets: Isaiah, Jeremiah, Lamentations, Ezekiel, Daniel;

the books of the twelve minor prophets: Hosea, Joel, Amos, Obadiah, Jonah, Micah, Nahum, Habakkuk, Zephaniah, Haggai,
Zechariah, Malachi.

In the New Testament,

the four Gospels: Matthew, Mark, Luke, John;

the Acts of the Apostles;

the thirteen letters of Paul: to the Romans; the two letters to the
Corinthians; to the Galatians, Ephesians, Philippians, Colossians;
the two letters to the Thessalonians; the two letters to Timothy;
to Titus, Philemon;

the letter to the Hebrews;

the seven letters of the other apostles: one of James; two of Peter;
three of John; one of Jude;

and the Revelation of the apostle John.

ARTICLE 5
The Authority of Scripture

We receive all these books and these only as holy and canonical, for
the regulating, founding, and establishing of our faith.

And we believe without a doubt all things contained in them—not
so much because the church receives and approves them as such but
above all because the Holy Spirit testifies in our hearts that they are
from God, and also because they prove themselves to be from God.

For even the blind themselves are able to see that the things predicted in them do happen.

ARTICLE 6
The Difference between Canonical
and Apocryphal Books

We distinguish between these holy books and the apocryphal ones, which are:

the third and fourth books of Esdras;
the books of Tobit, Judith, Wisdom, Jesus Sirach, Baruch;
what was added to the Story of Esther;
the Song of the Three Children in the Furnace;
the Story of Susannah;
the Story of Bel and the Dragon;
the Prayer of Manasseh;
and the two books of Maccabees.

The church may certainly read these books and learn from them as far as they agree with the canonical books. But they do not have such power and virtue that one could confirm from their testimony any point of faith or of the Christian religion. Much less can they detract from the authority of the other holy books.

ARTICLE 7
The Sufficiency of Scripture

We believe that this Holy Scripture contains the will of God completely and that everything one must believe to be saved is sufficiently taught in it.

For since the entire manner of service which God requires of us is described in it at great length, no one—even an apostle or an angel from heaven, as Paul says[a]—ought to teach other than what the Holy Scriptures have already taught us.

For since it is forbidden to add to or subtract from the Word of God,[b] this plainly demonstrates that the teaching is perfect and complete in all respects.

Therefore we must not consider human writings—no matter how holy their authors may have been—equal to the divine writings; nor may we put custom, nor the majority, nor age, nor the passage of time or persons, nor councils, decrees, or official decisions above the truth of God, for truth is above everything else.

For all human beings are liars by nature and more vain than vanity itself.

Therefore we reject with all our hearts everything that does not agree with this infallible rule, as we are taught to do by the apostles when they say, "Test the spirits to see if they are of God,"[c] and also, "If anyone comes to you and does not bring this teaching, do not receive him into your house."[d]

a Gal. 1:8   b Deut. 12:32; Rev. 22:18–19   c 1 John 4:1   d 2 John 10

ARTICLE 8
The Trinity

In keeping with this truth and Word of God we believe in one God, who is one single essence, in whom there are three persons, really, truly, and eternally distinct according to their incommunicable properties—namely, Father, Son, and Holy Spirit.

The Father is the cause, origin, and source of all things, visible as well as invisible.

The Son is the Word, the Wisdom, and the image of the Father.

The Holy Spirit is the eternal power and might, proceeding from the Father and the Son.

Nevertheless, this distinction does not divide God into three, since Scripture teaches us that the Father, the Son, and the Holy Spirit each has his own subsistence distinguished by characteristics—yet in such a way that these three persons are only one God.

It is evident then that the Father is not the Son and that the Son is not the Father, and that likewise the Holy Spirit is neither the Father nor the Son.

Nevertheless, these persons, thus distinct, are neither divided nor fused or mixed together. For the Father did not take on flesh, nor did the Spirit, but only the Son.

The Father was never without his Son, nor without his Holy Spirit, since all these are equal from eternity, in one and the same essence.

There is neither a first nor a last, for all three are one in truth and power, in goodness and mercy.

ARTICLE 9
The Scriptural Witness on the Trinity

All these things we know from the testimonies of Holy Scripture as well as from the effects of the persons, especially from those we feel within ourselves.

The testimonies of the Holy Scriptures, which teach us to believe in this Holy Trinity, are written in many places of the Old Testament, which need not be enumerated but only chosen with discretion.

In the book of Genesis God says, "Let us make man in our image, according to our likeness." So "God created man in his own image"—indeed, "male and female he created them."[a] "Behold, man has become like one of us."[b]

It appears from this that there is a plurality of persons within the Deity, when he says, "Let us make man in our image"—and afterward he indicates the unity when he says, "God created."

It is true that he does not say here how many persons there are—but what is somewhat obscure to us in the Old Testament is very clear in the New.

For when our Lord was baptized in the Jordan, the voice of the Father was heard saying, "This is my dear Son";[c] the Son was seen in the water; and the Holy Spirit appeared in the form of a dove.

So, in the baptism of all believers this form was prescribed by Christ: "Baptize all people in the name of the Father, and of the Son, and of the Holy Spirit."[d]

In the Gospel according to Luke the angel Gabriel says to Mary, the mother of our Lord: "The Holy Spirit will come upon you, and the power of the Most High will overshadow you; and therefore that holy one to be born of you shall be called the Son of God."[e]

And in another place it says: "The grace of our Lord Jesus Christ, and the love of God, and the fellowship of the Holy Spirit be with you."[f]

"There are three who bear witness in heaven—the Father, the Word, and the Holy Spirit—and these three are one."[g]

In all these passages we are fully taught that there are three persons in the one and only divine essence. And although this doctrine surpasses human understanding, we nevertheless believe it now, through the Word, waiting to know and enjoy it fully in heaven.

Furthermore, we must note the particular works and activities of these three persons in relation to us. The Father is called our Creator, by reason of his power. The Son is our Savior and Redeemer, by his blood. The Holy Spirit is our Sanctifier, by his living in our hearts.

This doctrine of the Holy Trinity has always been maintained in the true church, from the time of the apostles until the present, against Jews, Muslims, and certain false Christians and heretics, such as Marcion, Mani, Praxeas, Sabellius, Paul of Samosata, Arius, and others like them, who were rightly condemned by the holy fathers.

And so, in this matter we willingly accept the three ecumenical creeds—the Apostles', Nicene, and Athanasian—as well as what the ancient fathers decided in agreement with them.

a Gen. 1:26–27 b Gen. 3:22 c Matt. 3:17 d Matt. 28:19 e Luke 1:35 f 2 Cor. 13:14 g 1 John 5:7 (KJV)

ARTICLE 10
The Deity of Christ

We believe that Jesus Christ, according to his divine nature, is the only Son of God—eternally begotten, not made nor created, for then he would be a creature.

He is one in essence with the Father; coeternal; the exact image of the person of the Father and the "reflection of his glory,"[a] being in all things like him.

He is the Son of God not only from the time he assumed our nature but from all eternity, as the following testimonies teach us when they are taken together.

Moses says that God "created the world";[b] and John says that "all things were created by the Word,"[c] which he calls God. The letter to the Hebrews says that "God made the world by his Son."[d] Paul says that "God created all things by Jesus Christ."[e]

And so it must follow that he who is called God, the Word, the Son, and Jesus Christ already existed when all things were created by him. Therefore the prophet Micah says that his origin is "from ancient times, from eternity."[f] And Hebrews says that he has "neither beginning of days nor end of life."[g]

So then, he is the true eternal God, the Almighty, whom we invoke, worship, and serve.

a Col. 1:15; Heb. 1:3 b Gen. 1:1 c John 1:3 d Heb. 1:2 e Col. 1:16 f Mic. 5:2 g Heb. 7:3

ARTICLE 11
The Deity of the Holy Spirit

We believe and confess also that the Holy Spirit proceeds eternally from the Father and the Son—neither made, nor created, nor begotten, but only proceeding from the two of them. In regard to order, he is the third person of the Trinity—of one and the same essence, and majesty, and glory, with the Father and the Son.

He is true and eternal God, as the Holy Scriptures teach us.

ARTICLE 12
The Creation of All Things

We believe that the Father created heaven and earth and all other creatures from nothing, when it seemed good to him, by his Word—that is to say, by his Son.

He has given all creatures their being, form, and appearance, and their various functions for serving their Creator.

Even now he also sustains and governs them all, according to his eternal providence, and by his infinite power, that they may serve man, in order that man may serve God.

He has also created the angels good, that they might be his messengers and serve his elect.

Some of them have fallen from the excellence in which God created them into eternal perdition; and the others have persisted and remained in their original state, by the grace of God. The devils and evil spirits are so corrupt that they are enemies of God and of everything good. They lie in wait for the church and every member of it like thieves, with all their power, to destroy and spoil everything by their deceptions.

So then, by their own wickedness they are condemned to everlasting damnation, daily awaiting their torments.

For that reason we detest the error of the Sadducees, who deny that there are spirits and angels, and also the error of the Manicheans, who say that the devils originated by themselves, being evil by nature, without having been corrupted.

ARTICLE 13
The Doctrine of God's Providence

We believe that this good God, after he created all things, did not abandon them to chance or fortune but leads and governs them according to his holy will, in such a way that nothing happens in this world without his orderly arrangement.

Yet God is not the author of, nor can he be charged with, the sin that occurs. For his power and goodness are so great and incomprehensible that he arranges and does his work very well and justly even when the devils and wicked men act unjustly.

We do not wish to inquire with undue curiosity into what he does that surpasses human understanding and is beyond our ability to comprehend. But in all humility and reverence we adore the just judgments of God, which are hidden from us, being content to be Christ's disciples, so as to learn only what he shows us in his Word, without going beyond those limits.

This doctrine gives us unspeakable comfort since it teaches us that nothing can happen to us by chance but only by the arrangement of our gracious heavenly Father. He watches over us with fatherly care, keeping all creatures under his control, so that not one of the hairs on our heads (for they are all numbered) nor even a little bird can fall to the ground[a] without the will of our Father.

In this thought we rest, knowing that he holds in check the devils and all our enemies, who cannot hurt us without his permission and will.

For that reason we reject the damnable error of the Epicureans, who say that God involves himself in nothing and leaves everything to chance.

a Matt. 10:29–30

ARTICLE 14
The Creation and Fall of Man

We believe that God created man from the dust of the earth and made and formed him in his image and likeness—good, just, and holy; able by his own will to conform in all things to the will of God.

But when he was in honor he did not understand it[a] and did not recognize his excellence. But he subjected himself willingly to sin and consequently to death and the curse, lending his ear to the word of the devil.

For he transgressed the commandment of life, which he had received, and by his sin he separated himself from God, who was his true life, having corrupted his entire nature.

So he made himself guilty and subject to physical and spiritual death, having become wicked, perverse, and corrupt in all his ways. He lost all his excellent gifts which he had received from God, and he retained none of them except for small traces which are enough to make him inexcusable.

Moreover, all the light in us is turned to darkness, as the Scripture teaches us: "The light shone in the darkness, and the darkness did not receive it."[b] Here John calls men "darkness."

Therefore we reject everything taught to the contrary concerning man's free will, since man is nothing but the slave of sin and cannot do a thing unless it is "given him from heaven."[c]

For who can boast of being able to do anything good by himself, since Christ says, "No one can come to me unless my Father who sent me draws him"?[d]

Who can glory in his own will when he understands that "the mind of the flesh is enmity against God"?[e] Who can speak of his own knowledge in view of the fact that "the natural man does not understand the things of the Spirit of God"?[f] In short, who can produce a single thought, since he knows that we are "not able to think a thing" about ourselves, by ourselves, but that "our ability is from God"?[g]

And therefore, what the apostle says ought rightly to stand fixed and firm: "God works within us both to will and to do according to his good pleasure."[h]

For there is no understanding nor will conforming to God's understanding and will apart from Christ's work, as he teaches us when he says, "Without me you can do nothing."[i]

a Ps. 49:20   b John 1:5   c John 3:27   d John 6:44   e Rom. 8:7   f 1 Cor. 2:14   g 2 Cor. 3:5   h Phil. 2:13   i John 15:5

ARTICLE 15
The Doctrine of Original Sin

We believe that by the disobedience of Adam original sin has been spread through the whole human race.[a]

It is a corruption of all nature—an inherited depravity which even infects small infants in their mother's womb, and the root which produces in man every sort of sin. It is therefore so vile and enormous in God's sight that it is enough to condemn the human race, and it is not abolished or wholly uprooted even by baptism, seeing that sin constantly boils forth as though from a contaminated spring.

Nevertheless, it is not imputed to God's children for their condemnation but is forgiven by his grace and mercy—not to put them to sleep but so that the awareness of this corruption might often make believers groan as they long to be set free from the "body of this death."[b]

Therefore we reject the error of the Pelagians who say that this sin is nothing else than a matter of imitation.

a Rom. 5:12–13 b Rom. 7:24

ARTICLE 16
The Doctrine of Election

We believe that—all Adam's descendants having thus fallen into perdition and ruin by the sin of the first man—God showed himself to be as he is: merciful and just.

He is merciful in withdrawing and saving from this perdition those whom he, in his eternal and unchangeable counsel, has elected and chosen in Jesus Christ our Lord by his pure goodness, without any consideration of their works.

He is just in leaving the others in their ruin and fall into which they plunged themselves.

ARTICLE 17
The Recovery of Fallen Man

We believe that our good God, by his marvelous wisdom and goodness, seeing that man had plunged himself in this manner into both physical and spiritual death and made himself completely miserable, set out to find him, though man, trembling all over, was fleeing from him.

And he comforted him, promising to give him his Son, "born of a woman,"[a] to crush the head of the serpent,[b] and to make him blessed.

a Gal. 4:4 b Gen. 3:15

So then we confess that God fulfilled the promise which he had made to the early fathers by the mouth of his holy prophets when he sent his only and eternal Son into the world at the time set by him.

The Son took the "form of a servant" and was made in the "likeness of man,"ᵃ truly assuming a real human nature, with all its weaknesses, except for sin; being conceived in the womb of the blessed Virgin Mary by the power of the Holy Spirit, without male participation.

And he not only assumed human nature as far as the body is concerned but also a real human soul, in order that he might be a real human being. For since the soul had been lost as well as the body he had to assume them both to save them both together.

Therefore we confess, against the heresy of the Anabaptists who deny that Christ assumed human flesh from his mother, that he "shared the very flesh and blood of children";ᵇ that he is "fruit of the loins of David" according to the flesh;ᶜ "born of the seed of David" according to the flesh;ᵈ "fruit of the womb of the Virgin Mary";ᵉ "born of a woman";ᶠ "the seed of David";ᵍ "a shoot from the root of Jesse";ʰ "the offspring of Judah,"ⁱ having descended from the Jews according to the flesh; "from the seed of Abraham"—for he "assumed Abraham's seed" and was "made like his brothers except for sin."ʲ

In this way he is truly our Immanuel—that is: "God with us."ᵏ

a Phil. 2:7 b Heb. 2:14 c Acts 2:30 d Rom. 1:3 e Luke 1:42 f Gal. 4:4 g 2 Tim. 2:8 h Rom. 15:12
i Heb. 7:14 j Heb. 2:17; 4:15 k Matt. 1:23

ARTICLE 19

The Two Natures of Christ

We believe that by being thus conceived the person of the Son has been inseparably united and joined together with human nature, in such a way that there are not two Sons of God, nor two persons, but two natures united in a single person, with each nature retaining its own distinct properties.

Thus his divine nature has always remained uncreated, "without beginning of days or end of life,"[a] filling heaven and earth.

His human nature has not lost its properties but continues to have those of a creature—it has a beginning of days; it is of a finite nature and retains all that belongs to a real body. And even though he, by his resurrection, gave it immortality, that nonetheless did not change the reality of his human nature; for our salvation and resurrection depend also on the reality of his body.

But these two natures are so united together in one person that they are not even separated by his death.

So then, what he committed to his Father when he died was a real human spirit which left his body. But meanwhile his divine nature remained united with his human nature even when he was lying in the grave; and his deity never ceased to be in him, just as it was in him when he was a little child, though for a while it did not show itself as such.

These are the reasons why we confess him to be true God and true man—true God in order to conquer death by his power, and true man that he might die for us in the weakness of his flesh.

a Heb. 7:3

ARTICLE 20

The Justice and Mercy of God in Christ

We believe that God—who is perfectly merciful and also very just—sent his Son to assume the nature in which the disobedience had been committed, in order to bear in it the punishment of sin by his most bitter passion and death.

So God made known his justice toward his Son, who was charged with our sin, and he poured out his goodness and mercy on us, who are guilty and worthy of damnation, giving to us his Son to die, by a most perfect love, and raising him to life for our justification, in order that by him we might have immortality and eternal life.

ARTICLE 21

The Atonement

We believe that Jesus Christ is a high priest forever according to the order of Melchizedek—made such by an oath—and that he presented himself in our name before his Father, to appease his wrath with full satisfaction by offering himself on the tree of the cross and pouring out his precious blood for the cleansing of our sins, as the prophets had predicted.

For it is written that "the chastisement of our peace" was placed on the Son of God and that "we are healed by his wounds." He was "led to death as a lamb"; he was "numbered among sinners"[a] and condemned as a criminal by Pontius Pilate, though Pilate had declared that he was innocent.

So he paid back what he had not stolen,[b] and he suffered—the "just for the unjust,"[c] in both his body and his soul—in such a way that when he sensed the horrible punishment required by our sins his sweat became like "big drops of blood falling on the ground."[d] He cried, "My God, my God, why have you abandoned me?"[e]

And he endured all this for the forgiveness of our sins.

Therefore we rightly say with Paul that we "know nothing but Jesus and him crucified";[f] we consider all things as "dung for the excellence of the knowledge of our Lord Jesus Christ."[g] We find all comforts in his wounds and have no need to seek or invent any other means to reconcile ourselves with God than this one and only sacrifice, once made, which renders believers perfect forever.

This is also why the angel of God called him Jesus—that is, "Savior"—because he would save his people from their sins.[h]

a Isa. 53:4–12 b Ps. 69:4 c 1 Pet. 3:18 d Luke 22:44 e Matt. 27:46 f 1 Cor. 2:2 g Phil. 3:8
h Matt. 1:21

ARTICLE 22
The Righteousness of Faith

We believe that for us to acquire the true knowledge of this great mystery the Holy Spirit kindles in our hearts a true faith that embraces Jesus Christ, with all his merits, and makes him its own, and no longer looks for anything apart from him.

For it must necessarily follow that either all that is required for our salvation is not in Christ or, if all is in him, then he who has Christ by faith has his salvation entirely.

Therefore, to say that Christ is not enough but that something else is needed as well is a most enormous blasphemy against God—for it then would follow that Jesus Christ is only half a Savior. And therefore we justly say with Paul that we are justified "by faith alone" or by faith "apart from works."[a]

However, we do not mean, properly speaking, that it is faith itself that justifies us—for faith is only the instrument by which we embrace Christ, our righteousness.

But Jesus Christ is our righteousness, crediting to us all his merits and all the holy works he has done for us and in our place. And faith is the instrument that keeps us in communion with him and with all his benefits.

When those benefits are made ours they are more than enough to absolve us of our sins.

a Rom. 3:28

The Justification of Sinners

We believe that our blessedness lies in the forgiveness of our sins because of Jesus Christ, and that in it our righteousness before God is contained, as David and Paul teach us when they declare that man blessed to whom God grants righteousness apart from works.[a]

And the same apostle says that we are justified "freely" or "by grace" through redemption in Jesus Christ.[b] And therefore we cling to this foundation, which is firm forever, giving all glory to God, humbling ourselves, and recognizing ourselves as we are; not claiming a thing for ourselves or our merits and leaning and resting only on the obedience of Christ crucified, which is ours when we believe in him.

That is enough to cover all our sins and to make us confident, freeing the conscience from the fear, dread, and terror of God's approach, without doing what our first father, Adam, did, who trembled as he tried to cover himself with fig leaves.

In fact, if we had to appear before God relying—no matter how little—on ourselves or some other creature, then, alas, we would be swallowed up.

Therefore everyone must say with David: "Lord, do not enter into judgment with your servants, for before you no living person shall be justified."[c]

a Ps. 32:1; Rom. 4:6 b Rom. 3:24 c Ps. 143:2

ARTICLE 24
The Sanctification of Sinners

We believe that this true faith, produced in man by the hearing of God's Word and by the work of the Holy Spirit, regenerates him and makes him a "new man,"[a] causing him to live the "new life"[b] and freeing him from the slavery of sin.

Therefore, far from making people cold toward living in a pious and holy way, this justifying faith, quite to the contrary, so works within them that apart from it they will never do a thing out of love for God but only out of love for themselves and fear of being condemned.

So then, it is impossible for this holy faith to be unfruitful in a human being, seeing that we do not speak of an empty faith but of what Scripture calls "faith working through love,"[c] which leads a man to do of himself the works that God has commanded in his Word.

These works, proceeding from the good root of faith, are good and acceptable to God, since they are all sanctified by his grace.

Yet they do not count toward our justification—for by faith in Christ we are justified, even before we do good works. Otherwise they could not be good, any more than the fruit of a tree could be good if the tree is not good in the first place.

So then, we do good works, but not for merit—for what would we merit? Rather, we are indebted to God for the good works we do, and not he to us, since it is he who "works in us both to will and do according to his good pleasure"[d]—thus keeping in mind what is written: "When you have done all that is commanded you, then you shall say, 'We are unworthy servants; we have done what it was our duty to do.'"[e] Yet we do not wish to deny that God rewards good works—but it is by his grace that he crowns his gifts.

Moreover, although we do good works we do not base our salvation on them; for we cannot do any work that is not defiled by our flesh and also worthy of punishment. And even if we could point to one, memory of a single sin is enough for God to reject that work.

So we would always be in doubt, tossed back and forth without any certainty, and our poor consciences would be tormented constantly if they did not rest on the merit of the suffering and death of our Savior.

a 2 Cor. 5:17 b Rom. 6:4 c Gal. 5:6 d Phil. 2:13 e Luke 17:10

ARTICLE 25
The Fulfillment of the Law

We believe that the ceremonies and symbols of the law have ended with the coming of Christ, and that all foreshadowings have come to an end, so that the use of them ought to be abolished among Christians. Yet the truth and substance of these things remain for us in Jesus Christ, in whom they have been fulfilled.

Nevertheless, we continue to use the witnesses drawn from the law and prophets to confirm us in the gospel and to regulate our lives with full integrity for the glory of God, according to his will.

ARTICLE 26
The Intercession of Christ

We believe that we have no access to God except through the one and only Mediator and Intercessor: Jesus Christ the Righteous.[a]

He therefore was made man, uniting together the divine and human natures, so that we human beings might have access to the divine Majesty. Otherwise we would have no access.

But this Mediator, whom the Father has appointed between himself and us, ought not terrify us by his greatness, so that we have to look for another one, according to our fancy. For neither in heaven nor among the creatures on earth is there anyone who loves us more than Jesus Christ does. Although he was "in the form of God," he nevertheless "emptied himself," taking the form of "a man" and "a servant" for us;[b] and he made himself "completely like his brothers."[c]

Suppose we had to find another intercessor. Who would love us more than he who gave his life for us, even though "we were his enemies"?[d] And suppose we had to find one who has prestige and power. Who has as much of these as he who is seated "at the right hand of the Father,"[e] and who has all power "in heaven and on earth"?[f] And who will be heard more readily than God's own dearly beloved Son?

So then, sheer unbelief has led to the practice of dishonoring the saints, instead of honoring them. That was something the saints never did nor asked for, but which in keeping with their duty, as appears from their writings, they consistently refused.

We should not plead here that we are unworthy—for it is not a question of offering our prayers on the basis of our own dignity but only on the basis of the excellence and dignity of Jesus Christ, whose righteousness is ours by faith.

Since the apostle for good reason wants us to get rid of this foolish fear—or rather, this unbelief—he says to us that Jesus Christ was "made like his brothers in all things," that he might be a high priest who is merciful and faithful to purify the sins of the people.[g] For since he suffered, being tempted, he is also able to help those who are tempted.[h]

And further, to encourage us more to approach him he says, "Since we have a high priest, Jesus the Son of God, who has entered into heaven, we maintain our confession. For we do not have a high priest who is unable to have compassion for our weaknesses, but one who was tempted in all things, just as we are, except for sin. Let us go then with confidence to the throne of grace that we may obtain mercy and find grace, in order to be helped."[i] The same apostle says that we "have liberty to enter into the holy place by the blood of Jesus. Let us go, then, in the assurance of faith. . . ."[j]

Likewise, "Christ's priesthood is forever. By this he is able to save completely those who draw near to God through him who always lives to intercede for them."[k]

What more do we need? For Christ himself declares: "I am the way, the truth, and the life; no one comes to my Father but by me."[l] Why should we seek another intercessor?

Since it has pleased God to give us his Son as our Intercessor, let us not leave him for another—or rather seek, without ever finding. For when God gave him to us he knew well that we were sinners.

Therefore, in following the command of Christ we call on the heavenly Father through Christ, our only Mediator, as we are taught by the Lord's Prayer, being assured that we shall obtain all we ask of the Father in his name.

a 1 John 2:1 b Phil. 2:6–8 c Heb. 2:17 d Rom. 5:10 e Rom. 8:34; Heb. 1:3 f Matt. 28:18 g Heb. 2:17 h Heb. 2:18 i Heb. 4:14–16 j Heb. 10:19, 22 k Heb. 7:24–25 l John 14:6

ARTICLE 27
The Holy Catholic Church

We believe and confess one single catholic or universal church—a holy congregation and gathering of true Christian believers, awaiting their entire salvation in Jesus Christ being washed by his blood, and sanctified and sealed by the Holy Spirit.

This church has existed from the beginning of the world and will last until the end, as appears from the fact that Christ is eternal King who cannot be without subjects.

And this holy church is preserved by God against the rage of the whole world, even though for a time it may appear very small in the eyes of men—as though it were snuffed out.

For example, during the very dangerous time of Ahab the Lord preserved for himself seven thousand men who did not bend their knees to Baal.[a]

And so this holy church is not confined, bound, or limited to a certain place or certain persons. But it is spread and dispersed throughout the entire world, though still joined and united in heart and will, in one and the same Spirit, by the power of faith.

a 1 Kings 19:18

ARTICLE 28
The Obligations of Church Members

We believe that since this holy assembly and congregation is the gathering of those who are saved and there is no salvation apart from it, no one ought to withdraw from it, content to be by himself, regardless of his status or condition.

But all people are obliged to join and unite with it, keeping the unity of the church by submitting to its instruction and discipline, by bending their necks under the yoke of Jesus Christ, and by serving to build up one another, according to the gifts God has given them as members of each other in the same body.

And to preserve this unity more effectively, it is the duty of all believers, according to God's Word, to separate themselves from those who do not belong to the church, in order to join this assembly wherever God has established it, even if civil authorities and royal decrees forbid and death and physical punishment result.

And so, all who withdraw from the church or do not join it act contrary to God's ordinance.

We believe that we ought to discern diligently and very carefully, by the Word of God, what is the true church—for all sects in the world today claim for themselves the name of "the church."

We are not speaking here of the company of hypocrites who are mixed among the good in the church and who nonetheless are not part of it, even though they are physically there. But we are speaking of distinguishing the body and fellowship of the true church from all sects that call themselves "the church."

The true church can be recognized if it has the following marks: the church engages in the pure preaching of the gospel; it makes use of the pure administration of the sacraments as Christ instituted them; it practices church discipline for correcting faults.

In short, it governs itself according to the pure Word of God, rejecting all things contrary to it and holding Jesus Christ as the only Head. By these marks one can be assured of recognizing the true church—and no one ought to be separated from it.

As for those who are of the church, we can recognize them by the distinguishing marks of Christians: namely by faith, and by their fleeing from sin and pursuing righteousness, once they have received the one and only Savior, Jesus Christ. They love the true God and their neighbors, without turning to the right or left, and they crucify the flesh and its works.

Though great weakness remains in them, they fight against it by the Spirit all the days of their lives, appealing constantly to the blood, suffering, death, and obedience of the Lord Jesus, in whom they have forgiveness of their sins, through faith in him.

As for the false church, it assigns more authority to itself and its ordinances than to the Word of God; it does not want to subject itself to the yoke of Christ; it does not administer the sacraments as Christ commanded in his Word; it rather adds to them or subtracts from them as it pleases; it bases itself on men, more than on Jesus Christ; it persecutes those who live holy lives according to the Word of God and who rebuke it for its faults, greed, and idolatry.

These two churches are easy to recognize and thus to distinguish from each other.

ARTICLE 30
The Government of the Church

We believe that this true church ought to be governed according to the spiritual order that our Lord has taught us in his Word. There should be ministers or pastors to preach the Word of God and administer the sacraments. There should also be elders and deacons, along with the pastors, to make up the council of the church.

By this means true religion is preserved; true doctrine is able to take its course; and evil men are corrected spiritually and held in check, so that also the poor and all the afflicted may be helped and comforted according to their need.

By this means everything will be done well and in good order in the church, when such men are elected who are faithful and are chosen according to the rule that Paul gave to Timothy.[a]

a 1 Timothy 3

ARTICLE 31
The Officers of the Church

We believe that ministers of the Word of God, elders, and deacons ought to be chosen to their offices by a legitimate election of the church, with prayer in the name of the Lord, and in good order, as the Word of God teaches.

So everyone must be careful not to push himself forward improperly, but he must wait for God's call, so that he may be assured of his calling and be certain and sure that he is chosen by the Lord.

As for the ministers of the Word, they all have the same power and authority, no matter where they may be, since they are all servants of Jesus Christ, the only universal bishop, and the only head of the church.

Moreover, to keep God's holy order from being violated or despised, we say that everyone ought, as much as possible, to hold the ministers of the Word and elders of the church in special esteem, because of the work they do, and be at peace with them, without grumbling, quarreling, or fighting.

ARTICLE 32
The Order and Discipline of the Church

We also believe that although it is useful and good for those who govern the churches to establish and set up a certain order among themselves for maintaining the body of the church, they ought always to guard against deviating from what Christ, our only Master, has ordained for us.

Therefore we reject all human innovations and all laws imposed on us, in our worship of God, which bind and force our consciences in any way.

So we accept only what is proper to maintain harmony and unity and to keep all in obedience to God.

To that end excommunication, with all it involves, according to the Word of God, is required.

ARTICLE 33
The Sacraments

We believe that our good God, mindful of our crudeness and weakness, has ordained sacraments for us to seal his promises in us, to pledge his good will and grace toward us, and also to nourish and sustain our faith.

He has added these to the Word of the gospel to represent better to our external senses both what he enables us to understand by his Word and what he does inwardly in our hearts, confirming in us the salvation he imparts to us.

For they are visible signs and seals of something internal and invisible, by means of which God works in us through the power of the Holy Spirit. So they are not empty and hollow signs to fool and deceive us, for their truth is Jesus Christ, without whom they would be nothing.

Moreover, we are satisfied with the number of sacraments that Christ our Master has ordained for us. There are only two: the sacrament of baptism and the Holy Supper of Jesus Christ.

ARTICLE 34
The Sacrament of Baptism

We believe and confess that Jesus Christ, in whom the law is fulfilled, has by his shed blood put an end to every other shedding of blood, which anyone might do or wish to do in order to atone or satisfy for sins.

Having abolished circumcision, which was done with blood, he established in its place the sacrament of baptism. By it we are received into God's church and set apart from all other people and alien religions, that we may be dedicated entirely to him, bearing his mark and sign. It also witnesses to us that he will be our God forever, since he is our gracious Father.

Therefore he has commanded that all those who belong to him be baptized with pure water "in the name of the Father, and the Son, and the Holy Spirit."[a] In this way he signifies to us that just as water washes away the dirt of the body when it is poured on us and also is seen on the body of the baptized when it is sprinkled on him, so too the blood of Christ does the same thing internally, in the soul, by the Holy Spirit. It washes and cleanses it from its sins and transforms us from being the children of wrath into the children of God.

This does not happen by the physical water but by the sprinkling of the precious blood of the Son of God, who is our Red Sea, through which we must pass to escape the tyranny of Pharaoh, who is the devil, and to enter the spiritual land of Canaan. So ministers, as far as their work is concerned, give us the sacrament and what is visible, but our Lord gives what the sacrament signifies—namely the invisible gifts and graces; washing, purifying, and cleansing our souls of all filth and unrighteousness; renewing our hearts and filling them with all comfort; giving us true assurance of his fatherly goodness; clothing us with the "new man" and stripping off the "old," with all its works.[b]

For this reason we believe that anyone who aspires to reach eternal life ought to be baptized only once without ever repeating it—for we cannot be born twice. Yet this baptism is profitable not only when the water is on us and when we receive it but throughout our entire lives.

For that reason we detest the error of the Anabaptists who are not content with a single baptism once received and also condemn the baptism of the children of believers. We believe our children ought to be baptized and sealed with the sign of the covenant, as little children were circumcised in Israel on the basis of the same promises made to our children.

And truly, Christ has shed his blood no less for washing the little children of believers than he did for adults.

Therefore they ought to receive the sign and sacrament of what Christ has done for them, just as the Lord commanded in the law that by offering a lamb for them the sacrament of the suffering and death of Christ would be granted them shortly after their birth. This was the sacrament of Jesus Christ.

Furthermore, baptism does for our children what circumcision did for the Jewish people. That is why Paul calls baptism the "circumcision of Christ."c

a Matt. 28:19   b Col. 3:9–10   c Col. 2:11

ARTICLE 35
The Sacrament of the Lord's Supper

We believe and confess that our Savior Jesus Christ has ordained and instituted the sacrament of the Holy Supper to nourish and sustain those who are already born again and ingrafted into his family: his church.

Now those who are born again have two lives in them. The one is physical and temporal—they have it from the moment of their first birth, and it is common to all. The other is spiritual and heavenly, and is given them in their second birth; it comes through the Word of the gospel in the communion of the body of Christ; and this life is common to God's elect only.

Thus, to support the physical and earthly life God has prescribed for us an appropriate earthly and material bread, which is as common to all as life itself also is. But to maintain the spiritual and heavenly life that belongs to believers he has sent a living bread that came down from heaven: namely Jesus Christ, who nourishes and maintains the spiritual life of believers when eaten—that is, when appropriated and received spiritually by faith.

To represent to us this spiritual and heavenly bread Christ has instituted an earthly and visible bread as the sacrament of his body and wine as the sacrament of his blood. He did this to testify to us that just as truly as we take and hold the sacraments in our hands and eat and drink it in our mouths, by which our life is then sustained, so truly we receive into our souls, for our spiritual life, the true body and true blood of Christ, our only Savior. We receive these by faith, which is the hand and mouth of our souls.

Now it is certain that Jesus Christ did not prescribe his sacraments for us in vain, since he works in us all he represents by these holy signs, although the manner in which he does it goes beyond our understanding and is incomprehensible to us, just as the operation of God's Spirit is hidden and incomprehensible.

Yet we do not go wrong when we say that what is eaten is Christ's own natural body and what is drunk is his own blood—but the manner in which we eat it is not by the mouth but by the Spirit, through faith. In that way Jesus Christ remains always seated at the right hand of God the Father in heaven—but he never refrains on that account to communicate himself to us through faith.

This banquet is a spiritual table at which Christ communicates himself to us with all his benefits. At that table he makes us enjoy himself as much as the merits of his suffering and death, as he nourishes, strengthens, and comforts our poor, desolate souls by the eating of his flesh, and relieves and renews them by the drinking of his blood.

Moreover, though the sacraments and the thing signified are joined together, not all receive both of them. The wicked person certainly takes the sacrament, to his condemnation, but does not receive the truth of the sacrament, just as Judas and Simon the Sorcerer both indeed received the sacrament, but not Christ, who was signified by it. He is communicated only to believers.

Finally, with humility and reverence we receive the holy sacrament in the gathering of God's people, as we engage together, with thanksgiving, in a holy remembrance of the death of Christ our Savior, and as we thus confess our faith and Christian religion. Therefore no one should come to this table without examining himself carefully, lest "by eating this bread and drinking this cup he eat and drink to his own judgment."[a]

In short, by the use of this holy sacrament we are moved to a fervent love of God and our neighbors.

Therefore we reject as desecrations of the sacraments all the muddled ideas and damnable inventions that men have added and mixed in with them. And we say that we should be content with the procedure that Christ and the apostles have taught us and speak of these things as they have spoken of them.

a 1 Cor. 11:27

ARTICLE 36
The Civil Government

We believe that because of the depravity of the human race our good God has ordained kings, princes, and civil officers. He wants the world to be governed by laws and policies so that human lawlessness may be restrained and that everything may be conducted in good order among human beings.

For that purpose he has placed the sword in the hands of the government, to punish evil people and protect the good.

And being called in this manner to contribute to the advancement of a society that is pleasing to God, the civil rulers have the task, subject to God's law, of removing every obstacle to the preaching of the gospel and to every aspect of divine worship.

They should do this while completely refraining from every tendency toward exercising absolute authority, and while functioning in the sphere entrusted to them, with the means belonging to them.

They should do it in order that the Word of God may have free course; the kingdom of Jesus Christ may make progress; and every anti-Christian power may be resisted.[1]

Moreover everyone, regardless of status, condition, or rank, must be subject to the government, and pay taxes, and hold its representatives in honor and respect, and obey them in all things that are not in conflict with God's Word, praying for them that the Lord may be willing to lead them in all their ways and that we may live a peaceful and quiet life in all piety and decency.

And on this matter we denounce the Anabaptists, other anarchists, and in general all those who want to reject the authorities and civil officers and to subvert justice by introducing common ownership of goods and corrupting the moral order that God has established among human beings.

ARTICLE 37
The Last Judgment

Finally, we believe, according to God's Word, that when the time appointed by the Lord is come (which is unknown to all creatures) and the number of the elect is complete, our Lord Jesus Christ will come

---

1 The preceding three paragraphs are a substitution for the original paragraph below, which various Reformed synods have judged to be unbiblical: *And the government's task is not limited to caring for and watching over the public domain but extends also to upholding the sacred ministry, with a view to removing and destroying all idolatry and false worship of the Antichrist; to promoting the kingdom of Jesus Christ; and to furthering the preaching of the gospel everywhere; to the end that God may be honored and served by everyone, as he requires in his Word.*

from heaven, bodily and visibly, as he ascended, with great glory and majesty, to declare himself the judge of the living and the dead. He will burn this old world, in fire and flame, in order to cleanse it.

Then all human creatures will appear in person before that great judge—men, women, and children, who have lived from the beginning until the end of the world. They will be summoned there by the voice of the archangel and by the sound of the divine trumpet.[a]

For all those who died before that time will be raised from the earth, their spirits being joined and united with their own bodies in which they lived. And as for those who are still alive, they will not die like the others but will be changed "in the twinkling of an eye" from "corruptible to incorruptible."[b]

Then "the books" (that is, the consciences) will be opened, and the dead will be judged according to the things they did in the world,[c] whether good or evil. Indeed, all people will give account of all the idle words they have spoken,[d] which the world regards as only playing games. And then the secrets and hypocrisies of men will be publicly uncovered in the sight of all.

Therefore, with good reason the thought of this judgment is horrible and dreadful to wicked and evil people. But it is very pleasant and a great comfort to the righteous and elect, since their total redemption will then be accomplished. They will then receive the fruits of their labor and of the trouble they have suffered; their innocence will be openly recognized by all; and they will see the terrible vengeance that God will bring on the evil ones who tyrannized, oppressed, and tormented them in this world.

The evil ones will be convicted by the witness of their own consciences, and shall be made immortal—but only to be tormented in the everlasting fire prepared for the devil and his angels.[e]

In contrast, the faithful and elect will be crowned with glory and honor. The Son of God will "confess their names"[f] before God his

Father and the holy and elect angels; all tears will be "wiped from their eyes";[g] and their cause—at present condemned as heretical and evil by many judges and civil officers—will be acknowledged as the "cause of the Son of God."

And as a gracious reward the Lord will make them possess a glory such as the heart of man could never imagine.

So we look forward to that great day with longing in order to enjoy fully the promises of God in Christ Jesus, our Lord.

a 1 Thess. 4:16   b 1 Cor. 15:51–53   c Rev. 20:12   d Matt. 12:36   e Matt. 25:41   f Matt. 10:32   g Rev. 7:17

The Thirty-Nine Articles of Religion

INTRODUCTION

The Articles of the Church of England are a series of relatively long sentences, with a few notably long paragraphs as exceptions to the rule. Although there is no formal division among the Thirty-nine Articles, the first eighteen deal with the doctrine of God and the way of salvation, the second eighteen discuss the church and the sacraments, and a final trio of articles treats the civil magistrate, personal property, and oaths.

The Articles of the Church of England reprinted here are a version of the final text approved both by the English church and by Parliament. They began life as the Forty-two Articles, written by Archbishop Thomas Cranmer in 1552. With subtractions and additions under the guiding hand of Archbishop Matthew Parker and others, these became the Thirty-nine Articles in 1562. Further changes to the wording of the Thirty-nine Articles were effected by Queen Elizabeth in 1563, but then the Articles were revised again by Bishop John Jewel, the two houses of the English clergy, and the two houses of Parliament in 1571.

Finalized after the conclusion of the Council of Trent (the main attempt at Roman Catholic reform against the developments of the Protestant Reformation), the Articles of Religion offer a careful balance of continuity with, and criticism of, the old faith. Statements concerning the doctrine of God and the person and work of Christ offer traditional content. Furthermore, Article 8 requires Anglicans to affirm the Nicene Creed, the Athanasian Creed, "and that which is commonly called the Apostles' Creed." In fact, the order of the articles follows the general drift of the Apostles' Creed, even to the point of an explicit affirmation of that creed's clause stating that Christ had descended into hell (Article 3).

Other articles begin to move away from pre-Reformation theology in emphasis or tone. The articles include significant discussion of Scripture, with high praise for its authority and sufficiency. The testimony of the church to the Scriptures is not dismissed, but the stress is on the testimony of the Holy Spirit to the believer and the self-attesting power of Scripture itself (Article 5). The books of the Apocrypha are declared to have some use—"for example of life and instruction of manners"—but they cannot be used "to establish any doctrine" (Article 6).

Still other articles clearly display their Protestant credentials. While it is clear from the Thirty-nine Articles that the English church would remain hierarchical and episcopal, and that many of its ceremonies would maintain continuity with the medieval church, clear statements about sin and justification signal the English church's move from Roman Catholic to Reformed sympathies. Further chapters implicitly criticize mainline Catholic concepts of the human will and good works before explicitly stating that both Eastern and Western churches have erred, including the Church of Rome. Errors identified include positions on purgatory, ministering in Latin, too long a list of sacraments, and Catholic conceptions of a sacrifice of the Mass. The articles end where the official break with Rome began: with an assertion of the power of the English monarch in matters not only of state but also of faith.

THE THIRTY-NINE
ARTICLES OF RELIGION

ARTICLE 1
Of Faith in the Holy Trinity

There is but one living and true God, everlasting, without body, parts, or passions; of infinite power, wisdom, and goodness; the Maker, and Preserver of all things both visible and invisible. And in unity of this Godhead there be three Persons, of one substance, power, and eternity; the Father, the Son, and the Holy Ghost.

ARTICLE 2
Of the Word or Son of God, Which Was Made Very Man

The Son, which is the Word of the Father, begotten from everlasting of the Father, the very and eternal God, and of one substance with the Father, took Man's nature in the womb of the blessed Virgin, of her substance: so that two whole and perfect Natures, that is to say, the Godhead and Manhood, were joined together in one Person, never to be divided, whereof is one Christ, very God, and very Man; who truly suffered, was crucified, dead, and buried, to reconcile his Father to us, and to be a sacrifice, not only for original guilt, but also for all actual sins of men.

ARTICLE 3
Of the Going Down of Christ into Hell

As Christ died for us, and was buried, so also it is to be believed, that he went down into Hell.

ARTICLE 4
Of the Resurrection of Christ

Christ did truly rise again from death, and took again his body, with flesh, bones, and all things appertaining to the perfection of Man's nature; wherewith he ascended into Heaven, and there sitteth, until he return to judge all Men at the last day.

ARTICLE 5
Of the Holy Ghost

The Holy Ghost, proceeding from the Father and the Son, is of one substance, majesty, and glory, with the Father and the Son, very and eternal God.

ARTICLE 6
Of the Sufficiency of the Holy Scriptures for Salvation

Holy Scripture containeth all things necessary to salvation: so that whatsoever is not read therein, nor may be proved thereby, is not to be required of any man, that it should be believed an article of the Faith, or be thought requisite or necessary to salvation. In the name of the holy Scripture we do understand those Canonical Books of the Old and New Testament, of whose authority was never any doubt in the Church.

Of the Names and Number of the Canonical Books.

Genesis

Exodus

Leviticus

Numbers

Deuteronomy

Joshua

Judges

Ruth

The First Book of Samuel

The Second Book of Samuel

The First Book of Kings

The Second Book of Kings

The First Book of
   Chronicles

The Second Book of
   Chronicles

The First Book of Esdras

The Second Book of Esdras

The Book of Esther

The Book of Job

The Psalms

The Proverbs

Ecclesiastes or Preacher

Cantica, or Songs of
   Solomon

Four Prophets the greater

Twelve Prophets the less

And the other Books (as Hierome saith) the Church doth read for example of life and instruction of manners; but yet doth not apply them to establish any doctrine; such are these following:

The Third Book of Esdras

The Fourth Book of Esdras

The Book of Tobias

The Book of Judith

The rest of the Book of
   Esther

The Book of Wisdom

Jesus the Son of Sirach

Baruch the Prophet

The Song of the Three
   Children

The Story of Susanna

Of Bel and the Dragon

The Prayer of Manasses

The First Book of Maccabees

The Second Book of
   Maccabees

All the Books of the New Testament, as they are commonly received, we do receive, and account them Canonical.

ARTICLE 7
Of the Old Testament

The Old Testament is not contrary to the New: for both in the Old and New Testament everlasting life is offered to Mankind by Christ, who is the only Mediator between God and Man, being both God and Man. Wherefore they are not to be heard, which feign that the old Fathers did look only for transitory promises. Although the Law given from God by Moses, as touching Ceremonies and Rites, do not bind Christian men, nor the Civil precepts thereof ought of necessity to be received in any commonwealth; yet notwithstanding, no Christian man whatsoever is free from the obedience of the Commandments which are called Moral.

ARTICLE 8
Of the Three Creeds

The Three Creeds, Nicene Creed, Athanasius's Creed, and that which is commonly called the Apostles' Creed, ought thoroughly to be received and believed: for they may be proved by most certain warrants of holy Scripture.

ARTICLE 9
Of Original or Birth Sin

Original Sin standeth not in the following of Adam, (as the Pelagians do vainly talk;) but it is the fault and corruption of the Nature of every man, that naturally is ingendered of the offspring of Adam; whereby man is very far gone from original righteousness, and is of his own nature inclined to evil, so that the flesh lusteth always contrary to the spirit; and therefore in every person born into this world, it deserveth God's wrath and damnation. And this infection of nature doth remain, yea in them that are regenerated; whereby the lust of the flesh, called in the Greek, Φρόνημα σαρκὸς, which some do expound the wisdom, some sensuality, some the affection, some the desire, of the flesh, is not subject to the Law of God. And although there is no condemnation for them that believe and are baptized, yet the Apostle doth confess, that concupiscence and lust hath of itself the nature of sin.

ARTICLE 10
Of Free Will

The condition of Man after the fall of Adam is such, that he cannot turn and prepare himself, by his own natural strength and good works, to faith, and calling upon God: Wherefore we have no power to do good works pleasant and acceptable to God, without the grace of God by Christ preventing us, that we may have a good will, and working with us, when we have that good will.

ARTICLE 11
Of the Justification of Man

We are accounted righteous before God, only for the merit of our Lord and Saviour Jesus Christ by Faith, and not for our own works or deservings. Wherefore, that we are justified by Faith only is a most wholesome Doctrine, and very full of comfort, as more largely is expressed in the Homily of Justification.

ARTICLE 12

Of Good Works

Albeit that Good Works, which are the fruits of Faith, and follow after Justification, cannot put away our sins, and endure the severity of God's Judgement; yet are they pleasing and acceptable to God in Christ, and do spring out necessarily of a true and lively Faith; insomuch that by them a lively Faith may be as evidently known as a tree discerned by the fruit.

ARTICLE 13

Of Works before Justification

Works done before the grace of Christ, and the Inspiration of his Spirit, are not pleasant to God, forasmuch as they spring not of faith in Jesus Christ, neither do they make men meet to receive grace, or (as the School-authors say) deserve grace of congruity: yea rather, for that they are not done as God willed and commanded them to be done, we doubt not but they have the nature of sin.

ARTICLE 14

Of Works of Supererogation

Voluntary Works besides, over and above, God's Commandments, which they call Works of Supererogation, cannot be taught without arrogancy and impiety: for by them men do declare, that they do not only render unto God as much as they are bound to do, but that they do more for his sake, than of bounden duty is required: whereas Christ saith plainly, When ye have done all that are commanded to you, say, We are unprofitable servants.

ARTICLE 15
Of Christ Alone without Sin

Christ in the truth of our nature was made like unto us in all things, sin only except, from which he was clearly void, both in his flesh, and in his spirit. He came to be the Lamb without spot, who, by sacrifice of himself once made, should take away the sins of the world, and sin, as Saint John saith, was not in him. But all we the rest, although baptized, and born again in Christ, yet offend in many things; and if we say we have no sin, we deceive ourselves, and the truth is not in us.

ARTICLE 16
Of Sin after Baptism

Not every deadly sin willingly committed after Baptism is sin against the Holy Ghost, and unpardonable. Wherefore the grant of repentance is not to be denied to such as fall into sin after Baptism. After we have received the Holy Ghost, we may depart from grace given, and fall into sin, and by the grace of God we may arise again, and amend our lives. And therefore they are to be condemned, which say, they can no more sin as long as they live here, or deny the place of forgiveness to such as truly repent.

ARTICLE 17
Of Predestination and Election

Predestination to Life is the everlasting purpose of God, whereby (before the foundations of the world were laid) he hath constantly decreed by his counsel secret to us, to deliver from curse and damnation those whom he hath chosen in Christ out of mankind, and to bring them by Christ to everlasting salvation, as vessels made to honour. Wherefore, they which be endued with so excellent a benefit of God be called according to God's purpose by his Spirit working in due season: they through Grace obey the calling: they be justified freely: they be made sons of God by adoption: they be made like the image of his only-begotten Son Jesus Christ: they walk religiously in good works, and at length, by God's mercy, they attain to everlasting felicity.

As the godly consideration of Predestination, and our Election in Christ, is full of sweet, pleasant, and unspeakable comfort to godly persons, and such as feel in themselves the working of the Spirit of Christ, mortifying the works of the flesh, and their earthly members, and drawing up their mind to high and heavenly things, as well because it doth greatly establish and confirm their faith of eternal Salvation to be enjoyed through Christ, as because it doth fervently kindle their love towards God: So, for curious and carnal persons, lacking the Spirit of Christ, to have continually before their eyes the sentence of God's Predestination, is a most dangerous downfall, whereby the Devil doth thrust them either into desperation, or into wretchlessness of most unclean living, no less perilous than desperation.

Furthermore, we must receive God's promises in such wise, as they be generally set forth to us in holy Scripture: and, in our doings, that Will of God is to be followed, which we have expressly declared unto us in the Word of God.

ARTICLE 18
Of Obtaining Eternal Salvation Only by the Name of Christ

They also are to be had accursed that presume to say, That every man shall be saved by the Law or Sect which he professeth, so that he be diligent to frame his life according to that Law, and the light of Nature.

For holy Scripture doth set out unto us only the Name of Jesus Christ, whereby men must be saved.

ARTICLE 19
Of the Church

The visible Church of Christ is a congregation of faithful men, in the which the pure Word of God is preached, and the sacraments be duly ministered according to Christ's ordinance in all those things that of necessity are requisite to the same.

As the Church of Jerusalem, Alexandria, and Antioch, have erred; so also the Church of Rome hath erred, not only in their living and manner of Ceremonies, but also in matters of Faith.

ARTICLE 20
Of the Authority of the Church

The Church hath power to decree Rites or Ceremonies, and authority in Controversies of Faith: And yet it is not lawful for the Church to ordain anything that is contrary to God's Word written, neither may it so expound one place of Scripture, that it be repugnant to another. Wherefore, although the Church be a witness and a keeper of holy Writ, yet, as it ought not to decree anything against the same, so besides the same ought it not to enforce anything to be believed for necessity of Salvation.

ARTICLE 21
Of the Authority of General Councils

General Councils may not be gathered together without the commandment and will of Princes. And when they be gathered together, (forasmuch as they be an assembly of men, whereof all be not governed with the Spirit and Word of God,) they may err, and sometimes have erred, even in things pertaining unto God. Wherefore things ordained by them as necessary to salvation have neither strength nor authority, unless it may be declared that they be taken out of holy Scripture.

ARTICLE 22
Of Purgatory

The Romish Doctrine concerning Purgatory, Pardons, Worshipping and Adoration, as well of Images as of Reliques, and also invocation of Saints, is a fond thing vainly invented, and grounded upon no warranty of Scripture, but rather repugnant to the Word of God.

ARTICLE 23
Of Ministering in the Congregation

It is not lawful for any man to take upon him the office of publick preaching, or ministering the Sacraments in the Congregation, before he be lawfully called, and sent to execute the same. And those we ought to judge lawfully called and sent, which be chosen and called to this work by men who have publick authority given unto them in the Congregation, to call and send Ministers into the Lord's vineyard.

ARTICLE 24
Of Speaking in the Congregation in Such a Tongue As the People Understandeth

It is a thing plainly repugnant to the Word of God, and the custom of the Primitive Church, to have publick Prayer in the Church, or to minister the Sacraments in a tongue not understood of the people.

ARTICLE 25
Of the Sacraments

Sacraments ordained of Christ be not only badges or tokens of Christian men's profession, but rather they be certain sure witnesses, and effectual signs of grace, and God's good will towards us, by the which he doth work invisibly in us, and doth not only quicken, but also strengthen and confirm our Faith in him.

There are two Sacraments ordained of Christ our Lord in the Gospel, that is to say, Baptism, and the Supper of the Lord.

Those five commonly called Sacraments, that is to say, Confirmation, Penance, Orders, Matrimony, and extreme Unction, are not to be counted for Sacraments of the Gospel, being such as have grown partly of the corrupt following of the Apostles, partly are states of life allowed in the Scriptures; but yet have not like nature of Sacraments with Baptism, and the Lord's Supper, for that they have not any visible sign or ceremony ordained of God.

The Sacraments were not ordained of Christ to be gazed upon, or to be carried about, but that we should duly use them. And in such only as worthily receive the same they have a wholesome effect or operation: but they that receive them unworthily purchase to themselves damnation, as Saint Paul saith.

ARTICLE 26
Of the Unworthiness of the Ministers,
Which Hinders Not the Effect of the Sacrament

Although in the visible Church the evil be ever mingled with the good, and sometimes the evil have chief authority in the Ministration of the Word and Sacraments, yet forasmuch as they do not the same in their own name, but in Christ's, and do minister by his commission and authority, we may use their Ministry, both in hearing the Word of God, and in the receiving of the Sacraments. Neither is the effect of Christ's ordinance taken away by their wickedness, nor the grace of God's gifts diminished from such as by faith and rightly do receive the Sacraments ministered unto them; which be effectual, because of Christ's institution and promise, although they be ministered by evil men.

Nevertheless, it appertaineth to the discipline of the Church, that inquiry be made of evil Ministers, and that they be accused by those that have knowledge of their offences; and finally being found guilty, by just judgement be deposed.

ARTICLE 27
Of Baptism

Baptism is not only a sign of profession, and mark of difference, whereby Christian men are discerned from others that be not christened, but it is also a sign of Regeneration or new Birth, whereby, as by an instrument, they that receive Baptism rightly are grafted into the Church; the promises of the forgiveness of sin, and of our adoption to be the sons of God by the Holy Ghost, are visibly signed and sealed; Faith is confirmed, and Grace increased by virtue of prayer unto God. The Baptism of young Children is in any wise to be retained in the Church, as most agreeable with the institution of Christ.

ARTICLE 28
Of the Lord's Supper

The Supper of the Lord is not only a sign of the love that Christians ought to have among themselves one to another; but rather it is a

Sacrament of our Redemption by Christ's death: insomuch that to such as rightly, worthily, and with faith, receive the same, the Bread which we break is a partaking of the Body of Christ; and likewise the Cup of Blessing is a partaking of the Blood of Christ.

Transubstantiation (or the change of the substance of Bread and Wine) in the Supper of the Lord, cannot be proved by holy Writ; but is repugnant to the plain words of Scripture, overthroweth the nature of a Sacrament, and hath given occasion to many superstitions.

The Body of Christ is given, taken, and eaten, in the Supper, only after an heavenly and spiritual manner. And the mean whereby the Body of Christ is received and eaten in the Supper is Faith.

The Sacrament of the Lord's Supper was not by Christ's ordinance reserved, carried about, lifted up, or worshipped.

ARTICLE 29
Of the Wicked Which Eat Not the Body of
Christ in the Use of the Lord's Supper

The Wicked, and such as be void of a lively faith, although they do carnally and visibly press with their teeth (as Saint Augustine saith) the Sacrament of the Body and Blood of Christ, yet in no wise are they partakers of Christ: but rather, to their condemnation, do eat and drink the sign or Sacrament of so great a thing.

ARTICLE 30
Of Both Kinds

The Cup of the Lord is not to be denied to the Lay-people: for both the parts of the Lord's Sacrament, by Christ's ordinance and command-ment, ought to be ministered to all Christian men alike.

ARTICLE 31

Of the One Oblation of Christ Finished upon the Cross

The Offering of Christ once made is that perfect redemption, propitiation, and satisfaction, for all the sins of the whole world, both original and actual; and there is none other satisfaction for sin, but that alone. Wherefore the sacrifices of Masses, in the which it was commonly said, that the Priest did offer Christ for the quick and the dead, to have remission of pain or guilt, were blasphemous fables, and dangerous deceits.

ARTICLE 32

Of the Marriage of Priests

Bishops, Priests, and Deacons, are not commanded by God's Law, either to vow the estate of single life, or to abstain from marriage: therefore it is lawful also for them, as for all other Christian men, to marry at their own discretion, as they shall judge the same to serve better to godliness.

ARTICLE 33

Of Excommunicate Persons, How They Are to Be Avoided

That person which by open denunciation of the Church is rightly cut off from the unity of the Church, and excommunicated, ought to be taken of the whole multitude of the faithful, as an Heathen and Publican, until he be openly reconciled by penance, and received into the Church by a Judge that hath authority thereunto.

ARTICLE 34
Of the Traditions of the Church

It is not necessary that Traditions and Ceremonies be in all places one, or utterly like; for at all times they have been divers, and may be changed according to the diversities of countries, times, and men's manners, so that nothing be ordained against God's Word. Whosoever through his private judgement, willingly and purposely, doth openly break the traditions and ceremonies of the Church, which be not repugnant to the Word of God, and be ordained and approved by common authority, ought to be rebuked openly, (that others may fear to do the like,) as he that offendeth against the common order of the Church, and hurteth the authority of the Magistrate, and woundeth the consciences of the weak brethren.

Every particular or national Church hath authority to ordain, change, and abolish, ceremonies or rites of the Church ordained only by man's authority, so that all things be done to edifying.

ARTICLE 35
Of Homilies

The second Book of Homilies, the several titles whereof we have joined under this Article, doth contain a godly and wholesome Doctrine, and necessary for these times, as doth the former Book of Homilies, which were set forth in the time of Edward the Sixth; and therefore we judge them to be read in Churches by the Ministers, diligently and distinctly, that they may be understood of the people.

Of the Names of the Homilies.

1. Of the right use of the Church.
2. Against peril of Idolatry.
3. Of repairing and keeping clean of churches.
4. Of good Works: first of Fasting.
5. Against Gluttony and Drunkenness.
6. Against Excess of Apparel.
7. Of Prayer.
8. Of the Place and Time of Prayer.
9. That Common Prayers and Sacraments ought to be ministered in a known tongue.
10. Of the reverend estimation of God's Word.
11. Of Alms-doing.
12. Of the Nativity of Christ.
13. Of the Passion of Christ.
14. Of the Resurrection of Christ.
15. Of the worthy receiving of the Sacrament of the Body and Blood of Christ.
16. Of the Gifts of the Holy Ghost.
17. For the Rogation-days.
18. Of the State of Matrimony.
19. Of Repentance.
20. Against Idleness.
21. Against Rebellion.

ARTICLE 36
Of Consecration of Bishops and Ministers

The Book of Consecration of Archbishops and Bishops, and Ordering of Priests and Deacons, lately set forth in the time of Edward the Sixth, and confirmed at the same time by authority of Parliament, doth contain all things necessary to such Consecration and Ordering:

neither hath it anything, that of itself is superstitious and ungodly. And therefore whosoever are consecrated and ordered according to the Rites of that Book, since the second year of the forenamed King Edward unto this time, or hereafter shall be consecrated or ordered according to the same Rites; we decree all such to be rightly, orderly, and lawfully consecrated and ordered.

ARTICLE 37
Of the Civil Magistrates

The King's Majesty hath the chief power in this Realm of England, and other his Dominions, unto whom the chief Government of all Estates of this Realm, whether they be Ecclesiastical or Civil, in all causes doth appertain, and is not, nor ought to be, subject to any foreign Jurisdiction.

Where we attribute to the King's Majesty the chief government, by which Titles we understand the minds of some slanderous folks to be offended; we give not to our Princes the ministering either of God's Word, or of the Sacraments, the which thing the Injunctions also lately set forth by Elizabeth our Queen do most plainly testify; but that only prerogative, which we see to have been given always to all godly Princes in holy Scriptures by God himself; that is, that they should rule all estates and degrees committed to their charge by God, whether they be Ecclesiastical or Temporal, and restrain with the civil sword the stubborn and evildoers.

The Bishop of Rome hath no jurisdiction in this Realm of England.

The Laws of the Realm may punish Christian men with death, for heinous and grievous offences.

It is lawful for Christian men, at the commandment of the Magistrate, to wear weapons, and serve in the wars.

ARTICLE 38
Of Christian Men's Goods, Which Are Not Common

The Riches and Goods of Christians are not common, as touching the right, title, and possession of the same as certain Anabaptists do falsely boast. Notwithstanding, every man ought, of such things as he possesseth, liberally to give alms to the poor, according to his ability.

ARTICLE 39
Of a Christian Man's Oath

As we confess that vain and rash Swearing is forbidden Christian men by our Lord Jesus Christ, and James his Apostle, so we judge, that Christian Religion doth not prohibit, but that a man may swear when the Magistrate requireth, in a cause of faith and charity, so it be done according to the Prophet's teaching, in justice, judgement, and truth.

The Canons of Dort

INTRODUCTION

Of all the confessions written during the Reformation period, the authorship of the Canons of Dort enjoyed the widest national diversity. Although under the control of the Dutch state, the organizers of the Synod of Dort (or Dordrecht; 1618–1619), as it came to be known, invited delegates from other national Reformed churches. Representatives came from eight countries or city-states of the Reformation. In remembrance of the French Reformed churches, which were not permitted by their Roman Catholic government to send representatives, empty chairs were reserved for their missing delegates.

The Canons of Dort were the third and final contribution to what would become known as the Three Forms of Unity—the doctrinal standards of Dutch and German churches in the Reformed tradition. The Canons are not an ordered discussion of doctrinal topics but an argument against a group of protestors called the Remonstrants, most of whom were followers or friends of Jacobus Arminius. The Canons make five points under four headings, each designed (as the conclusion explains) to refute "five articles in dispute in the Netherlands, as well as the rejection of the errors by which the Dutch churches have for some time been disturbed." The famous "five points of Calvinism" are a simplification of these Canons.

The first main point of doctrine asserts a biblical position with regard to election and reprobation: the cause of a sinner's judgment is found in his or her own sin and unbelief; in contrast, the cause of election is found in God's good pleasure alone, not in anything pleasing in the sinner's life or in something in the sinner's future, including a foreseen faith. Furthermore, assurance of this election is a blessing, one that can extend to a believer's child who dies in infancy.

The second main point of doctrine treats the Savior's death as well as human redemption through him alone. The infinite value of Christ's death, as in the Heidelberg Catechism, is attributed to the fact the Jesus Christ is not only man but also God. As with every head of doctrine, the canon begins by providing positive teaching in the form of numbered articles. These are followed in each case by a series of rejected errors, with biblical reasons supplied for the rejection of these errors.

The third and fourth main points of doctrine address two related issues in one canon: human corruption and saving conversion. A proper doctrine of regeneration can never be developed without a proper doctrine of humanity. One first needs to understand the effects of the fall, including the spread of corruption and our total inability, as well as the inadequacy of keeping the law or learning from the light of nature. Only then can we see our need for the work of a powerful and Holy Spirit to raise the spiritually dead and draw us to our living Redeemer.

The final main point of doctrine presents the Bible's teaching on the perseverance of the saints, since Christian disciples are not preserved in a dormant state, without the fruits of faith. Rather, we are preserved by God in a life of faith and repentance, seeking continually to turn from sin to our Savior. The benefit of an assurance of salvation is laid out for the believer in this final point, and the canon argues that assurance of salvation is the best encouragement to godly living.

THE CANONS OF DORT

The First Main Point of Doctrine
Divine Election and Reprobation

The Judgment concerning Divine Predestination
Which the Synod Declares to Be in Agreement with
the Word of God and Accepted till Now in the
Reformed Churches, Set Forth in Several Articles

ARTICLE 1
God's Right to Condemn All People

Since all people have sinned in Adam and have come under the sentence of the curse and eternal death, God would have done no one an injustice if it had been his will to leave the entire human race in sin and under the curse, and to condemn them on account of their sin. As the apostle says: "The whole world is liable to the condemnation of God" (Rom. 3:19), "All have sinned and are deprived of the glory of God" (Rom. 3:23), and "The wages of sin is death" (Rom. 6:23).

ARTICLE 2

The Manifestation of God's Love

But this is how God showed his love: he sent his only begotten Son into the world, so that whoever believes in him should not perish but have eternal life (1 John 4:9; John 3:16).

ARTICLE 3

The Preaching of the Gospel

In order that people may be brought to faith, God mercifully sends proclaimers of this very joyful message to the people he wishes and at the time he wishes. By this ministry people are called to repentance and faith in Christ crucified. For "how shall they believe in him of whom they have not heard? And how shall they hear without someone preaching? And how shall they preach unless they have been sent?" (Rom. 10:14–15).

ARTICLE 4

A Twofold Response to the Gospel

God's anger remains on those who do not believe this gospel. But those who do receive it and embrace Jesus the Savior with a true and living faith are delivered through him from God's anger and from destruction, and receive the gift of eternal life.

ARTICLE 5

The Sources of Unbelief and of Faith

The cause or blame for this unbelief, as well as for all other sins, is not at all in God, but in man. Faith in Jesus Christ, however, and salvation through him is a free gift of God. As Scripture says, "It is by grace you have been saved, through faith, and this not from yourselves; it is a gift of God" (Eph. 2:8). Likewise: "It has been freely given to you to believe in Christ" (Phil. 1:29).

ARTICLE 6
God's Eternal Decision

The fact that some receive from God the gift of faith within time, and that others do not, stems from his eternal decision. For "all his works are known to God from eternity" (Acts 15:18; Eph. 1:11). In accordance with this decision he graciously softens the hearts, however hard, of his chosen ones and inclines them to believe, but by his just judgment he leaves in their wickedness and hardness of heart those who have not been chosen. And in this especially is disclosed to us his act—unfathomable, and as merciful as it is just—of distinguishing between people equally lost. This is the well-known decision of election and reprobation revealed in God's Word. This decision the wicked, impure, and unstable distort to their own ruin, but it provides holy and godly souls with comfort beyond words.

ARTICLE 7
Election

Election [or choosing] is God's unchangeable purpose by which he did the following: Before the foundation of the world, by sheer grace, according to the free good pleasure of his will, he chose in Christ to salvation a definite number of particular people out of the entire human race, which had fallen by its own fault from its original innocence into sin and ruin. Those chosen were neither better nor more deserving than the others, but lay with them in the common misery. He did this in Christ, whom he also appointed from eternity to be the mediator, the head of all those chosen, and the foundation of their salvation. And so he decided to give the chosen ones to Christ to be saved, and to call and draw them effectively into Christ's fellowship through his Word and Spirit. In other words, he decided to grant them true faith in Christ, to justify them, to sanctify them, and finally, after powerfully preserving them in the fellowship of his Son, to glorify them. God did all this in order to demonstrate his mercy, to the praise of the riches of his glorious grace.

As Scripture says, "God chose us in Christ, before the foundation of the world, so that we should be holy and blameless before him with love; he predestined us whom he adopted as his children through Jesus Christ, in himself, according to the good pleasure of his will, to the praise of his glorious grace, by which he freely made us pleasing to himself in his beloved" (Eph. 1:4–6). And elsewhere, "Those whom he predestined, he also called; and those whom he called, he also justified; and those whom he justified, he also glorified" (Rom. 8:30).

ARTICLE 8
A Single Decision of Election

This election is not of many kinds; it is one and the same election for all who were to be saved in the Old and the New Testament. For Scripture declares that there is a single good pleasure, purpose, and plan of God's will, by which he chose us from eternity both to grace and to glory, both to salvation and to the way of salvation, which he prepared in advance for us to walk in.

ARTICLE 9
Election Not Based on Foreseen Faith

This same election took place, not on the basis of foreseen faith, of the obedience of faith, of holiness, or of any other good quality and disposition, as though it were based on a prerequisite cause or condition in the person to be chosen, but rather for the purpose of faith, of the obedience of faith, of holiness, and so on. Accordingly, election is the source of each of the benefits of salvation. Faith, holiness, and the other saving gifts, and at last eternal life itself, flow forth from election as its fruits and effects. As the apostle says, "He chose us" (not because we were, but) "so that we should be holy and blameless before him in love" (Eph. 1:4).

ARTICLE 10
Election Based on God's Good Pleasure

But the cause of this undeserved election is exclusively the good pleasure of God. This does not involve his choosing certain human qualities or actions from among all those possible as a condition of salvation, but rather involves his adopting certain particular persons from among the common mass of sinners as his own possession. As Scripture says, "When the children were not yet born, and had done nothing either good or bad . . . , she [Rebecca] was told, 'The older will serve the younger.' As it is written, 'Jacob I loved, but Esau I hated'" (Rom. 9:11–13). Also, "All who were appointed for eternal life believed" (Acts 13:48).

ARTICLE 11
Election Unchangeable

Just as God himself is most wise, unchangeable, all-knowing, and almighty, so the election made by him can neither be suspended nor altered, revoked, or annulled; neither can his chosen ones be cast off, nor their number reduced.

ARTICLE 12
The Assurance of Election

Assurance of this their eternal and unchangeable election to salvation is given to the chosen in due time, though by various stages and in differing measure. Such assurance comes not by inquisitive searching into the hidden and deep things of God, but by noticing within themselves, with spiritual joy and holy delight, the unmistakable fruits of election pointed out in God's Word—such as a true faith in Christ, a childlike fear of God, a godly sorrow for their sins, a hunger and thirst for righteousness, and so on.

ARTICLE 13
The Fruit of This Assurance

In their awareness and assurance of this election God's children daily find greater cause to humble themselves before God, to adore the fathomless depth of his mercies, to cleanse themselves, and to give fervent love in return to him who first so greatly loved them. This is far from saying that this teaching concerning election, and reflection upon it, make God's children lax in observing his commandments or carnally self-assured. By God's just judgment this does usually happen to those who casually take for granted the grace of election or engage in idle and brazen talk about it but are unwilling to walk in the ways of the chosen.

ARTICLE 14
Teaching Election Properly

Just as, by God's wise plan, this teaching concerning divine election has been proclaimed through the prophets, Christ himself, and the apostles, in Old and New Testament times, and has subsequently been committed to writing in the Holy Scriptures, so also today in God's church, for which it was specifically intended, this teaching must be set forth—with a spirit of discretion, in a godly and holy manner, at the appropriate time and place, without inquisitive searching into the ways of the Most High. This must be done for the glory of God's most holy name, and for the lively comfort of his people.

ARTICLE 15
Reprobation

Moreover, Holy Scripture most especially highlights this eternal and undeserved grace of our election and brings it out more clearly for us, in that it further bears witness that not all people have been chosen but that some have not been chosen or have been passed by in God's eternal election—those, that is, concerning whom God, on the basis of his entirely free, most just, irreproachable, and unchangeable good pleasure, made the following decision: to leave them in the common misery into which, by their own fault, they have plunged themselves; not to grant them saving faith and the grace of conversion; but finally to condemn and eternally punish them (having been left in their own ways and under his just judgment), not only for their unbelief but also for all their other sins, in order to display his justice. And this is the decision of reprobation, which does not at all make God the author of sin (a blasphemous thought!) but rather its fearful, irreproachable, just judge and avenger.

ARTICLE 16

Responses to the Teaching of Reprobation

Those who do not yet actively experience within themselves a living faith in Christ or an assured confidence of heart, peace of conscience, a zeal for childlike obedience, and a glorying in God through Christ, but who nevertheless use the means by which God has promised to work these things in us—such people ought not to be alarmed at the mention of reprobation, nor to count themselves among the reprobate; rather they ought to continue diligently in the use of the means, to desire fervently a time of more abundant grace, and to wait for it in reverence and humility. On the other hand, those who seriously desire to turn to God, to be pleasing to him alone, and to be delivered from the body of death, but are not yet able to make such progress along the way of godliness and faith as they would like—such people ought much less to stand in fear of the teaching concerning reprobation, since our merciful God has promised that he will not snuff out a smoldering wick and that he will not break a bruised reed. However, those who have forgotten God and their Savior Jesus Christ and have abandoned themselves wholly to the cares of the world and the pleasures of the flesh—such people have every reason to stand in fear of this teaching, as long as they do not seriously turn to God.

ARTICLE 17

The Salvation of Deceased Infants of Believers

Since we must make judgments about God's will from his Word, which testifies that the children of believers are holy, not by nature but by virtue of the gracious covenant in which they together with their parents are included, godly parents ought not to doubt the election and salvation of their children whom God calls out of this life in infancy.

ARTICLE 18

The Proper Attitude toward Election and Reprobation

To those who complain about this grace of an undeserved election and about the severity of a just reprobation, we reply with the words of the apostle, "Who are you, O man, to talk back to God?" (Rom. 9:20), and with the words of our Savior, "Have I no right to do what I want with my own?" (Matt. 20:15). We, however, with reverent adoration of these secret things, cry out with the apostle: "Oh, the depths of the riches both of the wisdom and the knowledge of God! How unsearchable are his judgments, and his ways beyond tracing out! For who has known the mind of the Lord? Or who has been his counselor? Or who has first given to God, that God should repay him? For from him and through him and to him are all things. To him be the glory forever! Amen" (Rom. 11:33–36).

Having set forth the orthodox teaching concerning election and reprobation, the Synod rejects the errors of those

I

Who teach that the will of God to save those who would believe and persevere in faith and in the obedience of faith is the whole and entire decision of election to salvation, and that nothing else concerning this decision has been revealed in God's Word.

For they deceive the simple and plainly contradict Holy Scripture in its testimony that God does not only wish to save those who would believe, but that he has also from eternity chosen certain particular people to whom, rather than to others, he would within time grant faith in Christ and perseverance. As Scripture says, "I have revealed your name to those whom you gave me" (John 17:6). Likewise, "All who were appointed for eternal life believed" (Acts 13:48), and "He chose us before the foundation of the world so that we should be holy . . ." (Eph. 1:4).

II

Who teach that God's election to eternal life is of many kinds: one general and indefinite, the other particular and definite; and the latter in turn either incomplete, revocable, nonperemptory (or conditional), or else complete, irrevocable, and peremptory (or absolute). Likewise, who teach that there is one election to faith and another to salvation, so that there can be an election to justifying faith apart from a peremptory election to salvation.

For this is an invention of the human brain, devised apart from the Scriptures, which distorts the teaching concerning election and breaks up this golden chain of salvation: "Those whom he predestined, he also called; and those whom he called, he also justified; and those whom he justified, he also glorified" (Rom. 8:30).

III

Who teach that God's good pleasure and purpose, which Scripture mentions in its teaching of election, does not involve God's choosing certain particular people rather than others, but involves God's choosing, out of all possible conditions (including the works of the law) or out of the whole order of things, the intrinsically unworthy act of faith, as well as the imperfect obedience of faith, to be a condition of salvation; and it involves his graciously wishing to count this as perfect obedience and to look upon it as worthy of the reward of eternal life.

For by this pernicious error the good pleasure of God and the merit of Christ are robbed of their effectiveness and people are drawn away, by unprofitable inquiries, from the truth of undeserved justification and from the simplicity of the Scriptures. It also gives the lie to these words of the apostle: "God called us with a holy calling, not in virtue of works, but in virtue of his own purpose and the grace which was given to us in Christ Jesus before the beginning of time" (2 Tim. 1:9).

IV

Who teach that in election to faith a prerequisite condition is that man should rightly use the light of nature, be upright, unassuming, humble, and disposed to eternal life, as though election depended to some extent on these factors.

For this smacks of Pelagius, and it clearly calls into question the words of the apostle: "We lived at one time in the passions of our flesh, following the will of our flesh and thoughts, and we were by nature children of wrath, like everyone else. But God, who is rich in mercy, out of the great love with which he loved us, even when we were dead in transgressions, made us alive with Christ, by whose grace you have been saved. And God raised us up with him and seated us with him in heaven in Christ Jesus, in order that in the coming ages we might show the surpassing riches of his grace, according to his kindness toward us in Christ Jesus. For it is by grace you have been saved, through faith (and this not from yourselves; it is the gift of God) not by works, so that no one can boast" (Eph. 2:3–9).

V

Who teach that the incomplete and non-peremptory election of particular persons to salvation occurred on the basis of a foreseen faith, repentance, holiness, and godliness, which has just begun or continued for some time; but that complete and peremptory election occurred on the basis of a foreseen perseverance to the end in faith, repentance, holiness, and godliness. And that this is the gracious and evangelical worthiness, on account of which the one who is chosen is more worthy than the one who is not chosen. And therefore that faith, the obedience of faith, holiness, godliness, and perseverance are not fruits or effects of an unchangeable election to glory, but indispensable conditions and causes, which are prerequisite in those who are to be chosen in the complete election, and which are foreseen as achieved in them.

This runs counter to the entire Scripture, which throughout impresses upon our ears and hearts these sayings among others: "Election is not by works, but by him who calls" (Rom. 9:11); "All who were appointed for eternal life believed" (Acts 13:48); "He chose us in himself so that we should be holy" (Eph. 1:4); "You did not choose me, but I chose you" (John 15:16); "If by grace, not by works" (Rom. 11:6); "In this is love, not that we loved God, but that he loved us and sent his Son" (1 John 4:10).

VI

Who teach that not every election to salvation is unchangeable, but that some of the chosen can perish and do in fact perish eternally, with no decision of God to prevent it.

By this gross error they make God changeable, destroy the comfort of the godly concerning the steadfastness of their election, and contradict the Holy Scriptures, which teach that "the elect cannot be led astray" (Matt. 24:24), that "Christ does not lose those given to him by the Father" (John 6:39), and that "those whom God predestined, called, and justified, he also glorifies" (Rom. 8:30).

VII

Who teach that in this life there is no fruit, no awareness, and no assurance of one's unchangeable election to glory, except as conditional upon something changeable and contingent.

For not only is it absurd to speak of an uncertain assurance, but these things also militate against the experience of the saints, who with the apostle rejoice from an awareness of their election and sing the praises of this gift of God; who, as Christ urged, "rejoice" with his disciples "that their names have been written in heaven" (Luke 10:20); and finally who hold up against the flaming arrows of the devil's temptations the awareness of their election, with the question "Who will bring any charge against those whom God has chosen?" (Rom. 8:33).

VIII

Who teach that it was not on the basis of his just will alone that God decided to leave anyone in the fall of Adam and in the common state of sin and condemnation or to pass anyone by in the imparting of grace necessary for faith and conversion.

For these words stand fast: "He has mercy on whom he wishes, and he hardens whom he wishes" (Rom. 9:18). And also: "To you it has been given to know the secrets of the kingdom of heaven, but to them it has not been given" (Matt. 13:11). Likewise: "I give glory to you, Father, Lord of heaven and earth, that you have hidden these things from the wise and understanding, and have revealed them to little children; yes, Father, because that was your pleasure" (Matt. 11:25–26).

IX

Who teach that the cause for God's sending the gospel to one people rather than to another is not merely and solely God's good pleasure, but rather that one people is better and worthier than the other to whom the gospel is not communicated.

For Moses contradicts this when he addresses the people of Israel as follows: "Behold, to Jehovah your God belong the heavens and the highest heavens, the earth and whatever is in it. But Jehovah was inclined in his affection to love your ancestors alone, and chose out their descendants after them, you above all peoples, as at this day" (Deut. 10:14–15). And also Christ: "Woe to you, Korazin! Woe to you, Bethsaida! for if those mighty works done in you had been done in Tyre and Sidon, they would have repented long ago in sackcloth and ashes" (Matt. 11:21).

The Second Main Point of Doctrine
Christ's Death and Human Redemption through It

ARTICLE 1
The Punishment Which God's Justice Requires

God is not only supremely merciful, but also supremely just. His justice requires (as he has revealed himself in the Word) that the sins we have committed against his infinite majesty be punished with both temporal and eternal punishments, of soul as well as body. We cannot escape these punishments unless satisfaction is given to God's justice.

ARTICLE 2
The Satisfaction Made by Christ

Since, however, we ourselves cannot give this satisfaction or deliver ourselves from God's anger, God in his boundless mercy has given us as a guarantee his only begotten Son, who was made to be sin and a curse for us, in our place, on the cross, in order that he might give satisfaction for us.

ARTICLE 3
The Infinite Value of Christ's Death

This death of God's Son is the only and entirely complete sacrifice and satisfaction for sins; it is of infinite value and worth, more than sufficient to atone for the sins of the whole world.

ARTICLE 4
Reasons for This Infinite Value

This death is of such great value and worth for the reason that the person who suffered it is—as was necessary to be our Savior—not only a true and perfectly holy man, but also the only begotten Son of God, of the same eternal and infinite essence with the Father and the Holy Spirit. Another reason is that this death was accompanied by the experience of God's anger and curse, which we by our sins had fully deserved.

ARTICLE 5
The Mandate to Proclaim the Gospel to All

Moreover, it is the promise of the gospel that whoever believes in Christ crucified shall not perish but have eternal life. This promise, together with the command to repent and believe, ought to be announced and declared without differentiation or discrimination to all nations and people, to whom God in his good pleasure sends the gospel.

ARTICLE 6
Unbelief Man's Responsibility

However, that many who have been called through the gospel do not repent or believe in Christ but perish in unbelief is not because the sacrifice of Christ offered on the cross is deficient or insufficient, but because they themselves are at fault.

ARTICLE 7
Faith God's Gift

But all who genuinely believe and are delivered and saved by Christ's death from their sins and from destruction receive this favor solely from God's grace—which he owes to no one—given to them in Christ from eternity.

ARTICLE 8
The Saving Effectiveness of Christ's Death

For it was the entirely free plan and very gracious will and intention of God the Father that the enlivening and saving effectiveness of his Son's costly death should work itself out in all his chosen ones, in order that he might grant justifying faith to them only and thereby lead them without fail to salvation. In other words, it was God's will that Christ through the blood of the cross (by which he confirmed the new covenant) should effectively redeem from every people, tribe, nation, and language all those and only those who were chosen from eternity to salvation and given to him by the Father; that he should grant them faith (which, like the Holy Spirit's other saving gifts, he acquired for them by his death); that he should cleanse them by his blood from all their sins, both original and actual, whether committed before or after their coming to faith; that he should faithfully preserve them to the very end; and that he should finally present them to himself, a glorious people, without spot or wrinkle.

ARTICLE 9
The Fulfillment of God's Plan

This plan, arising out of God's eternal love for his chosen ones, from the beginning of the world to the present time has been powerfully carried out and will also be carried out in the future, the gates of hell seeking vainly to prevail against it. As a result the chosen are gathered into one, all in their own time, and there is always a church of believers founded on Christ's blood, a church which steadfastly loves, persistently worships, and—here and in all eternity—praises him as her Savior who laid down his life for her on the cross, as a bridegroom for his bride.

Having set forth the orthodox teaching, the Synod rejects the errors of those

I

Who teach that God the Father appointed his Son to death on the cross without a fixed and definite plan to save anyone by name, so that the necessity, usefulness, and worth of what Christ's death obtained could have stood intact and altogether perfect, complete and whole, even if the redemption that was obtained had never in actual fact been applied to any individual.

For this assertion is an insult to the wisdom of God the Father and to the merit of Jesus Christ, and it is contrary to Scripture. For the Savior speaks as follows: "I lay down my life for the sheep, and I know them" (John 10:15, 27). And Isaiah the prophet says concerning the Savior: "When he shall make himself an offering for sin, he shall see his offspring, he shall prolong his days, and the will of Jehovah shall prosper in his hand" (Isa. 53:10). Finally, this undermines the article of the creed in which we confess what we believe concerning the church.

II

Who teach that the purpose of Christ's death was not to establish in actual fact a new covenant of grace by his blood, but only to acquire for the Father the mere right to enter once more into a covenant with men, whether of grace or of works.

For this conflicts with Scripture, which teaches that Christ "has become the guarantee and mediator of a better"—that is, "a new"—"covenant" (Heb. 7:22; 9:15), and that "a will is in force only when someone has died" (Heb. 9:17).

III

Who teach that Christ, by the satisfaction which he gave, did not certainly merit for anyone salvation itself and the faith by which this satisfaction of Christ is effectively applied to salvation, but only acquired for the Father the authority or plenary will to relate in a new way with men and to impose such new conditions as he chose, and that the satisfying of these conditions depends on the free choice of man; consequently, that it was possible that either all or none would fulfill them.

For they have too low an opinion of the death of Christ, do not at all acknowledge the foremost fruit or benefit which it brings forth, and summon back from hell the Pelagian error.

IV

Who teach that what is involved in the new covenant of grace which God the Father made with men through the intervening of Christ's death is not that we are justified before God and saved through faith, insofar as it accepts Christ's merit, but rather that God, having withdrawn his demand for perfect obedience to the law, counts faith itself, and the imperfect obedience of faith, as perfect obedience to the law, and graciously looks upon this as worthy of the reward of eternal life.

For they contradict Scripture: "They are justified freely by his grace through the redemption that came by Jesus Christ, whom God presented as a sacrifice of atonement, through faith in his blood" (Rom. 3:24–25). And along with the ungodly Socinus, they introduce a new and foreign justification of man before God, against the consensus of the whole church.

V

Who teach that all people have been received into the state of reconciliation and into the grace of the covenant, so that no one on account of original sin is liable to condemnation, or is to be condemned, but that all are free from the guilt of this sin.

For this opinion conflicts with Scripture which asserts that we are by nature children of wrath.

VI

Who make use of the distinction between obtaining and applying in order to instill in the unwary and inexperienced the opinion that God, as far as he is concerned, wished to bestow equally upon all people the benefits which are gained by Christ's death; but that the distinction by which some rather than others come to share in the forgiveness of sins and eternal life depends on their own free choice (which applies itself to the grace offered indiscriminately) but does not depend on the unique gift of mercy which effectively works in them, so that they, rather than others, apply that grace to themselves.

For, while pretending to set forth this distinction in an acceptable sense, they attempt to give the people the deadly poison of Pelagianism.

VII

Who teach that Christ neither could die, nor had to die, nor did die for those whom God so dearly loved and chose to eternal life, since such people do not need the death of Christ.

For they contradict the apostle, who says: "Christ loved me and gave himself up for me" (Gal. 2:20), and likewise: "Who will bring any charge against those whom God has chosen? It is God who justifies. Who is he that condemns? It is Christ who died," that is, for them (Rom. 8:33–34). They also contradict the Savior, who asserts: "I lay down my life for the sheep" (John 10:15), and "My command is this: Love one another as I have loved you. Greater love has no one than this, that one lay down his life for his friends" (John 15:12–13).

The Third and Fourth Main Points of Doctrine
Human Corruption, Conversion to God, and the Way It Occurs

ARTICLE 1
The Effect of the Fall on Human Nature

Man was originally created in the image of God and was furnished in his mind with a true and salutary knowledge of his Creator and things spiritual, in his will and heart with righteousness, and in all his emotions with purity; indeed, the whole man was holy. However, rebelling against God at the devil's instigation and by his own free will, he deprived himself of these outstanding gifts. Rather, in their place he brought upon himself blindness, terrible darkness, futility, and distortion of judgment in his mind; perversity, defiance, and hardness in his heart and will; and finally impurity in all his emotions.

ARTICLE 2
The Spread of Corruption

Man brought forth children of the same nature as himself after the fall. That is to say, being corrupt he brought forth corrupt children. The corruption spread, by God's just judgment, from Adam to all his descendants—except for Christ alone—not by way of imitation (as in former times the Pelagians would have it) but by way of the propagation of his perverted nature.

ARTICLE 3
Total Inability

Therefore, all people are conceived in sin and are born children of wrath, unfit for any saving good, inclined to evil, dead in their sins, and slaves to sin; without the grace of the regenerating Holy Spirit they are neither willing nor able to return to God, to reform their distorted nature, or even to dispose themselves to such reform.

ARTICLE 4
The Inadequacy of the Light of Nature

There is, to be sure, a certain light of nature remaining in man after the fall, by virtue of which he retains some notions about God, natural things, and the difference between what is moral and immoral, and demonstrates a certain eagerness for virtue and for good outward behavior. But this light of nature is far from enabling man to come to a saving knowledge of God and conversion to him—so far, in fact, that man does not use it rightly even in matters of nature and society. Instead, in various ways he completely distorts this light, whatever its precise character, and suppresses it in unrighteousness. In doing so he renders himself without excuse before God.

ARTICLE 5
The Inadequacy of the Law

In this respect, what is true of the light of nature is true also of the Ten Commandments given by God through Moses specifically to the Jews. For man cannot obtain saving grace through the Decalogue, because, although it does expose the magnitude of his sin and increasingly convict him of his guilt, yet it does not offer a remedy or enable him to escape from his misery, and, indeed, weakened as it is by the flesh, leaves the offender under the curse.

ARTICLE 6
The Saving Power of the Gospel

What, therefore, neither the light of nature nor the law can do, God accomplishes by the power of the Holy Spirit, through the Word or the ministry of reconciliation. This is the gospel about the Messiah, through which it has pleased God to save believers, in both the Old and the New Testament.

ARTICLE 7
God's Freedom in Revealing the Gospel

In the Old Testament, God revealed this secret of his will to a small number; in the New Testament (now without any distinction between peoples) he discloses it to a large number. The reason for this difference must not be ascribed to the greater worth of one nation over another, or to a better use of the light of nature, but to the free good pleasure and undeserved love of God. Therefore, those who receive so much grace, beyond and in spite of all they deserve, ought to acknowledge it with humble and thankful hearts; on the other hand, with the apostle they ought to adore (but certainly not inquisitively search into) the severity and justice of God's judgments on the others, who do not receive this grace.

ARTICLE 8
The Serious Call of the Gospel

Nevertheless, all who are called through the gospel are called seriously. For seriously and most genuinely God makes known in his Word what is pleasing to him: that those who are called should come to him. Seriously he also promises rest for their souls and eternal life to all who come to him and believe.

ARTICLE 9
Human Responsibility for Rejecting the Gospel

The fact that many who are called through the ministry of the gospel do not come and are not brought to conversion must not be blamed on the gospel, nor on Christ, who is offered through the gospel, nor on God, who calls them through the gospel and even bestows various gifts on them, but on the people themselves who are called. Some in self-assurance do not even entertain the Word of life; others do entertain it but do not take it to heart, and for that reason, after the fleeting joy of a temporary faith, they relapse; others choke the seed of the Word with the thorns of life's cares and with the pleasures of the world and bring forth no fruits. This our Savior teaches in the parable of the sower (Matthew 13).

ARTICLE 10
Conversion as the Work of God

The fact that others who are called through the ministry of the gospel do come and are brought to conversion must not be credited to man, as though one distinguishes himself by free choice from others who are furnished with equal or sufficient grace for faith and conversion (as the proud heresy of Pelagius maintains). No, it must be credited to God: just as from eternity he chose his own in Christ, so within time he effectively calls them, grants them faith and repentance, and, having rescued them from the dominion of darkness, brings them into the kingdom of his Son, in order that they may declare the wonderful deeds of him who called them out of darkness into this marvelous light, and may boast not in themselves, but in the Lord, as apostolic words frequently testify in Scripture.

The Holy Spirit's Work in Conversion

Moreover, when God carries out this good pleasure in his chosen ones, or works true conversion in them, he not only sees to it that the gospel is proclaimed to them outwardly, and enlightens their minds powerfully by the Holy Spirit so that they may rightly understand and discern the things of the Spirit of God, but, by the effective operation of the same regenerating Spirit, he also penetrates into the inmost being of man, opens the closed heart, softens the hard heart, and circumcises the heart that is uncircumcised. He infuses new qualities into the will, making the dead will alive, the evil one good, the unwilling one willing, and the stubborn one compliant; he activates and strengthens the will so that, like a good tree, it may be enabled to produce the fruits of good deeds.

ARTICLE 12
Regeneration a Supernatural Work

And this is the regeneration, the new creation, the raising from the dead, and the making alive so clearly proclaimed in the Scriptures, which God works in us without our help. But this certainly does not happen only by outward teaching, by moral persuasion, or by such a way of working that, after God has done his work, it remains in man's power whether or not to be reborn or converted. Rather, it is an entirely supernatural work, one that is at the same time most powerful and most pleasing, a marvelous, hidden, and inexpressible work, which is not lesser than or inferior in power to that of creation or of raising the dead, as Scripture (inspired by the author of this work) teaches. As a result, all those in whose hearts God works in this marvelous way are certainly, unfailingly, and effectively reborn and do actually believe. And then the will, now renewed, is not only activated and motivated by God but in being activated by God is also itself active. For this reason, man himself, by that grace which he has received, is also rightly said to believe and to repent.

ARTICLE 13
The Incomprehensible Way of Regeneration

In this life believers cannot fully understand the way this work occurs; meanwhile, they rest content with knowing and experiencing that by this grace of God they do believe with the heart and love their Savior.

ARTICLE 14
The Way God Gives Faith

In this way, therefore, faith is a gift of God, not in the sense that it is offered by God for man to choose, but that it is in actual fact bestowed on man, breathed and infused into him. Nor is it a gift in the sense that God bestows only the potential to believe, but then awaits assent—the act of believing—from man's choice; rather, it is a gift in the sense that he who works both willing and acting and, indeed, works all things in all people produces in man both the will to believe and the belief itself.

ARTICLE 15
Responses to God's Grace

God does not owe this grace to anyone. For what could God owe to one who has nothing to give that can be paid back? Indeed, what could God owe to one who has nothing of his own to give but sin and falsehood? Therefore the person who receives this grace owes and gives eternal thanks to God alone; the person who does not receive it either does not care at all about these spiritual things and is satisfied with himself in his condition, or else in self-assurance foolishly boasts about having something which he lacks. Furthermore, following the example of the apostles, we are to think and to speak in the most favorable way about those who outwardly profess their faith and better their lives, for the inner chambers of the heart are unknown to us. But for others who have not yet been called, we are to pray to the God who calls things that do not exist as though they did. In no way, however, are we to pride ourselves as better than they, as though we had distinguished ourselves from them.

ARTICLE 16
Regeneration's Effect

However, just as by the fall man did not cease to be man, endowed with intellect and will, and just as sin, which has spread through the whole human race, did not abolish the nature of the human race but distorted and spiritually killed it, so also this divine grace of regeneration does not act in people as if they were blocks and stones; nor does it abolish the will and its properties or coerce a reluctant will by force, but spiritually revives, heals, reforms, and—in a manner at once pleasing and powerful—bends it back. As a result, a ready and sincere obedience of the Spirit now begins to prevail where before the rebellion and resistance of the flesh were completely dominant. It is in this that the true and spiritual restoration and freedom of our will consists. Thus, if the marvelous Maker of every good thing were not dealing with us, man would have no hope of getting up from his fall by his free choice, by which he plunged himself into ruin when still standing upright.

ARTICLE 17

God's Use of Means in Regeneration

Just as the almighty work of God by which he brings forth and sustains our natural life does not rule out but requires the use of means, by which God, according to his infinite wisdom and goodness, has wished to exercise his power, so also the aforementioned supernatural work of God by which he regenerates us in no way rules out or cancels the use of the gospel, which God in his great wisdom has appointed to be the seed of regeneration and the food of the soul. For this reason, the apostles and the teachers who followed them taught the people in a godly manner about this grace of God, to give him the glory and to humble all pride, and yet did not neglect meanwhile to keep the people, by means of the holy admonitions of the gospel, under the administration of the Word, the sacraments, and discipline. So even today it is out of the question that the teachers or those taught in the church should presume to test God by separating what he in his good pleasure has wished to be closely joined together. For grace is bestowed through admonitions, and the more readily we perform our duty, the more lustrous the benefit of God working in us usually is and the better his work advances. To him alone, both for the means and for their saving fruit and effectiveness, all glory is owed forever. Amen.

Rejection of the Errors

Having set forth the orthodox teaching, the Synod rejects the errors of those

I

Who teach that, properly speaking, it cannot be said that original sin in itself is enough to condemn the whole human race or to warrant temporal and eternal punishments.

For they contradict the apostle when he says: "Sin entered the world through one man, and death through sin, and in this way death passed on to all men because all sinned" (Rom. 5:12); also: "The guilt followed one sin and brought condemnation" (Rom. 5:16); likewise: "The wages of sin is death" (Rom. 6:23).

II

Who teach that the spiritual gifts or the good dispositions and virtues such as goodness, holiness, and righteousness could not have resided in man's will when he was first created, and therefore could not have been separated from the will at the fall.

For this conflicts with the apostle's description of the image of God in Ephesians 4:24, where he portrays the image in terms of righteousness and holiness, which definitely reside in the will.

III

Who teach that in spiritual death the spiritual gifts have not been separated from man's will, since the will in itself has never been corrupted but only hindered by the darkness of the mind and the unruliness of the emotions, and since the will is able to exercise its innate free capacity once these hindrances are removed, which is to say, it is able of itself to will or choose whatever good is set before it—or else not to will or choose it.

This is a novel idea and an error and has the effect of elevating the power of free choice, contrary to the words of Jeremiah the prophet: "The heart itself is deceitful above all things and wicked" (Jer. 17:9); and of the words of the apostle: "All of us also lived among them [the sons of disobedience] at one time in the passions of our flesh, following the will of our flesh and thoughts" (Eph. 2:3).

IV

Who teach that unregenerate man is not strictly or totally dead in his sins or deprived of all capacity for spiritual good but is able to hunger and thirst for righteousness or life and to offer the sacrifice of a broken and contrite spirit which is pleasing to God.

For these views are opposed to the plain testimonies of Scripture: "You were dead in your transgressions and sins" (Eph. 2:1, 5); "The imagination of the thoughts of man's heart is only evil all the time" (Gen. 6:5; 8:21). Besides, to hunger and thirst for deliverance from misery and for life, and to offer God the sacrifice of a broken spirit is characteristic only of the regenerate and of those called blessed (Ps. 51:17; Matt. 5:6).

V

Who teach that corrupt and natural man can make such good use of common grace (by which they mean the light of nature) or of the gifts remaining after the fall that he is able thereby gradually to obtain a greater grace—evangelical or saving grace—as well as salvation itself; and that in this way God, for his part, shows himself ready to reveal Christ to all people, since he provides to all, to a sufficient extent and in an effective manner, the means necessary for the revealing of Christ, for faith, and for repentance.

For Scripture, not to mention the experience of all ages, testifies that this is false: "He makes known his words to Jacob, his statutes and his laws to Israel; he has done this for no other nation, and they do not know his laws" (Ps. 147:19–20); "In the past God let all nations go their own way" (Acts 14:16); "They [Paul and his companions] were kept by the Holy Spirit from speaking God's word in Asia"; and "When they had come to Mysia, they tried to go to Bithynia, but the Spirit would not allow them to" (Acts 16:6–7).

VI

Who teach that in the true conversion of man new qualities, dispositions, or gifts cannot be infused or poured into his will by God, and indeed that the faith [or believing] by which we first come to conversion and from which we receive the name "believers" is not a quality or gift infused by God, but only an act of man, and that it cannot be called a gift except in respect to the power of attaining faith.

For these views contradict the Holy Scriptures, which testify that God does infuse or pour into our hearts the new qualities of faith, obedience, and the experiencing of his love: "I will put my law in their minds, and write it on their hearts" (Jer. 31:33); "I will pour water on the thirsty land, and streams on the dry ground; I will pour out my Spirit on your offspring" (Isa. 44:3); "The love of God has been poured out in our hearts by the Holy Spirit, who has been given to us" (Rom. 5:5). They also conflict with the continuous practice of the church, which prays with the prophet: "Convert me, Lord, and I shall be converted" (Jer. 31:18).

VII

Who teach that the grace by which we are converted to God is nothing but a gentle persuasion, or (as others explain it) that the way of God's acting in man's conversion that is most noble and suited to human nature is that which happens by persuasion, and that nothing prevents this grace of moral suasion even by itself from making natural men spiritual; indeed, that God does not produce the assent of the will except in this manner of moral suasion, and that the effectiveness of God's work by which it surpasses the work of Satan consists in the fact that God promises eternal benefits while Satan promises temporal ones.

For this teaching is entirely Pelagian and contrary to the whole of Scripture, which recognizes besides this persuasion also another, far more effective and divine way in which the Holy Spirit acts in man's conversion. As Ezekiel 36:26 puts it: "I will give you a new heart and put a new spirit in you; and I will remove your heart of stone and give you a heart of flesh. . . ."

VIII

Who teach that God in regenerating man does not bring to bear that power of his omnipotence whereby he may powerfully and unfailingly bend man's will to faith and conversion, but that even when God has accomplished all the works of grace which he uses for man's conversion, man nevertheless can, and in actual fact often does, so resist God and the Spirit in their intent and will to regenerate him, that man completely thwarts his own rebirth; and, indeed, that it remains in his own power whether or not to be reborn.

For this does away with all effective functioning of God's grace in our conversion and subjects the activity of Almighty God to the will of man; it is contrary to the apostles, who teach that "we believe by virtue of the effective working of God's mighty strength" (Eph. 1:19), and that "God fulfills the undeserved good will of his kindness and the work of faith in us with power" (2 Thess. 1:11), and likewise that "his divine power has given us everything we need for life and godliness" (2 Pet. 1:3).

IX

Who teach that grace and free choice are concurrent partial causes which cooperate to initiate conversion, and that grace does not precede—in the order of causality—the effective influence of the will; that is to say, that God does not effectively help man's will to come to conversion before man's will itself motivates and determines itself.

For the early church already condemned this doctrine long ago in the Pelagians, on the basis of the words of the apostle: "It does not depend on man's willing or running but on God's mercy" (Rom. 9:16); also: "Who makes you different from anyone else?" and "What do you have that you did not receive?" (1 Cor. 4:7); likewise: "It is God who works in you to will and act according to his good pleasure" (Phil. 2:13).

The Fifth Main Point of Doctrine
The Perseverance of the Saints

ARTICLE 1
The Regenerate Not Entirely Free from Sin

Those people whom God according to his purpose calls into fellowship with his Son Jesus Christ our Lord and regenerates by the Holy Spirit, he also sets free from the reign and slavery of sin, though in this life not entirely from the flesh and from the body of sin.

ARTICLE 2
The Believer's Reaction to Sins of Weakness

Hence daily sins of weakness arise, and blemishes cling to even the best works of God's people, giving them continual cause to humble themselves before God, to flee for refuge to Christ crucified, to put the flesh to death more and more by the Spirit of supplication and by holy exercises of godliness, and to strain toward the goal of perfection, until they are freed from this body of death and reign with the Lamb of God in heaven.

ARTICLE 3
God's Preservation of the Converted

Because of these remnants of sin dwelling in them and also because of the temptations of the world and Satan, those who have been converted could not remain standing in this grace if left to their own resources. But God is faithful, mercifully strengthening them in the grace once conferred on them and powerfully preserving them in it to the end.

ARTICLE 4
The Danger of True Believers'
Falling into Serious Sins

Although that power of God strengthening and preserving true believers in grace is more than a match for the flesh, yet those converted are not always so activated and motivated by God that in certain specific actions they cannot by their own fault depart from the leading of grace, be led astray by the desires of the flesh, and give in to them. For this reason they must constantly watch and pray that they may not be led into temptations. When they fail to do this, not only can they be carried away by the flesh, the world, and Satan into sins, even serious and outrageous ones, but also by God's just permission they sometimes are so carried away—witness the sad cases, described in Scripture, of David, Peter, and other saints falling into sins.

ARTICLE 5

The Effects of Such Serious Sins

By such monstrous sins, however, they greatly offend God, deserve the sentence of death, grieve the Holy Spirit, suspend the exercise of faith, severely wound the conscience, and sometimes lose the awareness of grace for a time—until, after they have returned to the way by genuine repentance, God's fatherly face again shines upon them.

ARTICLE 6

God's Saving Intervention

For God, who is rich in mercy, according to his unchangeable purpose of election does not take his Holy Spirit from his own completely, even when they fall grievously. Neither does he let them fall down so far that they forfeit the grace of adoption and the state of justification, or commit the sin which leads to death (the sin against the Holy Spirit), and plunge themselves, entirely forsaken by him, into eternal ruin.

ARTICLE 7

Renewal to Repentance

For, in the first place, God preserves in those saints when they fall his imperishable seed from which they have been born again, lest it perish or be dislodged. Secondly, by his Word and Spirit he certainly and effectively renews them to repentance so that they have a heartfelt and godly sorrow for the sins they have committed; seek and obtain, through faith and with a contrite heart, forgiveness in the blood of the Mediator; experience again the grace of a reconciled God; through faith adore his mercies; and from then on more eagerly work out their own salvation with fear and trembling.

ARTICLE 8

The Certainty of This Preservation

So it is not by their own merits or strength but by God's undeserved mercy that they neither forfeit faith and grace totally nor remain in their downfalls to the end and are lost. With respect to themselves this not only easily could happen, but also undoubtedly would happen; but with respect to God it cannot possibly happen, since his plan cannot be changed, his promise cannot fail, the calling according to his purpose cannot be revoked, the merit of Christ as well as his interceding and preserving cannot be nullified, and the sealing of the Holy Spirit can neither be invalidated nor wiped out.

ARTICLE 9

The Assurance of This Preservation

Concerning this preservation of those chosen to salvation and concerning the perseverance of true believers in faith, believers themselves can and do become assured in accordance with the measure of their faith, by which they firmly believe that they are and always will remain true and living members of the church, and that they have the forgiveness of sins and eternal life.

ARTICLE 10

The Ground of This Assurance

Accordingly, this assurance does not derive from some private revelation beyond or outside the Word, but from faith in the promises of God which he has very plentifully revealed in his Word for our comfort, from the testimony of "the Holy Spirit testifying with our spirit that we are God's children and heirs" (Rom. 8:16–17), and finally from a serious and holy pursuit of a clear conscience and of good works. And if God's chosen ones in this world did not have this well-founded comfort that the victory will be theirs and this reliable guarantee of eternal glory, they would be of all people most miserable.

ARTICLE 11
Doubts concerning This Assurance

Meanwhile, Scripture testifies that believers have to contend in this life with various doubts of the flesh and that under severe temptation they do not always experience this full assurance of faith and certainty of perseverance. But God, the Father of all comfort, "does not let them be tempted beyond what they can bear, but with the temptation he also provides a way out" (1 Cor. 10:13), and by the Holy Spirit revives in them the assurance of their perseverance.

ARTICLE 12
This Assurance as an Incentive to Godliness

This assurance of perseverance, however, so far from making true believers proud and carnally self-assured, is rather the true root of humility, of childlike respect, of genuine godliness, of endurance in every conflict, of fervent prayers, of steadfastness in crossbearing and in confessing the truth, and of well-founded joy in God. Reflecting on this benefit provides an incentive to a serious and continual practice of thanksgiving and good works, as is evident from the testimonies of Scripture and the examples of the saints.

ARTICLE 13
Assurance No Inducement to Carelessness

Neither does the renewed confidence of perseverance produce immorality or lack of concern for godliness in those put back on their feet after a fall, but it produces a much greater concern to observe carefully the ways of the Lord which he prepared in advance. They observe these ways in order that by walking in them they may maintain the assurance of their perseverance, lest, by their abuse of his fatherly goodness, the face of the gracious God (for the godly, looking upon his face is sweeter than life, but its withdrawal is more bitter than death) turn away from them again, with the result that they fall into greater anguish of spirit.

ARTICLE 14
God's Use of Means in Perseverance

And, just as it has pleased God to begin this work of grace in us by the proclamation of the gospel, so he preserves, continues, and completes his work by the hearing and reading of the gospel, by meditation on it, by its exhortations, threats, and promises, and also by the use of the sacraments.

ARTICLE 15
Contrasting Reactions to the Teaching of Perseverance

This teaching about the perseverance of true believers and saints, and about their assurance of it—a teaching which God has very richly revealed in his Word for the glory of his name and for the comfort of the godly and which he impresses on the hearts of believers—is something which the flesh does not understand, Satan hates, the world ridicules, the ignorant and the hypocrites abuse, and the spirits of error attack. The bride of Christ, on the other hand, has always loved this teaching very tenderly and defended it steadfastly as a priceless treasure; and God, against whom no plan can avail and no strength can prevail, will ensure that she will continue to do this. To this God alone, Father, Son, and Holy Spirit, be honor and glory forever. Amen.

Rejection of the Errors

Having set forth the orthodox teaching, the Synod rejects the errors of those

I

Who teach that the perseverance of true believers is not an effect of election or a gift of God produced by Christ's death, but a condition of the new covenant which man, before what they call his "peremptory" election and justification, must fulfill by his free will.

For Holy Scripture testifies that perseverance follows from election and is granted to the chosen by virtue of Christ's death, resurrection, and intercession: "The chosen obtained it; the others were hardened" (Rom. 11:7); likewise, "He who did not spare his own son, but gave him up for us all—how will he not, along with him, grant us all things? Who will bring any charge against those whom God has chosen? It is God who justifies. Who is he that condemns? It is Christ Jesus who died—more than that, who was raised—who also sits at the right hand of God, and is also interceding for us. Who shall separate us from the love of Christ?" (Rom. 8:32–35).

II

Who teach that God does provide the believer with sufficient strength to persevere and is ready to preserve this strength in him if he performs his duty, but that even with all those things in place which are necessary to persevere in faith and which God is pleased to use to preserve faith, it still always depends on the choice of man's will whether or not he perseveres.

For this view is obviously Pelagian; and though it intends to make men free it makes them sacrilegious. It is against the enduring consensus of evangelical teaching which takes from man all cause for boasting and ascribes the praise for this benefit only to God's grace. It is also against the testimony of the apostle: "It is God who keeps us strong to the end, so that we will be blameless on the day of our Lord Jesus Christ" (1 Cor. 1:8).

III

Who teach that those who truly believe and have been born again not only can forfeit justifying faith as well as grace and salvation totally and to the end, but also in actual fact do often forfeit them and are lost forever.

For this opinion nullifies the very grace of justification and regeneration as well as the continual preservation by Christ, contrary to the plain words of the apostle Paul: "If Christ died for us while we were still sinners, we will therefore much more be saved from God's wrath through him, since we have now been justified by his blood" (Rom. 5:8–9); and contrary to the apostle John: "No one who is born of God is intent on sin, because God's seed remains in him, nor can he sin, because he has been born of God" (1 John 3:9); also contrary to the words of Jesus Christ: "I give eternal life to my sheep, and they shall never perish; no one can snatch them out of my hand. My Father, who has given them to me, is greater than all; no one can snatch them out of my Father's hand" (John 10:28–29).

Who teach that those who truly believe and have been born again can commit the sin that leads to death (the sin against the Holy Spirit).

For the same apostle John, after making mention of those who commit the sin that leads to death and forbidding prayer for them (1 John 5:16–17), immediately adds: "We know that anyone born of God does not commit sin [that is, that kind of sin], but the one who was born of God keeps himself safe, and the evil one does not touch him" (v. 18).

V

Who teach that apart from a special revelation no one can have the assurance of future perseverance in this life.

For by this teaching the well-founded consolation of true believers in this life is taken away and the doubting of the Romanists is reintroduced into the church. Holy Scripture, however, in many places derives the assurance not from a special and extraordinary revelation but from the marks peculiar to God's children and from God's completely reliable promises. So especially the apostle Paul: "Nothing in all creation can separate us from the love of God that is in Christ Jesus our Lord" (Rom. 8:39); and John: "They who obey his commands remain in him and he in them. And this is how we know that he remains in us: by the Spirit he gave us" (1 John 3:24).

VI

Who teach that the teaching of the assurance of perseverance and of salvation is by its very nature and character an opiate of the flesh and is harmful to godliness, good morals, prayer, and other holy exercises, but that, on the contrary, to have doubt about this is praiseworthy.

For these people show that they do not know the effective operation of God's grace and the work of the indwelling Holy Spirit, and they contradict the apostle John, who asserts the opposite in plain words:

"Dear friends, now we are children of God, but what we will be has not yet been made known. But we know that when he is made known, we shall be like him, for we shall see him as he is. Everyone who has this hope in him purifies himself, just as he is pure" (1 John 3:2–3). Moreover, they are refuted by the examples of the saints in both the Old and the New Testament, who though assured of their perseverance and salvation yet were constant in prayer and other exercises of godliness.

VII

Who teach that the faith of those who believe only temporarily does not differ from justifying and saving faith except in duration alone.

For Christ himself in Matthew 13:20ff. and Luke 8:13ff. clearly defines these further differences between temporary and true believers: he says that the former receive the seed on rocky ground, and the latter receive it in good ground, or a good heart; the former have no root, and the latter are firmly rooted; the former have no fruit, and the latter produce fruit in varying measure, with steadfastness, or perseverance.

VIII

Who teach that it is not absurd that a person, after losing his former regeneration, should once again, indeed quite often, be reborn.

For by this teaching they deny the imperishable nature of God's seed by which we are born again, contrary to the testimony of the apostle Peter: "Born again, not of perishable seed, but of imperishable" (1 Pet. 1:23).

IX

Who teach that Christ nowhere prayed for an unfailing perseverance of believers in faith.

For they contradict Christ himself when he says: "I have prayed for you, Peter, that your faith may not fail" (Luke 22:32); and John the gospel writer when he testifies in John 17 that it was not only for the apostles, but also for all those who were to believe by their message that Christ prayed: "Holy Father, preserve them in your name" (v. 11); and "My prayer is not that you take them out of the world, but that you preserve them from the evil one" (v. 15).

Conclusion
Rejection of False Accusations

And so this is the clear, simple, and straightforward explanation of the orthodox teaching on the five articles in dispute in the Netherlands, as well as the rejection of the errors by which the Dutch churches have for some time been disturbed. This explanation and rejection the Synod declares to be derived from God's Word and in agreement with the confessions of the Reformed churches. Hence it clearly appears that those of whom one could hardly expect it have shown no truth, equity, and charity at all in wishing to make the public believe:

- that the teaching of the Reformed churches on predestination and on the points associated with it by its very nature and tendency draws the minds of people away from all godliness and religion, is an opiate of the flesh and the devil, and is a stronghold of Satan where he lies in wait for all people, wounds most of them, and fatally pierces many of them with the arrows of both despair and self-assurance;
- that this teaching makes God the author of sin, unjust, a tyrant, and a hypocrite; and is nothing but a refurbished Stoicism, Manicheism, Libertinism, and Mohammedanism;
- that this teaching makes people carnally self-assured, since it persuades them that nothing endangers the salvation of the

chosen, no matter how they live, so that they may commit the most outrageous crimes with self-assurance; and that on the other hand nothing is of use to the reprobate for salvation even if they have truly performed all the works of the saints;

- that this teaching means that God predestined and created, by the bare and unqualified choice of his will, without the least regard or consideration of any sin, the greatest part of the world to eternal condemnation; that in the same manner in which election is the source and cause of faith and good works, reprobation is the cause of unbelief and ungodliness; that many infant children of believers are snatched in their innocence from their mothers' breasts and cruelly cast into hell so that neither the blood of Christ nor their baptism nor the prayers of the church at their baptism can be of any use to them;

and very many other slanderous accusations of this kind which the Reformed churches not only disavow but even denounce with their whole heart.

Therefore this Synod of Dort in the name of the Lord pleads with all who devoutly call on the name of our Savior Jesus Christ to form their judgment about the faith of the Reformed churches, not on the basis of false accusations gathered from here or there, or even on the basis of the personal statements of a number of ancient and modern authorities—statements which are also often either quoted out of context or misquoted and twisted to convey a different meaning—but on the basis of the churches' own official confessions and of the present explanation of the orthodox teaching which has been endorsed by the unanimous consent of the members of the whole Synod, one and all.

Moreover, the Synod earnestly warns the false accusers themselves to consider how heavy a judgment of God awaits those who give false testimony against so many churches and their confessions, trouble the consciences of the weak, and seek to prejudice the minds of many against the fellowship of true believers.

Finally, this Synod urges all fellow ministers in the gospel of Christ to deal with this teaching in a godly and reverent manner, in the academic institutions as well as in the churches; to do so, both in their speaking and writing, with a view to the glory of God's name, holiness of life, and the comfort of anxious souls; to think and also speak with Scripture according to the analogy of faith; and, finally, to refrain from all those ways of speaking which go beyond the bounds set for us by the genuine sense of the Holy Scriptures and which could give impertinent sophists a just occasion to scoff at the teaching of the Reformed churches or even to bring false accusations against it.

May God's Son Jesus Christ, who sits at the right hand of God and gives gifts to men, sanctify us in the truth, lead to the truth those who err, silence the mouths of those who lay false accusations against sound teaching, and equip faithful ministers of his Word with a spirit of wisdom and discretion, that all they say may be to the glory of God and the building up of their hearers. Amen.

The Westminster Confession of Faith

INTRODUCTION

The Westminster Confession of Faith was written in 1646 by a gathering of pastor-theologians. They met in Westminster Abbey during England's bloodiest civil war, and it is from the name of the abbey (or from the English Parliament, meeting in the city of Westminster) that the confession derives its name. From the perspective of most Reformed Christians, England's Reformation had been left incomplete by Queen Elizabeth. Given that war had broken out in part for religious reasons, the English Parliament chose to call an assembly of theologians to advise it concerning the reform of the English church, especially in its worship and government. The so-called Westminster Assembly, meeting from 1643 to 1653, ended up changing the church's theological texts, too. Helped by Scottish theologians from the autumn of 1643, the texts written by the assembly ended up being endorsed more heartily and used more faithfully by that northern church and its missionaries than they ever were in England.

The Westminster Confession of Faith became the dominant confession of Reformed Christianity. Terms and phrases found in the Confession almost immediately became the preferred parlance of English-speaking Reformed churches, and when Congregationalists, Baptists, and Methodists wished to create confessional or catechetical texts of their own, they often resorted to revising and reissuing works produced by the Westminster Assembly.

In thirty-three chapters, the Westminster Confession of Faith builds on the foundations of the Christian faith (the self-revelation of God, God's character, and God's decree) to the outworking of his decrees in creation and providence. Of special interest in the realm of providence is the history of humanity's fall in Adam and rescue in Christ, our new representative. Redemption accomplished by Christ is outlined in one chapter before redemption applied by the Holy Spirit is detailed in many more.

The chapters of the Westminster Confession of Faith are clustered in a manner generically similar to that of the Thirty-nine Articles, the second Helvetic Confession (a Swiss confession of the 1560s), the Irish Articles of 1615, and Protestant systems of doctrine generally, with the structure of the Apostles' Creed always in the background. Thus chapters on the church, the sacraments, and eschatology conclude the confession, with chapters on the civil magistrate mixed in as well.

Presbyterians in the New World embraced the confession but found two ideas expressed in the original document particularly problematic. The first was that the civil magistrate had a duty to defend and promote gospel truth. The second was that civil magistrates should exercise godly control by calling synods or councils, even to the point of guiding the work of synods to ensure that they decide matters "according to the mind of God." After decades of permitting ministers to take exception to these statements in the Confession, American Presbyterians, meeting in Philadelphia in 1788, concluded that the civil government should not "in the least, interfere in matters of faith." The differences between the 1646 Westminster and the 1788 Philadelphia texts are identified in footnotes in the following texts.

THE WESTMINSTER
CONFESSION OF FAITH

I. Of the Holy Scripture

1. Although the light of nature, and the works of creation and providence do so far manifest the goodness, wisdom, and power of God, as to leave men unexcusable;[a] yet are they not sufficient to give that knowledge of God, and of his will, which is necessary unto salvation.[b] Therefore it pleased the Lord, at sundry times, and in divers manners, to reveal himself, and to declare that his will unto his church;[c] and afterwards, for the better preserving and propagating of the truth, and for the more sure establishment and comfort of the church against the corruption of the flesh, and the malice of Satan and of the world, to commit the same wholly unto writing:[d] which maketh the Holy Scripture to be most necessary;[e] those former ways of God's revealing his will unto his people being now ceased.[f]

a Rom. 2:14–15; Rom. 1:19–20; Ps. 19:1–4; Rom. 1:32–2:1 *b* John 17:3; 1 Cor. 1:21; 1 Cor. 2:13–14
c Heb. 1:1–2 *d* Luke 1:3–4; Rom. 15:4; Matt. 4:4, 7, 10; Isa. 8:20 *e* 2 Tim. 3:15; 2 Pet. 1:19 *f* John 20:31;
1 Cor. 14:37; 1 John 5:13; 1 Cor. 10:11; Heb. 1:1–2; Heb. 2:2–4

2. Under the name of Holy Scripture, or the Word of God written, are now contained all the books of the Old and New Testament, which are these:

Of the Old Testament:

Genesis	Ecclesiastes
Exodus	The Song of Songs
Leviticus	Isaiah
Numbers	Jeremiah
Deuteronomy	Lamentations
Joshua	Ezekiel
Judges	Daniel
Ruth	Hosea
I Samuel	Joel
II Samuel	Amos
I Kings	Obadiah
II Kings	Jonah
I Chronicles	Micah
II Chronicles	Nahum
Ezra	Habakkuk
Nehemiah	Zephaniah
Esther	Haggai
Job	Zechariah
Psalms	Malachi
Proverbs	

Of the New Testament:

The Gospels according to	the Romans
Matthew	the Corinthians I
Mark	the Corinthians II
Luke	the Galatians
John	the Ephesians
The Acts of the Apostles	the Philippians
Paul's Epistles to	the Colossians

the Thessalonians I	The Epistle of James
the Thessalonians II	The first and second Epistles
Timothy I	of Peter
Timothy II	The first, second, and third
Titus	Epistles of John
Philemon	The Epistle of Jude
The Epistle to the Hebrews	The Revelation of John

All which are given by inspiration of God to be the rule of faith and life.[a]

a Luke 16:29, 31; Luke 24:27, 44; 2 Tim. 3:15–16; John 5:46–47

3. The books commonly called Apocrypha, not being of divine inspiration, are no part of the canon of the Scripture, and therefore are of no authority in the church of God, nor to be any otherwise approved, or made use of, than other human writings.[a]

a Rev. 22:18–19; Rom. 3:2; 2 Pet. 1:21

4. The authority of the Holy Scripture, for which it ought to be believed, and obeyed, dependeth not upon the testimony of any man, or church; but wholly upon God (who is truth itself) the author thereof: and therefore it is to be received, because it is the Word of God.[a]

a 2 Pet. 1:19–20; 2 Tim. 3:16; 1 John 5:9; 1 Thess. 2:13; Rev. 1:1–2

5. We may be moved and induced by the testimony of the church to an high and reverent esteem of the Holy Scripture.[a] And the heavenliness of the matter, the efficacy of the doctrine, the majesty of the style, the consent of all the parts, the scope of the whole (which is, to give all glory to God), the full discovery it makes of the only way of man's salvation, the many other incomparable excellencies, and the

entire perfection thereof, are arguments whereby it doth abundantly evidence itself to be the Word of God: yet notwithstanding, our full persuasion and assurance of the infallible truth and divine authority thereof, is from the inward work of the Holy Spirit bearing witness by and with the Word in our hearts.[b]

a 1 Tim. 3:15 b 1 Cor. 2:9–10; Heb. 4:12; John 10:35; Isa. 55:11; Rom. 11:36; Ps. 19:7–11; 2 Tim. 3:15; 1 Cor. 2:4–5; 1 Thess. 1:5; 1 John 2:20, 27; Isa. 59:21

6. The whole counsel of God concerning all things necessary for his own glory, man's salvation, faith and life, is either expressly set down in Scripture, or by good and necessary consequence may be deduced from Scripture: unto which nothing at any time is to be added, whether by new revelations of the Spirit, or traditions of men.[a] Nevertheless, we acknowledge the inward illumination of the Spirit of God to be necessary for the saving understanding of such things as are revealed in the Word:[b] and that there are some circumstances concerning the worship of God, and government of the church, common to human actions and societies, which are to be ordered by the light of nature, and Christian prudence, according to the general rules of the Word, which are always to be observed.[c]

a 2 Tim. 3:16–17; Gal. 1:8–9; 2 Thess. 2:2 b John 6:45; 1 Cor. 2:12, 14–15; Eph. 1:18; 2 Cor. 4:6 c 1 Cor. 11:13–14; 1 Cor. 14:26, 40

7. All things in Scripture are not alike plain in themselves, nor alike clear unto all:[a] yet those things which are necessary to be known, believed, and observed for salvation, are so clearly propounded, and opened in some place of Scripture or other, that not only the learned, but the unlearned, in a due use of the ordinary means, may attain unto a sufficient understanding of them.[b]

a 2 Pet. 3:16 b Ps. 119:105, 130; Deut. 29:29; Deut. 30:10–14; Acts 17:11

8. The Old Testament in Hebrew (which was the native language of the people of God of old), and the New Testament in Greek (which, at the time of the writing of it, was most generally known to the nations), being immediately inspired by God, and, by his singular care and providence, kept pure in all ages, are therefore authentical;[a] so as, in all controversies of religion, the church is finally to appeal unto them.[b] But, because these original tongues are not known to all the people of God, who have right unto, and interest in the Scriptures, and are commanded, in the fear of God, to read and search them,[c] therefore they are to be translated into the vulgar language of every nation unto which they come,[d] that, the Word of God dwelling plentifully in all, they may worship him in an acceptable manner;[e] and, through patience and comfort of the Scriptures, may have hope.[f]

a Matt. 5:18; Ps. 119:89 b Isa. 8:20; Matt. 15:3, 6; Acts 15:15; Luke 16:31 c John 5:39; Acts 17:11; Rev. 1:3; 2 Tim. 3:14–15 d Matt. 28:19–20; 1 Cor. 14:6; Mark 15:34 e Col. 3:16; Ex. 20:4–6; Matt. 15:7–9 f Rom. 15:4

9. The infallible rule of interpretation of Scripture is the Scripture itself: and therefore, when there is a question about the true and full sense of any Scripture (which is not manifold, but one), it must be searched and known by other places that speak more clearly.[a]

a Acts 15:15; John 5:46; 2 Pet. 1:20–21

10. The supreme judge by which all controversies of religion are to be determined, and all decrees of councils, opinions of ancient writers, doctrines of men, and private spirits, are to be examined, and in whose sentence we are to rest, can be no other but the Holy Spirit speaking in the Scripture.[a]

a Matt. 22:29, 31; Acts 28:25; 1 John 4:1–6

1. There is but one only,[a] living, and true God,[b] who is infinite in being and perfection,[c] a most pure spirit,[d] invisible,[e] without body, parts,[f] or passions;[g] immutable,[h] immense,[i] eternal,[j] incomprehensible,[k] almighty,[l] most wise,[m] most holy,[n] most free,[o] most absolute;[p] working all things according to the counsel of his own immutable and most righteous will,[q] for his own glory;[r] most loving,[s] gracious, merciful, long-suffering, abundant in goodness and truth, forgiving iniquity, transgression, and sin;[t] the rewarder of them that diligently seek him;[u] and withal, most just, and terrible in his judgments,[v] hating all sin,[w] and who will by no means clear the guilty.[x]

a Deut. 6:4; 1 Cor. 8:4, 6; Gal. 3:20 b 1 Thess. 1:9; Jer. 10:10 c Job 11:7–9; Job 26:14; Ps. 139:6 d John 4:24 e 1 Tim. 1:17; John 1:18 f Deut. 4:15–16; John 4:24; Luke 24:39 g Acts 14:11, 15 h James 1:17; Mal. 3:6 i 1 Kings 8:27; Jer. 23:23–24 j Ps. 90:2; 1 Tim. 1:17 k Ps. 145:3; Rom. 11:34 l Gen. 17:1; Rev. 4:8 m Rom. 16:27 n Isa. 6:3; Rev. 4:8 o Ps. 115:3; Isa. 14:24 p Isa. 45:5–6; Ex. 3:14 q Eph. 1:11 r Prov. 16:4; Rom. 11:36; Rev. 4:11 s 1 John 4:8; 1 John 4:16; John 3:16 t Ex. 34:6–7 u Heb. 11:6 v Neh. 9:32–33; Heb. 10:28–31 w Rom. 1:18; Ps. 5:5–6; Ps. 11:5 x Ex. 34:7a; Nah. 1:2–3, 6

2. God hath all life,[a] glory,[b] goodness,[c] blessedness,[d] in and of himself; and is alone in and unto himself all-sufficient, not standing in need of any creatures which he hath made,[e] nor deriving any glory from them,[f] but only manifesting his own glory in, by, unto, and upon them. He is the alone fountain of all being, of whom, through whom, and to whom are all things;[g] and hath most sovereign dominion over them, to do by them, for them, or upon them whatsoever himself pleaseth.[h] In his sight all things are open and manifest,[i] his knowledge is infinite, infallible, and independent upon the creature,[j] so as nothing is to him contingent, or uncertain.[k] He is most holy in all his counsels, in all his works, and in all his commands.[l] To him is due from angels and men, and every other

creature, whatsoever worship, service, or obedience he is pleased to require of them.[m]

a Jer. 10:10; John 5:26 b Acts 7:2 c Ps. 119:68 d 1 Tim. 6:15; Rom. 9:5 e Acts 17:24–25 f Luke 17:10 g Rom. 11:36 h Rev. 4:11; Dan. 4:25, 35; 1 Tim. 6:15 i Heb. 4:13 j Rom. 11:33–34; Ps. 147:5 k Acts 15:18; Ezek. 11:5 l Ps. 145:17; Rom. 7:12 m Rev. 5:12–14

3. In the unity of the Godhead there be three persons, of one substance, power, and eternity: God the Father, God the Son, and God the Holy Ghost:[a] the Father is of none, neither begotten, nor proceeding; the Son is eternally begotten of the Father;[b] the Holy Ghost eternally proceeding from the Father and the Son.[c]

a Matt. 3:16–17; Matt. 28:19; 2 Cor. 13:14; Eph. 2:18 b John 1:14, 18; Heb. 1:2–3; Col. 1:15 c John 15:26; Gal. 4:6

III. Of God's Eternal Decree

1. God, from all eternity, did, by the most wise and holy counsel of his own will, freely, and unchangeably ordain whatsoever comes to pass:[a] yet so, as thereby neither is God the author of sin,[b] nor is violence offered to the will of the creatures; nor is the liberty or contingency of second causes taken away, but rather established.[c]

a Ps. 33:11; Eph. 1:11; Heb. 6:17 b Ps. 5:4; James 1:13–14; 1 John 1:5; Hab. 1:13 c Acts 2:23; Matt. 17:12; Acts 4:27–28; John 19:11; Prov. 16:33

2. Although God knows whatsoever may or can come to pass upon all supposed conditions,[a] yet hath he not decreed anything because he foresaw it as future, or as that which would come to pass upon such conditions.[b]

a 1 Sam. 23:11–12; Matt. 11:21, 23 b Rom. 9:11, 13, 16, 18

3. By the decree of God, for the manifestation of his glory, some men and angels[a] are predestinated unto everlasting life; and others foreordained to everlasting death.[b]

a 1 Tim. 5:21; Jude 6; Matt. 25:31, 41 b Eph. 1:5–6; Rom. 9:22–23; Prov. 16:4

4. These angels and men, thus predestinated, and foreordained, are particularly and unchangeably designed, and their number so certain and definite, that it cannot be either increased or diminished.[a]

a John 13:18; 2 Tim. 2:19; John 10:14–16, 27–28; 17:2, 6, 9–12

5. Those of mankind that are predestinated unto life, God, before the foundation of the world was laid, according to his eternal and immutable purpose, and the secret counsel and good pleasure of his will, hath chosen, in Christ, unto everlasting glory,[a] out of his mere free grace and love, without any foresight of faith, or good works, or perseverance in either of them, or any other thing in the creature, as conditions, or causes moving him thereunto;[b] and all to the praise of his glorious grace.[c]

a Eph. 1:4, 9, 11; Rom. 8:28–30; 2 Tim. 1:9; 1 Thess. 5:9 b Rom. 9:11, 13, 15–16; Eph. 2:8–9; Eph. 1:5, 9, 11 c Eph. 1:6, 12

6. As God hath appointed the elect unto glory, so hath he, by the eternal and most free purpose of his will, foreordained all the means thereunto.[a] Wherefore, they who are elected, being fallen in Adam, are redeemed by Christ,[b] are effectually called unto faith in Christ by his Spirit working in due season, are justified, adopted, sanctified,[c] and kept by his power, through faith, unto salvation.[d] Neither are any other redeemed by Christ, effectually called, justified, adopted, sanctified, and saved, but the elect only.[e]

a 1 Pet. 1:2; Eph. 2:10; 2 Thess. 2:13 b 1 Thess. 5:9–10; Titus 2:14 c Rom. 8:30; Eph. 1:5; 2 Thess. 2:13 d 1 Pet. 1:5 e John 10:14–15, 26; John 6:64–65; Rom. 8:28–39; John 8:47; 17:9; 1 John 2:19

7. The rest of mankind God was pleased, according to the unsearchable counsel of his own will, whereby he extendeth or withholdeth mercy, as he pleaseth, for the glory of his sovereign power over his creatures, to pass by; and to ordain them to dishonor and wrath for their sin, to the praise of his glorious justice.[a]

a Matt. 11:25–26; Rom. 9:17–18, 21–22; Jude 4; 1 Pet. 2:8; 2 Tim. 2:19–20

8. The doctrine of this high mystery of predestination is to be handled with special prudence and care,[a] that men, attending the will of God revealed in his Word, and yielding obedience thereunto, may, from the certainty of their effectual vocation, be assured of their eternal election.[b] So shall this doctrine afford matter of praise, reverence, and admiration of God;[c] and of humility, diligence, and abundant consolation to all that sincerely obey the gospel.[d]

a Rom. 9:20; Rom. 11:33; Deut. 29:29 b 2 Pet. 1:10; 1 Thess. 1:4–5 c Eph. 1:6; Rom. 11:33 d Rom. 11:5–6, 20; Rom. 8:33; Luke 10:20; 2 Pet. 1:10

IV. Of Creation

1. It pleased God the Father, Son, and Holy Ghost,[a] for the manifestation of the glory of his eternal power, wisdom, and goodness,[b] in the beginning, to create, or make of nothing, the world, and all things therein whether visible or invisible, in the space of six days; and all very good.[c]

a Rom. 11:36; 1 Cor. 8:6; Heb. 1:2; John 1:2–3; Gen. 1:2; Job 33:4 b Rom. 1:20; Jer. 10:12; Ps. 104:24; Ps. 33:5 c Gen. 1:1–31; Ps. 33:6; Heb. 11:3; Col. 1:16; Acts 17:24; Ex. 20:11

2. After God had made all other creatures, he created man, male and female,[a] with reasonable and immortal souls,[b] endued with knowledge, righteousness, and true holiness, after his own image;[c] having the law of God written in their hearts,[d] and power to fulfill it:[e] and yet

under a possibility of transgressing, being left to the liberty of their own will, which was subject unto change.*f* Beside this law written in their hearts, they received a command, not to eat of the tree of the knowledge of good and evil; which while they kept, they were happy in their communion with God,*g* and had dominion over the creatures.*h*

a Gen. 1:27 b Gen. 2:7; Eccles. 12:7; Luke 23:43; Matt. 10:28 c Gen. 1:26; Col. 3:10; Eph. 4:24
d Rom. 2:14–15 e Gen. 2:17; Eccles. 7:29 f Gen. 3:6, 17 g Gen. 2:17; Gen. 2:15–3:24 h Gen. 1:28;
Gen. 1:29–30; Ps. 8:6–8

V. Of Providence

1. God the great Creator of all things doth uphold,*a* direct, dispose, and govern all creatures, actions, and things,*b* from the greatest even to the least,*c* by his most wise and holy providence,*d* according to his infallible foreknowledge,*e* and the free and immutable counsel of his own will,*f* to the praise of the glory of his wisdom, power, justice, goodness, and mercy.*g*

a Neh. 9:6; Ps. 145:14–16; Heb. 1:3 b Dan. 4:34–35; Ps. 135:6; Acts 17:25–28; Job 38–41 c Matt.
10:29–31; Matt. 6:26–32 d Prov. 15:3; 2 Chron. 16:9; Ps. 104:24; Ps. 145:17 e Acts 15:18; Isa. 42:9; Ezek.
11:5 f Eph. 1:11; Ps. 33:10–11 g Isa. 63:14; Eph. 3:10; Rom. 9:17; Gen. 45:7; Ps. 145:7

2. Although, in relation to the foreknowledge and decree of God, the First Cause, all things come to pass immutably, and infallibly;*a* yet, by the same providence, he ordereth them to fall out, according to the nature of second causes, either necessarily, freely, or contingently.*b*

a Acts 2:23; Isa. 14:24, 27 b Gen. 8:22; Jer. 31:35; Isa. 10:6–7; Ex. 21:13; Deut. 19:5; 1 Kings 22:28–34

3. God, in his ordinary providence, maketh use of means,*a* yet is free to work without,*b* above,*c* and against them, at his pleasure.*d*

a Acts 27:24, 31, 44b; Isa. 55:10–11 b Hos. 1:7; Matt. 4:4; Job 34:20 c Rom. 4:19–21 d 2 Kings 6:6;
Dan. 3:27

4. The almighty power, unsearchable wisdom, and infinite goodness of God so far manifest themselves in his providence, that it extendeth itself even to the first fall, and all other sins of angels and men;[a] and that not by a bare permission,[b] but such as hath joined with it a most wise and powerful bounding,[c] and otherwise ordering, and governing of them, in a manifold dispensation, to his own holy ends;[d] yet so, as the sinfulness thereof proceedeth only from the creature, and not from God, who, being most holy and righteous, neither is nor can be the author or approver of sin.[e]

a Isa. 45:7; Rom. 11:32–34; 2 Sam. 16:10; Acts 2:23; Acts 4:27–28; 2 Sam. 24:1; 1 Chron. 21:1; 1 Kings 22:22–23; 1 Chron. 10:4, 13–14 b John 12:40; 2 Thess. 2:11 c Ps. 76:10; 2 Kings 19:28 d Gen. 50:20; Isa. 10:12; Isa. 10:6–7, 13–15 e James 1:13–14, 17; 1 John 2:16; Ps. 50:21

5. The most wise, righteous, and gracious God doth oftentimes leave, for a season, his own children to manifold temptations, and the corruption of their own hearts, to chastise them for their former sins, or to discover unto them the hidden strength of corruption and deceitfulness of their hearts, that they may be humbled;[a] and, to raise them to a more close and constant dependence for their support upon himself, and to make them more watchful against all future occasions of sin, and for sundry other just and holy ends.[b]

a 2 Chron. 32:25–26, 31; Deut. 8:2–3, 5; Luke 22:31–32; 2 Sam. 24:1, 25 b 2 Cor. 12:7–9; Ps. 73:1–28; 77:1–12; Mark 14:66–72; John 21:15–19

6. As for those wicked and ungodly men whom God, as a righteous Judge, for former sins, doth blind and harden,[a] from them he not only withholdeth his grace whereby they might have been enlightened in their understandings, and wrought upon in their hearts;[b] but sometimes also withdraweth the gifts which they had,[c] and exposeth them to such objects as their corruption makes occasions of sin;[d] and, withal, gives them over to their own lusts, the temptations of the

world, and the power of Satan,[e] whereby it comes to pass that they harden themselves, even under those means which God useth for the softening of others.[f]

a Rom. 1:24, 26, 28; Rom. 11:7–8 b Deut. 29:4; Mark 4:11–12 c Matt. 13:12; Matt. 25:29; Acts 13:10–11
d Gen. 4:8; 2 Kings 8:12–13; Matt. 26:14–16 e Ps. 109:6; Luke 22:3; 2 Thess. 2:10–12 f Ex. 8:15, 32;
2 Cor. 2:15–16; Isa. 8:14; 1 Pet. 2:7–8; Ex. 7:3; Isa. 6:9–10; Acts 28:26–27

7. As the providence of God doth, in general, reach to all creatures; so, after a most special manner, it taketh care of his church, and disposeth all things to the good thereof.[a]

a 1 Tim. 4:10; Amos 9:8–9; Matt. 16:18; Rom. 8:28; Isa. 43:3–5, 14

VI. Of the Fall of Man, of Sin, and of the Punishment Thereof

1. Our first parents, being seduced by the subtilty and temptation of Satan, sinned, in eating the forbidden fruit.[a] This their sin, God was pleased, according to his wise and holy counsel, to permit, having purposed to order it to his own glory.[b]

a Gen. 3:13; 2 Cor. 11:3 b See chapter 5, section 4

2. By this sin they fell from their original righteousness and communion with God,[a] and so became dead in sin,[b] and wholly defiled in all the parts and faculties of soul and body.[c]

a Gen. 3:6–8; Rom. 3:23 b Gen. 2:17; Eph. 2:1–3; Rom. 5:12 c Gen. 6:5; Jer. 17:9; Titus 1:15; Rom. 3:10–19

3. They being the root of all mankind, the guilt of this sin was imputed;[a] and the same death in sin, and corrupted nature, conveyed to all their posterity descending from them by ordinary generation.[b]

a Acts 17:26; Rom. 5:12, 15–19; 1 Cor. 15:21–22, 49 b Ps. 51:5; John 3:6; Gen. 5:3; Job 15:14

4. From this original corruption, whereby we are utterly indisposed, disabled, and made opposite to all good,[a] and wholly inclined to all evil,[b] do proceed all actual transgressions.[c]

a Rom. 5:6; Rom. 7:18; Rom. 8:7; Col. 1:21 b Gen. 8:21; Gen. 6:5; Rom. 3:10–12 c Matt. 15:19; James 1:14–15; Eph. 2:2–3

5. This corruption of nature, during this life, doth remain in those that are regenerated;[a] and although it be, through Christ, pardoned, and mortified; yet both itself, and all the motions thereof, are truly and properly sin.[b]

a Prov. 20:9; Eccles. 7:20; Rom. 7:14, 17–18, 21–23; 1 John 1:8, 10 b Rom. 7:7–8, 25; Gal. 5:17

6. Every sin, both original and actual, being a transgression of the righteous law of God, and contrary thereunto,[a] doth, in its own nature, bring guilt upon the sinner,[b] whereby he is bound over to the wrath of God,[c] and curse of the law,[d] and so made subject to death,[e] with all miseries spiritual,[f] temporal,[g] and eternal.[h]

a 1 John 3:4 b Rom. 2:15; Rom. 3:9, 19 c Eph. 2:3 d Gal. 3:10 e Rom. 6:23 f Eph. 4:18 g Rom. 8:20; Lam. 3:39 h Matt. 25:41; 2 Thess. 1:9

VII. Of God's Covenant with Man

1. The distance between God and the creature is so great, that although reasonable creatures do owe obedience unto him as their Creator, yet they could never have any fruition of him as their blessedness and reward, but by some voluntary condescension on God's part, which he hath been pleased to express by way of covenant.[a]

a Isa. 40:13–17; Job 9:32–33; Ps. 113:5–6; Job 22:2–3; Job 35:7–8; Luke 17:10; Acts 17:24–25

2. The first covenant made with man was a covenant of works,[a] wherein life was promised to Adam; and in him to his posterity,[b] upon condition of perfect and personal obedience.[c]

a Gen. 2:16–17; Hos. 6:7; Gal. 3:12 b Gen. 3:22; Rom. 10:5; Rom. 5:12–14; Rom. 5:15–20 c Gen. 2:17; Gal. 3:10

3. Man, by his fall, having made himself uncapable of life by that covenant, the Lord was pleased to make a second,[a] commonly called the covenant of grace; wherein he freely offereth unto sinners life and salvation by Jesus Christ; requiring of them faith in him, that they may be saved,[b] and promising to give unto all those that are ordained unto eternal life his Holy Spirit, to make them willing, and able to believe.[c]

a Gal. 3:21; Rom. 3:20–21; Rom. 8:3; Gen. 3:15; Isa. 42:6 b John 3:16; Rom. 10:6, 9; Rev. 22:17 c Acts 13:48; Ezek. 36:26–27; John 6:37, 44–45; 1 Cor. 12:3

4. This covenant of grace is frequently set forth in Scripture by the name of a testament, in reference to the death of Jesus Christ the Testator, and to the everlasting inheritance, with all things belonging to it, therein bequeathed.[a]

a Heb. 9:15–17

5. This covenant was differently administered in the time of the law, and in the time of the gospel:[a] under the law, it was administered by promises, prophecies, sacrifices, circumcision, the paschal lamb, and other types and ordinances delivered to the people of the Jews, all foresignifying Christ to come;[b] which were, for that time, sufficient and efficacious, through the operation of the Spirit, to instruct and build up the elect in faith in the promised Messiah,[c] by whom they had full remission of sins, and eternal salvation; and is called the old testament.[d]

a 2 Cor. 3:6–9 b Heb. 8:1–10:39; Rom. 4:11; Col. 2:11–12; 1 Cor. 5:7 c 1 Cor. 10:1–4; Heb. 11:13; John 8:56 d Gal. 3:7–9, 14; Ps. 32:1–2, 5

6. Under the gospel, when Christ, the substance,[a] was exhibited, the ordinances in which this covenant is dispensed are the preaching of the Word, and the administration of the sacraments of baptism and the Lord's Supper:[b] which, though fewer in number, and administered with more simplicity, and less outward glory, yet, in them, it is held forth in more fullness, evidence, and spiritual efficacy,[c] to all nations, both Jews and Gentiles;[d] and is called the new testament.[e] There are not therefore two covenants of grace, differing in substance, but one and the same, under various dispensations.[f]

a Col. 2:17 b 1 Cor. 1:21; Matt. 28:19–20; 1 Cor. 11:23–25 c Heb. 12:22–24; 2 Cor. 3:9–11; Jer. 31:33–34
d Luke 2:32; Acts 10:34; Eph. 2:15–19 e Luke 22:20 f Gal. 3:8–9, 14, 16; Rom. 3:21–22, 30; Rom. 4:3,
6–8; Gen. 15:6; Ps. 32:1–2; Rom. 4:16–17, 23–24; Heb. 4:2; Rom. 10:6–10; 1 Cor. 10:3–4

VIII. Of Christ the Mediator

1. It pleased God, in his eternal purpose, to choose and ordain the Lord Jesus, his only begotten Son, to be the Mediator between God and man,[a] the Prophet,[b] Priest,[c] and King,[d] the Head and Savior of his church,[e] the Heir of all things,[f] and Judge of the world:[g] unto whom he did from all eternity give a people, to be his seed,[h] and to be by him in time redeemed, called, justified, sanctified, and glorified.[i]

a Isa. 42:1; 1 Pet. 1:19–20; John 3:16; 1 Tim. 2:5 b Acts 3:20, 22; Deut. 18:15 c Heb. 5:5–6 d Ps. 2:6;
Luke 1:33; Isa. 9:5–6; Acts 2:29–36; Col. 1:13 e Eph. 5:23 f Heb. 1:2 g Acts 17:31 h John 17:6; Ps.
22:30; Isa. 53:10; Eph. 1:4 i 1 Tim. 2:6; Isa. 55:4–5; 1 Cor. 1:30; Rom. 8:30

2. The Son of God, the second person in the Trinity, being very and eternal God, of one substance and equal with the Father, did, when the fullness of time was come, take upon him man's nature,[a] with all the essential properties, and common infirmities thereof, yet without sin;[b] being conceived by the power of the Holy Ghost, in the womb of the virgin Mary, of her substance.[c] So that two whole, perfect, and distinct natures, the Godhead and the manhood, were inseparably

joined together in one person, without conversion, composition, or confusion.[d] Which person is very God, and very man, yet one Christ, the only Mediator between God and man.[e]

a John 1:1, 14; 1 John 5:20; Phil. 2:6; Gal. 4:4 b Phil. 2:7; Heb. 2:14, 16–17; Heb. 4:15 c Luke 1:27, 31, 35; Gal. 4:4; Matt. 1:18, 20–21 d Matt. 16:16; Col. 2:9; Rom. 9:5; 1 Tim. 3:16 e Rom. 1:3–4; 1 Tim. 2:5

3. The Lord Jesus, in his human nature thus united to the divine, was sanctified, and anointed with the Holy Spirit, above measure,[a] having in him all the treasures of wisdom and knowledge;[b] in whom it pleased the Father that all fullness should dwell;[c] to the end that, being holy, harmless, undefiled, and full of grace and truth,[d] he might be thoroughly furnished to execute the office of a mediator, and surety.[e] Which office he took not unto himself, but was thereunto called by his Father,[f] who put all power and judgment into his hand, and gave him commandment to execute the same.[g]

a Ps. 45:7; John 3:34; Isa. 61:1; Luke 4:18; Heb. 1:8–9 b Col. 2:3 c Col. 1:19 d Heb. 7:26; John 1:14 e Acts 10:38; Heb. 12:24; Heb. 7:22 f Heb. 5:4–5 g John 5:22, 27; Matt. 28:18; Acts 2:36

4. This office the Lord Jesus did most willingly undertake;[a] which that he might discharge, he was made under the law,[b] and did perfectly fulfill it;[c] endured most grievous torments immediately in his soul,[d] and most painful sufferings in his body;[e] was crucified, and died,[f] was buried, and remained under the power of death, yet saw no corruption.[g] On the third day he arose from the dead,[h] with the same body in which he suffered,[i] with which also he ascended into heaven, and there sitteth at the right hand of his Father,[j] making intercession,[k] and shall return, to judge men and angels, at the end of the world.[l]

a Ps. 40:7–8; Heb. 10:5–10; John 4:34; John 10:18; Phil. 2:8 b Gal. 4:4 c Matt. 3:15; Matt. 5:17; Heb. 5:8–9 d Matt. 26:37–38; Luke 22:44; Matt. 27:46 e Matt. 26:67–68; Matt. 27:27–50 f Mark 15:24, 37; Phil. 2:8 g Matt. 27:60; Acts 2:24, 27; Acts 13:29, 37; Rom. 6:9 h 1 Cor. 15:3–4 i Luke 24:39; John 20:25, 27 j Luke 24:50–51; 1 Pet. 3:22 k Rom. 8:34; Heb. 7:25; Heb. 9:24 l Acts 1:11; John 5:28–29; Rom. 14:10b; Acts 10:42; Matt. 13:40–42; Jude 6; 2 Pet. 2:4

5. The Lord Jesus, by his perfect obedience, and sacrifice of himself, which he, through the eternal Spirit, once offered up unto God, hath fully satisfied the justice of his Father;[a] and purchased, not only reconciliation, but an everlasting inheritance in the kingdom of heaven, for all those whom the Father hath given unto him.[b]

a Rom. 5:19; Heb. 9:14; Heb. 10:14; Eph. 5:2; Rom. 3:25–26 b Dan. 9:24; 2 Cor. 5:18; Col. 1:20; Eph. 1:11, 14; Heb. 9:12, 15; John 17:2

6. Although the work of redemption was not actually wrought by Christ till after his incarnation, yet the virtue, efficacy, and benefits thereof were communicated unto the elect, in all ages successively from the beginning of the world, in and by those promises, types, and sacrifices, wherein he was revealed, and signified to be the seed of the woman which should bruise the serpent's head; and the Lamb slain from the beginning of the world; being yesterday and today the same, and forever.[a]

a Gal. 4:4–5; Gen. 3:15; 1 Cor. 10:4; Rev. 13:8; Heb. 13:8; Rom. 3:25; Heb. 9:15

7. Christ, in the work of mediation, acts according to both natures, by each nature doing that which is proper to itself;[a] yet, by reason of the unity of the person, that which is proper to one nature is sometimes in Scripture attributed to the person denominated by the other nature.[b]

a John 10:17–18; 1 Pet. 3:18; Heb. 1:3; Heb. 9:14 b Acts 20:28; Luke 1:43; Rom. 9:5

8. To all those for whom Christ hath purchased redemption, he doth certainly and effectually apply and communicate the same;[a] making intercession for them,[b] and revealing unto them, in and by the Word, the mysteries of salvation;[c] effectually persuading them by his Spirit to believe and obey, and governing their hearts by his Word and Spirit;[d] overcoming all their enemies by his almighty power and wisdom, in

such manner, and ways, as are most consonant to his wonderful and unsearchable dispensation.[e]

a John 6:37, 39; John 10:15–16, 27–28 b 1 John 2:1; Rom. 8:34 c John 15:15; Eph. 1:9; John 17:6 d John 14:26; 2 Cor. 4:13; Rom. 8:9, 14; Rom. 15:18–19; John 17:17 e Ps. 110:1; 1 Cor. 15:25–26; Col. 2:15; Luke 10:19

IX. Of Free Will

1. God hath endued the will of man with that natural liberty, that it is neither forced, nor, by any absolute necessity of nature, determined to good, or evil.[a]

a James 1:13–14; Deut. 30:19; Isa. 7:11–12; Matt. 17:12; John 5:40; James 4:7

2. Man, in his state of innocency, had freedom, and power to will and to do that which was good and well pleasing to God;[a] but yet, mutably, so that he might fall from it.[b]

a Eccles. 7:29; Gen. 1:26, 31; Col. 3:10 b Gen. 2:16–17; Gen. 3:6, 17

3. Man, by his fall into a state of sin, hath wholly lost all ability of will to any spiritual good accompanying salvation:[a] so as, a natural man, being altogether averse from that good,[b] and dead in sin,[c] is not able, by his own strength, to convert himself, or to prepare himself thereunto.[d]

a Rom. 8:7–8; John 6:44, 65; John 15:5; Rom. 5:5 b Rom. 3:9–10, 12, 23 c Eph. 2:1, 5; Col. 2:13
d John 6:44, 65; John 3:3, 5–6; 1 Cor. 2:14; Titus 3:3–5

4. When God converts a sinner, and translates him into the state of grace, he freeth him from his natural bondage under sin;[a] and, by his grace alone, enables him freely to will and to do that which is spiritually good;[b] yet so, as that by reason of his remaining corruption, he doth not perfectly, nor only, will that which is good, but doth also will that which is evil.[c]

a Col. 1:13; John 8:34, 36; Rom. 6:6–7 b Phil. 2:13; Rom. 6:14, 17–19, 22 c Gal. 5:17; Rom. 7:14–25;
1 John 1:8, 10

5. The will of man is made perfectly and immutably free to good alone, in the state of glory only.[a]

a Heb. 12:23; 1 John 3:2; Jude 24; Rev. 21:27

X. Of Effectual Calling

1. All those whom God hath predestinated unto life, and those only, he is pleased, in his appointed and accepted time, effectually to call,[a] by his Word and Spirit,[b] out of that state of sin and death, in which they are by nature, to grace and salvation, by Jesus Christ;[c] enlightening their minds spiritually and savingly to understand the things of God,[d] taking away their heart of stone, and giving unto them a heart of flesh;[e] renewing their wills, and, by his almighty power, determining them to that which is good,[f] and effectually drawing them to Jesus Christ:[g] yet so, as they come most freely, being made willing by his grace.[h]

a Acts 13:48; Rom. 8:28, 30; Rom. 11:7; Eph. 1:5, 11; 2 Tim. 1:9–10 b 2 Thess. 2:13–14; James 1:18; 2 Cor. 3:3, 6; 1 Cor. 2:12 c 2 Tim. 1:9–10; 1 Pet. 2:9; Rom. 8:2; Eph. 2:1–10 d Acts 26:18; 1 Cor. 2:10, 12; Eph. 1:17–18; 2 Cor. 4:6 e Ezek. 36:26 f Ezek. 11:19; Deut. 30:6; Ezek. 36:27; John 3:5; Titus 3:5; 1 Pet. 1:23 g John 6:44–45; Acts 16:14 h Ps. 110:3; John 6:37; Matt. 11:28; Rev. 22:17; Rom. 6:16–18; Eph. 2:8; Phil. 1:29

2. This effectual call is of God's free and special grace alone, not from anything at all foreseen in man,[a] who is altogether passive therein, until, being quickened and renewed by the Holy Spirit,[b] he is thereby enabled to answer this call, and to embrace the grace offered and conveyed in it.[c]

a 2 Tim. 1:9; Eph. 2:8–9; Rom. 9:11 b 1 Cor. 2:14; Rom. 8:7–9; Titus 3:4–5 c John 6:37; Ezek. 36:27; 1 John 5:1; 1 John 3:9

3. Elect infants, dying in infancy, are regenerated, and saved by Christ, through the Spirit,[a] who worketh when, and where, and how he

pleaseth:[b] so also are all other elect persons who are uncapable of being outwardly called by the ministry of the Word.[c]

a Gen. 17:7; Luke 18:15–16; Acts 2:39; John 3:3, 5; 1 John 5:12; Luke 1:15 b John 3:8 c John 16:7–8; 1 John 5:12; Acts 4:12

4. Others, not elected, although they may be called by the ministry of the Word,[a] and may have some common operations of the Spirit,[b] yet they never truly come unto Christ, and therefore cannot be saved:[c] much less can men, not professing the Christian religion, be saved in any other way whatsoever, be they never so diligent to frame their lives according to the light of nature, and the laws of that religion they do profess.[d] And, to assert and maintain that they may, is very pernicious, and to be detested.[e]

a Matt. 13:14–15; Acts 28:24; Acts 13:48; Matt. 22:14 b Matt. 13:20–21; Matt. 7:22; Heb. 6:4–5 c John 6:37, 64–66; John 8:44; John 13:18; John 17:12 d Acts 4:12; 1 John 4:2–3; 2 John 9; John 14:6; Eph. 2:12–13; John 4:22; John 17:3; Rom. 10:13–17 e 2 John 9–11; 1 Cor. 16:22; Gal. 1:6–8

XI. Of Justification

1. Those whom God effectually calleth, he also freely justifieth:[a] not by infusing righteousness into them, but by pardoning their sins, and by accounting and accepting their persons as righteous; not for anything wrought in them, or done by them, but for Christ's sake alone; nor by imputing faith itself, the act of believing, or any other evangelical obedience to them, as their righteousness; but by imputing the obedience and satisfaction of Christ unto them,[b] they receiving and resting on him and his righteousness, by faith; which faith they have not of themselves, it is the gift of God.[c]

a Rom. 8:30; Rom. 3:24; Rom. 5:15–16 b Rom. 4:5–8; 2 Cor. 5:19, 21; Rom. 3:22–28; Titus 3:5, 7; Eph. 1:7; Jer. 23:6; 1 Cor. 1:30–31; Rom. 5:17–19 c John 1:12; Acts 10:43; Acts 13:38–39; Phil. 3:9; Eph. 2:7–8; John 6:44–45, 65; Phil. 1:29

2. Faith, thus receiving and resting on Christ and his righteousness, is the alone instrument of justification:[a] yet is it not alone in the person justified, but is ever accompanied with all other saving graces, and is no dead faith, but worketh by love.[b]

a John 3:18, 36; Rom. 3:28; Rom. 5:1 b James 2:17, 22, 26; Gal. 5:6

3. Christ, by his obedience and death, did fully discharge the debt of all those that are thus justified, and did make a proper, real, and full satisfaction to his Father's justice in their behalf.[a] Yet, inasmuch as he was given by the Father for them;[b] and his obedience and satisfaction accepted in their stead;[c] and both, freely, not for anything in them; their justification is only of free grace;[d] that both the exact justice and rich grace of God might be glorified in the justification of sinners.[e]

a Mark 10:45; Rom. 5:8–10, 18–19; Gal. 3:13; 1 Tim. 2:5–6; Heb. 1:3; Heb. 10:10, 14; Dan. 9:24, 26; Isa. 52:13–53:12 b Rom. 8:32; John 3:16 c 2 Cor. 5:21; Eph. 5:2; Phil. 2:6–9; Isa. 53:10–11 d Rom. 3:24; Eph. 1:7 e Rom. 3:26; Eph. 2:7; Zech. 9:9; Isa. 45:21

4. God did, from all eternity, decree to justify all the elect,[a] and Christ did, in the fullness of time, die for their sins, and rise again for their justification:[b] nevertheless, they are not justified, until the Holy Spirit doth, in due time, actually apply Christ unto them.[c]

a Rom. 8:29–30; Gal. 3:8; 1 Pet. 1:2, 19–20 b Gal. 4:4; 1 Tim. 2:6; Rom. 4:25 c Eph. 2:3; Titus 3:3–7; Gal. 2:16; Col. 1:21–22

5. God doth continue to forgive the sins of those that are justified;[a] and, although they can never fall from the state of justification,[b] yet they may, by their sins, fall under God's fatherly displeasure, and not have the light of his countenance restored unto them, until they humble themselves, confess their sins, beg pardon, and renew their faith and repentance.[c]

a Matt. 6:12; 1 John 1:7, 9; 1 John 2:1–2 b Rom. 5:1–5; Rom. 8:30–39; Heb. 10:14; Luke 22:32; John 10:28 c Ps. 89:30–33; Ps. 51:1–19; Ps. 32:5; Matt. 26:75; Luke 1:20; 1 Cor. 11:30, 32

6. The justification of believers under the old testament was, in all these respects, one and the same with the justification of believers under the new testament.[a]

a Gal. 3:9, 13–14; Rom. 4:6–8, 22–24; Rom. 10:6–13; Heb. 13:8

XII. Of Adoption

1. All those that are justified, God vouchsafeth, in and for his only Son Jesus Christ, to make partakers of the grace of adoption,[a] by which they are taken into the number, and enjoy the liberties and privileges of the children of God,[b] have his name put upon them,[c] receive the Spirit of adoption,[d] have access to the throne of grace with boldness,[e] are enabled to cry, Abba, Father,[f] are pitied,[g] protected,[h] provided for,[i] and chastened by him, as by a father:[j] yet never cast off,[k] but sealed to the day of redemption;[l] and inherit the promises,[m] as heirs of everlasting salvation.[n]

a Eph. 1:5; Gal. 4:4–5 b Rom. 8:17; John 1:12 c Num. 6:24–26; Jer. 14:9; Amos 9:12; Acts 15:17; 2 Cor. 6:18; Rev. 3:12 d Rom. 8:15 e Eph. 3:12; Heb. 4:16 f Rom. 8:15; Gal. 4:6; Rom. 8:16 g Ps. 103:13 h Prov. 14:26 i Matt. 6:30, 32; 1 Pet. 5:7 j Heb. 12:6 k Lam. 3:31–32; Ps. 89:30–35 l Eph. 4:30 m Heb. 6:12 n 1 Pet. 1:3–4; Heb. 1:14

XIII. Of Sanctification

1. They, who are once effectually called, and regenerated, having a new heart, and a new spirit created in them, are further sanctified, really and personally, through the virtue of Christ's death and resurrection,[a] by his Word and Spirit dwelling in them:[b] the dominion of the whole body of sin is destroyed,[c] and the several lusts thereof are more and more weakened and mortified;[d] and they more and more quickened and strengthened in all saving graces,[e] to the practice of true holiness, without which no man shall see the Lord.[f]

a 1 Thess. 5:23–24; 2 Thess. 2:13–14; Ezek. 36:22–28; Titus 3:5; Acts 20:32; Phil. 3:10; Rom. 6:5–6 b John 17:17, 19; Eph. 5:26; Rom. 8:13–14; 2 Thess. 2:13 c Rom. 6:6, 14 d Gal. 5:24; Rom. 8:13 e Col. 1:10–11; Eph. 3:16–19 f 2 Cor. 7:1; Col. 1:28; Col. 4:12; Heb. 12:14

2. This sanctification is throughout, in the whole man;[a] yet imperfect in this life, there abiding still some remnants of corruption in every part;[b] whence ariseth a continual and irreconcilable war, the flesh lusting against the Spirit, and the Spirit against the flesh.[c]

a 1 Thess. 5:23; Rom. 12:1–2 *b* 1 John 1:8–10; Rom. 7:14–25; Phil. 3:12 *c* Gal. 5:17

3. In which war, although the remaining corruption, for a time, may much prevail;[a] yet, through the continual supply of strength from the sanctifying Spirit of Christ, the regenerate part doth overcome;[b] and so, the saints grow in grace,[c] perfecting holiness in the fear of God.[d]

a Rom. 7:23 *b* Rom. 6:14; 1 John 5:4; Eph. 4:15–16; Rom. 8:2 *c* 2 Pet. 3:18; 2 Cor. 3:18 *d* 2 Cor. 7:1

XIV. Of Saving Faith

1. The grace of faith, whereby the elect are enabled to believe to the saving of their souls,[a] is the work of the Spirit of Christ in their hearts,[b] and is ordinarily wrought by the ministry of the Word,[c] by which also, and by the administration of the sacraments, and prayer, it is increased and strengthened.[d]

a Titus 1:1; Heb. 10:39 *b* 1 Cor. 12:3; John 3:5; Titus 3:5; John 6:44–45, 65; Eph. 2:8; Phil. 1:29; 2 Pet. 1:1; 1 Pet. 1:2 *c* Matt. 28:19–20; Rom. 10:14, 17; 1 Cor. 1:21 *d* 1 Pet. 2:2; Acts 20:32; Rom. 1:16–17; Matt. 28:19; Acts 2:38; 1 Cor. 10:16; 1 Cor. 11:23–29; Luke 17:5; Phil. 4:6–7

2. By this faith, a Christian believeth to be true whatsoever is revealed in the Word, for the authority of God himself speaking therein;[a] and acteth differently upon that which each particular passage thereof containeth; yielding obedience to the commands,[b] trembling at the threatenings,[c] and embracing the promises of God for this life, and that which is to come.[d] But the principal acts of saving faith are accepting, receiving, and resting upon Christ

alone for justification, sanctification, and eternal life, by virtue of the covenant of grace.[e]

a 2 Pet. 1:20–21; John 4:42; 1 Thess. 2:13; 1 John 5:9–10; Acts 24:14 b Ps. 119:10–11, 48, 97–98, 167–168; John 14:15 c Ezra 9:4; Isa. 66:2; Heb. 4:1 d Heb. 11:13; 1 Tim. 4:8 e John 1:12; Acts 16:31; Gal. 2:20; Acts 15:11; 2 Tim. 1:9–10

3. This faith is different in degrees, weak or strong;[a] may be often and many ways assailed, and weakened, but gets the victory:[b] growing up in many to the attainment of a full assurance, through Christ,[c] who is both the author and finisher of our faith.[d]

a Heb. 5:13–14; Rom. 14:1–2; Matt. 6:30; Rom. 4:19–20; Matt. 8:10 b Luke 22:31–32; Eph. 6:16; 1 John 5:4–5 c Heb. 6:11–12; Heb. 10:22; Col. 2:2 d Heb. 12:2

XV. Of Repentance unto Life

1. Repentance unto life is an evangelical grace,[a] the doctrine whereof is to be preached by every minister of the gospel, as well as that of faith in Christ.[b]

a Acts 11:18; 2 Cor. 7:10; Zech. 12:10 b Luke 24:47; Mark 1:15; Acts 20:21

2. By it, a sinner, out of the sight and sense not only of the danger, but also of the filthiness and odiousness of his sins, as contrary to the holy nature, and righteous law of God; and upon the apprehension of his mercy in Christ to such as are penitent, so grieves for, and hates his sins, as to turn from them all unto God,[a] purposing and endeavoring to walk with him in all the ways of his commandments.[b]

a Ezek. 18:30–31; Ezek. 36:31; Isa. 30:22; Ps. 51:4; Jer. 31:18–19; Joel 2:12–13; Amos 5:15; Ps. 119:128; 2 Cor. 7:11; 1 Thess. 1:9 b Ps. 119:6, 59, 106; 2 Kings 23:25; Luke 1:6

3. Although repentance be not to be rested in, as any satisfaction for sin, or any cause of the pardon thereof,[a] which is the act of God's free

grace in Christ;[b] yet it is of such necessity to all sinners, that none may expect pardon without it.[c]

a Ezek. 36:31–32; Ezek. 16:61–63; Isa. 43:25 b Hos. 14:2, 4; Rom. 3:24; Eph. 1:7 c Luke 13:3, 5; Mark 1:4; Acts 17:30–31

4. As there is no sin so small, but it deserves damnation;[a] so there is no sin so great, that it can bring damnation upon those who truly repent.[b]

a Rom. 6:23; Gal. 3:10; Matt. 12:36 b Isa. 55:7; Rom. 8:1; Isa. 1:16–18

5. Men ought not to content themselves with a general repentance, but it is every man's duty to endeavor to repent of his particular sins, particularly.[a]

a Ps. 19:13; Matt. 26:75; Luke 19:8; 1 Tim. 1:13, 15

6. As every man is bound to make private confession of his sins to God, praying for the pardon thereof;[a] upon which, and the forsaking of them, he shall find mercy;[b] so, he that scandalizeth his brother, or the church of Christ, ought to be willing, by a private or public confession, and sorrow for his sin, to declare his repentance to those that are offended,[c] who are thereupon to be reconciled to him, and in love to receive him.[d]

a Ps. 32:5–6; Ps. 51:1–14 b Prov. 28:13; Isa. 55:7; 1 John 1:9 c James 5:16; Luke 17:3–4; Josh. 7:19; Matt. 18:15–18 d 2 Cor. 2:7–8; Gal. 6:1–2

XVI. Of Good Works

1. Good works are only such as God hath commanded in his holy Word,[a] and not such as, without the warrant thereof, are devised by men, out of blind zeal, or upon any pretense of good intention.[b]

a Mic. 6:8; Rom. 12:2; Heb. 13:21 b Matt. 15:9; Isa. 29:13; 1 Pet. 1:18; John 16:2; Rom. 10:2; 1 Sam. 15:21–23; Deut. 10:12–13; Col. 2:16–17, 20–23

2. These good works, done in obedience to God's commandments, are the fruits and evidences of a true and lively faith:[a] and by them believers manifest their thankfulness,[b] strengthen their assurance,[c] edify their brethren,[d] adorn the profession of the gospel,[e] stop the mouths of the adversaries,[f] and glorify God,[g] whose workmanship they are, created in Christ Jesus thereunto,[h] that, having their fruit unto holiness, they may have the end, eternal life.[i]

a James 2:18, 22 b Ps. 116:12–14; Col. 3:15–17; 1 Pet. 2:9 c 1 John 2:3, 5; 2 Pet. 1:5–10 d 2 Cor. 9:2; Matt. 5:16; 1 Tim. 4:12 e Titus 2:5, 9–12; 1 Tim. 6:1 f 1 Pet. 2:15 g 1 Pet. 2:12; Phil. 1:11; John 15:8 h Eph. 2:10 i Rom. 6:22

3. Their ability to do good works is not at all of themselves, but wholly from the Spirit of Christ.[a] And that they may be enabled thereunto, beside the graces they have already received, there is required an actual influence of the same Holy Spirit, to work in them to will, and to do, of his good pleasure:[b] yet are they not hereupon to grow negligent, as if they were not bound to perform any duty unless upon a special motion of the Spirit; but they ought to be diligent in stirring up the grace of God that is in them.[c]

a John 15:4–6; Rom. 8:4–14; Ezek. 36:26–27 b Phil. 2:13; Phil. 4:13; 2 Cor. 3:5; Eph. 3:16 c Phil. 2:12; Heb. 6:11–12; 2 Pet. 1:3, 5, 10–11; Isa. 64:7; 2 Tim. 1:6; Acts 26:6–7; Jude 20–21

4. They who, in their obedience, attain to the greatest height which is possible in this life, are so far from being able to supererogate, and to do more than God requires, as that they fall short of much which in duty they are bound to do.[a]

a Luke 17:10; Neh. 13:22; Rom. 8:21–25; Gal. 5:17

5. We cannot by our best works merit pardon of sin, or eternal life at the hand of God, by reason of the great disproportion that is between them and the glory to come; and the infinite distance that

is between us and God, whom, by them, we can neither profit, nor satisfy for the debt of our former sins,[a] but when we have done all we can, we have done but our duty, and are unprofitable servants:[b] and because, as they are good, they proceed from his Spirit;[c] and as they are wrought by us, they are defiled, and mixed with so much weakness and imperfection, that they cannot endure the severity of God's judgment.[d]

a Rom. 3:20; Rom. 4:2, 4, 6; Eph. 2:8–9; Titus 3:5–7; Rom. 8:18, 22–24; Ps. 16:2; Job 22:2–3; Job 35:7–8 b Luke 17:10 c Rom. 8:13–14; Gal. 5:22–23 d Isa. 64:6; Gal. 5:17; Rom. 7:15, 18; Ps. 143:2; Ps. 130:3

6. Notwithstanding, the persons of believers being accepted through Christ, their good works also are accepted in him;[a] not as though they were in this life wholly unblamable and unreprovable in God's sight;[b] but that he, looking upon them in his Son, is pleased to accept and reward that which is sincere, although accompanied with many weaknesses and imperfections.[c]

a Eph. 1:6; 1 Pet. 2:5; Ex. 28:38; Gen. 4:4; Heb. 11:4 b Job 9:20; Ps. 143:2; 1 John 1:8 c Heb. 13:20–21; 2 Cor. 8:12; Heb. 6:10; Matt. 25:21, 23; 1 Cor. 3:14; 1 Cor. 4:5

7. Works done by unregenerate men, although for the matter of them they may be things which God commands; and of good use both to themselves and others:[a] yet, because they proceed not from an heart purified by faith;[b] nor are done in a right manner, according to the Word;[c] nor to a right end, the glory of God,[d] they are therefore sinful, and cannot please God, or make a man meet to receive grace from God:[e] and yet, their neglect of them is more sinful and displeasing unto God.[f]

a 2 Kings 10:30–31; 1 Kings 21:27, 29; Luke 6:32–34; Luke 18:2–7; Rom. 13:4 b Heb. 11:4, 6; Gen. 4:3–5 c 1 Cor. 13:3; Isa. 1:12 d Matt. 6:2, 5, 16; 1 Cor. 10:31 e Prov. 21:27; Hag. 2:14; Titus 1:15; Amos 5:21–22; Mark 7:6–7; Hos. 1:4; Rom. 9:16; Titus 3:5 f Ps. 14:4; Ps. 36:3; Matt. 25:41–45; Matt. 23:23; Rom. 1:21–32

1. They, whom God hath accepted in his Beloved, effectually called, and sanctified by his Spirit, can neither totally nor finally fall away from the state of grace, but shall certainly persevere therein to the end, and be eternally saved.[a]

a Phil. 1:6; 2 Pet. 1:10; Rom. 8:28–30; John 10:28–29; 1 John 3:9; 1 John 5:18; 1 Pet. 1:5, 9

2. This perseverance of the saints depends not upon their own free will, but upon the immutability of the decree of election, flowing from the free and unchangeable love of God the Father;[a] upon the efficacy of the merit and intercession of Jesus Christ,[b] the abiding of the Spirit, and of the seed of God within them,[c] and the nature of the covenant of grace:[d] from all which ariseth also the certainty and infallibility thereof.[e]

a Ps. 89:3–4, 28–33; 2 Tim. 2:18–19; Jer. 31:3   b Heb. 10:10, 14; Heb. 13:20–21; Heb. 9:12–15; Rom. 8:33–39; John 17:11, 24; Luke 22:32; Heb. 7:25   c John 14:16–17; 1 John 2:27; 1 John 3:9   d Jer. 32:40; Ps. 89:34–37; Jer. 31:31–34   e John 6:38–40; John 10:28; 2 Thess. 3:3; 1 John 2:19

3. Nevertheless, they may, through the temptations of Satan and of the world, the prevalency of corruption remaining in them, and the neglect of the means of their preservation, fall into grievous sins;[a] and, for a time, continue therein:[b] whereby they incur God's displeasure,[c] and grieve his Holy Spirit,[d] come to be deprived of some measure of their graces and comforts,[e] have their hearts hardened,[f] and their consciences wounded;[g] hurt and scandalize others,[h] and bring temporal judgments upon themselves.[i]

a Ex. 32:21; Jonah 1:3, 10; Ps. 51:14; Matt. 26:70, 72, 74   b 2 Sam. 12:9, 13; Gal. 2:11–14   c Num. 20:12; 2 Sam. 11:27; Isa. 64:7, 9   d Eph. 4:30   e Ps. 51:8, 10, 12; Rev. 2:4; Matt. 26:75   f Isa. 63:17   g Ps. 32:3–4; Ps. 51:8   h Gen. 12:10–20; 2 Sam. 12:14; Gal. 2:13   i Ps. 89:31–32; 1 Cor. 11:32

XVIII. Of the Assurance of Grace and Salvation

1. Although hypocrites and other unregenerate men may vainly deceive themselves with false hopes and carnal presumptions of being in the favor of God, and estate of salvation[a] (which hope of theirs shall perish[b]): yet such as truly believe in the Lord Jesus, and love him in sincerity, endeavoring to walk in all good conscience before him, may, in this life, be certainly assured that they are in the state of grace,[c] and may rejoice in the hope of the glory of God, which hope shall never make them ashamed.[d]

a Mic. 3:11; Deut. 29:19; John 8:41   b Amos 9:10; Matt. 7:22–23   c 1 John 5:13; 1 John 2:3; 1 John 3:14, 18–19, 21, 24   d Rom. 5:2, 5

2. This certainty is not a bare conjectural and probable persuasion grounded upon a fallible hope;[a] but an infallible assurance of faith founded upon the divine truth of the promises of salvation,[b] the inward evidence of those graces unto which these promises are made,[c] the testimony of the Spirit of adoption witnessing with our spirits that we are the children of God,[d] which Spirit is the earnest of our inheritance, whereby we are sealed to the day of redemption.[e]

a Heb. 6:11, 19   b Heb. 6:17–18   c 2 Pet. 1:4–11; 1 John 2:3; 1 John 3:14; 2 Cor. 1:12   d Rom. 8:15–16
e Eph. 1:13–14; Eph. 4:30; 2 Cor. 1:21–22

3. This infallible assurance doth not so belong to the essence of faith, but that a true believer may wait long, and conflict with many difficulties, before he be partaker of it:[a] yet, being enabled by the Spirit to know the things which are freely given him of God, he may, without extraordinary revelation, in the right use of ordinary means, attain thereunto.[b] And therefore it is the duty of everyone to give all diligence to make his calling and election sure,[c] that thereby his heart may be enlarged in peace and joy in the Holy Ghost, in love and thankfulness

to God, and in strength and cheerfulness in the duties of obedience, the proper fruits of this assurance;[d] so far is it from inclining men to looseness.[e]

a 1 John 5:13 b 1 Cor. 2:12; 1 John 4:13; Heb. 6:11–12; Eph. 3:17–18 c 2 Pet. 1:10 d Rom. 5:1–2, 5; Rom. 14:17; Rom. 15:13; Eph. 1:3–4; Ps. 4:6–7; Ps. 119:32 e 1 John 2:1–2; Rom. 6:1–2; Titus 2:11–12, 14; 2 Cor. 7:1; Rom. 8:1, 12; 1 John 3:2–3; Ps. 130:4; 1 John 1:6–7

4. True believers may have the assurance of their salvation divers ways shaken, diminished, and intermitted; as, by negligence in preserving of it, by falling into some special sin which woundeth the conscience and grieveth the Spirit; by some sudden or vehement temptation, by God's withdrawing the light of his countenance, and suffering even such as fear him to walk in darkness and to have no light:[a] yet are they never utterly destitute of that seed of God, and life of faith, that love of Christ and the brethren, that sincerity of heart, and conscience of duty, out of which, by the operation of the Spirit, this assurance may, in due time, be revived;[b] and by the which, in the meantime, they are supported from utter despair.[c]

a Ps. 51:8, 12, 14; Eph. 4:30–31; Ps. 77:1–10; Ps. 31:22; Matt. 26:69–72; Luke 22:31–34 b 1 John 3:9; Luke 22:32; Ps. 51:8, 12; Ps. 73:15 c Mic. 7:7–9; Jer. 32:40; Isa. 54:7–14; 2 Cor. 4:8–10

XIX. Of the Law of God

1. God gave to Adam a law, as a covenant of works, by which he bound him and all his posterity to personal, entire, exact, and perpetual obedience, promised life upon the fulfilling, and threatened death upon the breach of it, and endued him with power and ability to keep it.[a]

a Gen. 1:26–27; Gen. 2:17; Eph. 4:24; Rom. 2:14–15; Rom. 10:5; Rom. 5:12, 19; Gal. 3:10, 12; Eccles. 7:29

2. This law, after his fall, continued to be a perfect rule of righteousness; and, as such, was delivered by God upon Mount Sinai, in ten

commandments, and written in two tables:[a] the first four commandments containing our duty towards God; and the other six, our duty to man.[b]

a James 1:25; James 2:8, 10–12; Rom. 3:19; Rom. 13:8–9; Deut. 5:32; Deut. 10:4; Ex. 34:1   b Ex. 20:3–17; Matt. 22:37–40

3. Beside this law, commonly called moral, God was pleased to give to the people of Israel, as a church under age, ceremonial laws, containing several typical ordinances, partly of worship, prefiguring Christ, his graces, actions, sufferings, and benefits;[a] and partly, holding forth divers instructions of moral duties.[b] All which ceremonial laws are now abrogated, under the new testament.[c]

a Heb. 10:1; Gal. 4:1–3; Col. 2:17; Heb. 9:1–28   b Lev. 19:9–10, 19, 23, 27; Deut. 24:19–21; 1 Cor. 5:7; 2 Cor. 6:17; Jude 23   c Col. 2:14, 16–17; Dan. 9:27; Eph. 2:15–16; Heb. 9:10; Acts 10:9–16; Acts 11:2–10

4. To them also, as a body politic, he gave sundry judicial laws, which expired together with the State of that people; not obliging any other now, further than the general equity thereof may require.[a]

a Ex. 21:1–23:19; Gen. 49:10; 1 Pet. 2:13–14; 1 Cor. 9:8–10

5. The moral law doth forever bind all, as well justified persons as others, to the obedience thereof;[a] and that, not only in regard of the matter contained in it, but also in respect of the authority of God the Creator, who gave it.[b] Neither doth Christ, in the gospel, any way dissolve, but much strengthen this obligation.[c]

a Rom. 13:8–10; Rom. 3:31; Rom. 7:25; 1 Cor. 9:21; Gal. 5:14; Eph. 6:2–3; 1 John 2:3–4, 7; Rom. 3:20; Rom. 7:7–8; 1 John 3:4; Rom. 6:15   b Deut. 6:4–5; Ex. 20:11; Rom. 3:19; James 2:8, 10–11; Matt. 19:4–6; Gen. 17:1   c Matt. 5:17–19; Rom. 3:31; 1 Cor. 9:21; Luke 16:17–18

6. Although true believers be not under the law, as a covenant of works, to be thereby justified, or condemned;[a] yet is it of great use

to them, as well as to others; in that, as a rule of life informing them of the will of God, and their duty, it directs and binds them to walk accordingly;[b] discovering also the sinful pollutions of their nature, hearts, and lives;[c] so as, examining themselves thereby, they may come to further conviction of, humiliation for, and hatred against sin,[d] together with a clearer sight of the need they have of Christ, and the perfection of his obedience.[e] It is likewise of use to the regenerate, to restrain their corruptions, in that it forbids sin:[f] and the threatenings of it serve to show what even their sins deserve; and what afflictions, in this life, they may expect for them, although freed from the curse thereof threatened in the law.[g] The promises of it, in like manner, show them God's approbation of obedience, and what blessings they may expect upon the performance thereof:[h] although not as due to them by the law as a covenant of works.[i] So as, a man's doing good, and refraining from evil, because the law encourageth to the one, and deterreth from the other, is no evidence of his being under the law; and, not under grace.[j]

a Rom. 6:14; Rom. 7:4; Gal. 2:16; Gal. 3:13; Gal. 4:4–5; Acts 13:38–39; Rom. 8:1, 33   b Rom. 7:12, 22, 25; Ps. 119:1–6; 1 Cor. 7:19; Gal. 5:14–23   c Rom. 7:7, 13; Rom. 3:20   d James 1:23–25; Rom. 7:9, 14, 24   e Gal. 3:24; Rom. 7:24–25; Rom. 8:3–4   f James 2:11–12; Ps. 119:101, 104, 128   g Ezra 9:13–14; Ps. 89:30–34; Gal. 3:13   h Ex. 19:5–6; Deut. 5:33; Lev. 18:5; Matt. 19:17; Lev. 26:1–13; 2 Cor. 6:16; Eph. 6:2–3; Ps. 19:11; Ps. 37:11; Matt. 5:5   i Gal. 2:16; Luke 17:10   j Rom. 6:12–15; 1 Pet. 3:8–12; Ps. 34:12–16; Heb. 12:28–29

7. Neither are the forementioned uses of the law contrary to the grace of the gospel, but do sweetly comply with it;[a] the Spirit of Christ subduing and enabling the will of man to do that freely, and cheerfully, which the will of God, revealed in the law, requireth to be done.[b]

a Rom. 3:31; Gal. 3:21; Titus 2:11–14   b Ezek. 36:27; Heb. 8:10; Jer. 31:33; Ps. 119:35, 47; Rom. 7:22

1. The liberty which Christ hath purchased for believers under the gospel consists in their freedom from the guilt of sin, the condemning wrath of God, the curse of the moral law;[a] and, in their being delivered from this present evil world, bondage to Satan, and dominion of sin;[b] from the evil of afflictions, the sting of death, the victory of the grave, and everlasting damnation;[c] as also, in their free access to God,[d] and their yielding obedience unto him, not out of slavish fear, but a childlike love and willing mind.[e] All which were common also to believers under the law.[f] But, under the new testament, the liberty of Christians is further enlarged, in their freedom from the yoke of the ceremonial law, to which the Jewish church was subjected;[g] and in greater boldness of access to the throne of grace,[h] and in fuller communications of the free Spirit of God, than believers under the law did ordinarily partake of.[i]

a Titus 2:14; 1 Thess. 1:10; Gal. 3:13 b Gal. 1:4; Col. 1:13; Acts 26:18; Rom. 6:14 c Rom. 8:28; Ps. 119:71; 2 Cor. 4:15–18; 1 Cor. 15:54–57; Rom. 5:9; Rom. 8:1; 1 Thess. 1:10 d Rom. 5:1–2 e Rom. 8:14–15; Gal. 4:6; 1 John 4:18 f Gal. 3:8–9, 14; Rom. 4:6–8; 1 Cor. 10:3–4; Heb. 11:1–40 g Gal. 4:1–7; Gal. 5:1; Acts 15:10–11 h Heb. 4:14–16; Heb. 10:19–22 i John 7:38–39; Acts 2:17–18; 2 Cor. 3:8, 13, 17–18; Jer. 31:31–34

2. God alone is Lord of the conscience,[a] and hath left it free from the doctrines and commandments of men, which are, in anything, contrary to his Word; or beside it, if matters of faith, or worship.[b] So that, to believe such doctrines, or to obey such commands, out of conscience, is to betray true liberty of conscience:[c] and the requiring of an implicit faith, and an absolute and blind obedience, is to destroy liberty of conscience, and reason also.[d]

a James 4:12; Rom. 14:4, 10; 1 Cor. 10:29 b Acts 4:19; Acts 5:29; 1 Cor. 7:22–23; Matt. 15:1–6; Matt. 23:8–10; 2 Cor. 1:24; Matt. 15:9 c Col. 2:20–23; Gal. 1:10; Gal. 2:4–5; Gal. 4:9–10; Gal. 5:1 d Rom. 10:17; Isa. 8:20; Acts 17:11; John 4:22; Rev. 13:12, 16–17; Jer. 8:9; 1 Pet. 3:15

3. They who, upon pretense of Christian liberty, do practice any sin, or cherish any lust, do thereby destroy the end of Christian liberty, which is, that being delivered out of the hands of our enemies, we might serve the Lord without fear, in holiness and righteousness before him, all the days of our life.[a]

a Gal. 5:13; 1 Pet. 2:16; 2 Pet. 2:19; Rom. 6:15; John 8:34; Luke 1:74–75

4. And because the powers which God hath ordained, and the liberty which Christ hath purchased, are not intended by God to destroy, but mutually to uphold and preserve one another, they who, upon pretense of Christian liberty, shall oppose any lawful power, or the lawful exercise of it, whether it be civil or ecclesiastical, resist the ordinance of God.[a] And, for their publishing of such opinions, or maintaining of such practices, as are contrary to the light of nature, or to the known principles of Christianity (whether concerning faith, worship, or conversation), or to the power of godliness; or, such erroneous opinions or practices, as either in their own nature, or in the manner of publishing or maintaining them, are destructive to the external peace and order which Christ hath established in the church, they may lawfully be called to account, and proceeded against, by the censures of the church.[b][1]

a 1 Pet. 2:13–14, 16; Rom. 13:1–8; Heb. 13:17; 1 Thess. 5:12–13 b Rom. 1:32; 1 Cor. 5:1, 5, 11–13; 2 John 10–11; 2 Thess. 3:6, 14; 1 Tim. 6:3–4; Titus 1:10–11, 13–14; Titus 3:10; Rom. 16:17; Matt. 18:15–17; 1 Tim. 1:19–20; Rev. 2:2, 14–15, 20

XXI. Of Religious Worship and the Sabbath Day

1. The light of nature showeth that there is a God, who hath lordship and sovereignty over all, is good, and doth good unto all, and is therefore to be feared, loved, praised, called upon, trusted in, and

1 Original edition includes "and by the power of the civil magistrate" at the end of this paragraph.

served, with all the heart, and with all the soul, and with all the might.[a] But the acceptable way of worshiping the true God is instituted by himself, and so limited by his own revealed will, that he may not be worshiped according to the imaginations and devices of men, or the suggestions of Satan, under any visible representation, or any other way not prescribed in the Holy Scripture.[b]

a Rom. 1:20; Ps. 19:1–4a; Ps. 50:6; Ps. 97:6; Ps. 145:9–12; Acts 14:17; Ps. 104:1–35; Ps. 86:8–10; Ps. 95:1–6; Ps. 89:5–7; Deut. 6:4–5 b Deut. 12:32; Matt. 15:9; Acts 17:23–25; Matt. 4:9–10; Deut. 4:15–20; Ex. 20:4–6; John 4:23–24; Col. 2:18–23

2. Religious worship is to be given to God, the Father, Son, and Holy Ghost; and to him alone;[a] not to angels, saints, or any other creature:[b] and, since the fall, not without a Mediator; nor in the mediation of any other but of Christ alone.[c]

a John 5:23; Matt. 28:19; 2 Cor. 13:14; Eph. 3:14; Rev. 5:11–14; Acts 10:25–26 b Col. 2:18; Rev. 19:10; Rom. 1:25 c John 14:6; 1 Tim. 2:5; Eph. 2:18; Col. 3:17

3. Prayer, with thanksgiving, being one special part of religious worship,[a] is by God required of all men:[b] and, that it may be accepted, it is to be made in the name of the Son,[c] by the help of his Spirit,[d] according to his will,[e] with understanding, reverence, humility, fervency, faith, love, and perseverance;[f] and, if vocal, in a known tongue.[g]

a Phil. 4:6; 1 Tim. 2:1; Col. 4:2 b Ps. 65:2; Ps. 67:3; Ps. 96:7–8; Ps. 148:11–13; Isa. 55:6–7 c John 14:13–14; 1 Pet. 2:5 d Rom. 8:26; Eph. 6:18 e 1 John 5:14 f Ps. 47:7; Eccles. 5:1–2; Heb. 12:28; Gen. 18:27; James 5:16; James 1:6–7; Mark 11:24; Matt. 6:12, 14–15; Col. 4:2; Eph. 6:18 g 1 Cor. 14:14

4. Prayer is to be made for things lawful;[a] and for all sorts of men living, or that shall live hereafter:[b] but not for the dead,[c] nor for those of whom it may be known that they have sinned the sin unto death.[d]

a 1 John 5:14, 16; John 15:7 b 1 Tim. 2:1–2; John 17:20; 2 Sam. 7:29; 2 Chron. 6:14–42 c Luke 16:25–26; Isa. 57:1–2; Ps. 73:24; 2 Cor. 5:8, 10; Phil. 1:21–24; Rev. 14:13 d 1 John 5:16

5. The reading of the Scriptures with godly fear,[a] the sound preaching[b] and conscionable hearing of the Word, in obedience unto God, with understanding, faith, and reverence,[c] singing of psalms with grace in the heart;[d] as also, the due administration and worthy receiving of the sacraments instituted by Christ, are all parts of the ordinary religious worship of God:[e] beside religious oaths,[f] vows,[g] solemn fastings,[h] and thanksgivings upon special occasions,[i] which are, in their several times and seasons, to be used in an holy and religious manner.[j]

a Luke 4:16–17; Acts 15:21; Col. 4:16; 1 Thess. 5:27; Rev. 1:3 b 2 Tim. 4:2; Acts 5:42 c James 1:22; Acts 10:33; Matt. 13:19; Heb. 4:2; Isa. 66:2 d Col. 3:16; Eph. 5:19; James 5:13; 1 Cor. 14:15 e Matt. 28:19; 1 Cor. 11:23–29; Acts 2:42 f Deut. 6:13; Neh. 10:29; 2 Cor. 1:23 g Ps. 116:14; Isa. 19:21; Eccles. 5:4–5 h Joel 2:12; Est. 4:16; Matt. 9:15; Acts 14:23 i Ex. 15:1–21; Ps. 107:1–43; Neh. 12:27–43; Est. 9:20–22 j Heb. 12:28

6. Neither prayer, nor any other part of religious worship, is now, under the gospel, either tied unto, or made more acceptable by any place in which it is performed, or towards which it is directed:[a] but God is to be worshiped everywhere,[b] in spirit and truth;[c] as, in private families[d] daily,[e] and in secret, each one by himself;[f] so, more solemnly in the public assemblies, which are not carelessly or willfully to be neglected, or forsaken, when God, by his Word or providence, calleth thereunto.[g]

a John 4:21 b Mal. 1:11; 1 Tim. 2:8 c John 4:23–24 d Jer. 10:25; Deut. 6:6–7; Job 1:5; 2 Sam. 6:18, 20 e Matt. 6:11; Job 1:5 f Matt. 6:6, 16–18; Neh. 1:4–11; Dan. 9:3–4a g Isa. 56:6–7; Heb. 10:25; Ps. 100:4; Ps. 122:1; Ps. 84:1–12; Luke 4:16; Acts 13:42, 44; Acts 2:42

7. As it is the law of nature, that, in general, a due proportion of time be set apart for the worship of God; so, in his Word, by a positive, moral, and perpetual commandment binding all men in all ages, he hath particularly appointed one day in seven, for a Sabbath, to be kept holy unto him:[a] which, from the beginning of the world to the resurrection of Christ, was the last day of the week; and, from the

resurrection of Christ, was changed into the first day of the week,[b] which, in Scripture, is called the Lord's Day,[c] and is to be continued to the end of the world, as the Christian Sabbath.[d]

a Ex. 20:8–11; Isa. 56:2–7 b Gen. 2:2–3; 1 Cor. 16:1–2; Acts 20:7 c Rev. 1:10 d Matt. 5:17–18; Mark 2:27–28; Rom. 13:8–10; James 2:8–12

8. This Sabbath is then kept holy unto the Lord, when men, after a due preparing of their hearts, and ordering of their common affairs beforehand, do not only observe an holy rest, all the day, from their own works, words, and thoughts about their worldly employments and recreations,[a] but also are taken up, the whole time, in the public and private exercises of his worship, and in the duties of necessity and mercy.[b]

a Ex. 20:8; Ex. 16:23–30; Ex. 31:15–17; Isa. 58:13–14; Neh. 13:15–22 b Isa. 58:13–14; Luke 4:16; Matt. 12:1–13; Mark 3:1–5

XXII. Of Lawful Oaths and Vows

1. A lawful oath is a part of religious worship,[a] wherein, upon just occasion, the person swearing solemnly calleth God to witness what he asserteth, or promiseth, and to judge him according to the truth or falsehood of what he sweareth.[b]

a Deut. 10:20; Isa. 45:23; Rom. 14:11; Phil. 2:10–11 b Ex. 20:7; Lev. 19:12; Rom. 1:9; 2 Cor. 1:23; 2 Cor. 11:31; Gal. 1:20; 2 Chron. 6:22–23

2. The name of God only is that by which men ought to swear, and therein it is to be used with all holy fear and reverence.[a] Therefore, to swear vainly, or rashly, by that glorious and dreadful Name; or, to swear at all by any other thing, is sinful, and to be abhorred.[b] Yet, as in matters of weight and moment, an oath is warranted by the Word of God, under the new testament as well as under the old;[c] so a lawful

oath, being imposed by lawful authority, in such matters, ought to be taken.[d]

a Deut. 6:13; Josh. 23:7 b Ex. 20:7; Jer. 5:7; Matt. 5:33–37; James 5:12 c Heb. 6:16; 2 Cor. 1:23; Isa. 65:16 d 1 Kings 8:31; Neh. 13:25; Ezra 10:5

3. Whosoever taketh an oath ought duly to consider the weightiness of so solemn an act, and therein to avouch nothing but what he is fully persuaded is the truth:[a] neither may any man bind himself by oath to anything but what is good and just, and what he believeth so to be, and what he is able and resolved to perform.[b][2]

a Ex. 20:7; Lev. 19:12; Jer. 4:2; Hos. 10:4 b Gen. 24:2–9; Neh. 5:12–13; Eccles. 5:2, 5

4. An oath is to be taken in the plain and common sense of the words, without equivocation, or mental reservation.[a] It cannot oblige to sin; but in anything not sinful, being taken, it binds to performance, although to a man's own hurt.[b] Nor is it to be violated, although made to heretics, or infidels.[c]

a Jer. 4:2; Ps. 24:4 b 1 Sam. 25:22, 32–34; Ps. 15:4 c Ezek. 17:16–19; Josh. 9:18–19; 2 Sam. 21:1

5. A vow is of the like nature with a promissory oath, and ought to be made with the like religious care, and to be performed with the like faithfulness.[a]

a Num. 30:2; Isa. 19:21; Eccles. 5:4–6; Ps. 61:8; Ps. 66:13–14

6. It is not to be made to any creature, but to God alone:[a] and, that it may be accepted, it is to be made voluntarily, out of faith, and conscience of duty, in way of thankfulness for mercy received, or for the obtaining of what we want, whereby we more strictly bind ourselves

2 Original edition includes, "Yet it is a sin to refuse an oath touching anything that is good and just, being imposed by lawful authority" at the end of this paragraph.

to necessary duties; or, to other things, so far and so long as they may fitly conduce thereunto.[b]

a Ps. 50:14; Ps. 76:11; Ps. 116:14   b Deut. 23:21–23; Gen. 28:20–22; 1 Sam. 1:11; Ps. 66:13–14; Ps. 132:2–5

7. No man may vow to do anything forbidden in the Word of God, or what would hinder any duty therein commanded, or which is not in his own power, and for the performance whereof he hath no promise of ability from God.[a] In which respects, popish monastical vows of perpetual single life, professed poverty, and regular obedience, are so far from being degrees of higher perfection, that they are superstitious and sinful snares, in which no Christian may entangle himself.[b]

a Acts 23:12–14; Mark 6:26; Num. 30:5, 8, 12–13   b Matt. 19:11–12; 1 Cor. 7:2, 9; Heb. 13:4; Eph. 4:28; 1 Thess. 4:11–12; 1 Cor. 7:23

XXIII. Of the Civil Magistrate

1. God, the supreme Lord and King of all the world, hath ordained civil magistrates, to be, under him, over the people, for his own glory, and the public good: and, to this end, hath armed them with the power of the sword, for the defense and encouragement of them that are good, and for the punishment of evildoers.[a]

a Rom. 13:1–4; 1 Pet. 2:13–14

2. It is lawful for Christians to accept and execute the office of a magistrate, when called thereunto:[a] in the managing whereof, as they ought especially to maintain piety, justice, and peace, according to the wholesome laws of each commonwealth;[b] so, for that end, they may lawfully, now under the new testament, wage war, upon just and necessary occasion.[c]

a Gen. 41:39–43; Neh. 12:26; Neh. 13:15–31; Dan. 2:48–49; Prov. 8:15–16; Rom. 13:1–4   b Ps. 2:10–12; 1 Tim. 2:2; Ps. 82:3–4; 2 Sam. 23:3; 1 Pet. 2:13   c Luke 3:14; Rom. 13:4; Matt. 8:9–10; Acts 10:1–2

3. Civil magistrates may not assume to themselves the administration of the Word and sacraments; or the power of the keys of the kingdom of heaven;[a] or, in the least, interfere in matters of faith.[b] Yet, as nursing fathers, it is the duty of civil magistrates to protect the church of our common Lord, without giving the preference to any denomination of Christians above the rest, in such a manner that all ecclesiastical persons whatever shall enjoy the full, free, and unquestioned liberty of discharging every part of their sacred functions, without violence or danger.[c] And, as Jesus Christ hath appointed a regular government and discipline in his church, no law of any commonwealth should interfere with, let, or hinder, the due exercise thereof, among the voluntary members of any denomination of Christians, according to their own profession and belief.[d] It is the duty of civil magistrates to protect the person and good name of all their people, in such an effectual manner as that no person be suffered, either upon pretense of religion or of infidelity, to offer any indignity, violence, abuse, or injury to any other person whatsoever: and to take order, that all religious and ecclesiastical assemblies be held without molestation or disturbance.[e][3]

a 2 Chron. 26:18; Matt. 18:17; Matt. 16:19; 1 Cor. 12:28–29; Eph. 4:11–12; 1 Cor. 4:1–2; Rom. 10:15; Heb. 5:4 b John 18:36; Acts 5:29; Eph. 4:11–12 c Isa. 49:23; Rom. 13:1–6 d Ps. 105:15 e Rom. 13:4; 1 Tim. 2:2

4. It is the duty of people to pray for magistrates,[a] to honor their persons,[b] to pay them tribute or other dues,[c] to obey their lawful com-

---

3 Original edition of this paragraph reads, "The civil magistrate may not assume to himself the administration of the Word and sacraments, or the power of the keys of the kingdom of heaven: yet he hath authority, and it is his duty, to take order, that unity and peace be preserved in the Church, that the truth of God be kept pure and entire; that all blasphemies and heresies be suppressed; all corruptions and abuses in worship and discipline prevented or reformed; and all the ordinances of God duly settled, administered, and observed. For the better effecting whereof, he hath power to call synods, be present at them, and to provide that whatsoever is transacted in them be according to the mind of God."

mands, and to be subject to their authority, for conscience' sake.[d] Infidelity, or difference in religion, doth not make void the magistrates' just and legal authority, nor free the people from their due obedience to them:[e] from which ecclesiastical persons are not exempted,[f] much less hath the pope any power and jurisdiction over them in their dominions, or over any of their people; and, least of all, to deprive them of their dominions, or lives, if he shall judge them to be heretics, or upon any other pretense whatsoever.[g]

a 1 Tim. 2:1–3 b 1 Pet. 2:17 c Matt. 22:21; Rom. 13:6–7 d Rom. 13:5; Titus 3:1 e 1 Pet. 2:13–16 f Rom. 13:1; Acts 25:9–11; 2 Pet. 2:1, 10–11; Jude 8–11 g Mark 10:42–44; Matt. 23:8–12; 2 Tim. 2:24; 1 Pet. 5:3

XXIV. Of Marriage and Divorce

1. Marriage is to be between one man and one woman: neither is it lawful for any man to have more than one wife, nor for any woman to have more than one husband, at the same time.[a]

a Gen. 2:24; Matt. 19:4–6; Rom. 7:3; Prov. 2:17

2. Marriage was ordained for the mutual help of husband and wife,[a] for the increase of mankind with legitimate issue, and of the church with an holy seed;[b] and for preventing of uncleanness.[c]

a Gen. 2:18; Eph. 5:28; 1 Pet. 3:7 b Gen. 1:28; Gen. 9:1; Mal. 2:15 c 1 Cor. 7:2, 9

3. It is lawful for all sorts of people to marry, who are able with judgment to give their consent.[a] Yet it is the duty of Christians to marry only in the Lord.[b] And therefore such as profess the true reformed religion should not marry with infidels, papists, or other idolaters: neither should such as are godly be unequally yoked, by marrying with such as are notoriously wicked in their life, or maintain damnable heresies.[c]

a Heb. 13:4; 1 Tim. 4:3; 1 Cor. 7:36–38; Gen. 24:57–58 b 1 Cor. 7:39 c Gen. 34:14; Ex. 34:16; 2 Cor. 6:14; Deut. 7:3–4; 1 Kings 11:4; Neh. 13:25–27; Mal. 2:11–12

4. Marriage ought not to be within the degrees of consanguinity or affinity forbidden by the Word.[a] Nor can such incestuous marriages ever be made lawful by any law of man or consent of parties, so as those persons may live together as man and wife.[b] [4]

a Lev. 18:6–17, 24–30; Lev. 20:19; 1 Cor. 5:1; Amos 2:7   b Mark 6:18; Lev. 18:24–28

5. Adultery or fornication committed after a contract, being detected before marriage, giveth just occasion to the innocent party to dissolve that contract.[a] In the case of adultery after marriage, it is lawful for the innocent party to sue out a divorce:[b] and, after the divorce, to marry another, as if the offending party were dead.[c]

a Matt. 1:18–20; Deut. 22:23–24   b Matt. 5:31–32   c Matt. 19:9; Rom. 7:2–3

6. Although the corruption of man be such as is apt to study arguments unduly to put asunder those whom God hath joined together in marriage: yet, nothing but adultery, or such willful desertion as can no way be remedied by the church, or civil magistrate, is cause sufficient of dissolving the bond of marriage:[a] wherein, a public and orderly course of proceeding is to be observed; and the persons concerned in it not left to their own wills, and discretion, in their own case.[b]

a Matt. 19:8–9; 1 Cor. 7:15; Matt. 19:6   b Deut. 24:1–4

XXV. Of the Church

1. The catholic or universal church, which is invisible, consists of the whole number of the elect, that have been, are, or shall be gathered

---

4   Original edition includes "The man may not marry any of his wife's kindred nearer in blood than he may of his own; nor the woman of her husband's kindred nearer in blood than of her own" at the end of this paragraph.

into one, under Christ the Head thereof; and is the spouse, the body, the fullness of him that filleth all in all.[a]

a Eph. 1:10, 22–23; Eph. 5:23, 27, 32; Col. 1:18

2. The visible church, which is also catholic or universal under the gospel (not confined to one nation, as before under the law), consists of all those throughout the world that profess the true religion;[a] and of their children:[b] and is the kingdom of the Lord Jesus Christ,[c] the house and family of God,[d] out of which there is no ordinary possibility of salvation.[e]

a 1 Cor. 1:2; 1 Cor. 12:12–13; Ps. 2:8; Rev. 7:9; Rom. 15:9–12 b 1 Cor. 7:14; Acts 2:39; Gen. 17:7–12; Ezek. 16:20–21; Rom. 11:16; Gal. 3:7, 9, 14; Rom. 4:12, 16, 24 c Matt. 13:47; Isa. 9:7; Luke 1:32–33; Acts 2:30–36; Col. 1:13 d Eph. 2:19; Eph. 3:15 e Acts 2:47

3. Unto this catholic visible church Christ hath given the ministry, oracles, and ordinances of God, for the gathering and perfecting of the saints, in this life, to the end of the world: and doth, by his own presence and Spirit, according to his promise, make them effectual thereunto.[a]

a 1 Cor. 12:28; Eph. 4:11–13; Matt. 28:19–20; Isa. 59:21

4. This catholic church hath been sometimes more, sometimes less visible.[a] And particular churches, which are members thereof, are more or less pure, according as the doctrine of the gospel is taught and embraced, ordinances administered, and public worship performed more or less purely in them.[b]

a Rom. 11:3–5; Acts 9:31; Acts 2:41, 47; Acts 18:8–10 b Acts 2:41–42; 1 Cor. 5:6–7; Rev. 2:1–3:22

5. The purest churches under heaven are subject both to mixture and error;[a] and some have so degenerated, as to become no churches of Christ, but synagogues of Satan.[b] Nevertheless, there

shall be always a church on earth, to worship God according to his will.[c]

a 1 Cor. 13:12; Rev. 2:1–3:22; Matt. 13:24–30, 47 b Matt. 23:37–39; Rom. 11:18–22 c Matt. 16:18; Ps. 45:16–17; Ps. 72:17; Matt. 28:19–20; 1 Cor. 15:51–52; 1 Thess. 4:17

6. There is no other head of the church but the Lord Jesus Christ.[a] Nor can the pope of Rome, in any sense, be head thereof.[b][5]

a Col. 1:18; Eph. 1:22 b Matt. 23:8–10; 1 Pet. 5:2–4

XXVI. Of the Communion of Saints

1. All saints, that are united to Jesus Christ their Head, by his Spirit, and by faith, have fellowship with him in his graces, sufferings, death, resurrection, and glory:[a] and, being united to one another in love, they have communion in each other's gifts and graces,[b] and are obliged to the performance of such duties, public and private, as do conduce to their mutual good, both in the inward and outward man.[c]

a 1 John 1:3; Eph. 3:16–18; John 1:16; Eph. 2:5–6; Phil. 3:10; Rom. 6:5–6; Rom. 8:17; 2 Tim. 2:12
b Eph. 4:15–16; 1 Cor. 12:7, 12; 1 Cor. 3:21–23; Col. 2:19 c 1 Thess. 5:11, 14; Rom. 1:11–12, 14; 1 John 3:16–18; Gal. 6:10

2. Saints by profession are bound to maintain an holy fellowship and communion in the worship of God, and in performing such other spiritual services as tend to their mutual edification;[a] as also in relieving each other in outward things, according to their several abilities and necessities. Which communion, as God offereth opportunity, is to be extended unto all those who, in every place, call upon the name of the Lord Jesus.[b]

a Heb. 10:24–25; Acts 2:42, 46; Isa. 2:3; 1 Cor. 11:20 b 1 John 3:17; 2 Cor. 8:1–9:15; Acts 11:29–30; Acts 2:44–45

5 Original edition includes "but is that Antichrist, that man of sin and son of perdition, that exalteth himself in the church, against Christ, and all that is called God" at the end of this paragraph.

3. This communion which the saints have with Christ, doth not make them in any wise partakers of the substance of his Godhead; or to be equal with Christ in any respect: either of which to affirm is impious and blasphemous.[a] Nor doth their communion one with another, as saints, take away, or infringe the title or propriety which each man hath in his goods and possessions.[b]

a Col. 1:18–19; 1 Cor. 8:6; Ps. 45:6–7; Heb. 1:6–9; John 1:14; John 20:17 b Ex. 20:15; Eph. 4:28; Acts 5:4

XXVII. Of the Sacraments

1. Sacraments are holy signs and seals of the covenant of grace,[a] immediately instituted by God,[b] to represent Christ, and his benefits; and to confirm our interest in him:[c] as also, to put a visible difference between those that belong unto the church, and the rest of the world;[d] and solemnly to engage them to the service of God in Christ, according to his Word.[e]

a Rom. 4:11; Gen. 17:7, 10–11 b Matt. 28:19; 1 Cor. 11:23 c Rom. 6:3–4; Col. 2:12; 1 Cor. 10:16; 1 Cor. 11:25–26; Gal. 3:27 d Ex. 12:48; Gen. 34:14; 1 Cor. 10:21 e Rom. 6:3–4; Gal. 3:27; 1 Pet. 3:21; 1 Cor. 10:16; 1 Cor. 5:7–8

2. There is, in every sacrament, a spiritual relation, or sacramental union, between the sign and the thing signified: whence it comes to pass, that the names and effects of the one are attributed to the other.[a]

a Gen. 17:10; Matt. 26:27–28; 1 Cor. 10:16–18

3. The grace which is exhibited in or by the sacraments rightly used, is not conferred by any power in them; neither doth the efficacy of a sacrament depend upon the piety or intention of him that doth administer it:[a] but upon the work of the Spirit,[b] and the word of institution, which contains, together with a precept authorizing the use thereof, a promise of benefit to worthy receivers.[c]

a Rom. 2:28–29; 1 Pet. 3:21 b 1 Cor. 12:13 c Matt. 26:26–28; Luke 22:19–20; Matt. 28:19–20; 1 Cor. 11:26

4. There be only two sacraments ordained by Christ our Lord in the gospel; that is to say, baptism, and the Supper of the Lord: neither of which may be dispensed by any, but by a minister of the Word lawfully ordained.[a]

a Matt. 28:19; 1 Cor. 11:20, 23; 1 Cor. 4:1; Eph. 4:11–12

5. The sacraments of the old testament, in regard of the spiritual things thereby signified and exhibited, were, for substance, the same with those of the new.[a]

a 1 Cor. 10:1–4; Rom. 4:11; Col. 2:11–12

XXVIII. Of Baptism

1. Baptism is a sacrament of the new testament, ordained by Jesus Christ,[a] not only for the solemn admission of the party baptized into the visible church;[b] but also, to be unto him a sign and seal of the covenant of grace,[c] of his ingrafting into Christ,[d] of regeneration,[e] of remission of sins,[f] and of his giving up unto God, through Jesus Christ, to walk in newness of life.[g] Which sacrament is, by Christ's own appointment, to be continued in his church until the end of the world.[h]

a Matt. 28:19   b 1 Cor. 12:13; Gal. 3:27–28   c Rom. 4:11; Col. 2:11–12   d Gal. 3:27; Rom. 6:5   e John 3:5; Titus 3:5   f Mark 1:4; Acts 2:38; Acts 22:16   g Rom. 6:3–4   h Matt. 28:19–20

2. The outward element to be used in this sacrament is water, wherewith the party is to be baptized, in the name of the Father, and of the Son, and of the Holy Ghost, by a minister of the gospel, lawfully called thereunto.[a]

a Acts 10:47; Acts 8:36, 38; Matt. 28:19

3. Dipping of the person into the water is not necessary; but baptism is rightly administered by pouring, or sprinkling water upon the person.[a]

a Heb. 9:10, 13, 19, 21; Mark 7:2–4; Luke 11:38

4. Not only those that do actually profess faith in and obedience unto Christ,[a] but also the infants of one, or both, believing parents, are to be baptized.[b]

a Acts 2:41; Acts 8:12–13; Acts 16:14–15 b Gen. 17:7–14; Gal. 3:9, 14; Col. 2:11–12; Acts 2:38–39; Rom. 4:11–12; Matt. 19:13; Mark 10:13–16; Luke 18:15–17; Matt. 28:19; 1 Cor. 7:14

5. Although it be a great sin to contemn or neglect this ordinance,[a] yet grace and salvation are not so inseparably annexed unto it, as that no person can be regenerated, or saved, without it;[b] or, that all that are baptized are undoubtedly regenerated.[c]

a Gen. 17:14; Matt. 28:19; Acts 2:38; Luke 7:30 b Rom. 4:11; Acts 10:2, 4, 22, 31, 45, 47 c Acts 8:13, 23

6. The efficacy of baptism is not tied to that moment of time wherein it is administered;[a] yet, notwithstanding, by the right use of this ordinance, the grace promised is not only offered, but really exhibited, and conferred, by the Holy Ghost, to such (whether of age or infants) as that grace belongeth unto, according to the counsel of God's own will, in his appointed time.[b]

a John 3:5, 8 b Rom. 6:3–6; Gal. 3:27; 1 Pet. 3:21; Acts 2:38, 41

7. The sacrament of baptism is but once to be administered unto any person.[a]

a Rom. 6:3–11

1. Our Lord Jesus, in the night wherein he was betrayed, instituted the sacrament of his body and blood, called the Lord's Supper, to be observed in his church, unto the end of the world, for the perpetual remembrance of the sacrifice of himself in his death; the sealing all benefits thereof unto true believers, their spiritual nourishment and growth in him, their further engagement in and to all duties which they owe unto him; and, to be a bond and pledge of their communion with him, and with each other, as members of his mystical body.[a]

a 1 Cor. 11:23–26; 1 Cor. 10:16–17, 21; 1 Cor. 12:13

2. In this sacrament, Christ is not offered up to his Father; nor any real sacrifice made at all, for remission of sins of the quick or dead;[a] but only a commemoration of that one offering up of himself, by himself, upon the cross, once for all: and a spiritual oblation of all possible praise unto God, for the same:[b] so that the popish sacrifice of the Mass (as they call it) is most abominably injurious to Christ's one, only sacrifice, the alone propitiation for all the sins of his elect.[c]

a Heb. 9:22, 25–26, 28; Heb. 10:10–14 b 1 Cor. 11:24–26; Matt. 26:26–27; Luke 22:19–20 c Heb. 7:23–24, 27; Heb. 10:11–12, 14, 18

3. The Lord Jesus hath, in this ordinance, appointed his ministers to declare his word of institution to the people; to pray, and bless the elements of bread and wine, and thereby to set them apart from a common to an holy use; and to take and break the bread, to take the cup, and (they communicating also themselves) to give both to the communicants;[a] but to none who are not then present in the congregation.[b]

a Matt. 26:26–28; Mark 14:22–24; Luke 22:19–20; 1 Cor. 10:16–17; 1 Cor. 11:23–27 b Acts 20:7; 1 Cor. 11:20

4. Private Masses, or receiving this sacrament by a priest, or any other, alone;[a] as likewise, the denial of the cup to the people,[b] worshiping the elements, the lifting them up, or carrying them about, for adoration, and the reserving them for any pretended religious use; are all contrary to the nature of this sacrament, and to the institution of Christ.[c]

a 1 Cor. 10:16 b Matt. 26:27–28; Mark 14:23; 1 Cor. 11:25–29 c Matt. 15:9

5. The outward elements in this sacrament, duly set apart to the uses ordained by Christ, have such relation to him crucified, as that, truly, yet sacramentally only, they are sometimes called by the name of the things they represent, to wit, the body and blood of Christ;[a] albeit, in substance and nature, they still remain truly and only bread and wine, as they were before.[b]

a Matt. 26:26–28 b 1 Cor. 11:26–28; Matt. 26:29

6. That doctrine which maintains a change of the substance of bread and wine, into the substance of Christ's body and blood (commonly called transubstantiation) by consecration of a priest, or by any other way, is repugnant, not to Scripture alone, but even to common sense, and reason; overthroweth the nature of the sacrament, and hath been, and is, the cause of manifold superstitions; yea, of gross idolatries.[a]

a Acts 3:21; 1 Cor. 11:24–26; Luke 24:6, 39

7. Worthy receivers, outwardly partaking of the visible elements, in this sacrament,[a] do then also, inwardly by faith, really and indeed, yet not carnally and corporally, but spiritually, receive, and feed upon, Christ crucified, and all benefits of his death: the body and blood of Christ being then, not corporally or carnally, in, with, or under the bread and wine; yet, as really, but spiritually, present to the faith of

believers in that ordinance, as the elements themselves are to their outward senses.[b]

a 1 Cor. 11:28 b 1 Cor. 10:16; 1 Cor. 10:3–4

8. Although ignorant and wicked men receive the outward elements in this sacrament; yet, they receive not the thing signified thereby; but, by their unworthy coming thereunto, are guilty of the body and blood of the Lord, to their own damnation. Wherefore, all ignorant and ungodly persons, as they are unfit to enjoy communion with him, so are they unworthy of the Lord's table; and cannot, without great sin against Christ, while they remain such, partake of these holy mysteries,[a] or be admitted thereunto.[b]

a 1 Cor. 11:27–29; 2 Cor. 6:14–16; 1 Cor. 10:21 b 1 Cor. 5:6–7, 13; 2 Thess. 3:6, 14–15; Matt. 7:6

XXX. Of Church Censures

1. The Lord Jesus, as King and Head of his church, hath therein appointed a government, in the hand of church officers, distinct from the civil magistrate.[a]

a Isa. 9:6–7; Col. 1:18; 1 Tim. 5:17; 1 Thess. 5:12; Acts 20:17, 28; Heb. 13:7, 17, 24; Eph. 4:11–12; 1 Cor. 12:28; Matt. 28:18–20; John 18:36

2. To these officers the keys of the kingdom of heaven are committed; by virtue whereof, they have power, respectively, to retain, and remit sins; to shut that kingdom against the impenitent, both by the Word, and censures; and to open it unto penitent sinners, by the ministry of the gospel; and by absolution from censures, as occasion shall require.[a]

a Matt. 16:19; Matt. 18:17–18; John 20:21–23; 2 Cor. 2:6–8

3. Church censures are necessary, for the reclaiming and gaining of offending brethren, for deterring of others from the like offenses, for purging out of that leaven which might infect the whole lump, for vindicating the honor of Christ, and the holy profession of the gospel, and for preventing the wrath of God, which might justly fall upon the church, if they should suffer his covenant, and the seals thereof, to be profaned by notorious and obstinate offenders.[a]

a 1 Cor. 5:1–13; 1 Tim. 5:20; Matt. 7:6; 1 Tim. 1:20; 1 Cor. 11:27–34; Jude 23

4. For the better attaining of these ends, the officers of the church are to proceed by admonition; suspension from the sacrament of the Lord's Supper for a season; and by excommunication from the church; according to the nature of the crime, and demerit of the person.[a]

a 1 Thess. 5:12; 2 Thess. 3:6, 14–15; 1 Cor. 5:4–5, 13; Matt. 18:17; Titus 3:10

XXXI. Of Synods and Councils

1. For the better government, and further edification of the church, there ought to be such assemblies as are commonly called synods or councils:[a][6] and it belongeth to the overseers and other rulers of the particular churches, by virtue of their office, and the power which Christ hath given them for edification and not for destruction, to appoint such assemblies;[b] and to convene together in them, as often as they shall judge it expedient for the good of the church.[c]

a Acts 15:2, 4, 6 b Acts 15:1–35 c Acts 15:1–35; Acts 20:17

6 Original paragraph ended here, adding the following as a second paragraph: "As magistrates may lawfully call a synod of ministers, and other fit persons, to consult and advise with about matters of religion; so if magistrates be open enemies to the church, the ministers of Christ, of themselves, by virtue of their office; or, they with other fit persons, upon delegation from their churches, may meet together in such assemblies."

2. It belongeth to synods and councils, ministerially to determine controversies of faith, and cases of conscience; to set down rules and directions for the better ordering of the public worship of God, and government of his church; to receive complaints in cases of maladministration, and authoritatively to determine the same: which decrees and determinations, if consonant to the Word of God, are to be received with reverence and submission; not only for their agreement with the Word, but also for the power whereby they are made, as being an ordinance of God appointed thereunto in his Word.[a]

a Acts 15:15, 19, 24, 27–31; Acts 16:4; Matt. 18:17–20

3. All synods or councils, since the apostles' times, whether general or particular, may err; and many have erred. Therefore they are not to be made the rule of faith, or practice; but to be used as a help in both.[a]

a Eph. 2:20; Acts 17:11; 1 Cor. 2:5; 2 Cor. 1:24; Isa. 8:19–20; Matt. 15:9

4. Synods and councils are to handle, or conclude nothing, but that which is ecclesiastical: and are not to intermeddle with civil affairs which concern the commonwealth, unless by way of humble petition in cases extraordinary; or, by way of advice, for satisfaction of conscience, if they be thereunto required by the civil magistrate.[a]

a Luke 12:13–14; John 18:36; Matt. 22:21

XXXII. Of the State of Men after Death, and of the Resurrection of the Dead

1. The bodies of men, after death, return to dust, and see corruption:[a] but their souls, which neither die nor sleep, having an immortal subsistence, immediately return to God who gave them:[b] the souls of the righteous, being then made perfect in holiness, are received

into the highest heavens, where they behold the face of God, in light and glory, waiting for the full redemption of their bodies.[c] And the souls of the wicked are cast into hell, where they remain in torments and utter darkness, reserved to the judgment of the great day.[d] Beside these two places, for souls separated from their bodies, the Scripture acknowledgeth none.

a Gen. 3:19; Acts 13:36 b Luke 23:43; Eccles. 12:7 c Heb. 12:23; 2 Cor. 5:1, 6, 8; Phil. 1:23; Acts 3:21; Eph. 4:10; Rom. 8:23 d Luke 16:23–24; Acts 1:25; Jude 6–7; 1 Pet. 3:19

2. At the last day, such as are found alive shall not die, but be changed:[a] and all the dead shall be raised up, with the selfsame bodies, and none other (although with different qualities), which shall be united again to their souls forever.[b]

a 1 Thess. 4:17; 1 Cor. 15:51–52 b John 5:25–29; Acts 24:15; Job 19:26–27; Dan. 12:2; 1 Cor. 15:42–44

3. The bodies of the unjust shall, by the power of Christ, be raised to dishonor: the bodies of the just, by his Spirit, unto honor; and be made conformable to his own glorious body.[a]

a Acts 24:15; John 5:25–29; 1 Cor. 15:43; Phil. 3:21

XXXIII. Of the Last Judgment

1. God hath appointed a day, wherein he will judge the world, in righteousness, by Jesus Christ,[a] to whom all power and judgment is given of the Father.[b] In which day, not only the apostate angels shall be judged,[c] but likewise all persons that have lived upon earth shall appear before the tribunal of Christ, to give an account of their thoughts, words, and deeds; and to receive according to what they have done in the body, whether good or evil.[d]

a Acts 17:31 b John 5:22, 27 c Jude 6; 2 Pet. 2:4 d 2 Cor. 5:10; Eccles. 12:14; Rom. 2:16; Rom. 14:10, 12; Matt. 12:36–37

2. The end of God's appointing this day is for the manifestation of the glory of his mercy, in the eternal salvation of the elect; and of his justice, in the damnation of the reprobate, who are wicked and disobedient. For then shall the righteous go into everlasting life, and receive that fullness of joy and refreshing, which shall come from the presence of the Lord: but the wicked, who know not God, and obey not the gospel of Jesus Christ, shall be cast into eternal torments, and be punished with everlasting destruction from the presence of the Lord, and from the glory of his power.[a]

a Matt. 25:31–46; Rom. 2:5–6; Rom. 9:22–23; Matt. 25:21; Acts 3:19; 2 Thess. 1:7–10; Mark 9:48

3. As Christ would have us to be certainly persuaded that there shall be a day of judgment, both to deter all men from sin; and for the greater consolation of the godly in their adversity:[a] so will he have that day unknown to men, that they may shake off all carnal security, and be always watchful, because they know not at what hour the Lord will come; and may be ever prepared to say, Come Lord Jesus, come quickly, Amen.[b]

a 2 Pet. 3:11, 14; 2 Cor. 5:10–11; 2 Thess. 1:5–7; Luke 21:27–28; Rom. 8:23–25   b Matt. 24:36, 42–44

The London Baptist Confession

INTRODUCTION

The classic Baptist summary of faith is the London Baptist Confession. The text of the confession, written in 1677 and formally adopted in 1689, was adapted from the 1658 Savoy Declaration of Faith and Order (a now little-used text), which was in turn a revision of the 1646 Westminster Confession of Faith. The London Baptist Confession remains a lodestone to many Baptists, its appeal being found chiefly in its usefulness as a teaching tool or even as a basis for association. It is sometimes called the Second London Baptist Confession to differentiate it from an earlier Baptist confession written in 1644.

The Savoy Declaration had been a meticulous modification of the Westminster Confession. Words and phrases were occasionally altered in the hope of doctrinal improvements; whole paragraphs were changed in places; a new chapter was added ("Of the Gospel, and of the Extent of Grace Thereof"); and two chapters on church government were removed, with congregationalist content inserted in the chapter on the church.

The London Baptist Confession was in turn another modest revision, designed to show Reformed Christians how much they held in common. The confession generally follows the Congregationalist Savoy revision rather than the more Presbyterian Westminster original. Further changes to the Savoy, where they can be found, offer a further clarification of concepts. For example, the second chapter boasts the attractive assertion that each of the persons of the Trinity has "the whole Divine Essence, yet the Essence undivided." The fourteenth chapter, on saving faith, is adjusted in a manner that makes it more Christ-centered.

Still other changes quite reasonably reflect differences in Baptist readings of the Bible from the paedobaptist convictions of the Presbyterians and Congregationalists. The first chapter deletes a reference to the Christian's accountability not only to the explicit statements of Scripture but also to truths logically deduced from Scripture (of which infant baptism is seen to be one). Chapters touching on covenant theology are revised. The most creative work is found in chapters on the church and the sacraments. These statements are remarkably compact, well organized, and to the point.

Perhaps the most lightly revised chapters are the final two: "Of the State of Man after Death and of the Resurrection of the Dead" and "Of the Last Judgment." Here a series of minor adjustments are made from the earlier confessions, but the ending remains powerful. In its closing paragraphs readers are called to offer praise: "God hath appointed a Day wherein he will judge the world in Righteousness, by Jesus Christ; to whom all power and judgment is given of the Father" (32.1); called to give thanks: "The Righteous go into Everlasting Life, and receive that fullness of Joy, and Glory, with everlasting reward, in the presence of the Lord" (32.2); and, above all, called to pay attention: "As Christ would have us to be certainly persuaded that there shall be a Day of judgment, both to deter all men from sin, and for the greater consolation of the godly, in their adversity; so will he have that day unknown to Men, that they may shake off all carnal security, and be always watchful, because they know not at what hour, the Lord will come; and may ever be prepared to say, Come Lord Jesus, Come quickly, Amen" (32.3).

THE LONDON
BAPTIST CONFESSION

I. Of the Holy Scriptures

1. The Holy Scripture is the only sufficient, certain, and infallible [a]rule of all saving Knowledge, Faith and Obedience; Although the [b]light of Nature, and the works of Creation and Providence do so far manifest the goodness, wisdom and power of God, as to leave men unexcusable; yet are they not sufficient to give that knowledge of God and His will, which is necessary unto Salvation. [c]Therefore it pleased the Lord at sundry times, and in divers manners, to reveal himself, and to declare that His will unto his Church; and afterward for the better preserving, and propagating of the Truth, and for the more sure Establishment, and Comfort of the Church against the corruption of the flesh, and the malice of Satan, and of the World, to commit the same wholly unto [d]writing; which maketh the Holy Scriptures to be most necessary, those former ways of God's revealing his will unto his people being now ceased.

a 2 Tim. 3:15–17; Isa. 8:20; Luke 16:29, 31; Eph. 2:20 b Rom. 1:19–23; Rom. 2:14–15; Ps. 19:1–3
c Heb. 1:1 d Prov. 22:19–21; Rom. 15:4; 2 Pet. 1:19–20

2. Under the Name of Holy Scripture or the Word of God written; are now contained all the Books of the Old and New Testament which are these,

Genesis, Exodus, Leviticus, Numbers, Deuteronomy, Joshua, Judges, Ruth, 1 Samuel, 2 Samuel, 1 Kings, 2 Kings, 1 Chronicles, 2 Chronicles, Ezra, Nehemiah, Esther, Job, Psalms, Proverbs, Ecclesiastes, the Song of Songs, Isaiah, Jeremiah, Lamentations, Ezekiel, Daniel, Hosea, Joel, Amos, Obadiah, Jonah, Micah, Nahum, Habakkuk, Zephaniah, Haggai, Zechariah, Malachi.

Of the New Testament

Matthew, Mark, Luke, John, The Acts of the Apostles, Paul's Epistle to the Romans, 1 Corinthians, 2 Corinthians, Galatians, Ephesians, Philippians, Colossians, 1 Thessalonians, 2 Thessalonians, 1 Timothy, 2 Timothy, to Titus, to Philemon, the Epistle to the Hebrews, the Epistle of James, the first and second Epistles of Peter, the first, second and third Epistles of John, the Epistle of Jude, the Revelation.

All which are given by the *a*inspiration of God, to be the rule of Faith and Life.

a 2 Tim. 3:16

3. The Books commonly called Apocrypha not being of *a*Divine inspiration, are no part of the Canon (or rule) of the Scripture, and therefore are of no authority to the Church of God, nor to be any otherwise approved or made use of, then other human writings.

a Luke 24:27, 44; Rom. 3:2

4. The Authority of the Holy Scripture for which it ought to be believed dependeth not upon the testimony of any man, or Church; but

wholly upon [a]God (who is truth itself) the Author thereof; therefore it is to be received, because it is the Word of God.

a 2 Pet. 1:19–21; 2 Tim. 3:16; 2 Thess. 2:13; 1 John 5:9

5. We may be moved and induced by the testimony of the Church of God, to an high and reverent esteem of the Holy Scriptures; and the heavenliness of the matter, the efficacy of the Doctrine, and the Majesty of the style, the consent of all the parts, the scope of the whole (which is to give all glory to God) the full discovery it makes of the only way of man's salvation, and many other incomparable Excellencies, and entire perfections thereof, are arguments whereby it doth abundantly evidence itself to be the Word of God; yet notwithstanding; our [a]full persuasion, and assurance of the infallible truth, and divine authority thereof, is from the inward work of the Holy Spirit, bearing witness by and with the Word in our Hearts.

a John 16:13–14; 1 Cor. 2:10–12; 1 John 2:20, 27

6. The whole Counsel of God concerning all things [a]necessary for his own Glory, Man's Salvation, Faith and Life, is either expressly set down or necessarily contained in the Holy Scripture; unto which nothing at any time is to be added, whether by new Revelation of the Spirit, or traditions of men.

Nevertheless we acknowledge the [b]inward illumination of the Spirit of God, to be necessary for the saving understanding of such things as are revealed in the Word, and that there are some circumstances concerning the worship of God, and government of the Church common to human actions and societies; which are to be [c]ordered by the light of nature, and Christian prudence according to the general rules of the Word, which are always to be observed.

a 2 Tim. 3:15–17; Gal. 1:8–9 b John 6:45; 1 Cor. 2:9–12 c 1 Cor. 11:13–14; 1 Cor. 14:26, 40

7. All things in Scripture are not alike ªplain in themselves, nor alike clear unto all; yet those things which are necessary to be known, believed, and observed for Salvation, are so ᵇclearly propounded, and opened in some place of Scripture or other, that not only the learned, but the unlearned, in a due use of ordinary means, may attain to a sufficient understanding of them.

a 2 Pet. 3:16 b Ps. 19:7; Ps. 119:130

8. The Old Testament in ªHebrew (which was the Native language of the people of God of old) and the New Testament in Greek (which at the time of the writing of it was most generally known to the Nations), being immediately inspired by God, and by his singular care and Providence kept pure in all Ages, are therefore ᵇauthentical; so as in all controversies of Religion the Church is finally to appeal unto them. ᶜBut because these original tongues are not known to all the people of God, who have a right unto, and interest in the Scriptures, and are commanded in the fear of God to read ᵈand search them, therefore they are to be translated into the vulgar language of every Nation, unto which they ᵉcome, that the Word of God dwelling ᶠplentifully in all, they may worship him in an acceptable manner, and through patience and comfort of the Scriptures may have hope.

a Rom. 3:2 b Isa. 8:20 c Acts 15:15 d John 5:39 e 1 Cor. 14:6, 9, 11–12, 24, 28 f Col. 3:16

9. The infallible rule of interpretation of Scripture is the ªScripture itself: And therefore when there is a question about the true and full sense of any Scripture (which is not manifold but one) it must be searched by other places that speak more clearly.

a 2 Pet. 1:20–21; Acts 15:15–16

10. The supreme judge by which all controversies of Religion are to be determined, and all Decrees of Councils, opinions of ancient Writers, Doctrines of men, and private Spirits, are to be examined, and in whose sentence we are to rest, can be no other but the Holy Scripture delivered by the Spirit, into which ªScripture so delivered, our faith is finally resolved.

a Matt. 22:29, 31; Eph. 2:20; Acts 28:23

II. Of God and of the Holy Trinity

1. The Lord our God is but ªone only, living, and true God; whose ᵇsubsistence is in and of himself, ᶜinfinite in being, and perfection, whose Essence cannot be comprehended by any but himself; ᵈa most pure spirit, ᵉinvisible, without body, parts, or passions, who only hath immortality, dwelling in the light, which no man can approach unto, who is ᶠimmutable, ᵍimmense, ʰeternal, incomprehensible, ⁱAlmighty, every way infinite, ʲmost holy, most wise, most free, most absolute, ᵏworking all things according to the counsel of his own immutable, and most righteous will, ˡfor his own glory, most loving, gracious, merciful, longsuffering, abundant in goodness and truth, forgiving iniquity, transgression, and sin, ᵐthe rewarder of them that diligently seek him, and withal most just, ⁿand terrible in his judgments, ºhating all sin, and who will by no means clear the ᵖguilty.

a 1 Cor. 8:4, 6; Deut. 6:4 b Jer. 10:10; Isa. 48:12 c Ex. 3:14 d John 4:24 e 1 Tim. 1:17; Deut. 4:15–16
f Mal. 3:6 g 1 Kings 8:27; Jer. 23:23 h Ps. 90:2 i Gen. 17:1 j Isa. 6:3 k Ps. 115:3; Isa. 46:10 l Prov.
16:4; Rom. 11:36 m Ex. 34:6–7; Heb. 11:6 n Neh. 9:32–33 o Ps. 5:5–6 p Ex. 34:7; Nah. 1:2, 3

2. God having all ªlife, ᵇglory, ᶜgoodness, blessedness, in and of himself: is alone in, and unto himself all-sufficient, not ᵈstanding in need of any Creature which he hath made, nor deriving any glory from them, but only manifesting his own glory in, by, unto, and upon them, he is the

alone fountain of all Being, ^cof whom, through whom, and to whom are all things, and he hath most sovereign ^fdominion over all creatures, to do by them, for them, or upon them, whatsoever himself pleaseth; in his sight^gall things are open and manifest, his knowledge is ^hinfinite, infallible, and independent upon the Creature, so as nothing is to him contingent, or uncertain; he is most holy in all his Counsels, in ⁱall his Works, and in all his Commands; to him is due^jfrom Angels and men, whatsoever worship, service, or obedience as Creatures they owe unto the Creator, and whatever he is further pleased to require of them.

a John 5:26 b Ps. 148:13 c Ps. 119:68 d Job 22:2–3 e Rom. 11:34–36 f Dan. 4:25, 34–35 g Heb. 4:13
h Ezek. 11:5; Acts 15:18 i Ps. 145:17 j Rev. 5:12–14

3. In this divine and infinite Being there are three subsistences, ^athe Father, the Word (or Son), and Holy Spirit, of one substance, power, and Eternity, each having the whole Divine Essence, ^byet the Essence undivided, the Father is of none neither begotten nor proceeding, the Son is ^cEternally begotten of the Father, the holy Spirit ^dproceeding from the Father and the Son, all infinite, without beginning, therefore but one God, who is not to be divided in nature and Being; but distinguished by several peculiar, relative properties, and personal relations; which doctrine of the Trinity is the foundation of all our Communion with God, and comfortable dependence on him.

a 1 John 5:7; Matt. 28:19; 2 Cor. 13:14 b Ex. 3:14; John 14:11; 1 Cor. 8:6 c John 1:14, 18 d John 15:26; Gal. 4:6

III. Of God's Decree

1. God hath ^aDecreed in himself from all Eternity, by the most wise and holy Counsel of his own will, freely and unchangeably, all things whatsoever comes to pass; yet so as thereby is God neither the author of sin, ^bnor hath fellowship with any therein, nor is violence offered to the will of the Creature, nor yet is the liberty, or contingency of

second causes taken away, but rather ᶜestablished, in which appears his wisdom in disposing all things, and power, and faithfulness ᵈin accomplishing his Decree.

a Isa. 46:10; Eph. 1:11; Heb. 6:17; Rom. 9:15, 18   *b* James 1:13, 17; 1 John 1:5   *c* Acts 4:27–28; John 19:11
d Num. 23:19; Eph. 1:3–5

2. Although God knoweth whatsoever may, or can come to pass upon all ᵃsupposed conditions; yet hath he not Decreed anything, ᵇbecause he foresaw it as future, or as that which would come to pass upon such conditions.

a Acts 15:18   *b* Rom. 9:11, 13, 16, 18

3. By the decree of God for the manifestation of his glory ᵃsome men and Angels, are predestinated, or foreordained to Eternal Life, through Jesus Christ to the ᵇpraise of his glorious grace; others being left to act in their sin to their ᶜjust condemnation, to the praise of his glorious justice.

a 1 Tim. 5:21; Matt. 25:34   *b* Eph. 1:5–6   *c* Rom. 9:22–23; Jude 4

4. These Angels and Men thus predestinated, and foreordained, are particularly, and unchangeably designed; and their ᵃnumber so certain, and definite, that it cannot be either increased, or diminished.

a 2 Tim. 2:19; John 13:18

5. Those of mankind ᵃthat are predestinated to life, God before the foundation of the world was laid, according to his eternal and immutable purpose, and the secret Counsel and good pleasure of his will, hath chosen in Christ unto everlasting glory, out of his mere free grace and love; ᵇwithout any other thing in the creature as a condition or cause moving him thereunto.

a Eph. 1:4, 9, 11; Rom. 8:30; 2 Tim. 1:9; 1 Thess. 5:9   *b* Rom. 9:13, 16; Eph. 2:5, 12

6. As God hath appointed the Elect unto glory, so he hath by the eternal and most free purpose of his will, foreordained ^aall the means thereunto, wherefore they who are elected, being fallen in Adam, ^bare redeemed by Christ, are effectually ^ccalled unto faith in Christ, by his spirit working in due season, are justified, adopted, sanctified, and kept by his power through faith ^dunto salvation; neither are any other redeemed by Christ, or effectually called, justified, adopted, sanctified, and saved, but the Elect ^eonly.

a 1 Pet. 1:2; 2 Thess. 2:13 b 1 Thess. 5:9–10 c Rom. 8:30; 2 Thess. 2:13 d 1 Pet. 1:5 e John 10:26; John 17:9; John 6:64

7. The Doctrine of this high mystery of predestination, is to be handled with special prudence, and care; that men attending the will of God revealed in his word, and yielding obedience thereunto, may from the certainty of their effectual vocation, be assured of their ^aeternal election; so shall this doctrine afford matter ^bof praise, reverence, and admiration of God, and ^cof humility, diligence, and abundant ^dconsolation, to all that sincerely obey the Gospel.

a 1 Thess. 1:4–5; 2 Pet. 1:10 b Eph. 1:6; Rom. 11:33 c Rom. 11:5–6 d Luke 10:20

IV. Of Creation

1. In the beginning it pleased God the Father, ^aSon, and Holy Spirit, for the manifestation of the glory of ^bhis eternal power, wisdom, and goodness, to Create or make the world, and all things therein, ^cwhether visible or invisible, in the space of six days, and all very good.

a John 1:2–3; Heb. 1:2; Job 26:13 b Rom. 1:20 c Col. 1:16; Gen. 2:1–2

2. After God had made all other Creatures, he Created ^aman, male and female, with ^breasonable and immortal souls, rendering them fit unto that life to God; for which they were Created; being ^cmade after the

image of God, in knowledge, righteousness, and true holiness; having the Law of God [d]written in their hearts, and power to fulfill it; and yet under a possibility of transgressing, being left to the liberty of their own will, which was [e]subject to change.

a Gen. 1:27 b Gen. 2:7 c Eccles. 7:29; Gen. 1:26 d Rom. 2:14–15 e Gen. 3:6

3. Besides the Law written in their hearts, they received [a]a command not to eat of the tree of knowledge of good and evil; which whilst they kept, they were happy in their Communion with God, and had dominion [b]over the Creatures.

a Gen. 2:17; Gen. 3:8–10 b Gen. 1:26, 28

V. Of Divine Providence

1. God the good Creator of all things, in his infinite power, and wisdom, doth [a]uphold, direct, dispose, and govern all Creatures, and things, from the greatest even to the [b]least, by his most wise and holy providence, to the end for the which they were Created; according unto his infallible foreknowledge, and the free and immutable Counsel of his [c]own will; to the praise of the glory of his wisdom, power, justice, infinite goodness and mercy.

a Heb. 1:3; Job 38:11; Isa. 46:10–11; Ps. 135:6 b Matt. 10:29–31 c Eph. 1:11

2. Although in relation to the foreknowledge and Decree of God, the first cause, all things come to pass [a]immutably and infallibly; so that there is not anything, befalls any [b]by chance, or without his Providence; yet by the same Providence he ordereth them to fall out, according to the nature of second causes, either [c]necessarily, freely, or contingently.

a Acts 2:23 b Prov. 16:33 c Gen. 8:22

3. God in his ordinary Providence ªmaketh use of means; yet is free ᵇto work, without, ᶜabove, and ᵈagainst them at his pleasure.

a Acts 27:31, 44; Isa. 55:10–11   *b* Hos. 1:7   *c* Rom. 4:19–21   *d* Dan. 3:27

4. The Almighty power, unsearchable wisdom, and infinite goodness of God, so far manifest themselves in his Providence, that his determinate Counsel ªextendeth itself even to the first fall, and all other sinful actions both of Angels, and Men; (and that not by a bare permission) which also he most wisely and powerfully ᵇboundeth, and otherwise ordereth, and governeth, in a manifold dispensation to his most holy ᶜends: yet so, as the sinfulness of their acts proceedeth only from the Creatures, and not from God; who being most holy and righteous, neither is nor can be, the author or ᵈapprover of sin.

a Rom. 11:32–34; 2 Sam. 24:1; 1 Chron. 21:1   *b* 2 Kings 19:28; Ps. 76:10   *c* Gen. 50:20; Isa. 10:6–7, 12
d Ps. 50:21; 1 John 2:16

5. The most wise, righteous, and gracious God, doth oftentimes, leave for a season his own children to manifold temptations, and the corruptions of their own heart, to chastise them for their former sins, or to discover unto them the hidden strength of corruption, and deceitfulness of their hearts, ªthat they may be humbled; and to raise them to a more close, and constant dependence for their support, upon himself; and to make them more watchful against all future occasions of sin, and for other just and holy ends.

So that whatsoever befalls any of his elect is by his appointment, for his glory, ᵇand their good.

a 2 Chron. 32:25–26, 31; 2 Sam. 24:1; 2 Cor. 12:7–9   *b* Rom. 8:28

6. As for those wicked and ungodly men, whom God as a righteous judge, for former sin doth ªblind and harden; from them he not only

withholdeth his [b]Grace, whereby they might have been enlightened in their understanding, and wrought upon in their hearts: But sometimes also withdraweth [c]the gifts which they had, and exposeth them to such [d]objects as their corruptions make occasion of sin; and withal [e]gives them over to their own lusts, the temptations of the world, and the power of Satan, whereby it comes to pass, that they [f]harden themselves, even under those means which God useth for the softening of others.

a Rom. 1:24, 26, 28; Rom. 11:7–8 b Deut. 29:4 c Matt. 13:12 d Deut. 2:30; 2 Kings 8:12–13 e Ps. 81:11–12; 2 Thess. 2:10–12 f Ex. 8:15, 32; Isa. 6:9–10; 1 Pet. 2:7–8

7. As the Providence of God doth in general reach to all Creatures, so after a most special manner it taketh care of his [a]Church, and disposeth of all things to the good thereof.

a 1 Tim. 4:10; Amos 9:8–9; Isa. 43:3–5

VI. Of the Fall of Man, of Sin, and of the Punishment Thereof

1. Although God created Man upright, and perfect, and gave him a righteous law, which had been unto life had he kept it, [a]and threatened death upon the breach thereof; yet he did not long abide in this honor; [b]Satan using the subtlety of the serpent to seduce Eve, then by her seducing Adam, who without any compulsion, did willfully transgress the Law of their Creation, and the command given unto them, in eating the forbidden fruit; which God was pleased according to his wise and holy Counsel to permit, having purposed to order it, to his own glory.

a Gen. 2:16–17 b Gen. 3:12–13; 2 Cor. 11:3

2. Our first Parents by this Sin, fell from their [a]original righteousness and communion with God, and we in them, whereby death came

upon all; [b]all becoming dead in Sin, and wholly defiled, [c]in all the faculties, and parts, of soul, and body.

a Rom. 3:23 b Rom. 5:12–17 c Titus 1:15; Gen. 6:5; Jer. 17:9; Rom. 3:10–19

3. They being the [a]root, and by God's appointment, standing in the room, and stead of all mankind; the guilt of the Sin was imputed, and corrupted nature conveyed, to all their posterity descending from them by ordinary generation, being now [b]conceived in Sin, and by nature children [c]of wrath, the servants of Sin, the subjects [d]of death and all other miseries, spiritual, temporal and eternal, unless the Lord Jesus [e]set them free.

a Rom. 5:12–19; 1 Cor. 15:21–22, 45, 49 b Ps. 51:5; Job 14:4 c Eph. 2:3 d Rom. 6:23; Rom. 5:12
e Heb. 2:14–15; 1 Thess. 1:10

4. From this original corruption, whereby we are [a]utterly indisposed, disabled, and made opposite to all good, and wholly inclined to all evil, do [b]proceed all actual transgressions.

a Rom. 8:7; Col. 1:21 b James 1:14–15; Matt. 15:19

5. The corruption of nature, during this Life, doth [a]remain in those that are regenerated: and although it be through Christ pardoned, and mortified, yet both itself, and the first motions thereof, are truly and properly [b]Sin.

a Rom. 7:18, 23; Eccles. 7:20; 1 John 1:8 b Rom. 7:23–25; Gal. 5:17

VII. Of God's Covenant

1. The distance between God and the Creature is so great, that although reasonable Creatures do owe obedience unto him as their Creator, yet they could never have attained the reward of Life, but by

some ^avoluntary condescension on God's part, which he hath been
pleased to express, by way of Covenant.

a Luke 17:10; Job 35:7–8

2. Moreover Man having brought himself ^aunder the curse of the Law
by his fall, it pleased the Lord to make a Covenant of Grace wherein
he freely offereth unto Sinners, ^bLife and Salvation by Jesus Christ,
requiring of them Faith in him, that they may be saved; and ^cpromis-
ing to give unto all those that are ordained unto eternal Life, his holy
Spirit, to make them willing, and able to believe.

a Gen. 2:17; Gal. 3:10; Rom. 3:20–21 b Rom. 8:3; Mark 16:15–16; John 3:16 c Ezek. 36:26–27; John
6:44–45; Ps. 110:3

3. This Covenant is revealed in the Gospel; first of all to Adam in the
promise of Salvation by the ^aseed of the woman, and afterwards by
farther steps, until the full ^bdiscovery thereof was completed in the
new Testament; and it is founded in that ^cEternal Covenant transac-
tion, that was between the Father and the Son, about the Redemption of the Elect; and it is alone by the Grace of this Covenant, that
all of the posterity of fallen Adam, that ever were ^dsaved, did obtain
life and a blessed immortality; Man being now utterly incapable of
acceptance with God upon those terms, on which Adam stood in his
state of innocency.

a Gen. 3:15 b Heb. 1:1 c 2 Tim. 1:9; Titus 1:2 d Heb. 11:6, 13; Rom. 4:1–25; Acts 4:12; John 8:56

VIII. Of Christ the Mediator

1. It pleased God in his eternal purpose, to choose and ordain the Lord
Jesus his only begotten Son, according to the Covenant made between
them both, ^ato be the Mediator between God and Man; the ^bProphet,
^cPriest and ^dKing; Head and Savior of his Church, the heir of all things,

and judge of the world: Unto whom he did from all Eternity *give a people to be his seed, and to be by him in time redeemed, called, justified, sanctified, and glorified.

a Isa. 42:1; 1 Pet. 1:19–20 *b* Acts 3:22 *c* Heb. 5:5–6 *d* Ps. 2:6; Luke 1:33; Eph. 1:22–23; Heb. 1:2; Acts 17:31 *e* Isa. 53:10; John 17:6; Rom. 8:30

2. The Son of God, the second Person in the Holy Trinity, being very and eternal God, the brightness of the Father's glory, of one substance and equal with him: who made the World, who upholdeth and governeth all things he hath made: did when the fullness of time was come take unto him *man's nature, with all the Essential properties, and common infirmities thereof, *byet without sin: being conceived by the Holy Spirit in the Womb of the Virgin Mary, the Holy Spirit coming down upon her, and the power of the most High overshadowing her, *and so was made of a Woman, of the Tribe of Judah, of the Seed of Abraham, and David according to the Scriptures: So that two whole, perfect, and distinct natures, were inseparably joined together in one Person: without conversion, composition, or confusion: which Person is very God, and very Man; yet one *dChrist, the only Mediator between God and Man.

a John 1:1, 14; Gal. 4:4 *b* Rom. 8:3; Heb. 2:14, 16–17; Heb. 4:15 *c* Luke 1:27, 31, 35 *d* Rom. 9:5; 1 Tim. 2:5

3. The Lord Jesus in his human nature thus united to the divine, in the Person of the Son, was sanctified, and anointed *with the Holy Spirit, above measure; having in him *ball the treasures of wisdom and knowledge; in whom it pleased the Father that *call fullness should dwell: To the end that being *dholy, harmless, undefiled, and full *of Grace, and Truth, he might be thoroughly furnished to execute the Office of a Mediator, and *Surety; which Office he took not upon himself, but was thereunto *called by his Father; who also put *hall

power and judgment in his hand, and gave him Commandment to execute the same.

a Ps. 45:7; Acts 10:38; John 3:34 b Col. 2:3 c Col. 1:19 d Heb. 7:26 e John 1:14 f Heb. 7:22 g Heb. 5:5 h John 5:22, 27; Matt. 28:18; Acts 2:36

4. This Office the Lord Jesus did most ^awillingly undertake, which that he might discharge he was made under the Law, ^band did perfectly fulfill it, and underwent the ^cpunishment due to us, which we should have born and suffered, being made ^dSin and a Curse for us: enduring most grievous sorrows ^ein his Soul; and most painful sufferings in his body; was crucified, and died, and remained in the state of the dead; yet saw no ^fcorruption: on the ^gthird day he arose from the dead, with the same ^hbody in which he suffered; with which he also ⁱascended into heaven: and there sitteth at the right hand of his Father, ^jmaking intercession; and shall ^kreturn to judge Men and Angels, at the end of the World.

a Ps. 40:7–8; Heb. 10:5–11; John 10:18 b Gal. 4:4; Matt. 3:15 c Gal. 3:13; Isa. 53:6; 1 Pet. 3:18 d 2 Cor. 5:21 e Matt. 26:37–38; Luke 22:44; Matt. 27:46 f Acts 13:37 g 1 Cor. 15:3–4 h John 20:25, 27 i Mark 16:19; Acts 1:9–11 j Rom. 8:34; Heb. 9:24 k Acts 10:42; Rom. 14:9–10; Acts 1:11

5. The Lord Jesus by his perfect obedience and sacrifice of himself, which he through the Eternal Spirit once offered up unto God, ^ahath fully satisfied the Justice of God, procured reconciliation, and purchased an Everlasting inheritance in the Kingdom of Heaven, ^bfor all those whom the Father hath given unto him.

a Heb. 9:14; Heb. 10:14; Rom. 3:25–26 b John 17:2; Heb. 9:15

6. Although the price of Redemption was not actually paid by Christ, till after his Incarnation, ^ayet the virtue, efficacy, and benefit thereof were communicated to the Elect in all ages successively, from the beginning of the World, in and by those Promises, Types, and Sacrifices,

wherein he was revealed, and signified to be the Seed of the Woman, which should bruise the Serpent's head; [b]and the Lamb slain from the foundation of the World: [c]Being the same yesterday, and today, and for ever.

a 1 Cor. 4:10; Heb. 4:2; 1 Pet. 1:10–11 b Rev. 13:8 c Heb. 13:8

7. Christ in the work of Mediation acteth according to both natures, by each nature doing that which is proper to itself; yet by reason of the Unity of the Person, that which is proper to one nature, is sometimes in Scripture attributed to the Person [a]denominated by the other nature.

a John 3:13; Acts 20:28

8. To all those for whom Christ hath obtained eternal redemption, he doth certainly, and effectually [a]apply, and communicate the same; making intercession for them, uniting them to himself by his spirit, [b]revealing unto them, in and by the word, the mystery of salvation; persuading them to believe, and obey; [c]governing their hearts by his word and spirit, and [d]overcoming all their enemies by his Almighty power, and wisdom; in such manner, and ways as are most consonant to his wonderful, and [e]unsearchable dispensation; and all of free, and absolute Grace, without any condition foreseen in them, to procure it.

a John 6:37; John 10:15–16; John 17:9; Rom. 5:10 b John 17:6, Eph. 1:9; 1 John 5:20 c Rom. 8:9, 14
d Ps. 110:1; 1 Cor. 15:25–26 e John 3:8; Eph. 1:8

9. This Office of Mediator between God and Man, is proper [a]only to Christ, who is the Prophet, Priest, and King of the Church of God; and may not be either in whole, or any part thereof transferred from him to any other.

a 1 Tim. 2:5

10. This number and order of Offices is necessary; for in respect of our [a]ignorance, we stand in need of his Prophetical Office; and in respect of our alienation from God, [b]and imperfection of the best of our services, we need his Priestly Office, to reconcile us, and present us acceptable unto God: and in respect of our averseness, and utter inability to return to God, and for our rescue, and security from our spiritual adversaries, we need his Kingly Office, [c]to convince, subdue, draw, uphold, deliver, and preserve us to his Heavenly Kingdom.

a John 1:18 b Col. 1:21; Gal. 5:17 c John 16:8; Ps. 110:3; Luke 1:74–75

IX. Of Free Will

1. God hath endued the Will of Man, with that natural liberty, and power of acting upon choice; that it is [a]neither forced, nor by any necessity of nature determined to do good or evil.

a Matt. 17:12; James 1:14; Deut. 30:19

2. Man in his state of innocency, had freedom, and power, to will, and to do that [a]which was good, and well-pleasing to God; but yet [b]was mutable, so that he might fall from it.

a Eccles. 7:29 b Gen. 3:6

3. Man by his fall into a state of sin hath wholly lost [a]all ability of Will, to any spiritual good accompanying salvation; so as a natural man, being altogether averse from that good, [b]and dead in Sin, is not able, by his own strength, to [c]convert himself; or to prepare himself thereunto.

a Rom. 5:6; Rom. 8:7 b Eph. 2:1, 5 c Titus 3:3–5; John 6:44

4. When God converts a sinner, and translates him into the state of Grace [a]he freeth him from his natural bondage under sin, and by

his grace alone, enables him [b]freely to will, and to do that which is spiritually good; yet so as that by reason of his [c]remaining corruptions he doth not perfectly nor only will that which is good; but doth also will that which is evil.

a Col. 1:13; John 8:36 b Phil. 2:13 c Rom. 7:15, 18–19, 21, 23

5. The Will of Man is made [a]perfectly, and immutably free to good alone, in the state of Glory only.

a Eph. 4:13

X. Of Effectual Calling

1. Those whom God hath predestinated unto Life, he is pleased in his appointed, and accepted time, [a]effectually to call by his word, and Spirit, out of that state of sin, and death, in which they are by nature, to grace and Salvation [b]by Jesus Christ; enlightening their minds, spiritually, and savingly to [c]understand the things of God; taking away their [d]heart of stone, and giving unto them an heart of flesh; renewing their wills, and by his Almighty power determining them [e]to that which is good, and effectually drawing them to Jesus Christ; yet so as they come [f]most freely, being made willing by his Grace.

a Rom. 8:30; Rom. 11:7; Eph. 1:10–11; 2 Thess. 3:13–14 b Eph. 2:1–6 c Acts 26:18; Eph. 1:17–18
d Ezek. 36:26 e Deut. 30:6; Ezek. 36:27; Eph. 1:19 f Ps. 110:3; Song 1:4

2. This Effectual Call is of God's free, and special grace alone, [a]not from anything at all foreseen in man, nor from any power, or agency in the Creature, coworking with his special Grace, [b]the Creature being wholly passive therein, being dead in sins and trespasses, until being quickened and renewed by the holy Spirit, he is thereby enabled to answer this call, and to embrace the Grace offered and conveyed in

it; and that by no less [c]power, then that which raised up Christ from the dead.

a 2 Tim. 1:9; Eph. 2:8   *b* 1 Cor. 2:14; Eph. 2:5; John 5:25   *c* Eph. 1:19–20

3. Elect Infants dying in infancy, are [a]regenerated and saved by Christ through the Spirit; who worketh when, and where, and [b]how he pleaseth: so also are all other elect persons, who are incapable of being outwardly called by the Ministry of the Word.

a John 3:3, 5–6   *b* John 3:8

4. Others not elected, although they may be called by the Ministry of the word, [a]and may have some common operations of the Spirit, yet not being effectually drawn by the Father, they neither will, nor can truly [b]come to Christ; and therefore cannot be saved: much less can men that receive not the Christian Religion [c]be saved; be they never so diligent to frame their lives according to the light of nature, and the Law of that Religion they do profess.

a Matt. 22:14; Matt. 13:20–21; Heb. 6:4–5   *b* John 6:44–45, 65; 1 John 2:24–25   *c* Acts 4:12; John 4:22; John 17:3

XI. *Of Justification*

1. Those whom God Effectually calleth, he also freely [a]justifieth, not by infusing Righteousness into them, but by [b]pardoning their sins, and by accounting, and accepting their Persons as [c]Righteous; not for anything wrought in them, or done by them, but for Christ's sake alone, not by imputing faith itself, the act of believing, or any other [d]evangelical obedience to them, as their Righteousness; but by imputing Christ's active obedience unto the whole Law, and passive obedience in his death, for their whole and sole Righteousness, they [e]receiving, and resting on him, and his

Righteousness, by Faith; which faith they have not of themselves, it is the gift of God.

a Rom. 3:24; Rom. 8:30 b Rom. 4:5–8; Eph. 1:7 c 1 Cor. 1:30–31; Rom. 5:17–19 d Phil. 3:8–9; Eph. 2:8–10 e John 1:12; Rom. 5:17

2. Faith thus receiving and resting on Christ, and his Righteousness, is the ªalone instrument of Justification: yet it is not alone in the person justified, but is ever accompanied with all other saving Graces, and is no dead faith, ᵇbut worketh by love.

a Rom. 3:28 b Gal. 5:6; James 2:17, 22, 26

3. Christ by his obedience, and death, did fully discharge the debt of all those that are justified; and did by the sacrifice of himself, in the blood of his cross, undergoing in their stead, the penalty due unto them: make a proper, real and full satisfaction ªto God's justice in their behalf: yet inasmuch as he was given by the Father for them, and his Obedience and Satisfaction accepted in their stead, and both ᵇfreely, not for anything in them; their Justification is only of Free Grace, that both the exact justice and rich Grace of God, might be ᶜglorified in the Justification of sinners.

a Heb. 10:14; 1 Pet. 1:18–19; Isa. 53:5–6 b Rom. 8:32; 2 Cor. 5:21 c Rom. 3:26; Eph. 1:6–7; Eph. 2:7

4. God did from all eternity decree to ªjustify all the Elect, and Christ did in the fullness of time die for their sins, and rise ᵇagain for their Justification; Nevertheless they are not justified personally, until the Holy Spirit, doth in due time ᶜactually apply Christ unto them.

a Gal. 3:8; 1 Pet. 1:2; 1 Tim. 2:6 b Rom. 4:25 c Col. 1:21–22; Titus 3:4–7

5. God doth continue to ªForgive the sins of those that are justified, and although they can never fall from the state of ᵇjustification; yet

they may by their sins fall under God's ᶠFatherly displeasure; and in that condition, they have not usually the light of his Countenance restored unto them, until they ᵈhumble themselves, confess their sins, beg pardon, and renew their faith, and repentance.

a Matt. 6:12; 1 John 1:7, 9 *b* John 10:28 *c* Ps. 89:31–33 *d* Ps. 32:5; Ps. 51:1–19; Matt. 26:75

6. The Justification of Believers under the Old Testament was in all these respects, ᵃone and the same with the justification of Believers under the New Testament.

a Gal. 3:9; Rom. 4:22–24

XII. Of Adoption

1. All those that are justified, God vouchsafed, in, and for the sake of his only Son Jesus Christ, to make partakers of the Grace ᵃof Adoption; by which they are taken into the number, and enjoy the Liberties, and ᵇPrivileges of Children of God; have his ᶜname put upon them, ᵈreceive the Spirit of Adoption, ᵉhave access to the throne of Grace with boldness, are enabled to cry *Abba*, Father, are ᶠpitied, ᵍprotected, ʰprovided for, and ⁱchastened by him, as by a Father; yet never ʲcast off; but sealed ᵏto the day of Redemption, and inherit the promises, ˡas heirs, of everlasting Salvation.

a Eph. 1:5; Gal. 4:4–5 *b* John 1:12; Rom. 8:17 *c* 2 Cor. 6:18; Rev. 3:12 *d* Rom. 8:15 *e* Gal. 4:6; Eph. 2:18 *f* Ps. 103:13 *g* Prov. 14:26 *h* 1 Pet. 5:7 *i* Heb. 12:6 *j* Isa. 54:8–9; Lam. 3:31 *k* Eph. 4:30 *l* Heb. 1:14; Heb. 6:12

XIII. Of Sanctification

1. They who are united to Christ, Effectually called, and regenerated, having a new heart, and a new Spirit created in them, through the virtue of Christ's death, and Resurrection; are also ᵃfarther sanctified,

really, and personally, through the same virtue, [b]by his word and Spirit dwelling in them; [c]the dominion of the whole body of sin is destroyed, [d]and the several lusts thereof, are more and more weakened, and mortified; and they more and more quickened, and [e]strengthened in all saving graces, to the [f]practice of all true holiness, without which no man shall see the Lord.

a Acts 20:32; Rom. 6:5–6 b John 17:17; Eph. 3:16–19; 1 Thess. 5:21–23 c Rom. 6:14 d Gal. 5:24
e Col. 1:11 f 2 Cor. 7:1; Heb. 12:14

2. This Sanctification is [a]throughout, in the whole man, yet imperfect [b]in this life; there abideth still some remnants of corruption in every part, whence ariseth a [c]continual, and irreconcilable war; the Flesh lusting against the Spirit, and the Spirit against the Flesh.

a 1 Thess. 5:23 b Rom. 7:18, 23 c Gal. 5:17; 1 Pet. 2:11

3. In which war, although the remaining corruption for a time may much [a]prevail; yet through the continual supply of strength from the sanctifying Spirit of Christ the [b]regenerate part doth overcome; and so the Saints grow in Grace, perfecting holiness in the fear of God, [c]pressing after an heavenly life, in Evangelical Obedience to all the commands which Christ as Head and King, in his Word hath prescribed to them.

a Rom. 7:23 b Rom. 6:14 c Eph. 4:15–16; 2 Cor. 3:18; 2 Cor. 7:1

XIV. Of Saving Faith

1. The Grace of Faith, whereby the Elect are enabled to believe to the saving of their souls, is the work of the Spirit of Christ [a]in their hearts; and is ordinarily wrought by the Ministry of the [b]Word; by which also, and by the administration of Baptism, and the Lord's

Supper, Prayer and other Means appointed of God, it is increased, ᶜand strengthened.

a 2 Cor. 4:13; Eph. 2:8 *b* Rom. 10:14, 17 *c* Luke 17:5; 1 Pet. 2:2; Acts 20:32

2. By this Faith, a Christian believeth to be true, ᵃwhatsoever is revealed in the Word, for the Authority of God himself; and also apprehendeth an excellency therein, ᵇabove all other Writings; and all things in the world: as it bears forth the Glory of God in his Attributes, the excellency of Christ in his Nature and Offices; and the Power and Fullness of the Holy Spirit in his Workings, and Operations; and so is enabled to ᶜcast his Soul upon the truth thus believed; and also acteth differently, upon that which each particular, passage thereof containeth; yielding obedience to the ᵈcommands, trembling at the ᵉthreatenings, and embracing the ᶠpromises of God, for this life, and that which is to come: But the principal acts of Saving Faith, have immediate relation to Christ, accepting, receiving, and resting upon ᵍhim alone, for Justification, Sanctification, and Eternal Life, by virtue of the Covenant of Grace.

a Acts 24:14 *b* Ps. 19:7–10; Ps. 119:72 *c* 2 Tim. 1:12 *d* John 15:14 *e* Isa. 66:2 *f* Heb. 11:13 *g* John 1:12; Acts 16:31; Gal. 2:20; Acts 15:11

3. This Faith although it be different in degrees, and may be weak, ᵃor strong; yet it is in the least degree of it, different in the kind, or nature of it (as is all other saving Grace) from the Faith, ᵇand common grace of temporary believers; and therefore though it may be many times assailed, and weakened; yet it gets ᶜthe victory; growing up in many, to the attainment of a full ᵈassurance through Christ, who is both the Author ᵉand finisher of our Faith.

a Heb. 5:13–14; Matt. 6:30; Rom. 4:19–20 *b* 2 Pet. 1:1 *c* Eph. 6:16; 1 John 5:4–5 *d* Heb. 6:11–12; Col. 2:2 *e* Heb. 12:2

1. Such of the Elect as are converted at riper years, having ᵃsome-times lived in the state of nature, and therein served divers lusts and pleasures, God in their Effectual Calling giveth them Repentance unto Life.

a Titus 3:2–5

2. Whereas there is none that doth good, and sinneth ᵃnot; and the best of men may through the power, and deceitfulness of their corruption dwelling in them, with the prevalency of temptation, fall into great sins, and provocations; God hath in the Covenant of Grace, mercifully provided that Believers so sinning, and falling, ᵇbe renewed through Repentance unto Salvation.

a Eccles. 7:20 b Luke 22:31–32

3. This saving Repentance is an ᵃevangelical Grace, whereby a person being by the Holy Spirit made sensible of the manifold evils of his sin, doth, by Faith in Christ, humble himself for it, with godly sor-row, detestation of it, and self-abhorrency; ᵇpraying for pardon, and strength of grace, with a purpose and endeavor by supplies of the Spirit, to ᶜwalk before God unto all well pleasing in all things.

a Zech. 12:10; Acts 11:18 b Ezek. 36:31; 2 Cor. 7:11 c Ps. 119:6, 128

4. As Repentance is to be continued through the whole course of our lives, upon the account of the body of death, and the motions thereof; so it is every man's duty, to repent of his ᵃparticular known sins, particularly.

a Luke 19:8; 1 Tim. 1:13, 15

5. Such is the provision which God hath made through Christ in the Covenant of Grace, for the preservation of Believers unto Salvation, that although there is no sin so small, but it deserves ᵃdamnation; yet there is no sin so great, that it shall bring damnation on them that ᵇrepent; which makes the constant preaching of Repentance necessary.

a Rom. 6:23 *b* Isa. 1:16, 18; Isa. 55:7

XVI. Of Good Works

1. Good Works are only such as God hath ᵃcommanded in his Holy word; and not such as without the warrant thereof, are devised by men, out of blind zeal, ᵇor upon any pretense of good intentions.

a Mic. 6:8; Heb. 13:21 *b* Matt. 15:9; Isa. 29:13

2. These good works, done in obedience to God's commandments, are the fruits, and evidences ᵃof a true, and lively faith; and by them Believers manifest their ᵇthankfulness, strengthen their ᶜassurance, edify their ᵈbrethren, adorn the profession of the Gospel, stop the mouths of the adversaries and glorify ᵉGod whose workmanship they are, created in Christ Jesus ᶠthereunto, that having their fruit unto holiness, they may have the end ᵍeternal life.

a James 2:18, 22 *b* Ps. 116:12–13 *c* 1 John 2:3, 5; 2 Pet. 1:5–11 *d* Matt. 5:16 *e* 1 Tim. 6:1; 1 Pet. 2:15; Phil. 1:11 *f* Eph. 2:10 *g* Rom. 6:22

3. Their ability to do good works, is not at all of themselves; but wholly from the Spirit ᵃof Christ; and that they may be enabled thereunto, besides the graces they have already received, there is necessary an ᵇactual influence of the same Holy Spirit, to work in them to will, and to do, of his good pleasure; yet are they not hereupon to grow negligent, as if they were not bound to perform any duty, unless upon a special

motion of the Spirit; but they ought to be diligent in 'stirring up the Grace of God that is in them.

a John 15:4–5   b 2 Cor. 3:5; Phil. 2:13   c Phil. 2:12; Heb. 6:11–12; Isa. 64:7

4. They who in their obedience attain to the greatest height which is possible in this life, are so far from being able to supererogate, and to do more then God requires, as that [a]they fall short of much which in duty they are bound to do.

a Job 9:2–3; Gal. 5:17; Luke 17:10

5. We cannot by our best works merit pardon of Sin or Eternal Life at the hand of God, by reason of the great disproportion that is between them and the glory to come; and the infinite distance that is between us and God, whom by them we can neither profit, nor satisfy for the debt of our [a]former sins; but when we have done all we can, we have done but our duty, and are unprofitable servants; and because as they are good they proceed from his [b]Spirit, and as they are wrought by us they are defiled [c]and mixed with so much weakness and imperfection that they cannot endure the severity of God's judgment.

a Rom. 3:20; Eph. 2:8–9; Rom. 4:6   b Gal. 5:22–23   c Isa. 64:6; Ps. 143:2

6. Yet notwithstanding the persons of Believers being accepted through Christ their good works also are accepted in [a]him; not as though they were in this life wholly unblameable and unreprovable in God's sight; but that he looking upon them in his Son is pleased to accept and reward that which is [b]sincere although accompanied with many weaknesses and imperfections.

a Eph. 1:6; 1 Pet. 2:5   b Matt. 25:21, 23; Heb. 6:10

7. Works done by unregenerate men although for the matter of them they may be things which God commands, and of good use, both to themselves and [a]others; yet because they proceed not from a heart purified by [b]faith, nor are done in a right manner according to the [c]word, nor to a right end the [d]glory of God; they are therefore sinful and cannot please God; nor make a man meet to receive grace from [e]God; and yet their neglect of them is more sinful and [f]displeasing to God.

a 2 Kings 10:30; 1 Kings 21:27, 29   b Gen. 4:5; Heb. 11:4, 6   c 1 Cor. 13:1   d Matt. 6:2, 5   e Amos 5:21–22; Rom. 9:16; Titus 3:5   f Job 21:14–15; Matt. 25:41–43

XVII. Of Perseverance of the Saints

1. Those whom God hath accepted in the beloved, effectually called and Sanctified by his Spirit, and given the precious faith of his Elect unto, can neither totally nor finally fall from the state of grace; [a]but shall certainly persevere therein to the end and be eternally saved, seeing the gifts and callings of God are without Repentance, (whence he still begets and nourisheth in them Faith, Repentance, Love, Joy, Hope, and all the graces of the Spirit unto immortality) and though many storms and floods arise and beat against them, yet they shall never be able to take them off that foundation and rock which by faith they are fastened upon: notwithstanding through unbelief and the temptations of Satan the sensible sight of the light and love of God, may for a time be clouded, and obscured from [b]them, yet he is still the same [c]and they shall be sure to be kept by the power of God unto Salvation, where they shall enjoy their purchased possession, they being engraven upon the palm of his hands, and their names having been written in the book of life from all Eternity.

a John 10:28–29; Phil. 1:6; 2 Tim. 2:19; 1 John 2:19   b Ps. 89:31–32; 1 Cor. 11:32   c Mal. 3:6

2. This perseverance of the Saints depends not upon their own free will; but upon the immutability of the decree of [a]Election flowing from the free and unchangeable love of God the Father; upon the efficacy of the merit and intercession of Jesus Christ [b]and Union with him, the [c]oath of God, the abiding of his Spirit and the [d]seed of God within them, and the nature of the [e]Covenant of Grace from all which ariseth also the certainty and infallibility thereof.

a Rom. 8:30; Rom. 9:11, 16   b Rom. 5:9–10; John 14:19   c Heb. 6:17–18   d 1 John 3:9   e Jer. 32:40

3. And though they may through the temptation of Satan and of the world, the prevalency of corruption remaining in them, and the neglect of means of their preservation fall into grievous [a]sins, and for a time continue therein; whereby they incur [b]God's displeasure, and grieve his holy Spirit, come to have their graces and [c]comforts impaired, have their hearts hardened, and their Consciences wounded, [d]hurt, and scandalize others, and bring temporal judgments [e]upon themselves: yet they shall renew their [f]repentance and be preserved through faith in Christ Jesus to the end.

a Matt. 26:70, 72, 74   b Isa. 64:5, 9; Eph. 4:30   c Ps. 51:10–12   d Ps. 32:3–4   e 2 Sam. 12:14   f Luke 22:32, 61–62

XVIII. Of the Assurance of Grace and Salvation

1. Although temporary Believers, and other unregenerate men, may vainly deceive themselves with false hopes, and carnal presumptions, of being in the favor of God, and state of salvation, [a]which hope of theirs shall perish; yet such as truly believe in the Lord Jesus, and love him in sincerity, endeavoring to walk in all good Conscience before him, may in this life be certainly assured [b]that they are in

the state of Grace; and may rejoice in the hope of the glory of God which hope shall never make them [c]ashamed.

a Job 8:13–14; Matt. 7:22–23 b 1 John 2:3; 1 John 3:14, 18–19, 21, 24; 1 John 5:13 c Rom. 5:2, 5

2. This certainty is not a bare conjectural, and probable persuasion, grounded upon [a]a fallible hope; but an infallible assurance of faith founded on the Blood and Righteousness of Christ [b]revealed in the Gospel; and also upon the inward [c]evidence of those graces of the Spirit unto which promises are made, and on the testimony of the [d]Spirit of adoption, witnessing with our Spirits that we are the children of God; and as a fruit thereof keeping the heart both [e]humble and holy.

a Heb. 6:11, 19 b Heb. 6:17–18 c 2 Pet. 1:4–5, 10–11 d Rom. 8:15–16 e 1 John 3:1–3

3. This infallible assurance doth not so belong to the essence of faith, but that a true Believer, may wait long and conflict with many difficulties before he be [a]partaker of it; yet being enabled by the Spirit to know the things which are freely given him of God, he may without extraordinary revelation in the right use of means [b]attain thereunto: and therefore it is the duty of everyone, to give all diligence to make their Calling and Election sure, that thereby his heart may be enlarged in peace and joy in the holy Spirit, in love and thankfulness to God, and in strength and cheerfulness in the duties of obedience, the proper [c]fruits of this Assurance; so far is it [d]from inclining men to looseness.

a Isa. 50:10; Ps. 88:1–18; Ps. 77:1–12 b 1 John 4:13; Heb. 6:11–12 c Rom. 5:1–2, 5; Rom. 14:17; Ps. 119:32
d Rom. 6:1–2; Titus 2:11–12, 14

4. True Believers may have the assurance of their Salvation divers ways shaken, diminished, and intermitted; as [a]by negligence in preserving of it, by [b]falling into some special Sin, which woundeth the Conscience, and grieveth the Spirit, by some sudden or [c]vehement temptation, by God's withdrawing the [d]light of his countenance

and suffering even such as fear him to walk in darkness and to have no light; yet are they never destitute of the ᶜseed of God, and Life ʄof Faith, that Love of Christ, and the brethren, that sincerity of Heart, and Conscience of duty, out of which by the operation of the Spirit, this Assurance may in due time be ᵍrevived: and by the which in the mean time they are ʰpreserved from utter despair.

a Song 5:2–3, 6   b Ps. 51:8, 12, 14   c Ps. 116:11; Ps. 77:7–8; Ps. 31:22   d Ps. 30:7   e 1 John 3:9   f Luke 22:32   g Ps. 42:5, 11   h Lam. 3:26–31

XIX. Of the Law of God

1. God gave to Adam a Law of universal obedience, ᵃwritten in his Heart, and a particular precept of not eating the Fruit of the tree of knowledge of good and evil; by which he bound him, and all his posterity to personal entire exact and perpetual ᵇobedience; promised life upon the fulfilling, and ᶜthreatened death upon the breach of it; and endued him with power and ability to keep it.

a Gen. 1:27; Eccles. 7:29   b Rom. 10:5   c Gal. 3:10, 12

2. The same Law that was first written in the heart of man, ᵃcontinued to be a perfect rule of Righteousness after the fall; and was delivered by God upon Mount Sinai, in ᵇTen Commandments and written in two Tables; the four first containing our duty towards God, and the other six our duty to man.

a Rom. 2:14–15   b Deut. 10:4

3. Besides this Law commonly called moral, God was pleased to give to the people of Israel Ceremonial Laws, containing several typical ordinances, partly of worship, ᵃprefiguring Christ, his graces, actions, sufferings, and benefits; and partly holding forth divers instructions ᵇof moral duties, all which Ceremonial Laws being appointed only

to the time of reformation, are by Jesus Christ the true Messiah and only Law-giver who was furnished with power from the Father, for that end, ^cabrogated and taken away.

a Heb. 10:1; Col. 2:17   *b* 1 Cor. 5:7   *c* Col. 2:14, 16–17; Eph. 2:14, 16

4. To them also he gave sundry judicial Laws, which expired together with the state of that people, not obliging any now by virtue of that institution; their general ^aequity only, being of moral use.

a 1 Cor. 9:8–10

5. The moral Law doth for ever bind all, ^aas well justified persons as others, to the obedience thereof, and that not only in regard of the matter contained in it, but also in respect of the ^bauthority of God the Creator; who gave it: Neither doth Christ in the Gospel any way dissolve, ^cbut much strengthen this obligation.

a Rom. 13:8–10; James 2:8, 10–12   *b* James 2:10–11   *c* Matt. 5:17–19; Rom. 3:31

6. Although true Believers be not under the Law, as a Covenant of Works, ^ato be thereby Justified or condemned; yet it is of great use to them as well as to others: in that, as a Rule of Life, informing them of the Will of God, and their Duty, it directs and binds them, to walk accordingly; ^bdiscovering also the sinful pollutions of their Natures, Hearts and Lives; so as Examining themselves thereby, they may come to further Conviction of, Humiliation for, and Hatred against Sin; together with a clearer sight of the need they have of Christ and the perfection of his Obedience: It is likewise of use to the Regenerate to restrain their Corruptions, in that it forbids Sin; and the Threatenings of it serve to show what even their Sins deserve; and what afflictions in this Life they may expect for them, although freed from the Curse and unallayed Rigor thereof. The Promises of it likewise show them

God's approbation of Obedience, and what blessings they may expect upon the performance thereof, though not as due to them by the Law as a Covenant of Works; so as man's doing Good and refraining from Evil, because the Law encourageth to the one and deterreth from the other, is no Evidence of his being ᶜunder the Law and not under Grace.

a Rom. 6:14; Gal. 2:16; Rom. 8:1; Rom. 10:4   b Rom. 3:20; Rom. 7:7–25   c Rom. 6:12–14; 1 Pet. 3:8–13

7. Neither are the forementioned uses of the Law ᵃcontrary to the Grace of the Gospel; but do sweetly comply with it; the Spirit of Christ subduing ᵇand enabling the Will of man, to do that freely and cheerfully, which the will of God revealed in the Law, requireth to be done.

a Gal. 3:21   b Ezek. 36:27

XX. Of the Gospel, and of the Extent of the Grace thereof

1. The Covenant of Works being broken by Sin, and made unprofitable unto Life; God was pleased to give forth the promise of Christ, ᵃthe Seed of the Woman, as the means of calling the Elect, and begetting in them Faith and Repentance; in this Promise, the ᵇGospel, as to the substance of it, was revealed, and therein Effectual, for the Conversion and Salvation of Sinners.

a Gen. 3:15   b Rev. 13:8

2. This Promise of Christ, and Salvation by him, is revealed only by ᵃthe Word of God; neither do the Works of Creation, or Providence, with the light of Nature, ᵇmake discovery of Christ, or of Grace by him; so much as in a general, or obscure way; much less that men destitute of the Revelation of him by the Promise, or Gospel; ᶜshould be enabled thereby, to attain saving Faith, or Repentance.

a Rom. 1:17   b Rom. 10:14–15, 17   c Prov. 29:18; Isa. 25:7; Isa. 60:2–3

3. The Revelation of the Gospel unto Sinners, made in divers times, and by sundry parts; with the addition of Promises, and Precepts for the Obedience required therein, as to the Nations, and Persons, to whom it is granted, is merely of the ᵃSovereign Will and good Pleasure of God; not being annexed by virtue of any Promise, to the due improvement of men's natural abilities, by virtue of Common light received, without it; which none ever did ᵇmake, or can so do: And therefore in all Ages the preaching of the Gospel hath been granted unto persons and Nations, as to the extent, or straitening of it, in great variety, according to the Counsel of the Will of God.

a Ps. 147:20; Acts 16:7 *b* Rom. 1:18–32

4. Although the Gospel be the only outward means, of revealing Christ, and saving Grace; and is, as such, abundantly sufficient thereunto; yet that men who are dead in Trespasses, may be born again, Quickened or Regenerated; there is moreover necessary, an effectual, insuperable ᵃwork of the Holy Spirit, upon the whole Soul, for the producing in them a new spiritual Life; without which no other means will effect ᵇtheir Conversion unto God.

a Ps. 110:3; 1 Cor. 2:14; Eph. 1:19–20 *b* John 6:44; 2 Cor. 4:4, 6

XXI. Of Christian Liberty and Liberty of Conscience

1. The Liberty which Christ hath purchased for Believers under the Gospel, consists in their freedom from the guilt of Sin, the condemning wrath of God, the Rigor and ᵃCurse of the Law; and in their being delivered from this present evil ᵇWorld, Bondage to ᶜSatan, and Dominion ᵈof Sin; from the ᵉEvil of Afflictions; the Fear, and Sting ᶠof Death, the Victory of the Grave, and ᵍEverlasting Damnation; as also in their ʰfree access to God; and their yielding

Obedience unto him not out of a slavish fear, 'but a Child-like love, and willing mind.

All which were common also to Believers under the Law ʲfor the substance of them; but under the new Testament, the Liberty of Christians is further enlarged in their freedom from the yoke of the Ceremonial Law, to which the Jewish Church was subjected; and in greater boldness of access to the Throne of Grace; and in fuller Communications of the ᵏFree Spirit of God, then Believers under the Law did ordinarily partake of.

a Gal. 3:13 b Gal. 1:4 c Acts 26:18 d Rom. 8:3 e Rom. 8:28 f 1 Cor. 15:54–57 g 2 Thess. 1:10
h Rom. 8:15 i Luke 1:74–75; 1 John 4:18 j Gal. 3:9, 14 k John 7:38–39; Heb. 10:19–21

2. God alone is ᵃLord of the Conscience, and hath left it free from the Doctrines and Commandments of men, ᵇwhich are in anything contrary to his Word, or not contained in it. So that to Believe such Doctrines, or obey such Commands out of Conscience, ᶜis to betray true liberty of Conscience; and the requiring of an ᵈimplicit Faith, and absolute and blind Obedience, is to destroy Liberty of Conscience, and Reason also.

a James 4:12; Rom. 14:4 b Acts 4:19; 5:29; 1 Cor. 7:23; Matt. 15:9 c Col. 2:20, 22–23 d 1 Cor. 3:5;
2 Cor. 1:24

3. They who upon pretense of Christian Liberty do practice any sin, or cherish any sinful lust; as they do thereby pervert the main design of the Grace of the Gospel, ᵃto their own Destruction; so they wholly destroy ᵇthe end of Christian Liberty, which is, that being delivered out of the hands of all our Enemies we might serve the Lord without fear in Holiness, and Righteousness before him, all the days of our Life.

a Rom. 6:1–2 b Gal. 5:13; 2 Pet. 2:18–21

XXII. Of Religious Worship and the Sabbath Day

1. The light of Nature shows that there is a God, who hath Lordship, and Sovereignty over all; is just, good, and doth good unto all; and is therefore to be feared, loved, praised, called upon, trusted in, and served, with all the Heart, and all the Soul, [a]and with all the Might. But the acceptable way of Worshiping the true God, is [b]instituted by himself; and so limited by his own revealed will, that he may not be Worshiped according to the imaginations, and devices of Men, or the suggestions of Satan, under any visible representations, or [c]any other way, not prescribed in the Holy Scriptures.

a Jer. 10:7; Mark 12:33   b Deut. 12:32   c Ex. 20:4–6

2. Religious Worship is to be given to God the Father, Son, and Holy Spirit, and to him [a]alone; not to Angels, Saints, or any other [b]Creatures; and since the fall, not without a [c]Mediator, nor in the Mediation of any other but [d]Christ alone.

a Matt. 4:9–10; John 6:23; Matt. 28:19   b Rom. 1:25; Col. 2:18; Rev. 19:10   c John 14:6   d 1 Tim. 2:5

3. Prayer with thanksgiving, being one special part of natural worship, is by God required of [a]all men. But that it may be accepted, it is to be made in the [b]Name of the Son, by the help [c]of the Spirit, according to [d]his Will; with understanding, reverence, humility, fervency, faith, love, and perseverance; and when with others, in a [e]known tongue.

a Ps. 95:1–7; Ps. 65:2   b John 14:13–14   c Rom. 8:26   d 1 John 5:14   e 1 Cor. 14:16–17

4. Prayer is to be made for things lawful, and for all sorts of men living, [a]or that shall live hereafter; but not [b]for the dead, nor for those of whom it may be known that they have sinned [c]the sin unto death.

a 1 Tim. 2:1–2; 2 Sam. 7:29   b 2 Sam. 12:21–23   c 1 John 5:16

5. The ᵃreading of the Scriptures, Preaching, and ᵇhearing the word of God, teaching and admonishing one another in Psalms, Hymns and Spiritual songs, singing with grace in our Hearts to ᶜthe Lord; as also the Administration ᵈof Baptism, and ᵉthe Lord's Supper are all parts of Religious worship of God, to be performed in obedience to him, with understanding, faith, reverence, and godly fear; moreover solemn humiliation ᶠwith fastings; and thanksgiving upon ᵍspecial occasions, ought to be used in an holy and religious manner.

a 1 Tim. 4:13 b 2 Tim. 4:2; Luke 8:18 c Col. 3:16; Eph. 5:19 d Matt. 28:19–20 e 1 Cor. 11:26 f Est. 4:16; Joel 2:12 g Ex. 15:1–21; Ps. 107:1–43

6. Neither Prayer, nor any other part of Religious worship, is now under the Gospel tied unto, or made more acceptable by, any place in which it is ᵃperformed, or towards which it is directed; but God is to be worshiped everywhere in Spirit, and in truth; as in ᵇprivate families ᶜdaily, and ᵈin secret each one by himself, so more solemnly in the public Assemblies, which are not carelessly, nor willfully, to be ᵉneglected, or forsaken, when God by his word, or providence calleth thereunto.

a John 4:21; Mal. 1:11; 1 Tim 2:8 b Acts 10:2 c Matt. 6:11; Ps. 55:17 d Matt. 6:6 e Heb. 10:25; Acts 2:42

7. As it is of the Law of nature, that in general a proportion of time by God's appointment, be set apart for the Worship of God; so by his Word in a positive, moral, and perpetual Commandment, binding all men, in all Ages, he hath particularly appointed one day in seven for a ᵃSabbath to be kept holy unto him, which from the beginning of the World to the Resurrection of Christ, was the last day of the week; and from the resurrection of Christ, was changed into the first day of the week ᵇwhich is called the Lord's day; and is to be continued to

the end of the World, as the Christian Sabbath; the observation of the last day of the week being abolished.

a Ex. 20:8   b 1 Cor. 16:1–2; Acts 20:7; Rev. 1:10

8. The Sabbath is then kept holy unto the Lord, when men after a due preparing of their hearts, and ordering their common affairs aforehand, do not only observe an holy ᵃrest all the day, from their own works, words, and thoughts, about their worldly employment, and recreations, but also are taken up the whole time in the public and private exercises of his worship, and in the duties ᵇof necessity and mercy.

a Isa. 58:13; Neh. 13:15–23   b Matt. 12:1–13

XXIII. Of Lawful Oaths and Vows

1. A lawful Oath is a part of religious worship, ᵃwherein the person swearing in Truth, Righteousness, and Judgment, solemnly calleth God to witness what he sweareth; ᵇand to judge him according to the Truth or falseness thereof.

a Ex. 20:7; Deut. 10:20; Jer. 4:2   b 2 Chron. 6:22–23

2. The Name of God only is that by which men ought to swear; and therein it is to be used, with all Holy Fear and reverence, therefore to swear vainly or rashly by that glorious, and dreadful name; or to swear at all by any other thing, is sinful and to be ᵃabhorred; yet as in matter of weight and moment for confirmation of truth, ᵇand ending all strife, an Oath is warranted by the Word of God; so a lawful Oath being imposed, ᶜby lawful Authority, in such matters, ought to be taken.

a Matt. 5:34, 37; James 5:12   b Heb. 6:16; 2 Cor. 1:23   c Neh. 13:25

3. Whosoever taketh an Oath warranted by the Word of God, ought duly to consider the weightiness of so solemn an act; and therein to avouch nothing, but what he knoweth to be the truth; for that by rash, false, and vain Oaths the ªLord is provoked, and for them this Land mourns.

a Lev. 19:12; Jer. 23:10

4. An Oath is to be taken in the plain, and ªcommon sense of the words; without equivocation, or mental reservation.

a Ps. 24:4

5. A Vow which is not to be made to any Creature, but to God alone, ªis to be made and performed with all Religious care, and faithfulness: But Popish Monastical Vows, ᵇof perpetual single life, professed ᶜpoverty, and regular obedience, are so far from being degrees of higher perfection, that they are superstitious, ᵈand sinful snares, in which no Christian may entangle himself.

a Ps. 76:11; Gen. 28:20–22   b 1 Cor. 7:2, 9   c Eph. 4:28   d Matt. 19:11

XXIV. Of the Civil Magistrate

1. God the supreme Lord, and King of all the World, hath ordained Civil ªMagistrates to be under him, over the people for his own glory, and the public good; and to this end hath armed them with the power of the Sword, for defense and encouragement of them that do good, and for the punishment of evil doers.

a Rom. 13:1–4

2. It is lawful for Christians to Accept, and Execute the Office of a Magistrate when called thereunto; in the management whereof, as

they ought especially to maintain [a]Justice, and Peace, according to the wholesome Laws of each Kingdom, and Commonwealth: so for that end they may lawfully now under the New Testament [b]wage war upon just and necessary occasions.

a 2 Sam. 23:3; Ps. 82:3–4 b Luke 3:14

3. Civil Magistrates being set up by God, for the ends aforesaid; subjection in all lawful things commanded by them, ought to be yielded by us, in the Lord; not only for wrath [a]but for Conscience sake; and we ought to make supplications and prayers for Kings, and all that are in Authority, [b]that under them we may live a quiet and peaceable life, in all godliness and honesty.

a Rom. 13:5–7; 1 Pet. 2:17 b 1 Tim. 2:1–2

XXV. Of Marriage

1. Marriage is to be between one Man and one Woman; [a]neither is it lawful for any man to have more then one Wife, nor for any Woman to have more then one Husband at the same time.

a Gen. 2:24; Mal. 2:15; Matt. 19:5–6

2. Marriage was ordained for the mutual help [a]of Husband and Wife, [b]for the increase of Mankind, with a legitimate issue, and for [c]preventing of uncleanness.

a Gen. 2:18 b Gen. 1:28 c 1 Cor. 7:2, 9

3. It is lawful for [a]all sorts of people to Marry, who are able with judgment to give their consent; yet it is the duty of Christians [b]to marry in the Lord, and therefore such as profess the true Religion, should not Marry with Infidels, [c]or Idolaters; neither should such as are godly be

unequally yoked, by marrying with such as are wicked, in their life, or maintain damnable Heresy.

a Heb. 13:4; 1 Tim. 4:3   *b* 1 Cor. 7:39   *c* Neh. 13:25–27

4. Marriage ought not to be within the degrees of consanguinity, [a]or Affinity forbidden in the word; nor can such incestuous Marriage ever be made lawful, by any law of Man or consent of parties, [b]so as those persons may live together as Man and Wife.

a Lev. 18:1–30   *b* Mark 6:18; 1 Cor. 5:1

XXVI. Of the Church

1. The Catholic or universal Church, which (with respect to the internal work of the Spirit, and truth of grace) may be called invisible, consists of the whole [a]number of the Elect, that have been, are, or shall be gathered into one, under Christ the head thereof; and is the spouse, the body, the fullness of him that filleth all in all.

a Heb. 12:23; Col. 1:18; Eph. 1:10, 22–23; Eph. 5:23, 27, 32

2. All persons throughout the world, professing the faith of the Gospel, and obedience unto God by Christ, according unto it; not destroying their own profession by any Errors everting the foundation, or unholiness of conversation, [a]are and may be called visible Saints; [b]and of such ought all particular Congregations to be constituted.

a 1 Cor. 1:2; Acts 11:26   *b* Rom. 1:7; Eph. 1:20–22

3. The purest Churches under heaven are subject [a]to mixture, and error; and some have so degenerated as to become [b]no Churches of Christ, but Synagogues of Satan; nevertheless Christ always hath had,

and ever shall have a ᶜKingdom in this world, to the end thereof, of such as believe in him, and make profession of his Name.

a 1 Cor. 15:1–58; Rev. 2:1–29; Rev. 3:1–22   b Rev. 18:2; 2 Thess. 2:11–12   c Matt. 16:18; Ps. 72:17; Ps. 102:28; Rev. 12:17

4. The Lord Jesus Christ is the Head of the Church, in whom by the appointment of the Father, ᵃall power for the calling, institution, order, or Government of the Church, is invested in a supreme and sovereign manner, neither can the Pope of Rome in any sense be head thereof, but is ᵇthat Antichrist, that Man of sin, and Son of perdition, that exalteth himself in the Church against Christ, and all that is called God; whom the Lord shall destroy with the brightness of his coming.

a Col. 1:18; Matt. 28:18–20; Eph. 4:11–12   b 2 Thess. 2:3–9

5. In the execution of this power wherewith he is so entrusted, the Lord Jesus calleth out of the World unto himself, through the Ministry of his word, by his Spirit, ᵃthose that are given unto him by his Father; that they may walk before him in all the ᵇways of obedience, which he prescribeth to them in his Word. Those thus called he commandeth to walk together in particular societies, or ᶜChurches, for their mutual edification; and the due performance of that public worship, which he requireth of them in the World.

a John 10:16; John 12:32   b Matt. 28:20   c Matt. 18:15–20

6. The Members of these Churches are ᵃSaints by calling, visibly manifesting and evidencing (in and by their profession and walking) their obedience unto that call of Christ; and do willingly consent to walk together according to the appointment of Christ, giving up themselves, to the Lord and one to another by the will of God, ᵇin professed subjection to the Ordinances of the Gospel.

a Rom. 1:7; 1 Cor. 1:2   b Acts 2:41–42; Acts 5:13–14; 2 Cor. 9:13

7. To each of these Churches thus gathered, according to his mind, declared in his word, he hath given all that ªpower and authority, which is any way needful, for their carrying on that order in worship, and discipline, which he hath instituted for them to observe; with commands, and rules, for the due and right exerting, and executing of that power.

a Matt. 18:17–18; 1 Cor. 5:4–5, 13; 2 Cor. 2:6–8

8. A particular Church gathered, and completely Organized, according to the mind of Christ, consists of Officers, and Members; And the Officers appointed by Christ to be chosen and set apart by the Church (so called and gathered) for the peculiar Administration of Ordinances, and Execution of Power, or Duty, which he entrusts them with, or calls them to, to be continued to the end of the World are ªBishops or Elders and Deacons.

a Acts 20:17, 28; Phil. 1:1

9. The way appointed by Christ for the Calling of any person, fitted, and gifted by the Holy Spirit, unto the Office of Bishop, or Elder, in a Church, is, that he be chosen thereunto by the common ªsuffrage of the Church itself; and Solemnly set apart by Fasting and Prayer, with imposition of hands of the ᵇEldership of the Church, if there be any before Constituted therein; And of a Deacon ꞇthat he be chosen by the like suffrage, and set apart by Prayer, and the like Imposition of hands.

a Acts 14:23 b 1 Tim. 4:14 c Acts 6:3, 5–6

10. The work of Pastors being constantly to attend the Service of Christ, in his Churches, in the Ministry of the Word, and Prayer, ªwith watching for their Souls, as they that must give an account to him; it is incumbent on the Churches to whom they Minister, not only

to give them all due respect, [b]but also to communicate to them of all their good things according to their ability, so as they may have a comfortable supply, without being themselves [c]entangled in Secular Affairs; and may also be capable of exercising [d]Hospitality toward others; and this is required by the [e]Law of Nature, and by the Express order of our Lord Jesus, who hath ordained that they that preach the Gospel, should live of the Gospel.

a Acts 6:4; Heb. 13:17 b 1 Tim. 5:17–18; Gal. 6:6–7 c 2 Tim. 2:4 d 1 Tim. 3:2 e 1 Cor. 9:6–14

11. Although it be incumbent on the Bishops or Pastors of the Churches to be instant in Preaching the Word, by way of Office; yet the work of Preaching the Word, is not so peculiarly confined to them; but that others also [a]gifted, and fitted by the Holy Spirit for it, and approved, and called by the Church, may and ought to perform it.

a Acts 11:19–21; 1 Pet. 4:10–11

12. As all Believers are bound to join themselves to particular Churches, when and where they have opportunity so to do; So all that are admitted unto the privileges of a Church, are also [a]under the Censures and Government thereof, according to the Rule of Christ.

a 1 Thess. 5:14; 2 Thess. 3:6, 14–15

13. No Church-members upon any offence taken by them, having performed their Duty required of them towards the person they are offended at, ought to disturb any Church order, or absent themselves from the Assemblies of the Church, or Administration of any Ordinances, upon the account of such offence at any of their fellow-members; but to wait upon Christ, [a]in the further proceeding of the Church.

a Matt. 18:15–17; Eph. 4:2–3

14. As each Church, and all the Members of it are bound to ªpray continually, for the good and prosperity of all the Churches of Christ, in all places; and upon all occasions to further it (everyone within the bounds of their places, and callings, in the Exercise of their Gifts and Graces) so the Churches (when planted by the providence of God so as they may enjoy opportunity and advantage for it) ought to hold ᵇcommunion amongst themselves for their peace, increase of love, and mutual edification.

a Eph. 6:18; Ps. 122:6 b Rom. 16:1–2; 3 John 8–10

15. In cases of difficulties or differences, either in point of Doctrine, or Administration; wherein either the Churches in general are concerned, or any one Church in their peace, union, and edification; or any member, or members, of any Church are injured, in or by any proceedings in censures not agreeable to truth, and order: it is according to the mind of Christ, that many Churches holding communion together, do by their messengers meet to consider, ªand give their advice, in or about that matter in difference, to be reported to all the Churches concerned; howbeit these messengers assembled are not entrusted with any Church-power properly so called; or with any jurisdiction over the Churches themselves, to exercise any censures either over any Churches, or Persons: or ᵇto impose their determination on the Churches, or Officers.

a Acts 15:2, 4, 6; Acts 15:22–23, 25 b 2 Cor. 1:24; 1 John 4:1

XXVII. Of the Communion of Saints

1. All Saints that are united to Jesus Christ their Head, by his Spirit, and Faith; although they are not made thereby one person with him, have ªfellowship in his Graces, sufferings, death, resurrection, and glory; and being united to one another in love, they ᵇhave communion in

each others gifts, and graces; and are obliged to the performance of such duties, public and private, in an orderly way, 'as do conduce to their mutual good, both in the inward and outward man.

a 1 John 1:3; John 1:16; Phil. 3:10; Rom. 6:5–6   b Eph. 4:15–16; 1 Cor. 12:7; 1 Cor. 3:21–23   c 1 Thess. 5:11, 14; Rom. 1:12; 1 John 3:17–18; Gal. 6:10

2. Saints by profession are bound to maintain an holy fellowship and communion in the worship of God, and in performing such other spiritual services, ^aas tend to their mutual edification; as also in relieving each other in ^boutward things according to their several abilities, and necessities; which communion according to the rule of the Gospel, though especially to be exercised by them, in the relations wherein they stand, whether in ^cfamilies, or ^dChurches; yet as God offereth opportunity is to be extended to all the household of faith, even all those who in every place call upon the name of the Lord Jesus; nevertheless their communion one with another as Saints, doth not take away or ^einfringe, the title or propriety, which each man hath in his goods and possessions.

a Heb. 10:24–25; Heb. 3:12–13   b Acts 11:29–30   c Eph. 6:4   d 1 Cor. 12:14–27   e Acts 5:4; Eph. 4:28

XXVIII. Of Baptism and the Lord's Supper

1. Baptism and the Lord's Supper are ordinances of positive, and sovereign institution; appointed by the Lord Jesus the only Lawgiver, to be continued in his Church ^ato the end of the world.

a Matt. 28:19–20; 1 Cor. 11:26

2. These holy appointments are to be administered by those only, who are qualified and thereunto called according ^ato the commission of Christ.

a Matt. 28:19; 1 Cor. 4:1

1. Baptism is an Ordinance of the New Testament, ordained by Jesus Christ, to be unto the party Baptized, a sign of his fellowship with him, in his death, [a]and resurrection; of his being engrafted into him; of [b]remission of sins; and of his [c]giving up unto God through Jesus Christ to live and walk in newness of Life.

a Rom. 6:3–5; Col. 2:12; Gal. 3:27   b Mark 1:4; Acts 26:16   c Rom. 6:2, 4

2. Those who do actually profess [a]repentance towards God, faith in, and obedience, to our Lord Jesus, are the only proper subjects of this ordinance.

a Mark 16:16; Acts 8:36–37

3. The outward element to be used in this ordinance [a]is water, wherein the party is to be baptized, in the name of the Father, and of the Son, and of the Holy Spirit.

a Matt. 28:19–20; Acts 8:38

4. Immersion, or dipping of the person [a]in water, is necessary to the due administration of this ordinance.

a Matt. 3:16; John 3:23

XXX. Of the Lord's Supper

1. The Supper of the Lord Jesus, was instituted by him, the same night wherein he was betrayed, to be observed in his Churches unto the end of the world, for the perpetual remembrance, and showing forth the sacrifice of himself in his death, [a]confirmation of the faith of believers in all the benefits thereof, their spiritual nourishment, and growth in

him, their further engagement in, and to, all duties which they owe unto him; [b]and to be a bond and pledge of their communion with him, and with each other.

a 1 Cor. 11:23–26   b 1 Cor. 10:16–17, 21

2. In this ordinance Christ is not offered up to his Father, nor any real sacrifice made at all, for remission of sin of the quick or dead; but only a memorial of that [a]one offering up of himself, by himself, upon the cross, once for all; and a spiritual oblation of all [b]possible praise unto God for the same; so that the Popish sacrifice of the Mass (as they call it) is most abominable, injurious to Christ's own only sacrifice, the alone propitiation for all the sins of the Elect.

a Heb. 9:25–26, 28   b 1 Cor. 11:24; Matt. 26:26–27

3. The Lord Jesus hath in this Ordinance, appointed his Ministers to Pray, and bless the Elements of Bread and Wine, and thereby to set them apart from a common to an holy use, and to take and break the Bread; to take the Cup, [a]and (they communicating also themselves) to give both to the Communicants.

a 1 Cor. 11:23–30

4. The denial of the Cup to the people, worshiping the Elements, the lifting them up, or carrying them about for adoration, and reserving them for any pretended religious use, [a]are all contrary to the nature of this Ordinance, and to the institution of Christ.

a Matt. 26:26–28; Matt. 15:9; Ex. 20:4–5

5. The outward Elements in this Ordinance, duly set apart to the uses ordained by Christ, have such relation to him crucified, as that truly, although in terms used figuratively, they are sometimes called

by the name of the things they represent, to wit the [a]body and Blood of Christ; albeit in substance, and nature, they still remain truly, and only [b]Bread, and Wine, as they were before.

a 1 Cor. 11:27 b 1 Cor. 11:26, 28

6. That doctrine which maintains a change of the substance of Bread and Wine, into the substance of Christ's body and blood (commonly called Transubstantiation) by consecration of a Priest, or by any other way, is repugnant not to Scripture [a]alone, but even to common sense and reason; overthroweth the [b]nature of the ordinance, and hath been and is the cause of manifold superstitions, yea, of gross Idolatries.

a Acts 3:21; Luke 24:6, 39 b 1 Cor. 11:24–25

7. Worthy receivers, outwardly partaking of the visible Elements in this Ordinance, do then also inwardly by faith, really and indeed, yet not carnally, and corporally, but spiritually receive, and feed upon Christ crucified [a]and all the benefits of his death: the Body and Blood of Christ, being then not corporally, or carnally, but spiritually present to the faith of Believers, in that Ordinance, as the Elements themselves are to their outward senses.

a 1 Cor. 10:16; 1 Cor. 11:23–26

8. All ignorant and ungodly persons, as they are unfit to enjoy communion [a]with Christ; so are they unworthy of the Lord's Table; and cannot without great sin against him, while they remain such, partake of these holy mysteries, [b]or be admitted thereunto: yea whosoever shall receive unworthily are guilty of the Body and Blood of the Lord, eating and drinking judgment to themselves.

a 2 Cor. 6:14–15 b 1 Cor. 11:29; Matt. 7:6

XXXI. Of the State of Man after Death and of the Resurrection of the Dead

1. The Bodies of Men after Death return to dust, [a]and see corruption; but their Souls (which neither die nor sleep) having an immortal subsistence, immediately [b]return to God who gave them: the Souls of the Righteous being then made perfect in holiness, are received into paradise where they are with Christ, and behold the face of God, in light [c]and glory; waiting for the full Redemption of their Bodies; and the souls of the wicked, are cast into hell; where they remain in torment and utter darkness, reserved to [d]the judgment of the great day; besides these two places for Souls separated from their bodies, the Scripture acknowledgeth none.

a Gen. 3:19; Acts 13:36 *b* Eccles. 12:7 *c* Luke 23:43; 2 Cor. 5:1, 6, 8; Phil. 1:23; Heb. 12:23 *d* Jude 6–7; 1 Pet. 3:19; Luke 16:23–24

2. At the last day such of the Saints as are found alive shall not sleep but be [a]changed; and all the dead shall be raised up with the self same bodies, and [b]none other; although with different [c]qualities, which shall be united again to their Souls forever.

a 1 Cor. 15:51–52; 1 Thess. 4:17 *b* Job 19:26–27 *c* 1 Cor. 15:42–43

3. The bodies of the unjust shall by the power of Christ, be raised to dishonor; the bodies of the just by his spirit unto honor, [a]and be made conformable to his own glorious Body.

a Acts 24:15; John 5:28–29; Phil. 3:21

XXXII. Of the Last Judgment

1. God hath appointed a Day wherein he will judge the world in Righteousness, by [a]Jesus Christ; to whom all power and judgment is

given of the Father; in which Day not only the [b]Apostate Angels shall be judged; but likewise all persons that have lived upon the Earth, shall appear before the Tribunal of Christ; [c]to give an account of their Thoughts, Words, and Deeds, and to receive according to what they have done in the body, whether good or evil.

a Acts 17:31; John 5:22, 27 *b* 1 Cor. 6:3; Jude 6 *c* 2 Cor. 5:10; Eccles. 12:14; Matt. 12:36; Rom. 14:10, 12; Matt. 25:32–46

2. The end of God's appointing this Day, is for the manifestation of the glory of his Mercy, in the Eternal Salvation of the Elect; [a]and of his Justice in the Eternal damnation of the Reprobate, who are wicked and disobedient; for then shall the Righteous go into Everlasting Life, and receive that fullness of Joy, and Glory, with everlasting reward, in the presence [b]of the Lord: but the wicked who know not God, and obey not the Gospel of Jesus Christ, shall be cast into Eternal torments, and [c]punished with everlasting destruction, from the presence of the Lord, and from the glory of his power.

a Rom. 9:22–23 *b* Matt. 25:21, 34; 2 Tim. 4:8 *c* Matt. 25:46; Mark 9:48; 2 Thess. 1:7–10

3. As Christ would have us to be certainly persuaded that there shall be a Day of judgment, both [a]to deter all men from sin, and for the greater [b]consolation of the godly, in their adversity; so will he have that day unknown to Men, that they may shake off all carnal security, and be always watchful, because they know not at what hour, the [c]Lord will come; and may ever be prepared to say, [d]Come Lord Jesus, Come quickly, Amen.

a 2 Cor. 5:10–11 *b* 2 Thess. 1:5–7 *c* Mark 13:35–37; Luke 12:35–40 *d* Rev. 22:20

The Heidelberg Catechism

INTRODUCTION

The chief influence in the development of the Heidelberg Catechism was Zacharias Ursinus. A new recruit at the University of Heidelberg (in modern-day Germany), the twenty-nine-year-old professor of theology was a leading figure in the university's golden age as a center for training ministers for the Protestant church. Ursinus's catechism, completed in 1563, was his most famous work. It was quickly translated into various languages and became a favorite among the Reformed. When the Synod of Dort approved the catechism in 1619, it was assured a special place among churches in the continental Reformed tradition.

The preface to the catechism (Questions 1 and 2) frames the discussion of the faith in terms of gospel comfort in the face of sin and suffering. In words that have thrilled generations of believers, the catechism offers a vocabulary to express confidence in Christ: "I am not my own, but belong—body and soul, in life and in death—to my faithful Savior, Jesus Christ." A conversation follows, all of it in question-and-answer form, organized under the headings of guilt, grace, and gratitude.

Questions 3–11 speak of our sin and the misery that accompanies a failure to keep God's law—a law summarized in the two great commandments of Matthew 22:34–40. The catechism concludes that the gravity of our sin and the pure severity of God's justice have left us in a desperate place.

Questions 12–85 then offer welcome relief. The catechism employs the Apostles' Creed to introduce our triune God and then trace the plan of salvation. Particularly useful is an explanation of the reason for the incarnation. With this catechism in hand, every believer is helped to answer the question, why did God become man? As expected in an exposition of the creed, this section also discusses the doctrine of the church (briefly) and the sacraments (at length).

The final questions, 86–129, ask how we might express our thankfulness for the grace of God in delivering us from our misery. The catechism colors in the details of the Christian life using the outlines provided by the Ten Commandments and the Lord's Prayer, considering one precept or petition at a time. Here as elsewhere, the catechism groups questions into "Lord's Days," coherent units that Reformed Christians were expected to consider on a weekly basis, often in an afternoon worship service. With fifty-two Lord's Days, church leaders could offer a summary of the whole of theology in one year, thus grounding believers in their understanding not only of the Bible itself but of the Bible's central themes as well.

THE HEIDELBERG CATECHISM

Lord's Day 1

1. *What is your only comfort in life and in death?*

    That I am not my own,[a] but belong—body and soul, in life and in death[b]—to my faithful Savior, Jesus Christ.[c]

    He has fully paid for all my sins with his precious blood,[d] and has delivered me from the tyranny of the devil.[e] He also watches over me in such a way[f] that not a hair can fall from my head without the will of my Father in heaven;[g] in fact, all things must work together for my salvation.[h]

    Because I belong to him, Christ, by his Holy Spirit, also assures me of eternal life[i] and makes me wholeheartedly willing and ready from now on to live for him.[j]

    a 1 Cor. 6:19–20 *b* Rom. 14:7–9 *c* 1 Cor. 3:23; Titus 2:14 *d* 1 Pet. 1:18–19; 1 John 1:7–9; 2:2 *e* John 8:34–36; Heb. 2:14–15; 1 John 3:1–11 *f* John 6:39–40; 10:27–30; 2 Thess. 3:3; 1 Pet. 1:5 *g* Matt. 10:29–31; Luke 21:16–18 *h* Rom. 8:28 *i* Rom. 8:15–16; 2 Cor. 1:21–22; 5:5; Eph. 1:13–14 *j* Rom. 8:1–17

2. *How many things must you know to live and die in the joy of this comfort?*

    Three: first, how great my sin and misery are;[a] second, how I am delivered from all my sins and misery;[b] third, how I am to thank God for such deliverance.[c]

    a Rom. 3:9–10; 1 John 1:10 *b* John 17:3; Acts 4:12; 10:43 *c* Matt. 5:16; Rom. 6:13; Eph. 5:8–10; 2 Tim. 2:15; 1 Pet. 2:9–10

3. *How do you come to know your misery?*
    The law of God tells me.[a]

    a Rom. 3:20; 7:7–25

4. *What does God's law require of us?*
    Christ teaches us this in summary in Matthew 22:37–40: "'You
    shall love the Lord your God with all your heart and with all
    your soul and with all your mind, and with all your strength.'[a]
    This is the greatest and first commandment. And a second is
    like it: 'You shall love your neighbor as yourself.'[b] On these two
    commandments hang all the law and the Prophets."

    a Deut. 6:5   b Lev. 19:18

5. *Can you live up to all this perfectly?*
    No.[a] I am inclined by nature to hate God and my neighbor.[b]

    a Rom. 3:9–20, 23; 1 John 1:8, 10   b Gen. 6:5; Jer. 17:9; Rom. 7:23–24; 8:7; Eph. 2:1–3;
    Titus 3:3

Lord's Day 3

6. *Did God create man so wicked and perverse?*
    No. God created man good[a] and in his own image,[b] that is, in
    true righteousness and holiness,[c] so that he might truly know
    God his creator,[d] love him with all his heart, and live with God
    in eternal happiness, for his praise and glory.[e]

    a Gen. 1:31   b Gen. 1:26–27   c Eph. 4:24   d Col. 3:10   e Ps. 8:1–9

7. *Then where does man's corrupt nature come from?*

From the fall and disobedience of our first parents, Adam and Eve, in Paradise.[a]

This fall has so poisoned our nature[b] that we are all conceived and born in sin.[c]

a Gen. 3:1–24 b Rom. 5:12, 18–19 c Ps. 51:5

8. *But are we so corrupt that we are totally unable to do any good and inclined toward all evil?*

Yes,[a] unless we are born again by the Spirit of God.[b]

a Gen. 6:5; 8:21; Job 14:4; Isa. 53:6 b John 3:3–5

Lord's Day 4

9. *But doesn't God do man an injustice by requiring in his law what man is unable to do?*

No, God created man with the ability to keep the law.[a] Man, however, at the instigation of the devil,[b] in willful disobedience,[c] robbed himself and all his descendants of these gifts.[d]

a Gen. 1:31; Eph. 4:24 b Gen. 3:13; John 8:44 c Gen. 3:6 d Rom. 5:12, 18–19

10. *Will God permit such disobedience and rebellion to go unpunished?*

Certainly not. He is terribly angry with the sin we are born with as well as our actual sins. God will punish them by a just judgment both now and in eternity,[a] having declared: "Cursed is everyone who does not observe and obey all the things written in the book of the law."[b]

a Ex. 34:7; Ps. 5:4–6; Nah. 1:2; Rom. 1:18; Eph. 5:6; Heb. 9:27 b Gal. 3:10 (Deut. 27:26)

11. *But isn't God also merciful?*

God is certainly merciful,[a] but he is also just.[b] His justice demands that sin, committed against his supreme majesty, be punished with the supreme penalty—eternal punishment of body and soul.[c]

a Ex. 34:6–7; Ps. 103:8–9   b Ex. 34:7; Deut. 7:9–11; Ps. 5:4–6; Heb. 10:30–31
c Matt. 25:35–46

Lord's Day 5

12. *According to God's righteous judgment we deserve punishment both now and in eternity: how then can we escape this punishment and return to God's favor?*

God requires that his justice be satisfied.[a] Therefore the claims of this justice must be paid in full, either by ourselves or by another.[b]

a Ex. 23:7; Rom. 2:1–11   b Isa. 53:11; Rom. 8:3–4

13. *Can we make this payment ourselves?*

Certainly not. Actually, we increase our debt every day.[a]

a Matt. 6:12; Rom. 2:4–5

14. *Can another creature—any at all—pay this debt for us?*

No. To begin with, God will not punish any other creature for what a human is guilty of.[a] Furthermore, no mere creature can bear the weight of God's eternal wrath against sin and deliver others from it.[b]

a Ezek. 18:4, 20; Heb. 2:14–18   b Ps. 49:7–9; 130:3

15. *What kind of mediator and deliverer should we look for then?*
One who is a true[a] and righteous[b] man, yet more powerful than all creatures, that is, one who is also true God.[c]

a Rom. 1:3; 1 Cor. 15:21; Heb. 2:17 b Isa. 53:9; 2 Cor. 5:21; Heb. 7:26 c Isa. 7:14; 9:6; Jer. 23:6; John 1:1

Lord's Day 6

16. *Why must the mediator be a true and righteous man?*
Because God's justice requires that human nature, which has sinned, must pay for its sin;[a] but a sinner could never pay for others.[b]

a Rom. 5:12, 15; 1 Cor. 15:21; Heb. 2:14–16 b Heb. 7:26–27; 1 Pet. 3:18

17. *Why must he also be true God?*
So that, by the power of his divinity, he might bear in his humanity the weight of God's wrath, and earn for us and restore to us righteousness and life.[a]

a Isa. 53:1–12; John 3:16; 2 Cor. 5:21

18. *Then who is this mediator—true God and at the same time a true and righteous man?*
Our Lord Jesus Christ,[a] who was given to us for our complete deliverance and righteousness.[b]

a Matt. 1:21–23; Luke 2:11; 1 Tim. 2:5 b 1 Cor. 1:30

19. *How do you come to know this?*
The holy gospel tells me. God himself began to reveal the gospel already in Paradise;[a] later, he proclaimed it by the holy patriarchs[b]

and prophets[c] and foreshadowed it by the sacrifices and other ceremonies of the law;[d] and finally he fulfilled it through his own beloved Son.[e]

a Gen. 3:15 b Gen. 22:18; 49:10 c Isa. 53:1–12; Jer. 23:5–6; Mic. 7:18–20; Acts 10:43; Heb. 1:1–2
d Lev. 1:1–7:38; John 5:46; Heb. 10:1–10 e Rom. 10:4; Gal. 4:4–5; Col. 2:17

Lord's Day 7

20. *Are all people then saved through Christ just as they were lost through Adam?*

No. Only those are saved who through true faith are grafted into Christ and accept all his benefits.[a]

a Matt. 7:14; John 3:16, 18, 36; Rom. 11:16–21

21. *What is true faith?*

True faith is not only a sure knowledge by which I hold as true all that God has revealed to us in his Word;[a] it is also a wholehearted trust,[b] which the Holy Spirit works in me[c] by the gospel,[d] that God has freely granted, not only to others but to me also,[e] forgiveness of sins, eternal righteousness, and salvation.[f]

These gifts are purely of grace, only because of Christ's merit.[g]

a John 17:3, 17; Heb. 11:1–3; James 2:19 b Rom. 4:18–21; 5:1; 10:10; Heb. 4:14–16 c Matt.
16:15–17; John 3:5; Acts 16:14 d Rom. 1:16; 10:17; 1 Cor. 1:21 e Gal. 2:20 f Rom. 1:17; Heb.
10:10 g Rom. 3:21–26; Gal. 2:16; Eph. 2:8–10

22. *What then must a Christian believe?*

All that is promised us in the gospel,[a] a summary of which is taught us in the articles of our catholic and undoubted Christian faith.

a Matt. 28:18–20; John 20:30–31

23. *What are these articles?*
I believe in God, the Father Almighty, Creator of heaven and earth.

I believe in Jesus Christ, his only begotten Son, our Lord, who was conceived by the Holy Spirit, born of the virgin Mary; suffered under Pontius Pilate, was crucified, dead, and buried; he descended into hell; the third day he rose again from the dead; he ascended to heaven, and sits at the right hand of God the Father Almighty; from there he will come to judge the living and the dead.

I believe in the Holy Spirit; the holy catholic church; the communion of saints; the forgiveness of sins; the resurrection of the body; and the life everlasting. Amen.

Lord's Day 8

24. *How are these articles divided?*
Into three parts: God the Father and our creation; God the Son and our deliverance; and God the Holy Spirit and our sanctification.

25. *Since there is only one divine being,[a] why do you speak of three: Father, Son, and Holy Spirit?*
Because that is how God has revealed himself in his Word:[b] these three distinct persons are one, true, eternal God.

a Deut. 6:4; 1 Cor. 8:4, 6   b Matt. 3:16–17; 28:18–19; Luke 4:18 (Isa. 61:1); John 14:26; 15:26; 2 Cor. 13:14; Gal. 4:6; Titus 3:5–6

26. *What do you believe when you say, "I believe in God, the Father Almighty, Creator of heaven and earth"?*

That the eternal Father of our Lord Jesus Christ, who out of nothing created heaven and earth and everything in them,ᵃ who still upholds and rules them by his eternal counsel and providence,ᵇ is my God and Father for the sake of Christ his Son.ᶜ

I trust God so much that I do not doubt he will provide whatever I need for body and soul,ᵈ and will turn to my good whatever adversity he sends upon me in this vale of tears.ᵉ

He is able to do this because he is almighty God;ᶠ he desires to do this because he is a faithful Father.ᵍ

a Gen. 1:1–2:25; Ex. 20:11; Ps. 33:6; Isa. 44:24; Acts 4:24; 14:15 b Ps. 104:1–35; Matt. 6:30; 10:29; Eph. 1:11 c John 1:12–13; Rom. 8:15–16 d Ps. 55:22; Matt. 6:25–26; Luke 12:22–31 e Rom. 8:28 f Gen. 18:14; Rom. 8:31–39 g Matt. 7:9–11

Lord's Day 10

27. *What do you understand by the providence of God?*

Providence is the almighty and ever-present power of Godᵃ by which God upholds, as with his hand, heaven and earth and all creatures,ᵇ and so rules them that leaf and blade, rain and drought, fruitful and lean years, food and drink, health and sickness, prosperity and povertyᶜ—all things, in fact, come to us not by chanceᵈ but by his fatherly hand.ᵉ

a Jer. 23:23–24; Acts 17:24–28 b Heb. 1:3 c Jer. 5:24; Acts 14:15–17; John 9:3; Prov. 22:2 d Prov. 16:33 e Matt. 10:29

28. *How does the knowledge of God's creation and providence help us?*

We can be patient in adversity,[a] thankful in prosperity,[b] and for the future we can have good confidence in our faithful God and Father that no creature will separate us from his love.[c] For all creatures are so completely in his hand that without his will they can neither move nor be moved.[d]

a Job 1:21–22; James 1:3 b Deut. 8:10; 1 Thess. 5:18 c Ps. 55:22; Rom. 5:3–5; 8:38–39 d Job 1:12; 2:6; Prov. 21:1; Acts 17:24–28

Lord's Day 11

29. *Why is the Son of God called "Jesus," meaning "savior"?*

Because he saves us from our sins;[a] and because salvation is not to be sought or found in anyone else.[b]

a Matt. 1:21; Heb. 7:25 b Isa. 43:11; John 15:5; Acts 4:11–12; 1 Tim. 2:5

30. *Do those who look for their salvation and security in saints, in themselves, or elsewhere really believe in the only savior Jesus?*

No. Although they boast of being his, by their actions they deny the only savior, Jesus.[a] Either Jesus is not a perfect savior, or those who in true faith accept this savior have in him all they need for their salvation.[b]

a 1 Cor. 1:12–13; Gal. 5:4 b Col. 1:19–20; 2:10; 1 John 1:7

Lord's Day 12

31. *Why is he called "Christ," meaning "anointed"?*

Because he has been ordained by God the Father and has been anointed with the Holy Spirit[a] to be our chief prophet and teacher[b] who fully reveals to us the secret counsel and will of God concerning our deliverance;[c] our only high priest[d] who has delivered us by the one sacrifice of his body,[e] and who continually intercedes for us before the Father;[f] and our eternal king[g] who governs us by his Word and Spirit, and who guards us and keeps us in the deliverance he has won for us.[h]

a Luke 3:21–22; 4:14–19 (Isa. 61:1); Heb. 1:9 (Ps. 45:7) b Acts 3:22 (Deut. 18:15) c John 1:18; 15:15 d Heb. 7:17 (Ps. 110:4) e Heb. 9:12; 10:11–14 f Rom. 8:34; Heb. 9:24 g Matt. 21:5 (Zech. 9:9) h Matt. 28:18–20; John 10:28; Rev. 12:10–11

32. But why are you called a Christian?

Because by faith I am a member of Christ[a] and so I share in his anointing.[b]

I am anointed to confess his name,[c] to present myself to him as a living sacrifice of thanks,[d] to strive with a free conscience against sin and the devil in this life,[e] and afterward to reign with Christ over all creation for eternity.[f]

a 1 Cor. 12:12–27 b Acts 2:17 (Joel 2:28); 1 John 2:27 c Matt. 10:32; Rom. 10:9–10; Heb. 13:15 d Rom. 12:1; 1 Pet. 2:5, 9 e Gal. 5:16–17; Eph. 6:11; 1 Tim. 1:18–19 f Matt. 25:34; 2 Tim. 2:12

Lord's Day 13

33. Why is he called God's "only begotten Son" when we also are God's children?

Because Christ alone is the eternal, natural Son of God.[a] We, however, are adopted children of God—adopted by grace for the sake of Christ.[b]

a John 1:1–3, 14, 18; Heb. 1:1–14 b John 1:12; Rom. 8:14–17; Eph. 1:5–6

34. *Why do you call him "our Lord"?*

Because—not with gold or silver, but with his precious blood[a]—he has delivered and purchased us body and soul from sin and from the tyranny of the devil,[b] to be his very own.[c]

a 1 Pet. 1:18–19 b Col. 1:13–14; Heb. 2:14–15 c 1 Cor. 6:20; 1 Tim. 2:5–6

Lord's Day 14

35. *What does it mean that he "was conceived by the Holy Spirit, born of the virgin Mary"?*

That the eternal Son of God, who is and remains true and eternal God,[a] took to himself, through the working of the Holy Spirit,[b] from the flesh and blood of the virgin Mary,[c] a true human nature so that he might also become David's true descendant,[d] like his brothers in all things[e] except for sin.[f]

a John 1:1; 10:30–36; Acts 13:33 (Ps. 2:7); Col. 1:15–17; 1 John 5:20 b Luke 1:35 c Matt. 1:18–23; John 1:14; Gal. 4:4; Heb. 2:14 d 2 Sam. 7:12–16; Ps. 132:11; Matt. 1:1; Rom. 1:3 e Phil. 2:7; Heb. 2:17 f Heb. 4:15; 7:26–27

36. *How does the holy conception and birth of Christ benefit you?*

He is our mediator[a] and, in God's sight, he covers with his innocence and perfect holiness my sin, in which I was conceived.[b]

a 1 Tim. 2:5–6; Heb. 9:13–15 b Rom. 8:3–4; 2 Cor. 5:21; Gal. 4:4–5; 1 Pet. 1:18–19

Lord's Day 15

37. *What do you understand by the word "suffered"?*

That during his whole life on earth, but especially at the end, Christ sustained in body and soul the wrath of God against the sin of the whole human race.[a]

This he did in order that, by his suffering as the only atoning sacrifice[b] he might deliver us, body and soul, from eternal condemnation,[c] and gain for us God's grace, righteousness, and eternal life.[d]

a Isa. 53:1–12; 1 Pet. 2:24; 3:18 b Rom. 3:25; Heb. 10:14; 1 John 2:2; 4:10 c Rom. 8:1–4; Gal. 3:13 d John 3:16; Rom. 3:24–26

38. *Why did he suffer "under Pontius Pilate" as judge?*
So that he, though innocent, might be condemned by an earthly judge,[a] and so free us from the severe judgment of God that was to fall on us.[b]

a Luke 23:13–24; John 19:4, 12–16 b Isa. 53:4–5; 2 Cor. 5:21; Gal. 3:13

39. *Is it significant that he was "crucified" instead of dying some other way?*
Yes. By this death I am convinced that he shouldered the curse which lay on me since death by crucifixion was cursed by God.[a]

a Gal. 3:10–13 (Deut. 21:23)

Lord's Day 16

40. *Why did Christ have to suffer death?*
Because God's justice and truth require it:[a] nothing else could pay for our sins except the death of the Son of God.[b]

a Gen. 2:17 b Rom. 8:3–4; Phil. 2:8; Heb. 2:9

41. *Why was he "buried"?*
His burial testifies that he really died.[a]

a Isa. 53:9; John 19:38–42; Acts 13:29; 1 Cor. 15:3–4

42. *Since Christ has died for us, why do we still have to die?*
Our death is not a payment for our sins,[a] but only a dying to sins and an entering into eternal life.[b]

a Ps. 49:7 b John 5:24; Phil. 1:21–23; 1 Thess. 5:9–10

43. *What further benefit do we receive from Christ's sacrifice and death on the cross?*
By his power our old man is crucified, put to death, and buried with him,[a] so that the evil desires of the flesh may no longer rule us,[b] but that instead we may offer ourselves as a sacrifice of thanksgiving to him.[c]

a Rom. 6:5–11; Col. 2:11–12 b Rom. 6:12–14 c Rom. 12:1; Eph. 5:1–2

44. *Why does the creed add, "He descended into hell"?*
To assure me during attacks of deepest dread and temptation that Christ my Lord, by suffering unspeakable anguish, pain, and terror of soul, on the cross but also earlier, has delivered me from hellish anguish and torment.[a]

a Isa. 53:1–12; Matt. 26:36–46; 27:45–46; Luke 22:44; Heb. 5:7–10

Lord's Day 17

45. *How does Christ's resurrection benefit us?*
First, by his resurrection he has overcome death, so that he might make us share in the righteousness he obtained for us by his death.[a]

Second, by his power we too are already raised to a new life.[b]

Third, Christ's resurrection is a sure pledge to us of our blessed resurrection.[c]

a Rom. 4:25; 1 Cor. 15:16–20; 1 Pet. 1:3–5 b Rom. 6:5–11; Eph. 2:4–6; Col. 3:1–4 c Rom. 8:11; 1 Cor. 15:12–23; Phil. 3:20–21

46. *What do you mean by saying, "He ascended to heaven"?*
That Christ, while his disciples watched, was taken up from the earth into heaven[a] and remains there on our behalf[b] until he comes again to judge the living and the dead.[c]

a Luke 24:50–51; Acts 1:9–11 b Rom. 8:34; Eph. 4:8–10; Heb. 7:23–25; 9:24 c Acts 1:11

47. *But isn't Christ with us until the end of the world as he promised us?* [a]
Christ is true man and true God. In his human nature Christ is not now on earth;[b] but in his divinity, majesty, grace, and Spirit he is never absent from us.[c]

a Matt. 28:20 b Acts 1:9–11; 3:19–21 c Matt. 28:18–20; John 14:16–19

48. *If his humanity is not present wherever his divinity is, then aren't the two natures of Christ separated from each other?*
Certainly not. Since divinity is not limited and is present everywhere,[a] it is evident that Christ's divinity is surely beyond the bounds of the humanity that has been taken on, but at the same time his divinity is in and remains personally united to his humanity.[b]

a Jer. 23:23–24; Acts 7:48–49 (Isa. 66:1) b John 1:14; 3:13; Col. 2:9

49. *How does Christ's ascension to heaven benefit us?*
First, he is our advocate in heaven in the presence of his Father.[a]

Second, we have our own flesh in heaven as a sure pledge that Christ our head will also take us, his members, up to himself.[b]

Third, he sends his Spirit to us on earth as a corresponding pledge.[c] By the Spirit's power we seek not earthly things but the things above, where Christ is, sitting at God's right hand.[d]

a Rom. 8:34; 1 John 2:1 b John 14:2; 17:24; Eph. 2:4–6 c John 14:16; 2 Cor. 1:21–22; 5:5
d Col. 3:1–4

Lord's Day 19

50. *Why the next words: "and sits at the right hand of God"?*
Christ ascended to heaven, there to show that he is head of his church,[a] the one through whom the Father governs all things.[b]

a Eph. 1:20–23; Col. 1:18 b Matt. 28:18; John 5:22–23

51. *How does this glory of Christ our head benefit us?*
First, through his Holy Spirit he pours out gifts from heaven upon us his members.[a]

Second, by his power he defends us and preserves us from all enemies.[b]

a Acts 2:33; Eph. 4:7–12 b Ps. 110:1–2; John 10:27–30; Rev. 19:11–16

52. *How does Christ's return "to judge the living and the dead" comfort you?*
In all distress and persecution, with uplifted head, I confidently await the very judge who has already offered himself to the judgment of God in my place and removed the whole curse from me.[a] Christ will cast all his enemies and mine into everlasting condemnation, but will take me and all his chosen ones to himself into the joy and glory of heaven.[b]

a Luke 21:28; Rom. 8:22–25; Phil. 3:20–21; Titus 2:13–14 b Matt. 25:31–46; 2 Thess. 1:6–10

53. *What do you believe concerning "the Holy Spirit"?*

First, that the Spirit, with the Father and the Son, is eternal God.[a]

Second, that he is given also to me,[b] so that, through true faith, he makes me share in Christ and all his benefits,[c] comforts me,[d] and will remain with me forever.[e]

a Gen. 1:1–2; Matt. 28:19; Acts 5:3–4 b 1 Cor. 6:19; 2 Cor. 1:21–22; Gal. 4:6 c Gal. 3:14
d John 15:26; Acts 9:31 e John 14:16–17; 1 Pet. 4:14

Lord's Day 21

54. *What do you believe concerning "the holy catholic church"?*

I believe that the Son of God through his Spirit and Word,[a] out of the entire human race,[b] from the beginning of the world to its end,[c] gathers, protects, and preserves for himself a community chosen for eternal life[d] and united in true faith.[e] And of this community I am[f] and always will be[g] a living member.

a John 10:14–16; Acts 20:28; Rom. 10:14–17; Col. 1:18 b Gen. 26:3b–4; Rev. 5:9 c Isa. 59:21;
1 Cor. 11:26 d Matt. 16:18; John 10:28–30; Rom. 8:28–30; Eph. 1:3–14 e Acts 2:42–47; Eph.
4:1–6 f 1 John 3:14, 19–21 g John 10:27–28; 1 Cor. 1:4–9; 1 Pet. 1:3–5

55. *What do you understand by "the communion of saints"?*

First, that believers one and all, as members of Christ the Lord, have communion with him and share in all his treasures and gifts.[a]

Second, that each member should consider it a duty to use these gifts readily and joyfully for the service and enrichment of the other members.[b]

a Rom. 8:32; 1 Cor. 6:17; 12:4–7, 12–13; 1 John 1:3 b Rom. 12:4–8; 1 Cor. 12:20–27; 13:1–7;
Phil. 2:4–8

56. *What do you believe concerning "the forgiveness of sins"?*

I believe that God, because of Christ's satisfaction, will no longer remember any of my sins[a] or my sinful nature which I need to struggle against all my life.[b] Rather, by his grace God grants me the righteousness of Christ that I may never come into judgment.[c]

a Ps. 103:3–4, 10, 12; Mic. 7:18–19; 2 Cor. 5:18–21; 1 John 1:7; 2:2   b Rom. 7:21–25   c John 3:17–18; Rom. 8:1–2

Lord's Day 22

57. *How does "the resurrection of the body" comfort you?*

Not only will my soul be taken immediately after this life to Christ its head,[a] but also my very flesh, raised by the power of Christ, will be reunited with my soul, and made like Christ's glorious body.[b]

a Luke 23:43; Phil. 1:21–23   b 1 Cor. 15:20, 42–46, 54; Phil. 3:21; 1 John 3:2

58. *How does the article concerning "life everlasting" comfort you?*

Even as I already now experience in my heart the beginning of eternal joy,[a] so after this life I will have perfect blessedness such as no eye has seen, no ear has heard, no heart has ever imagined: a blessedness in which to praise God eternally.[b]

a Rom. 14:17   b John 17:3; 1 Cor. 2:9

Lord's Day 23

59. *But how does it help you now that you believe all this?*

That I am righteous in Christ before God and an heir to life everlasting.[a]

a John 3:36; Rom. 1:17 (Hab. 2:4); Rom. 5:1–2

60. *How are you righteous before God?*

Only by true faith in Jesus Christ.[a]

Even though my conscience accuses me of having grievously sinned against all God's commandments, of never having kept any of them,[b] and of still being inclined toward all evil,[c] nevertheless, without any merit of my own,[d] out of sheer grace,[e] God grants and credits to me the perfect satisfaction, righteousness, and holiness of Christ,[f] as if I had never sinned nor been a sinner, and as if I had been as perfectly obedient as Christ was obedient for me[g]—if only I accept this gift with a believing heart.[h]

a Rom. 3:21–28; Gal. 2:16; Eph. 2:8–9; Phil. 3:8–11 b Rom. 3:9–10 c Rom. 7:23 d Titus 3:4–5
e Rom. 3:24; Eph. 2:8 f Rom. 4:3–5 (Gen. 15:6); 2 Cor. 5:17–19; 1 John 2:1–2 g Rom. 4:24–25;
2 Cor. 5:21 h John 3:18; Acts 16:30–31

61. *Why do you say that through faith alone you are righteous?*

Not because I please God by the worthiness of my faith, for only Christ's satisfaction, righteousness, and holiness are my righteousness before God,[a] and I can receive this righteousness and make it mine in no other way than by faith alone.[b]

a 1 Cor. 1:30–31 b Rom. 10:10; 1 John 5:10–12

Lord's Day 24

62. *Why can't our good works be our righteousness before God, or at least a part of our righteousness?*

Because the righteousness which can pass God's judgment must be entirely perfect and must in every way measure up to the divine law.[a] But even our best works in this life are all imperfect and stained with sin.[b]

a Rom. 3:20; Gal. 3:10 (Deut. 27:26) b Isa. 64:6

63. *How can our good works be said to merit nothing when God promises to reward them in this life and the next?*[a]

This reward is not merited; it is a gift of grace.[b]

a Matt. 5:12; Heb. 11:6 b Luke 17:10; 2 Tim. 4:7–8

64. *But doesn't this teaching make people indifferent and wicked?*

No. It is impossible for those grafted into Christ by true faith not to produce fruits of gratitude.[a]

a Luke 6:43–45; John 15:5

Lord's Day 25

65. *It is by faith alone that we share in Christ and all his benefits: where then does that faith come from?*

The Holy Spirit works it in our hearts[a] by the preaching of the holy gospel,[b] and confirms it by the use of the holy sacraments.[c]

a John 3:5; 1 Cor. 2:10–14; Eph. 2:8 b Rom. 10:17; 1 Pet. 1:23–25 c Matt. 28:19–20; 1 Cor. 10:16

66. *What are sacraments?*

Sacraments are visible, holy signs and seals.

They were instituted by God so that by our use of them he might make us understand more clearly the promise of the gospel, and seal that promise.[a]

And this is God's gospel promise: he grants us forgiveness of sins and eternal life by grace because of Christ's one sacrifice accomplished on the cross.[b]

a Gen. 17:11; Deut. 30:6; Rom. 4:11 b Matt. 26:27–28; Acts 2:38; Heb. 10:10

67. *Are both the word and the sacraments then intended to focus our faith on the sacrifice of Jesus Christ on the cross as the only ground of our salvation?*

Yes indeed! The Holy Spirit teaches us in the gospel and confirms by the holy sacraments that our entire salvation rests on Christ's one sacrifice for us on the cross.[a]

a Rom. 6:3; 1 Cor. 11:26; Gal. 3:27

68. *How many sacraments did Christ institute in the New Testament?*

Two: holy baptism and the holy supper.[a]

a Matt. 28:19–20; 1 Cor. 11:23–26

Lord's Day 26

69. *How does holy baptism remind and assure you that Christ's one sacrifice on the cross benefits you personally?*

In this way: Christ instituted this outward washing[a] and with it promised that, as surely as water washes away the dirt from the body, so certainly his blood and his Spirit wash away my soul's impurity, that is, all my sins.[b]

a Acts 2:38 b Matt. 3:11; Rom. 6:3–10; 1 Pet. 3:21

70. *What does it mean to be washed with Christ's blood and Spirit?*

To be washed with Christ's blood means that God, by grace, has forgiven our sins because of Christ's blood poured out for us in his sacrifice on the cross.[a]

To be washed with Christ's Spirit means that the Holy Spirit has renewed and sanctified us to be members of Christ, so that more and more we die to sin and live holy and blameless lives.[b]

a Zech. 13:1; Eph. 1:7–8; Heb. 12:24; 1 Pet. 1:2; Rev. 1:5 b Ezek. 36:25–27; John 3:5–8; Rom. 6:4; 1 Cor. 6:11; Col. 2:11–12

71. *Where does Christ promise that we are washed with his blood and Spirit as surely as we are washed with the water of baptism?*

In the institution of baptism, where he says: "Go therefore and make disciples of all nations, baptizing them in the name of the Father and of the Son and of the Holy Spirit."[a] "Whoever believes and is baptized will be saved; but whoever does not believe will be condemned."[b]

This promise is repeated when Scripture calls baptism "the washing of regeneration"[c] and the washing away of sins.[d]

a Matt. 28:19 b Mark 16:16 c Titus 3:5 d Acts 22:16

Lord's Day 27

72. *Does this outward washing with water itself wash away sins?*

No, only Jesus Christ's blood and the Holy Spirit cleanse us from all sins.[a]

a Matt. 3:11; 1 Pet. 3:21; 1 John 1:7

73. *Why then does the Holy Spirit call baptism the water of rebirth and the washing away of sins?*

God has good reason for these words.

To begin with, he wants to teach us that the blood and Spirit of Christ take away our sins just as water removes dirt from the body.[a]

But more importantly, he wants to assure us, by this divine pledge and sign, that we are as truly washed of our sins spiritually as our bodies are washed with water physically.[b]

a 1 Cor. 6:11; Rev. 1:5; 7:14 b Acts 2:38; Rom. 6:3–4; Gal. 3:27

74. *Should infants also be baptized?*

Yes. Infants as well as adults are included in God's covenant and people,[a] and they, no less than adults, are promised deliverance from sin through Christ's blood and the Holy Spirit who works faith.[b]

Therefore, by baptism, the sign of the covenant, they too should be incorporated into the Christian church and distinguished from the children of unbelievers.[c]

This was done in the Old Testament by circumcision,[d] which was replaced in the New Testament by baptism.[e]

a Gen. 17:7; Matt. 19:14 b Isa. 44:1–3; Acts 2:38–39; 16:31 c Acts 10:47; 1 Cor. 7:14 d Gen. 17:9–14 e Col. 2:11–13

Lord's Day 28

75. *How does the holy supper remind and assure you that you share in Christ's one sacrifice on the cross and in all his benefits?*

In this way: Christ has commanded me and all believers to eat this broken bread and to drink this cup in remembrance of him. With this command come these promises:[a]

First, as surely as I see with my eyes the bread of the Lord broken for me and the cup shared with me, so surely his body was offered and broken for me and his blood poured out for me on the cross.

Second, as surely as I receive from the hand of him who serves, and taste with my mouth the bread and cup of the Lord, given me as sure signs of Christ's body and blood, so surely he nourishes and refreshes my soul for eternal life with his crucified body and poured-out blood.

a Matt. 26:26–28; Mark 14:22–24; Luke 22:19–20; 1 Cor. 11:23–25

76. *What does it mean to eat the crucified body of Christ and to drink his poured-out blood?*

It means to accept with a believing heart the entire suffering and death of Christ and in this way to receive forgiveness of sins and eternal life.[a]

But it means more. Through the Holy Spirit, who lives both in Christ and in us, we are united more and more to Christ's blessed body.[b] And so, although he is in heaven[c] and we are on earth, we are flesh of his flesh and bone of his bone.[d] And we forever live on and are governed by one Spirit, as the members of our body are by one soul.[e]

a John 6:35, 40, 50–54 b John 6:55–56; 1 Cor. 12:13 c Acts 1:9–11; 1 Cor. 11:26; Col. 3:1
d 1 Cor. 6:15–17; Eph. 5:29–30; 1 John 4:13 e John 6:56–58; 15:1–6; Eph. 4:15–16; 1 John 3:24

77. *Where does Christ promise to nourish and refresh believers with his body and blood as surely as they eat this broken bread and drink this cup?*

In the institution of the Lord's Supper: "The Lord Jesus on the night when he was betrayed took bread, and when he had given thanks he broke it, and said, 'Take, eat, this is my body which is broken for you. Do this in remembrance of me.' In the same way also he took the cup, after supper, saying, 'This cup is the new covenant in my blood. Do this, as often as you drink it, in remembrance of me.' For as often as you eat this bread and drink the cup, you proclaim the Lord's death until he comes."[a]

This promise is repeated by Paul in these words: "The cup of blessing that we bless, is it not a participation in the blood of Christ? The bread that we break, is it not a participation in the body of Christ? Because there is one bread, we who are many are one body, for we all partake of the one bread."[b]

a 1 Cor. 11:23–26 b 1 Cor. 10:16–17

78. *Do the bread and wine become the real body and blood of Christ?*

No. Just as the water of baptism is not changed into Christ's blood and does not itself wash away sins but is simply a divine sign and assurance[a] of these things, so too the holy bread of the Lord's Supper does not become the body of Christ itself,[b] even though it is called the body of Christ[c] in keeping with the nature and language of sacraments.[d]

a Eph. 5:26; Titus 3:5 b Matt. 26:26–29 c 1 Cor. 10:16–17; 11:26–28 d Gen. 17:10–11; Ex. 12:11, 13; 1 Cor. 10:1–4

79. *Why then does Christ call the bread his body and the cup his blood, or the new covenant in his blood, and Paul use the words, a participation in Christ's body and blood?*

Christ has good reason for these words.

He wants to teach us that just as bread and wine nourish the temporal life, so too his crucified body and poured-out blood are the true food and drink of our souls for eternal life.[a]

But more important, he wants to assure us, by this visible sign and pledge, that we, through the Holy Spirit's work, share in his true body and blood as surely as our mouths receive these holy signs in his remembrance,[b] and that all of his suffering and obedience are as definitely ours as if we personally had suffered and made satisfaction for our sins.[c]

a John 6:51, 55 b 1 Cor. 10:16–17; 11:26 c Rom. 6:5–11

80. *How does the Lord's Supper differ from the Roman Catholic Mass?*

The Lord's Supper declares to us that all our sins are completely forgiven through the one sacrifice of Jesus Christ, which he himself accomplished on the cross once for all.[a] It also declares to us that the Holy Spirit grafts us into Christ,[b] who with his true body is now in heaven at the right hand of the Father[c] where he wants us to worship him.[d]

But the Mass teaches that the living and the dead do not have their sins forgiven through the suffering of Christ unless Christ is still offered for them daily by the priests. It also teaches that Christ is bodily present under the form of bread and wine where Christ is therefore to be worshiped.

Thus the Mass is basically nothing but a denial of the one sacrifice and suffering of Jesus Christ and a condemnable idolatry.

a John 19:30; Heb. 7:27; 9:12, 25–26; 10:10–18   b 1 Cor. 6:17; 10:16–17   c Acts 7:55–56; Heb. 1:3; 8:1   d Matt. 6:20–21; John 4:21–24; Phil. 3:20; Col. 3:1–3

81. *Who should come to the Lord's table?*

Those who are displeased with themselves because of their sins, but who nevertheless trust that their sins are pardoned and that their remaining weakness is covered by the suffering and death of Christ, and who also desire more and more to strengthen their faith and to lead a better life.

Hypocrites and those who are unrepentant, however, eat and drink judgment on themselves.[a]

a 1 Cor. 10:19–22; 11:26–32

82. *Should those be admitted to the Lord's Supper who show by what they profess and how they live that they are unbelieving and ungodly?*

No, that would dishonor God's covenant and bring down God's wrath upon the entire congregation.[a]

Therefore, according to the instruction of Christ and his apostles, the Christian church is duty-bound to exclude such people, by the official use of the keys of the kingdom, until they reform their lives.

a 1 Cor. 11:17–32; Ps. 50:14–16; Isa. 1:11–17

Lord's Day 31

83. *What are the keys of the kingdom?*

The preaching of the holy gospel and Christian discipline toward repentance.

Both of them open the kingdom of heaven to believers and close it to unbelievers.[a]

a Matt. 16:19; John 20:22–23

84. *How does preaching the holy gospel open and close the kingdom of heaven?*

According to the command of Christ: The kingdom of heaven is opened by proclaiming and publicly declaring to all believers, each and every one, that, as often as they accept the gospel promise in true faith, God, because of Christ's merit, truly forgives all their sins.

The kingdom of heaven is closed, however, by proclaiming and publicly declaring to unbelievers and hypocrites that, as long as they do not repent, the wrath of God and eternal condemnation rest on them.

God's judgment, both in this life and in the life to come, is based on this gospel testimony.[a]

a Matt. 16:19; John 3:31–36; 20:21–23

85. *How is the kingdom of heaven closed and opened by Christian discipline?*
According to the command of Christ: Those who, though called Christians, profess unchristian teachings or live unchristian lives, and who after repeated personal and loving admonitions, refuse to abandon their errors and evil ways, and who after being reported to the church, that is, to those ordained by the church for that purpose, fail to respond also to the church's admonitions—such persons the church excludes from the Christian community by withholding the sacraments from them, and God also excludes them from the kingdom of Christ.[a]

Such persons, when promising and demonstrating genuine reform, are received again as members of Christ and of his church.[b]

a Matt. 18:15–20; 1 Cor. 5:3–5, 11–13; 2 Thess. 3:14–15 b Luke 15:20–24; 2 Cor. 2:6–11

Lord's Day 32

86. *Since we have been delivered from our misery by grace through Christ without any merit of our own, why then should we do good works?*
Because Christ, having redeemed us by his blood, is also renewing us by his Spirit into his image, so that with our whole lives we may show that we are thankful to God for his benefits,[a] and that he may be praised through us,[b] and further, so that we may be assured of our faith by its fruits,[c] and by our godly living our neighbors may be won over to Christ.[d]

a Rom. 6:13; 12:1–2; 1 Pet. 2:5–10 b Matt. 5:16; 1 Cor. 6:19–20 c Matt. 7:17–18; Gal. 5:22–24; 2 Pet. 1:10–11 d Matt. 5:14–16; Rom. 14:17–19; 1 Pet. 2:12; 3:1–2

87. *Can those be saved who do not turn to God from their ungrateful and unrepentant ways?*

By no means. Scripture tells us that no unchaste person, no idolater, adulterer, thief, no covetous person, no drunkard, slanderer, robber, or the like will inherit the kingdom of God.[a]

a 1 Cor. 6:9–10; Gal. 5:19–21; Eph. 5:1–20; 1 John 3:14

Lord's Day 33

88. *What is involved in genuine repentance or conversion?*

Two things: the dying-away of the old self, and the rising-to-life of the new.[a]

a Rom. 6:1–11; 2 Cor. 5:17; Eph. 4:22–24; Col. 3:5–10

89. *What is the dying-away of the old self?*

To be genuinely sorry for sin and more and more to hate and run away from it.[a]

a Ps. 51:3–4, 17; Joel 2:12–13; Rom. 8:12–13; 2 Cor. 7:10

90. *What is the rising-to-life of the new self?*

Wholehearted joy in God through Christ[a] and a love and delight to live according to the will of God by doing every kind of good work.[b]

a Ps. 51:8, 12; Isa. 57:15; Rom. 5:1; 14:17 b Rom. 6:10–11; Gal. 2:20

91. *But what are good works?*

Only those which are done out of true faith,[a] conform to God's law,[b] and are done for his glory;[c] and not those based on our own opinion or human tradition.[d]

a John 15:5; Heb. 11:6 b Lev. 18:4; 1 Sam. 15:22; Eph. 2:10 c 1 Cor. 10:31 d Deut. 12:32; Isa. 29:13; Ezek. 20:18–19; Matt. 15:7–9

92. *What is God's law?*
God spoke all these words:

The First Commandment
I am the Lord your God, who brought you out of the land of Egypt, out of the house of slavery; you shall have no other gods before me.

The Second Commandment
You shall not make for yourself an idol, whether in the form of anything that is in heaven above, or that is on the earth beneath, or that is in the water under the earth. You shall not bow down to them or worship them; for I the Lord your God am a jealous God, punishing children for the iniquity of parents, to the third and fourth generation of those who reject me, but showing love to the thousandth generation of those who love me and keep my commandments.

The Third Commandment
You shall not make wrongful use of the name of the Lord your God, for the Lord will not acquit anyone who misuses his name.

The Fourth Commandment
Remember the Sabbath day and keep it holy. Six days you shall labor and do all your work. But the seventh day is a Sabbath to the Lord your God; you shall not do any work—you, your son or your daughter, your male or female servant, your livestock, or the alien resident in your towns. For in six days the Lord made the heaven and earth, the sea, and all that is in them, but rested

the seventh day; therefore the Lord blessed the Sabbath day and consecrated it.

The Fifth Commandment
Honor your father and your mother, so that your days may be long in the land that the Lord your God is giving to you.

The Sixth Commandment
You shall not murder.

The Seventh Commandment
You shall not commit adultery.

The Eighth Commandment
You shall not steal.

The Ninth Commandment
You shall not bear false witness against your neighbor.

The Tenth Commandment
You shall not covet your neighbor's house; you shall not covet your neighbor's wife, or male or female servant, or ox, or donkey, or anything that belongs to your neighbor.[a]

a Ex. 20:1–17; Deut. 5:6–21

93. *How are these commandments divided?*
Into two tables.

The first has four commandments, teaching us how we should live in relation to God.

The second has six commandments, teaching us what we owe our neighbor.[a]

a Matt. 22:37–39

94. *What does the Lord require in the first commandment?*

That I, not wanting to endanger my own salvation, avoid and shun all idolatry,[a] sorcery,[b] superstitious rites, and prayer to saints or to other creatures.[c]

That I rightly know the only true God,[d] trust him alone,[e] and look to God for every good thing[f] humbly[g] and patiently,[h] and love,[i] fear,[j] and honor[k] him with all my heart.

In short, that I renounce all created things rather than go against God's will in any way.[l]

a 1 Cor. 6:9–10; 10:5–14; 1 John 5:21 b Lev. 19:31; Deut. 18:9–12 c Matt. 4:10; Rev. 19:10; 22:8–9 d John 17:3 e Jer. 17:5, 7 f Ps. 104:27–28; James 1:17 g 1 Pet. 5:5–6 h Col. 1:11; Heb. 10:36 i Matt. 22:37 (Deut. 6:5) j Prov. 9:10; 1 Pet. 1:17 k Matt. 4:10 (Deut. 6:13) l Matt. 5:29–30; 10:37–39

95. *What is idolatry?*

Idolatry is having or inventing something in which one trusts in place of or alongside of the only true God, who has revealed himself in his Word.[a]

a 1 Chron. 16:26; Gal. 4:8–9; Eph. 5:5; Phil. 3:19

Lord's Day 35

96. *What is God's will for us in the second commandment?*

That we in no way make any image of God[a] nor worship him in any other way than has been commanded in God's Word.[b]

a Deut. 4:15–19; Isa. 40:18–25; Acts 17:29; Rom. 1:22–23 b Lev. 10:1–7; 1 Sam. 15:22–23; John 4:23–24

97. *May we then not make any image at all?*

God cannot and may not be visibly portrayed in any way. Although creatures may be portrayed, yet God forbids making or having such images in order to worship them or serve God through them.[a]

a Ex. 34:13–14, 17; 2 Kings 18:4–5

98. *But may not images, as books for the unlearned, be permitted in churches?*
No, we should not try to be wiser than God. He wants the Christian community instructed by the living preaching of his Word[a]—not by idols that cannot even talk.[b]

a Rom. 10:14–15, 17; 2 Tim. 3:16–17; 2 Pet. 1:19 b Jer. 10:8; Hab. 2:18–20

Lord's Day 36

99. *What is God's will for us in the third commandment?*
That we neither blaspheme nor misuse the name of God by cursing,[a] perjury,[b] or unnecessary oaths,[c] nor share in such horrible sins by being silent bystanders.[d]

In summary, we must use the holy name of God only with reverence and awe,[e] so that we may properly confess him,[f] call upon him,[g] and praise him in everything we do and say.[h]

a Lev. 24:10–17 b Lev. 19:12 c Matt. 5:37; James 5:12 d Lev. 5:1; Prov. 29:24 e Ps. 99:1–5; Jer. 4:2 f Matt. 10:32–33; Rom. 10:9–10 g Ps. 50:14–15; 1 Tim. 2:8 h Col. 3:17

100. *Is blasphemy of God's name by swearing and cursing really such serious sin that God is angry also with those who do not do all they can to help prevent and forbid it?*
Yes, indeed.[a] No sin is greater or provokes God's wrath more than blaspheming his name. That is why he commanded it to be punished with death.[b]

a Lev. 5:1 b Lev. 24:10–17

101. *But may we swear an oath in God's name if we do it reverently?*

Yes, when the government demands it, or when necessity requires it, in order to maintain and promote truth and trustworthiness for God's glory and our neighbor's good. Such oath-taking is grounded in God's Word[a] and was rightly used by the saints in the Old and New Testaments.[b]

a Deut. 6:13; 10:20; Jer. 4:1–2; Heb. 6:16 b Gen. 21:24; Josh. 9:15; 1 Kings 1:29–30; Rom. 1:9; 2 Cor. 1:23

102. *May we also swear by saints or other created things?*

No. A legitimate oath is calling upon God as the one who knows my heart to witness to the truth and to punish me if I swear falsely.[a] No created thing is worthy of such honor.[b]

a Rom. 9:1; 2 Cor. 1:23 b Matt. 5:34–37; 23:16–22; James 5:12

Lord's Day 38

103. *What is God's will for you in the fourth commandment?*

First, that the gospel ministry and schools for it be maintained,[a] and that, especially on the festive day of rest, I diligently attend the assembly of God's people[b] to learn what God's Word teaches,[c] to participate in the sacraments,[d] to pray to the Lord publicly,[e] and to bring Christian offerings for the poor.[f]

Second, that every day of my life I rest from my evil ways, let the Lord work in me through his Spirit, and so begin in this life the eternal Sabbath.[g]

a Deut. 6:4–9, 20–25; 1 Cor. 9:13–14; 2 Tim. 2:2; 3:13–17; Titus 1:5 b Deut. 12:5–12; Ps. 40:9–10; 68:26; Acts 2:42–47; Heb. 10:23–25 c Rom. 10:14–17; 1 Cor. 14:31–32; 1 Tim. 4:13 d 1 Cor. 11:23–25 e Col. 3:16; 1 Tim. 2:1 f Ps. 50:14; 1 Cor. 16:2; 2 Cor. 8:1–9:15 g Isa. 66:23; Heb. 4:9–11

104. *What is God's will for you in the fifth commandment?*

That I show honor, love, and faithfulness to my father and mother and all those in authority over me; submit myself with proper obedience to all their good teaching and discipline;[a] and also that I be patient with their failings[b]—for by their hand God wills to rule us.[c]

a Ex. 21:17; Prov. 1:8; 4:1; Rom. 13:1–2; Eph. 5:21–22; 6:1–9; Col. 3:18–4:1 b Prov. 20:20; 23:22; 1 Pet. 2:18 c Matt. 22:21; Rom. 13:1–8; Eph. 6:1–9; Col. 3:18–21

Lord's Day 40

105. *What is God's will for you in the sixth commandment?*

I am not to belittle, hate, insult, or kill my neighbor—not by my thoughts, my words, my look or gesture, and certainly not by actual deeds—and I am not to be party to this in others;[a] rather, I am to put away all desire for revenge.[b] I am not to harm or recklessly endanger myself either.[c]

Prevention of murder is also why government is armed with the sword.[d]

a Gen. 9:6; Lev. 19:17–18; Matt. 5:21–22; 26:52 b Prov. 25:21–22; Matt. 18:35; Rom. 12:19; Eph. 4:26 c Matt. 4:7; 26:52; Rom. 13:11–14 d Gen. 9:6; Ex. 21:14; Rom. 13:4

106. *Does this commandment refer only to murder?*

By forbidding murder God teaches us that he hates the root of murder: envy, hatred, anger, vengefulness.[a] In God's sight all such are disguised forms of murder.[b]

a Prov. 14:30; Rom. 1:29; 12:19; Gal. 5:19–21; 1 John 2:9–11 b 1 John 3:15

107. *Is it enough then that we do not murder our neighbor in any such way?*

No. By condemning envy, hatred, and anger God wants us to love our neighbors as ourselves,[a] to be patient, peace-loving, gentle, merciful, and friendly toward them,[b] to protect them from harm as much as we can, and to do good even to our enemies.[c]

a Matt. 7:12; 22:39; Rom. 12:10 *b* Matt. 5:3–12; Luke 6:36; Rom. 12:10, 18; Gal. 6:1–2; Eph. 4:2; Col. 3:12; 1 Pet. 3:8 *c* Ex. 23:4–5; Matt. 5:44–45; Rom. 12:20–21 (Prov. 25:21–22)

Lord's Day 41

108. *What is God's will for us in the seventh commandment?*

That God condemns all unchastity,[a] and that we should therefore detest it wholeheartedly[b] and live decent and chaste lives,[c] within or outside of the holy state of marriage.

a Lev. 18:30; Eph. 5:3–5 *b* Jude 22–23 *c* 1 Cor. 7:1–9; 1 Thess. 4:3–8; Heb. 13:4

109. *Does God, in this commandment, forbid only such scandalous sins as adultery?*

We are temples of the Holy Spirit, body and soul, and God wants both to be kept clean and holy. That is why God forbids all unchaste actions, looks, talk, thoughts, or desires,[a] and whatever may incite someone to them.[b]

a Matt. 5:27–29; 1 Cor. 6:18–20; Eph. 5:3–4 *b* 1 Cor. 15:33; Eph. 5:18

Lord's Day 42

110. *What does God forbid in the eighth commandment?*

He forbids not only outright theft and robbery, which governing authorities punish,[a] but in God's sight theft also includes all evil tricks and schemes designed to get our neighbor's goods for ourselves, whether by force or means that appear legitimate,[b] such as inaccurate measurements of weight, size, or volume; fraudulent merchandising; counterfeit money; excessive interest; or any other means forbidden by God.[c]

In addition God forbids all greed[d] and pointless squandering of his gifts.[e]

a Ex. 22:1; 1 Cor. 5:9–10; 6:9–10 b Mic. 6:9–11; Luke 3:14; James 5:1–6 c Deut. 25:13–16; Ps. 15:5; Prov. 11:1; 12:22; Ezek. 45:9–12; Luke 6:35 d Luke 12:15; Eph. 5:5 e Prov. 21:20; 23:20–21; Luke 16:10–13

111. *What does God require of you in this commandment?*
That I do whatever I can and may for my neighbor's good, that I treat others as I would like them to treat me, and that I work faithfully so that I may help the needy in their hardship.[a]

a Isa. 58:5–10; Matt. 7:12; Gal. 6:9–10; Eph. 4:28

Lord's Day 43

112. *What is God's will for you in the ninth commandment?*
That I never give false testimony against anyone, twist no one's words, not gossip or slander, nor join in condemning anyone rashly or without a hearing.[a]

Rather, I should avoid, under penalty of God's wrath,[b] every kind of lying and deceit as the very works of the devil; and, in court and everywhere else, I should love the truth, speak it candidly, and openly acknowledge it.[c]

And I should do what I can to defend and advance my neighbor's honor and reputation.[d]

a Ps. 15:1–5; Prov. 19:5; Matt. 7:1; Luke 6:37; Rom. 1:28–32 b Lev. 19:11–12; Prov. 12:22; 13:5; John 8:44; Rev. 21:8a c 1 Cor. 13:6; Eph. 4:25 d 1 Pet. 3:8–9; 4:8

113. *What is God's will for you in the tenth commandment?*
That not even the slightest desire or thought contrary to any one of God's commandments should ever arise in our hearts.

Rather, with all our hearts we should always hate sin and delight in all righteousness.[a]

a Ps. 19:7–14; 139:23–24; Rom. 7:7–8

114. *But can those converted to God keep these commandments perfectly?*
No. In this life even the holiest have only a small beginning of this obedience.[a]

Nevertheless, with all seriousness of purpose, they do begin to live according to all, not only some, of God's commandments.[b]

a Eccles. 7:20; Rom. 7:14–15; 1 Cor. 13:9; 1 John 1:8–10 b Ps. 1:1–2; Rom. 7:22–25; Phil. 3:12–16

115. *Since no one in this life can keep the Ten Commandments perfectly, why does God want them preached so pointedly?*
First, so that all our life long we may more and more come to know our sinful nature and thus more eagerly seek the forgiveness of sins and righteousness in Christ.[a]

Second, so that we may never stop striving and never stop praying to God for the grace of the Holy Spirit, so that we may be renewed more and more after God's image, until after this life we reach our goal: perfection.[b]

a Ps. 32:5; Rom. 3:19–26; 7:7, 24–25; 1 John 1:9 b 1 Cor. 9:24; Phil. 3:12–14; 1 John 3:1–3

116. *Why do Christians need to pray?*

Because prayer is the most important part of the thankfulness God requires of us.[a]

And also because God will give his grace and Holy Spirit only to those who continually and with heartfelt longing ask God for these gifts and thank him for them.[b]

a Ps. 50:14–15; 116:12–19; 1 Thess. 5:16–18 b Matt. 7:7–8; Luke 11:9–13

117. *How does God want us to pray so that he will listen to us?*

First, we must pray from the heart to no other than the one true God, who has revealed himself to us in his Word, asking for everything he has commanded us to ask of him.[a]

Second, we must fully recognize our need and misery, so that we humble ourselves in God's majestic presence.[b]

Third, we must rest on this unshakable foundation: even though we do not deserve it, God will surely listen to our prayer because of Christ our Lord, as he has promised us in his Word.[c]

a Ps. 145:18–20; John 4:22–24; Rom. 8:26–27; James 1:5; 1 John 5:14–15 b 2 Chron. 7:14; Ps. 2:11; 34:18; 62:8; Isa. 66:2; Rev. 4:1–11 c Dan. 9:17–19; Matt. 7:8; John 14:13–14; 16:23; Rom. 10:13; James 1:6

118. *What has God commanded us to ask of him?*

Everything we need, spiritually and physically,[a] as embraced in the prayer Christ our Lord himself taught us.

a James 1:17; Matt. 6:33

119. *What is this prayer?*

Our Father who is in heaven, hallowed be your name.

Your kingdom come.

Your will be done, on earth as it is in heaven.

Give us this day our daily bread,

and forgive us our debts, as we forgive our debtors.

And lead us not into temptation, but deliver us

from evil.

For yours is the kingdom and the power and the glory,

forever. Amen.[a]

a Matt. 6:9–13; Luke 11:2–4

Lord's Day 46

120. *Why has Christ commanded us to address God as "our Father"?*

To awaken in us at the very beginning of our prayer what should be basic to our prayer—a childlike reverence and trust that through Christ God has become our Father, and will much less refuse to give us what we ask in faith than will our parents refuse us the things of this life.[a]

a Matt. 7:9–11; Luke 11:11–13

121. *Why the words "who is in heaven"?*

These words teach us not to think of God's heavenly majesty in an earthly way,[a] and to expect from his almighty power everything needed for body and soul.[b]

a Jer. 23:23–24; Acts 17:24–25 b Matt. 6:25–34; Rom. 8:31–32

122. *What does the first petition mean?*

"Hallowed be your name" means: Help us to truly know you,[a] to honor, glorify, and praise you for all your works and for all that shines forth from them: your almighty power, wisdom, kindness, justice, mercy, and truth.[b]

And it means: Help us to direct all our living—what we think, say, and do—so that your name will never be blasphemed because of us but always honored and praised.[c]

a Jer. 9:23–24; 31:33–34; Matt. 16:17; John 17:3 b Ex. 34:5–8; Ps. 145:1–21; Jer. 32:16–20; Luke 1:46–55, 68–75; Rom. 11:33–36 c Ps. 115:1; Matt. 5:16

Lord's Day 48

123. *What does the second petition mean?*

"Your kingdom come" means: Rule us by your Word and Spirit in such a way that more and more we submit to you.[a] Preserve and increase your church.[b] Destroy the devil's work; destroy every force which revolts against you and every conspiracy against your holy Word.[c]

Do all this until your kingdom fully comes, when you will be all in all.[d]

a Ps. 119:5, 105; 143:10; Matt. 6:33 b Ps. 122:6–9; Matt. 16:18; Acts 2:42–47 c Rom. 16:20; 1 John 3:8 d Rom. 8:22–23; 1 Cor. 15:28; Rev. 22:17, 20

124. *What does the third petition mean?*

"Your will be done on earth as it is in heaven" means: Help us and all people to renounce our own wills and without any back talk to obey your will, for it alone is good.[a]

Help everyone carry out his office and calling,[b] as willingly and faithfully as the angels in heaven.[c]

a Matt. 7:21; 16:24–26; Luke 22:42; Rom. 12:1–2; Titus 2:11–12 b 1 Cor. 7:17–24; Eph. 6:5–9
c Ps. 103:20–21

Lord's Day 50

125. *What does the fourth petition mean?*

"Give us this day our daily bread" means: Provide for all our physical needs[a] so that we may recognize that you are the only source of everything good,[b] and that neither our care and work nor your gifts can do us any good without your blessing.[c] Therefore may we withdraw our trust from all creatures and place it in you alone.[d]

a Ps. 104:27–30; 145:15–16; Matt. 6:25–34 b Acts 14:17; 17:25; James 1:17 c Deut. 8:3; Ps. 37:16;
127:1–2; 1 Cor. 15:58 d Ps. 55:22; 62:1–12; 146:1–10; Jer. 17:5–8; Heb. 13:5–6

Lord's Day 51

126. *What does the fifth petition mean?*

"Forgive us our debts as we forgive our debtors" means: Because of Christ's blood, do not impute to us, poor sinners that we are, any of the transgressions we do or the evil that constantly clings to us.[a]

Forgive us just as we are fully determined, as evidence of your grace in us, wholeheartedly to forgive our neighbors.[b]

a Ps. 51:1–7; 143:2; Rom. 8:1; 1 John 2:1–2 b Matt. 6:14–15; 18:21–35

Lord's Day 52

127. *What does the sixth petition mean?*

"And lead us not into temptation, but deliver us from evil" means: We are so weak that we cannot stand on our own for a moment,[a] and our sworn enemies—the devil,[b] the world,[c] and our own flesh[d]—never stop attacking us.

And so, Lord, uphold us and make us strong by the power of your Holy Spirit, so that we may not be defeated in this spiritual fight,[e] but may firmly resist our enemies until we finally win the complete victory.[f]

a Ps. 103:14–16; John 15:1–5 b 2 Cor. 11:14; Eph. 6:10–13; 1 Pet. 5:8 c John 15:18–21
d Rom. 7:23; Gal. 5:17 e Matt. 10:19–20; 26:41; Mark 13:33; Rom. 5:3–5 f 1 Cor. 10:13;
1 Thess. 3:13; 5:23

128. *How do you conclude this prayer?*

"For yours is the kingdom and the power and the glory forever."

This means we have made all these petitions of you because, as our all-powerful king, you are both willing and able to give us all that is good;[a] and because your holy name, and not we ourselves, should receive all the praise, forever.[b]

a Rom. 10:11–13; 2 Pet. 2:9 b Ps. 115:1; John 14:13

129. *What does that little word "Amen" express?*

"Amen" means: This shall truly and surely be!

For it is much more certain that God has heard my prayer than I feel in my heart that I desire such things from him.[a]

a Isa. 65:24; 2 Cor. 1:20; 2 Tim. 2:13

The Westminster Larger Catechism

INTRODUCTION

The Westminster Catechisms (both written in 1647) offer questions and answers covering a full range of doctrinal topics, but with special focus on the doctrine of salvation and the Christian life. The voice of the catechisms is, for the most part, in the third person, declaring what God's Word says, instead of the first person, sharing what Christians believe. Nonetheless, passages often carry a tone of praise, awe, or exhortation.

The catechisms are designed to be companion texts to the Westminster Confession of Faith. Together they form a relative rarity in the Reformation: a confessional-catechetical package designed to fit together. In fact, parallel presentations of the 1646 Confession and the 1647 Catechisms show extensive verbal dependence of the later texts on the earlier: the Shorter Catechism leans on the Larger; the Larger Catechism is derived largely from the Confession.

Of these three texts, the Larger Catechism is the least known and most forgotten in the church today. The Larger Catechism is actually the lengthiest text among the Westminster Standards. What is more, its statements benefit from an additional year of the Westminster Assembly's debates. The Larger Catechism offers the ripest fruit of the assembly's deliberations but lives in the shadows of the Confession of Faith. Admittedly, its formulations mostly mirror that of the confession, yet there are places in which it further develops its ideas in the confession, not least in the ethical realm. In fact, unique to the Larger Catechism is a thoughtful interpretive guide to the Ten Commandments, putting into words the principles of interpretation commonly used among Reformed theologians.

The structure of the catechisms is at once more straightforward yet also subtler than that of the confession. On the face of both catechisms is a programmatic statement: "What do the Scriptures principally teach? The Scriptures principally teach, what man is to believe concerning God, and what duty God requires of man" (WLC 5; WSC 3). The remainder of each catechism discusses who God is and what he has done. The catechisms then explain what Christians must do in response.

Nonetheless, if this is their overt structure, it is also true that both catechisms follow a traditional pattern of expounding the Apostles' Creed (although the creed is not mentioned explicitly), the Ten Commandments, and the Lord's Prayer. This structure is significant, as the focus on the law and on Christian piety gives these texts moral and spiritual emphases not found in the Westminster Confession. As well, the Larger Catechism offers an ecclesial perspective distinct from the more individualist emphasis of the Shorter Catechism, resulting in an accent on the practical importance of church life for the Christian community.

THE WESTMINSTER
LARGER CATECHISM

1. *What is the chief and highest end of man?*
   Man's chief and highest end is to glorify God,[a] and fully to enjoy
   him forever.[b]

   a Rom. 11:36; 1 Cor. 6:20; 1 Cor. 10:31; Ps. 86:9, 12   b Ps. 73:24–28; John 17:21–23; Ps. 16:5–11;
   Rev. 21:3–4

2. *How doth it appear that there is a God?*
   The very light of nature in man, and the works of God, declare
   plainly that there is a God;[a] but his Word and Spirit only do sufficiently and effectually reveal him unto men for their salvation.[b]

   a Rom. 1:19–20; Acts 17:28; Ps. 19:1–3   b 1 Cor. 2:9–10; 1 Cor. 1:20–21; 2 Tim. 3:15–17; Isa. 59:21

3. *What is the Word of God?*
   The Holy Scriptures of the Old and New Testament are the Word
   of God,[a] the only rule of faith and obedience.[b]

   a 2 Tim. 3:16; 2 Pet. 1:19–21; 2 Pet. 3:2, 15–16; Matt. 19:4–5; Gen. 2:24   b Deut. 4:2; Eph. 2:20;
   Rev. 22:18–19; Isa. 8:20; Luke 16:29, 31; Gal. 1:8–9; 2 Tim. 3:15–16

4. *How doth it appear that the Scriptures are the Word of God?*
   The Scriptures manifest themselves to be the Word of God, by their
   majesty[a] and purity;[b] by the consent of all the parts,[c] and the scope
   of the whole, which is to give all glory to God;[d] by their light and
   power to convince and convert sinners, to comfort and build up

believers unto salvation:[e] but the Spirit of God bearing witness by and with the Scriptures in the heart of man, is alone able fully to persuade it that they are the very Word of God.[f]

a Hos. 8:12; 1 Cor. 2:6–7, 13; Ps. 119:18, 129 b Ps. 12:6; Ps. 119:140 c Luke 24:27; Acts 10:43; Acts 26:22 d Rom. 3:19, 27; Rom. 16:25–27; 2 Cor. 3:6–11 e Acts 18:28; Heb. 4:12; James 1:18; Ps. 19:7–9; Rom. 15:4; Acts 20:32 f John 16:13–14; 1 John 2:20, 27; John 20:31

5. *What do the Scriptures principally teach?*
The Scriptures principally teach, what man is to believe concerning God,[a] and what duty God requires of man.[b]

a Gen. 1:1; Ex. 34:5–7; Ps. 48:1; John 20:31; 2 Tim. 3:15 b Deut. 10:12–13; 2 Tim. 3:15–17; Acts 16:30–31

What Man Ought to Believe concerning God

6. *What do the Scriptures make known of God?*
The Scriptures make known what God is,[a] the persons in the Godhead,[b] his decrees,[c] and the execution of his decrees.[d]

a John 4:24; Ex. 34:6–7; Isa. 40:18, 21–23, 25, 28; Heb. 11:6 b Matt. 3:16–17; Deut. 6:4–6; 1 Cor. 8:4, 6; Matt. 28:19–20; 2 Cor. 13:14 c Acts 15:14–15, 18; Isa. 46:9–10 d Acts 4:27–28

7. *What is God?*
God is a Spirit,[a] in and of himself infinite in being,[b] glory,[c] blessedness,[d] and perfection;[e] all-sufficient,[f] eternal,[g] unchangeable,[h] incomprehensible,[i] everywhere present,[j] almighty,[k] knowing all things,[l] most wise,[m] most holy,[n] most just,[o] most merciful and gracious, long-suffering, and abundant in goodness and truth.[p]

a John 4:24 b Ex. 3:14; Job 11:7–9; Ps. 145:3; Ps. 147:5 c Acts 7:2 d 1 Tim. 6:15 e Matt. 5:48 f Ex. 3:14; Gen. 17:1; Rom. 11:35–36 g Ps. 90:2; Deut. 33:27 h Mal. 3:6 i 1 Kings 8:27; Ps. 145:3; Rom. 11:34 j Ps. 139:1–13 k Rev. 4:8; Gen. 17:1; Matt. 19:26 l Heb. 4:13; Ps. 147:5 m Rom. 11:33–34; Rom. 16:27 n 1 Pet. 1:15–16; Rev. 15:4; Isa. 6:3 o Deut. 32:4; Rom. 3:5, 26 p Ex. 34:6; Ps. 117:2; Deut. 32:4

8. *Are there more Gods than one?*

There is but one only,[a] the living and true God.[b]

a Deut. 6:4; 1 Cor. 8:4, 6; Isa. 45:21–22; Isa. 44:6 b Jer. 10:10; John 17:3; 1 Thess. 1:9; 1 John 5:20

9. *How many persons are there in the Godhead?*

There be three persons in the Godhead, the Father, the Son, and the Holy Ghost;[a] and these three are one true, eternal God, the same in substance, equal in power and glory; although distinguished by their personal properties.[b]

a Matt. 3:16–17; Matt. 28:19; 2 Cor. 13:14 b John 1:1; Gen. 1:1–3; John 17:5; John 10:30; Ps. 45:6; Heb. 1:8–9; Acts 5:3–4; Rom. 9:5; Col. 2:9

10. *What are the personal properties of the three persons in the Godhead?*

It is proper to the Father to beget the Son,[a] and to the Son to be begotten of the Father,[b] and to the Holy Ghost to proceed from the Father and the Son from all eternity.[c]

a Heb. 1:5–6, 8 b John 1:14, 18 c John 15:26; Gal. 4:6

11. *How doth it appear that the Son and the Holy Ghost are God equal with the Father?*

The Scriptures manifest that the Son and the Holy Ghost are God equal with the Father, ascribing unto them such names,[a] attributes,[b] works,[c] and worship,[d] as are proper to God only.

a Isa. 6:3, 5, 8; John 12:41; Acts 28:25; 1 John 5:20; Acts 5:3–4 b John 1:1; Isa. 9:6; John 2:24–25; 1 Cor. 2:10–11 c Col. 1:16; Gen. 1:2 d Matt. 28:19; 2 Cor. 13:14

12. *What are the decrees of God?*

God's decrees are the wise, free, and holy acts of the counsel of his will,[a] whereby, from all eternity, he hath, for his own glory, unchangeably foreordained whatsoever comes to pass in time,[b] especially concerning angels and men.

a Isa. 45:6–7; Eph. 1:11; Rom. 11:33; Rom. 9:14–15, 18 b Ps. 33:11; Isa. 14:24; Acts 2:23; Acts 4:27–28; Rom. 9:22–23; Eph. 1:4, 11

13. *What hath God especially decreed concerning angels and men?*

God, by an eternal and immutable decree, out of his mere love, for the praise of his glorious grace, to be manifested in due time, hath elected some angels to glory;[a] and in Christ hath chosen some men to eternal life, and the means thereof:[b] and also, according to his sovereign power, and the unsearchable counsel of his own will (whereby he extendeth or withholdeth favor as he pleaseth) hath passed by and foreordained the rest to dishonor and wrath, to be for their sin inflicted, to the praise of the glory of his justice.[c]

a 1 Tim. 5:21 b Eph. 1:4–6; Eph. 2:10; 2 Thess. 2:13–14; 1 Pet. 1:2 c Rom. 9:17–18, 21–22; Matt. 11:25–26; 2 Tim. 2:20; Jude 4; 1 Pet. 2:8

14. *How doth God execute his decrees?*

God executeth his decrees in the works of creation and providence,[a] according to his infallible foreknowledge, and the free and immutable counsel of his own will.[b]

a Rev. 4:11; Isa. 40:12–31 b Eph. 1:11; Ps. 148:8; Dan. 4:35; Acts 4:24–28

15. *What is the work of creation?*

The work of creation is that wherein God did in the beginning, by the word of his power, make of nothing the world, and all things therein, for himself, within the space of six days, and all very good.[a]

a Gen. 1:1–31; Ps. 33:6, 9; Heb. 11:3; Rev. 4:11; Rom. 11:36

16. *How did God create angels?*

God created all the angels[a] spirits,[b] immortal,[c] holy,[d] excelling in knowledge,[e] mighty in power,[f] to execute his commandments, and to praise his name,[g] yet subject to change.[h]

a Col. 1:16 *b* Ps. 104:4 *c* Matt. 22:30; Luke 20:36 *d* Matt. 25:31 *e* 2 Sam. 14:17; Matt. 24:36
f 2 Thess. 1:7 *g* Ps. 91:11–12; Ps. 103:20–21 *h* 2 Pet. 2:4

17. *How did God create man?*

After God had made all other creatures, he created man male and female;[a] formed the body of the man of the dust of the ground,[b] and the woman of the rib of the man,[c] endued them with living, reasonable, and immortal souls;[d] made them after his own image,[e] in knowledge,[f] righteousness, and holiness;[g] having the law of God written in their hearts,[h] and power to fulfill it,[i] and dominion over the creatures;[j] yet subject to fall.[k]

a Gen. 1:27; Matt. 19:4 *b* Gen. 2:7 *c* Gen. 2:22 *d* Gen. 2:7; Job 35:11; Eccles. 12:7; Matt.
10:28; Luke 23:43 *e* Gen. 1:26–27 *f* Col. 3:10 *g* Eph. 4:24 *h* Rom. 2:14–15 *i* Eccles. 7:29
j Gen. 1:28; Ps. 8:6–8 *k* Gen. 2:16–17; Gen. 3:6; Eccles. 7:29

18. *What are God's works of providence?*

God's works of providence are his most holy,[a] wise,[b] and powerful preserving[c] and governing[d] all his creatures; ordering them, and all their actions,[e] to his own glory.[f]

a Ps. 145:17; Lev. 21:8 *b* Ps. 104:24; Isa. 28:29 *c* Heb. 1:3; Ps. 36:6; Neh. 9:6 *d* Ps. 103:19; Job
38:1–41:34; Ps. 145:14–16 *e* Matt. 10:29–31; Gen. 45:7; Ps. 135:6 *f* Rom. 11:36; Isa. 63:14

19. *What is God's providence towards the angels?*

God by his providence permitted some of the angels, willfully and irrecoverably, to fall into sin and damnation,[a] limiting and ordering that, and all their sins, to his own glory;[b] and established the rest in holiness and happiness;[c] employing them all,[d] at his pleasure, in the administrations of his power, mercy, and justice.[e]

a Jude 6; 2 Pet. 2:4; Heb. 2:16; John 8:44 b Job 1:12; Matt. 8:31; Luke 10:17 c 1 Tim. 5:21; Mark 8:38; Heb. 12:22 d Ps. 103:20; Ps. 104:4 e Heb. 1:14; 2 Kings 19:35

20. *What was the providence of God toward man in the estate in which he was created?*

The providence of God toward man in the estate in which he was created, was the placing him in paradise, appointing him to dress it, giving him liberty to eat of the fruit of the earth;[a] putting the creatures under his dominion,[b] and ordaining marriage for his help;[c] affording him communion with himself;[d] instituting the Sabbath;[e] entering into a covenant of life with him, upon condition of personal, perfect, and perpetual obedience,[f] of which the tree of life was a pledge;[g] and forbidding to eat of the tree of the knowledge of good and evil, upon the pain of death.[h]

a Gen. 2:8, 15–16 b Gen. 1:28 c Gen. 2:18; Matt. 19:3–9; Eph. 5:31 d Gen. 1:26–29; Gen. 3:8 e Gen. 2:3; Ex. 20:11 f Gen. 2:16–17; Gal. 3:12; Rom. 10:5 g Gen. 2:9; Gen. 3:22–24 h Gen. 2:17; James 2:10

21. *Did man continue in that estate wherein God at first created him?*

Our first parents being left to the freedom of their own will, through the temptation of Satan, transgressed the commandment of God in eating the forbidden fruit; and thereby fell from the estate of innocency wherein they were created.[a]

a Gen. 3:6–8, 13; Eccles. 7:29; 2 Cor. 11:3

22. *Did all mankind fall in that first transgression?*

The covenant being made with Adam as a public person, not for himself only, but for his posterity, all mankind descending from him by ordinary generation,[a] sinned in him, and fell with him in that first transgression.[b]

a Acts 17:26; Rom. 3:23 *b* Gen. 2:16–17; James 2:10; Rom. 5:12–20; 1 Cor. 15:21–22

23. *Into what estate did the fall bring mankind?*
The fall brought mankind into an estate of sin and misery.[a]

a Gen. 3:16–19; Rom. 5:12; Eph. 2:1; Rom. 3:16, 23

24. *What is sin?*
Sin is any want of conformity unto, or transgression of, any law of God, given as a rule to the reasonable creature.[a]

a Lev. 5:17; James 4:17; 1 John 3:4; Gal. 3:10, 12

25. *Wherein consisteth the sinfulness of that estate whereinto man fell?*
The sinfulness of that estate whereinto man fell, consisteth in the guilt of Adam's first sin,[a] the want of that righteousness wherein he was created, and the corruption of his nature, whereby he is utterly indisposed, disabled, and made opposite unto all that is spiritually good, and wholly inclined to all evil, and that continually;[b] which is commonly called original sin, and from which do proceed all actual transgressions.[c]

a Rom. 5:12, 19; 1 Cor. 15:22 *b* Rom. 3:10–19; Eph. 2:1–3; Rom. 5:6; Rom. 8:7–8; Gen. 6:5; Col. 3:10; Eph. 4:24 *c* James 1:14–15; Ps. 53:1–3; Matt. 15:19; Rom. 3:10–18, 23; Gal. 5:19–21

26. *How is original sin conveyed from our first parents unto their posterity?*
Original sin is conveyed from our first parents unto their posterity by natural generation, so as all that proceed from them in that way are conceived and born in sin.[a]

a Ps. 51:5; Job 14:4; John 3:6

27. *What misery did the fall bring upon mankind?*

The fall brought upon mankind the loss of communion with God,[a] his displeasure and curse;[b] so as we are by nature children of wrath,[c] bond slaves to Satan,[d] and justly liable to all punishments in this world, and that which is to come.[e]

a Gen. 3:8, 10, 24; John 8:34, 42, 44; Eph. 2:12 b Gen. 3:16–19; Job 5:7; Eccles. 2:22–23; Rom. 8:18–23 c Eph. 2:2–3; John 3:36; Rom. 1:18; Eph. 5:6 d 2 Tim. 2:26 e Gen. 2:17; Lam. 3:39; Rom. 6:23; Matt. 25:41, 46; Jude 7

28. *What are the punishments of sin in this world?*

The punishments of sin in this world are either inward, as blindness of mind,[a] a reprobate sense,[b] strong delusions,[c] hardness of heart,[d] horror of conscience,[e] and vile affections;[f] or outward, as the curse of God upon the creatures for our sakes,[g] and all other evils that befall us in our bodies, names, estates, relations, and employments;[h] together with death itself.[i]

a Eph. 4:18 b Rom. 1:28 c 2 Thess. 2:11 d Rom. 2:5 e Isa. 33:14; Gen. 4:13; Matt. 27:4 f Rom. 1:26 g Gen. 3:17 h Deut. 28:15–68 i Rom. 6:21, 23

29. *What are the punishments of sin in the world to come?*

The punishments of sin in the world to come, are everlasting separation from the comfortable presence of God, and most grievous torments in soul and body, without intermission, in hellfire forever.[a]

a 2 Thess. 1:9; Mark 9:43–44, 46, 48; Luke 16:24, 26; Matt. 25:41, 46; Rev. 14:11; John 3:36

30. *Doth God leave all mankind to perish in the estate of sin and misery?*

God doth not leave all men to perish in the estate of sin and misery,[a] into which they fell by the breach of the first covenant, commonly called the covenant of works;[b] but of his mere love and mercy delivereth his elect out of it, and bringeth them into an estate of salvation by the second covenant, commonly called the covenant of grace.[c]

a 1 Thess. 5:9 b Gen. 3:17; Rom. 5:12, 15; Gal. 3:10, 12 c Titus 3:4–7; Gal. 3:21; Rom. 3:20–22; 2 Thess. 2:13–14; Acts 13:48; Eph. 1:4–5

31. *With whom was the covenant of grace made?*
The covenant of grace was made with Christ as the second Adam, and in him with all the elect as his seed.[a]

a Gal. 3:16; Rom. 5:15–21; Isa. 53:10–11; Isa. 59:20–21

32. *How is the grace of God manifested in the second covenant?*
The grace of God is manifested in the second covenant, in that he freely provideth and offereth to sinners a Mediator,[a] and life and salvation by him;[b] and requiring faith as the condition to interest them in him,[c] promiseth and giveth his Holy Spirit[d] to all his elect, to work in them that faith,[e] with all other saving graces;[f] and to enable them unto all holy obedience,[g] as the evidence of the truth of their faith[h] and thankfulness to God,[i] and as the way which he hath appointed them to salvation.[j]

a Gen. 3:15; Isa. 42:6; John 3:16; John 6:27; 1 Tim. 2:5 b 1 John 5:11–12 c John 3:16, 36; John 1:12 d Isa. 59:21; Luke 11:13; John 14:16–20; 1 Cor. 12:13; Rom. 8:4, 9, 11, 14–16 e 2 Cor. 4:13; 1 Cor. 12:3, 9; Eph. 2:8–10; Acts 16:14; 2 Pet. 1:1 f Gal. 5:22–23 g Ezek. 36:27; Eph. 2:10 h James 2:18, 22 i 2 Cor. 5:14–15 j Eph. 2:10; Titus 2:14

33. *Was the covenant of grace always administered after one and the same manner?*
The covenant of grace was not always administered after the same manner, but the administrations of it under the old testament were different from those under the new.[a]

a 2 Cor. 3:6–9; Heb. 8:7–13

34. How was the covenant of grace administered under the old testament?

The covenant of grace was administered under the old testament, by promises,[a] prophecies,[b] sacrifices,[c] circumcision,[d] the Passover,[e] and other types and ordinances, which did all foresignify Christ then to come, and were for that time sufficient to build up the elect in faith in the promised Messiah,[f] by whom they then had full remission of sin, and eternal salvation.[g]

a Rom. 15:8; Gen. 3:15; Gen. 12:1–3; Gen. 15:5 b Acts 3:20, 24; Isa. 52:13–53:12 c Heb. 10:1; Lev. 1:1–7:38 d Rom. 4:11; Gen. 17:1–14 e 1 Cor. 5:7; Ex. 12:1–51 f Heb. 8:1–10:39; Heb. 11:13 g Gal. 3:7–9, 14

35. How is the covenant of grace administered under the new testament?

Under the new testament, when Christ the substance was exhibited, the same covenant of grace was and still is to be administered in the preaching of the Word,[a] and the administration of the sacraments of baptism[b] and the Lord's Supper;[c] in which grace and salvation are held forth in more fullness, evidence, and efficacy, to all nations.[d]

a Luke 24:47–48; Matt. 28:19–20 b Matt. 28:19–20 c Matt. 26:28; 1 Cor. 11:23–25 d Rom. 1:16; 2 Cor. 3:6–9; Heb. 8:6, 10–11; Matt. 28:19; Eph. 3:1–12

36. Who is the Mediator of the covenant of grace?

The only Mediator of the covenant of grace is the Lord Jesus Christ,[a] who, being the eternal Son of God, of one substance and equal with the Father,[b] in the fullness of time became man,[c] and so was and continues to be God and man, in two entire distinct natures, and one person, forever.[d]

a 1 Tim. 2:5; John 14:6; Acts 4:12 b John 1:1, 14, 18; John 10:30; Phil. 2:6; Ps. 2:7; Matt. 3:17; Matt. 17:5 c Gal. 4:4; Matt. 1:23; John 1:14 d Luke 1:35; Acts 1:11; Rom. 9:5; Col. 2:9; Heb. 7:24–25; Heb. 13:8; Phil. 2:5–11

37. How did Christ, being the Son of God, become man?

Christ the Son of God became man, by taking to himself a true body, and a reasonable soul,[a] being conceived by the power of the Holy Ghost in the womb of the virgin Mary, of her substance, and born of her,[b] yet without sin.[c]

a John 1:14; Matt. 26:38; Phil. 2:7; Heb. 2:14–17; Luke 2:40, 52; John 11:33   b Luke 1:27, 31, 35; Gal. 4:4   c Heb. 4:15; Heb. 7:26; 2 Cor. 5:21; 1 John 3:5

38. Why was it requisite that the Mediator should be God?

It was requisite that the Mediator should be God, that he might sustain and keep the human nature from sinking under the infinite wrath of God, and the power of death;[a] give worth and efficacy to his sufferings, obedience, and intercession;[b] and to satisfy God's justice,[c] procure his favor,[d] purchase a peculiar people,[e] give his Spirit to them,[f] conquer all their enemies,[g] and bring them to everlasting salvation.[h]

a Acts 2:24–25; Rom. 1:4; Rom. 4:25; Heb. 9:14   b Acts 20:28; Heb. 9:14; Heb. 7:25–28; John 17:1–26   c Rom. 3:24–26   d Eph. 1:6; Matt. 3:17   e Titus 2:13–14   f Gal. 4:6; John 15:26; John 16:7; John 14:26   g Luke 1:68–69, 71, 74   h Heb. 5:8–9; Heb. 9:11–15

39. Why was it requisite that the Mediator should be man?

It was requisite that the Mediator should be man, that he might advance our nature,[a] perform obedience to the law,[b] suffer and make intercession for us in our nature,[c] have a fellow feeling of our infirmities;[d] that we might receive the adoption of sons,[e] and have comfort and access with boldness unto the throne of grace.[f]

a Heb. 2:16; 2 Pet. 1:4   b Gal. 4:4; Matt. 5:17; Rom. 5:19; Phil. 2:8   c Heb. 2:14; Heb. 7:24–25   d Heb. 4:15   e Gal. 4:5   f Heb. 4:16

40. Why was it requisite that the Mediator should be God and man in one person?

It was requisite that the Mediator, who was to reconcile God and man, should himself be both God and man, and this in one person, that the proper works of each nature might be accepted of God for us,[a] and relied on by us, as the works of the whole person.[b]

a Matt. 1:21, 23; Matt. 3:17; Heb. 9:14 b 1 Pet. 2:6

41. *Why was our Mediator called Jesus?*
Our Mediator was called Jesus, because he saveth his people from their sins.[a]

a Matt. 1:21

42. *Why was our Mediator called Christ?*
Our Mediator was called Christ, because he was anointed with the Holy Ghost above measure;[a] and so set apart, and fully furnished with all authority and ability,[b] to execute the offices of prophet,[c] priest,[d] and king of his church,[e] in the estate both of his humiliation and exaltation.

a Matt. 3:16; Acts 10:37–38; John 3:34; Ps. 45:7 b John 6:27; Matt. 28:18–20; Rom. 1:3–4
c Acts 3:21–22; Luke 4:18, 21; Heb. 1:1–2; Deut. 18:18 d Heb. 5:5–7; Heb. 4:14–15 e Ps. 2:6;
Luke 1:32–34; John 18:37; Matt. 21:5; Isa. 9:6–7; Phil. 2:8–11

43. *How doth Christ execute the office of a prophet?*
Christ executeth the office of a prophet, in his revealing to the church,[a] in all ages, by his Spirit and Word,[b] in divers ways of administration,[c] the whole will of God,[d] in all things concerning their edification and salvation.[e]

a John 1:18 b 1 Pet. 1:10–12 c Heb. 1:1–2 d John 15:15 e Acts 20:32; Eph. 4:11–13;
John 20:31

44. *How doth Christ execute the office of a priest?*
Christ executeth the office of a priest, in his once offering himself a sacrifice without spot to God,[a] to be a reconciliation for

the sins of his people;[b] and in making continual intercession for them.[c]

a Heb. 9:14, 28; Heb. 10:12; Isa. 53:1–12 b Heb. 2:17; 2 Cor. 5:18; Col. 1:21–22 c Heb. 7:25; Heb. 9:24

45. *How doth Christ execute the office of a king?*
Christ executeth the office of a king, in calling out of the world a people to himself,[a] and giving them officers,[b] laws,[c] and censures, by which he visibly governs them;[d] in bestowing saving grace upon his elect,[e] rewarding their obedience,[f] and correcting them for their sins,[g] preserving and supporting them under all their temptations and sufferings,[h] restraining and overcoming all their enemies,[i] and powerfully ordering all things for his own glory,[j] and their good;[k] and also in taking vengeance on the rest, who know not God, and obey not the gospel.[l]

a Acts 15:14–16; Gen. 49:10; Ps. 110:3; John 17:2 b Eph. 4:11–12; 1 Cor. 12:28 c Isa. 33:22
d Matt. 18:17–18; 1 Cor. 5:4–5 e Acts 5:31 f Rev. 22:12; Rev. 2:10 g Rev. 3:19 h Isa. 63:9
i 1 Cor. 15:25; Ps. 110:1–2 j Rom. 14:10–11 k Rom. 8:28 l 2 Thess. 1:8–9; Ps. 2:8–9

46. *What was the estate of Christ's humiliation?*
The estate of Christ's humiliation was that low condition, wherein he for our sakes, emptying himself of his glory, took upon him the form of a servant,[a] in his conception[b] and birth,[c] life,[d] death,[e] and after his death,[f] until his resurrection.[g]

a Phil. 2:6–8 b Luke 1:31 c Luke 2:7 d Gal. 4:4; 2 Cor. 8:9; Luke 9:58; Heb. 2:18; Isa.
53:3 e Ps. 22:1; Matt. 27:46; Isa. 53:10; 1 John 2:2; Phil. 2:8 f Matt. 12:40; 1 Cor. 15:3–4
g Acts 2:24–27, 31

47. *How did Christ humble himself in his conception and birth?*
Christ humbled himself in his conception and birth, in that, being from all eternity the Son of God, in the bosom of the Father, he was pleased in the fullness of time to become the son

of man, made of a woman of low estate, and to be born of her; with divers circumstances of more than ordinary abasement.[a]

a John 1:14, 18; Gal. 4:4; Luke 2:7

48. **How did Christ humble himself in his life?**

Christ humbled himself in his life, by subjecting himself to the law,[a] which he perfectly fulfilled;[b] and by conflicting with the indignities of the world,[c] temptations of Satan,[d] and infirmities in his flesh, whether common to the nature of man, or particularly accompanying that his low condition.[e]

a Gal. 4:4 b Matt. 5:17; Rom. 5:19 c Ps. 22:6; Isa. 53:2–3; Heb. 12:2–3 d Matt. 4:1–11; Luke 4:13 e Heb. 2:17–18; Heb. 4:15; Isa. 52:13–14

49. **How did Christ humble himself in his death?**

Christ humbled himself in his death, in that having been betrayed by Judas,[a] forsaken by his disciples,[b] scorned and rejected by the world,[c] condemned by Pilate, and tormented by his persecutors;[d] having also conflicted with the terrors of death, and the powers of darkness, felt and borne the weight of God's wrath,[e] he laid down his life an offering for sin,[f] enduring the painful, shameful, and cursed death of the cross.[g]

a Matt. 27:4 b Matt. 26:56 c Isa. 53:2–3 d Matt. 27:26–50; John 19:34; Luke 22:63–64 e Luke 22:44; Matt. 27:46 f Isa. 53:10; Matt. 20:28; Mark 10:45 g Phil. 2:8; Heb. 12:2; Gal. 3:13

50. **Wherein consisted Christ's humiliation after his death?**

Christ's humiliation after his death consisted in his being buried,[a] and continuing in the state of the dead, and under the power of death till the third day;[b] which hath been otherwise expressed in these words, *He descended into hell.*

a 1 Cor. 15:3–4 b Ps. 16:10; Acts 2:24–27, 31; Rom. 6:9; Matt. 12:40

51. *What was the estate of Christ's exaltation?*

The estate of Christ's exaltation comprehendeth his resurrection,[a] ascension,[b] sitting at the right hand of the Father,[c] and his coming again to judge the world.[d]

a 1 Cor. 15:4 b Ps. 68:18; Acts 1:11; Eph. 4:8 c Eph. 1:20; Ps. 110:1; Acts 2:33–34; Heb. 1:3
d Acts 1:11; Acts 17:31; Matt. 16:27

52. *How was Christ exalted in his resurrection?*

Christ was exalted in his resurrection, in that, not having seen corruption in death (of which it was not possible for him to be held[a]) and having the very same body in which he suffered, with the essential properties thereof[b] (but without mortality, and other common infirmities belonging to this life) really united to his soul,[c] he rose again from the dead the third day by his own power;[d] whereby he declared himself to be the Son of God,[e] to have satisfied divine justice,[f] to have vanquished death, and him that had the power of it,[g] and to be Lord of quick and dead:[h] all which he did as a public person,[i] the head of his church,[j] for their justification,[k] quickening in grace,[l] support against enemies,[m] and to assure them of their resurrection from the dead at the last day.[n]

a Acts 2:24, 27 b Luke 24:39 c Rom. 6:9; Rev. 1:18 d John 10:18 e Rom. 1:4 f Rom.
8:34; Rom. 3:25–26; Heb. 9:13–14 g Heb. 2:14 h Rom. 14:9 i 1 Cor. 15:21–22; Isa. 53:10–11
j Eph. 1:20–23; Col. 1:18 k Rom. 4:25 l Eph. 2:1, 5–6; Col. 2:12 m 1 Cor. 15:25–27; Ps. 2:7–9
n 1 Cor. 15:20; 1 Thess. 4:14

53. *How was Christ exalted in his ascension?*

Christ was exalted in his ascension, in that having after his resurrection often appeared unto and conversed with his apostles, speaking to them of the things pertaining to the kingdom of God,[a] and giving them commission to preach the gospel to all nations,[b] forty days after his resurrection, he, in our nature, and as our head,[c] triumphing over enemies,[d] visibly went up into the highest heavens, there to receive gifts for men,[e] to raise up our affections thither,[f] and to prepare a place for us,[g] where himself is, and shall continue till his second coming at the end of the world.[h]

a Acts 1:2–3 b Matt. 28:19–20 c John 20:17; Heb. 6:20 d Eph. 4:8 e Acts 1:9–11; Eph. 4:7–8; Ps. 68:18; Eph. 4:10; Acts 2:33 f Col. 3:1–2 g John 14:3 h Acts 3:21

54.   *How is Christ exalted in his sitting at the right hand of God?*
Christ is exalted in his sitting at the right hand of God, in that as God-man he is advanced to the highest favor with God the Father,[a] with all fullness of joy,[b] glory,[c] and power over all things in heaven and earth;[d] and doth gather and defend his church, and subdue their enemies; furnisheth his ministers and people with gifts and graces,[e] and maketh intercession for them.[f]

a Phil. 2:9 b Acts 2:28; Ps. 16:11 c John 17:5 d Dan. 7:13–14; Eph. 1:22; 1 Pet. 3:22 e Eph. 4:10–12; Ps. 110:1; Heb. 10:12–14; Ezek. 37:24 f Rom. 8:34; 1 John 2:1; Heb. 7:25

55.   *How doth Christ make intercession?*
Christ maketh intercession, by his appearing in our nature continually before the Father in heaven,[a] in the merit of his obedience and sacrifice on earth,[b] declaring his will to have it applied to all believers;[c] answering all accusations against them,[d] and procuring for them quiet of conscience, notwithstanding daily failings,[e] access with boldness to the throne of grace,[f] and acceptance of their persons[g] and services.[h]

a Heb. 9:12, 24 b Isa. 53:12; Heb. 1:3 c John 3:16; John 17:9, 20, 24 d Rom. 8:33–34 e Rom. 5:1–2; 1 John 2:1–2 f Heb. 4:16 g Eph. 1:6 h 1 Pet. 2:5

56. *How is Christ to be exalted in his coming again to judge the world?*
Christ is to be exalted in his coming again to judge the world, in that he, who was unjustly judged and condemned by wicked men,[a] shall come again at the last day in great power,[b] and in the full manifestation of his own glory, and of his Father's, with all his holy angels,[c] with a shout, with the voice of the archangel, and with the trumpet of God,[d] to judge the world in righteousness.[e]

a Acts 3:14–15 b Matt. 24:30; 2 Thess. 1:9–10 c Luke 9:26; Matt. 25:31 d 1 Thess. 4:16
e Acts 17:31; 2 Thess. 1:6–8

57. *What benefits hath Christ procured by his mediation?*
Christ, by his mediation, hath procured redemption,[a] with all other benefits of the covenant of grace.[b]

a 1 Tim. 2:5–6; Heb. 9:12; Eph. 1:7 b 2 Cor. 1:20; Eph. 1:3–6; 2 Pet. 1:3–4

58. *How do we come to be made partakers of the benefits which Christ hath procured?*
We are made partakers of the benefits which Christ hath procured, by the application of them unto us,[a] which is the work especially of God the Holy Ghost.[b]

a John 1:11–12 b Titus 3:4–7; John 16:14–15; John 3:3–8

59. *Who are made partakers of redemption through Christ?*
Redemption is certainly applied, and effectually communicated, to all those for whom Christ hath purchased it;[a] who are in time by the Holy Ghost enabled to believe in Christ according to the gospel.[b]

a Eph. 1:13–14; John 6:37, 39; John 10:15–16 b Rom. 10:17; 1 Cor. 2:12–16; Eph. 2:8;
Rom. 8:9, 14

60. Can they who have never heard the gospel, and so know not Jesus Christ, nor believe in him, be saved by their living according to the light of nature?

They who, having never heard the gospel,[a] know not Jesus Christ,[b] and believe not in him, cannot be saved,[c] be they never so diligent to frame their lives according to the light of nature,[d] or the laws of that religion which they profess;[e] neither is there salvation in any other, but in Christ alone,[f] who is the Savior only of his body the church.[g]

a Rom. 10:14 b 2 Thess. 1:8–9; Eph. 2:12; John 1:10–12 c John 8:24; John 3:18 d 1 Cor. 1:20–24 e John 4:22; Rom. 9:31–32; Phil. 3:4–9 f Acts 4:12 g Eph. 5:23

61. Are all they saved who hear the gospel, and live in the church?

All that hear the gospel, and live in the visible church, are not saved; but they only who are true members of the church invisible.[a]

a John 12:38–40; Rom. 9:6; Matt. 22:14; Matt. 7:21; Rom. 11:7; 1 Cor. 10:2–5

62. What is the visible church?

The visible church is a society made up of all such as in all ages and places of the world do profess the true religion,[a] and of their children.[b]

a 1 Cor. 1:2; 1 Cor. 12:13; Rom. 15:9–12; Rev. 7:9; Ps. 2:8; Ps. 22:27–31; Ps. 45:17; Matt. 28:19–20; Isa. 59:21 b 1 Cor. 7:14; Acts 2:39; Rom. 11:16; Gen. 17:7

63. What are the special privileges of the visible church?

The visible church hath the privilege of being under God's special care and government;[a] of being protected and preserved in all ages, notwithstanding the opposition of all enemies;[b] and of enjoying the communion of saints, the ordinary means of salvation,[c] and offers of grace by Christ to all the members of it in the ministry of the gospel, testifying, that whosoever believes in him shall be saved,[d] and excluding none that will come unto him.[e]

a Isa. 4:5–6; 1 Tim. 4:10; Eph. 4:11–13 b Ps. 115:1–2, 9; Isa. 31:4–5; Zech. 12:2–4, 8–9; Matt. 16:18 c Acts 2:39, 42; Matt. 28:19–20; 1 Cor. 12:12–13 d Ps. 147:19–20; Rom. 9:4; Eph. 4:11–12; Acts 22:16; Acts 2:21; Joel 2:32; Rom. 10:10–13, 17 e Matt. 11:28–29; John 6:37

64. *What is the invisible church?*
The invisible church is the whole number of the elect, that have been, are, or shall be gathered into one under Christ the head.[a]

a Eph. 1:10; Eph. 1:22–23; John 10:16; John 11:52; Eph. 5:23, 27, 32

65. *What special benefits do the members of the invisible church enjoy by Christ?*
The members of the invisible church by Christ enjoy union and communion with him in grace and glory.[a]

a John 17:21; Eph. 2:5–6; John 17:24; 1 John 1:3; John 1:16; Eph. 3:16–19; Phil. 3:10; Rom. 6:5–6

66. *What is that union which the elect have with Christ?*
The union which the elect have with Christ is the work of God's grace,[a] whereby they are spiritually and mystically, yet really and inseparably, joined to Christ as their head and husband;[b] which is done in their effectual calling.[c]

a Eph. 2:6–7 b Eph. 1:22; 1 Cor. 6:17; John 10:28; Eph. 5:23, 30; John 15:5; Eph. 3:17 c 1 Pet. 5:10; 1 Cor. 1:9

67. *What is effectual calling?*
Effectual calling is the work of God's almighty power and grace,[a] whereby (out of his free and special love to his elect, and from nothing in them moving him thereunto[b]) he doth, in his accepted time, invite and draw them to Jesus Christ, by his Word and Spirit;[c] savingly enlightening their minds,[d] renewing and powerfully determining their wills,[e] so as they (although in

themselves dead in sin) are hereby made willing and able freely to answer his call, and to accept and embrace the grace offered and conveyed therein.[f]

a Ezek. 37:9, 14; John 5:25; Eph. 1:18–20; 2 Tim. 1:8–9 b Titus 3:4–5; Eph. 2:4–5, 7–9; Rom. 9:11; Deut. 9:5 c John 3:5; Titus 3:5; 2 Cor. 5:20; 2 Cor. 6:1–2; John 6:44–45; Acts 16:14; 2 Thess. 2:13–14 d Acts 26:18; 1 Cor. 2:10, 12; 2 Cor. 4:6; Eph. 1:17–18 e Ezek. 11:19; Ezek. 36:26–27; John 6:45 f Eph. 2:5; Phil. 2:13; Deut. 30:6; Isa. 45:22; Matt. 11:28–30; Rev. 22:17

68. *Are the elect only effectually called?*

All the elect, and they only, are effectually called;[a] although others may be, and often are, outwardly called by the ministry of the Word,[b] and have some common operations of the Spirit;[c] who, for their willful neglect and contempt of the grace offered to them, being justly left in their unbelief, do never truly come to Jesus Christ.[d]

a Acts 13:48 b Matt. 22:14; Acts 8:13, 20–21 c Matt. 7:22; Matt. 13:20–21; Heb. 6:4–6 d John 12:38–40; Acts 28:25–27; John 6:64–65; Ps. 81:11–12; Heb. 10:29; 1 John 2:19

69. *What is the communion in grace which the members of the invisible church have with Christ?*

The communion in grace which the members of the invisible church have with Christ, is their partaking of the virtue of his mediation, in their justification,[a] adoption,[b] sanctification, and whatever else, in this life, manifests their union with him.[c]

a Rom. 8:30 b Eph. 1:5 c 1 Cor. 1:30; 1 Cor. 6:11

70. *What is justification?*

Justification is an act of God's free grace unto sinners,[a] in which he pardoneth all their sins, accepteth and accounteth their persons righteous in his sight;[b] not for anything wrought in them, or done by them,[c] but only for the perfect obedience and full

satisfaction of Christ, by God imputed to them,[d] and received
by faith alone.[e]

a Rom. 3:22, 24–25; Rom. 4:5 b Jer. 23:6; Rom. 4:6–8; 2 Cor. 5:19, 21; Rom. 3:22, 24–25, 27–
28 c Titus 3:5, 7; Eph. 1:7 d Rom. 4:6–8, 11; Rom. 5:17–19 e Acts 10:43; Gal. 2:16; Phil. 3:9

71. *How is justification an act of God's free grace?*

Although Christ, by his obedience and death, did make a proper,
real, and full satisfaction to God's justice in the behalf of them
that are justified;[a] yet inasmuch as God accepteth the satisfaction from a surety, which he might have demanded of them,
and did provide this surety, his own only Son,[b] imputing his
righteousness to them,[c] and requiring nothing of them for their
justification but faith,[d] which also is his gift,[e] their justification
is to them of free grace.[f]

a Rom. 5:8–10, 19 b 1 Tim. 2:5–6; Heb. 10:10; Matt. 20:28; Dan. 9:24, 26; Isa. 53:4–6, 10–12;
Heb. 7:22; Rom. 8:32; 1 Pet. 1:18–19 c 2 Cor. 5:21; Rom. 4:6, 11 d Rom. 3:24–25 e Eph. 2:8
f Eph. 1:7; Rom. 3:24–25

72. *What is justifying faith?*

Justifying faith is a saving grace,[a] wrought in the heart of a
sinner by the Spirit[b] and Word of God,[c] whereby he, being convinced of his sin and misery, and of the disability in himself
and all other creatures to recover him out of his lost condition,[d]
not only assenteth to the truth of the promise of the gospel,[e]
but receiveth and resteth upon Christ and his righteousness,
therein held forth, for pardon of sin,[f] and for the accepting
and accounting of his person righteous in the sight of God for
salvation.[g]

a Heb. 10:39 b 2 Cor. 4:13; Eph. 1:17–19; 1 Cor. 12:3; 1 Pet. 1:2 c Rom. 10:14–17; 1 Cor. 1:21
d Acts 2:37; Acts 16:30; John 16:8–9; Rom. 6:6; Eph. 2:1; Acts 4:12 e Eph. 1:13; Heb. 11:13
f John 1:12; Acts 16:31; Acts 10:43; Zech. 3:8–9 g Phil. 3:9; Acts 15:11

73. *How doth faith justify a sinner in the sight of God?*

Faith justifies a sinner in the sight of God, not because of those other graces which do always accompany it, or of good works that are the fruits of it,[a] nor as if the grace of faith, or any act thereof, were imputed to him for his justification;[b] but only as it is an instrument by which he receiveth and applieth Christ and his righteousness.[c]

a Gal. 3:11; Rom. 3:28 b Rom. 4:5; Rom. 10:10 c John 1:12; Phil. 3:9; Gal. 2:16

74. *What is adoption?*

Adoption is an act of the free grace of God,[a] in and for his only Son Jesus Christ,[b] whereby all those that are justified are received into the number of his children,[c] have his name put upon them,[d] the Spirit of his Son given to them,[e] are under his fatherly care and dispensations,[f] admitted to all the liberties and privileges of the sons of God, made heirs of all the promises, and fellow heirs with Christ in glory.[g]

a 1 John 3:1 b Eph. 1:5; Gal. 4:4–5 c John 1:12; Rom. 8:15–16 d Num. 6:24–27; Amos 9:12; 2 Cor. 6:18; Rev. 3:12 e Gal. 4:6 f Ps. 103:13; Prov. 14:26; Matt. 6:32; Heb. 12:5–7, 11 g Heb. 6:12; Rom. 8:17; 1 Pet. 1:3–4

75. *What is sanctification?*

Sanctification is a work of God's grace, whereby they whom God hath, before the foundation of the world, chosen to be holy, are in time, through the powerful operation of his Spirit[a] applying the death and resurrection of Christ unto them,[b] renewed in their whole man after the image of God;[c] having the seeds of repentance unto life, and all other saving graces, put into their hearts,[d] and those graces so stirred up, increased, and strengthened,[e] as that they more and more die unto sin, and rise unto newness of life.[f]

a Ezek. 36:27; Phil. 2:13; 2 Thess. 2:13; Eph. 1:4; 1 Cor. 6:11 b Rom. 6:4–6; Col. 3:1–3;
Phil. 3:10 c 2 Cor. 5:17; Eph. 4:23–24; 1 Thess. 5:23 d Acts 11:18; 1 John 3:9 e Jude 20;
Heb. 6:11–12; Eph. 3:16–19; Col. 1:10–11 f Ezek. 36:25–27; Rom. 6:4, 6, 12–14; 2 Cor. 7:1;
1 Pet. 2:24; Gal. 5:24

76. **What is repentance unto life?**

Repentance unto life is a saving grace,[a] wrought in the heart of a
sinner by the Spirit[b] and Word of God,[c] whereby, out of the sight
and sense, not only of the danger,[d] but also of the filthiness and
odiousness of his sins,[e] and upon the apprehension of God's
mercy in Christ to such as are penitent,[f] he so grieves for[g] and
hates his sins,[h] as that he turns from them all to God,[i] purposing
and endeavoring constantly to walk with him in all the ways of
new obedience.[j]

a 2 Tim. 2:25; Acts 11:18 b Zech. 12:10 c Acts 11:18, 20–21 d Ezek. 18:28, 30, 32; Luke
15:17–18; Hos. 2:6–7 e Ezek. 36:31; Isa. 30:22; Phil. 3:7–8 f Joel 2:12–13; Ps. 51:1–4; Luke
15:7, 10; Acts 2:37 g Jer. 31:18–19; Ps. 32:5 h 2 Cor. 7:11 i Luke 1:16–17; 1 Thess. 1:9; Acts
26:18; Ezek. 14:6; 1 Kings 8:47–48 j 2 Chron. 7:14; Ps. 119:57–64; Matt. 3:8; 2 Cor. 7:10;
Luke 1:6

77. **Wherein do justification and sanctification differ?**

Although sanctification be inseparably joined with justification,[a]
yet they differ, in that God in justification imputeth the righteousness of Christ;[b] in sanctification his Spirit infuseth grace,
and enableth to the exercise thereof;[c] in the former, sin is
pardoned;[d] in the other, it is subdued:[e] the one doth equally
free all believers from the revenging wrath of God, and that
perfectly in this life, that they never fall into condemnation;[f]
the other is neither equal in all,[g] nor in this life perfect in any,[h]
but growing up to perfection.[i]

a 1 Cor. 6:11; 1 Cor. 1:30 b Rom. 4:6, 8 c Ezek. 36:27; Heb. 9:13–14 d Rom. 3:24–25
e Rom. 6:6, 14 f Rom. 8:33–34 g 1 John 2:12–14; Heb. 5:12–14 h 1 John 1:8, 10 i 2 Cor. 7:1;
Phil. 3:12–14

78. *Whence ariseth the imperfection of sanctification in believers?*

The imperfection of sanctification in believers ariseth from the remnants of sin abiding in every part of them, and the perpetual lustings of the flesh against the spirit; whereby they are often foiled with temptations, and fall into many sins,[a] are hindered in all their spiritual services,[b] and their best works are imperfect and defiled in the sight of God.[c]

a Rom. 7:18, 23; Mark 14:66–72; Gal. 2:11–12 *b* Heb. 12:1 *c* Isa. 64:6; Ex. 28:38; Gal. 5:16–18

79. *May not true believers, by reason of their imperfections, and the many temptations and sins they are overtaken with, fall away from the state of grace?*

True believers, by reason of the unchangeable love of God,[a] and his decree and covenant to give them perseverance,[b] their inseparable union with Christ,[c] his continual intercession for them,[d] and the Spirit and seed of God abiding in them,[e] can neither totally nor finally fall away from the state of grace,[f] but are kept by the power of God through faith unto salvation.[g]

a Jer. 31:3 *b* 2 Tim. 2:19; Heb. 13:20–21; 2 Sam. 23:5 *c* 1 Cor. 1:8–9 *d* Heb. 7:25; Luke 22:32
e 1 John 3:9; 1 John 2:27 *f* Jer. 32:40; John 10:28 *g* 1 Pet. 1:5

80. *Can true believers be infallibly assured that they are in the estate of grace, and that they shall persevere therein unto salvation?*

Such as truly believe in Christ, and endeavor to walk in all good conscience before him,[a] may, without extraordinary revelation, by faith grounded upon the truth of God's promises, and by the Spirit enabling them to discern in themselves those graces to which the promises of life are made,[b] and bearing witness with their spirits that they are the children of God,[c] be infallibly assured that they are in the estate of grace, and shall persevere therein unto salvation.[d]

a 1 John 2:3; Heb. 10:19–23 *b* 1 Cor. 2:12; 1 John 3:14, 18–19, 21, 24; 1 John 4:13, 16; Heb. 6:11–12 *c* Rom. 8:15–16 *d* 1 John 5:13; Heb. 6:19–20; 2 Pet. 1:5–11

81. *Are all true believers at all times assured of their present being in the estate of grace, and that they shall be saved?*

Assurance of grace and salvation not being of the essence of faith,[a] true believers may wait long before they obtain it;[b] and, after the enjoyment thereof, may have it weakened and intermitted, through manifold distempers, sins, temptations, and desertions;[c] yet are they never left without such a presence and support of the Spirit of God as keeps them from sinking into utter despair.[d]

a Eph. 1:13 *b* Isa. 50:10; Ps. 88:1–3, 6–7, 9–10, 13–15 *c* Ps. 77:1–12; Ps. 51:8, 12; Ps. 31:22; Ps. 22:1; Eph. 4:30; Luke 22:31–34 *d* 1 John 3:9; Ps. 73:15, 23; Isa. 54:7–10; 1 Pet. 4:12–14

82. *What is the communion in glory which the members of the invisible church have with Christ?*

The communion in glory which the members of the invisible church have with Christ, is in this life,[a] immediately after death,[b] and at last perfected at the resurrection and day of judgment.[c]

a 2 Cor. 3:18 *b* Luke 23:43 *c* 1 Thess. 4:17

83. *What is the communion in glory with Christ which the members of the invisible church enjoy in this life?*

The members of the invisible church have communicated to them in this life the firstfruits of glory with Christ, as they are members of him their head, and so in him are interested in that glory which he is fully possessed of;[a] and, as an earnest thereof, enjoy the sense of God's love,[b] peace of conscience, joy in the Holy Ghost, and hope of glory;[c] as, on the contrary, sense of God's revenging wrath, horror of conscience, and a fearful expectation of judgment, are to the wicked the beginning of their torments which they shall endure after death.[d]

a Eph. 2:5–6 *b* Rom. 5:5; 2 Cor. 1:22 *c* Rom. 5:1–2; Rom. 14:17; 2 Pet. 3:18 *d* Gen. 4:13; Matt. 27:4; Heb. 10:27; Rom. 2:9; Mark 9:44

84. *Shall all men die?*

Death being threatened as the wages of sin,[a] it is appointed unto all men once to die;[b] for that all have sinned.[c]

a Rom. 6:23   b Heb. 9:27   c Rom. 5:12

85. *Death being the wages of sin, why are not the righteous delivered from death, seeing all their sins are forgiven in Christ?*

The righteous shall be delivered from death itself at the last day, and even in death are delivered from the sting and curse of it;[a] so that, although they die, yet it is out of God's love,[b] to free them perfectly from sin and misery,[c] and to make them capable of further communion with Christ in glory, which they then enter upon.[d]

a 1 Cor. 15:26, 55–57; Heb. 2:15; John 11:25–26   b Isa. 57:1–2; 2 Kings 22:20   c Rev. 14:13; Eph. 5:27   d Luke 23:43; Phil. 1:23

86. *What is the communion in glory with Christ, which the members of the invisible church enjoy immediately after death?*

The communion in glory with Christ, which the members of the invisible church enjoy immediately after death, is, in that their souls are then made perfect in holiness,[a] and received into the highest heavens,[b] where they behold the face of God in light and glory,[c] waiting for the full redemption of their bodies,[d] which even in death continue united to Christ,[e] and rest in their graves as in their beds,[f] till at the last day they be again united to their souls.[g] Whereas the souls of the wicked are at their death cast into hell, where they remain in torments and utter darkness, and their bodies kept in their graves, as in their prisons, till the resurrection and judgment of the great day.[h]

a Heb. 12:23; Acts 7:55, 59   b 2 Cor. 5:1, 6, 8; Phil. 1:23; Acts 3:21; Eph. 4:10; Luke 23:43
c 1 John 3:2; 1 Cor. 13:12   d Rom. 8:23; Ps. 16:9   e 1 Thess. 4:14, 16   f Isa. 57:2   g Job 19:26–27
h Luke 16:23–24; Acts 1:25; Jude 6–7

87. *What are we to believe concerning the resurrection?*

We are to believe, that at the last day there shall be a general resurrection of the dead, both of the just and unjust:[a] when they that are then found alive shall in a moment be changed; and the selfsame bodies of the dead which were laid in the grave, being then again united to their souls forever, shall be raised up by the power of Christ.[b] The bodies of the just, by the Spirit of Christ, and by virtue of his resurrection as their head, shall be raised in power, spiritual, incorruptible, and made like to his glorious body;[c] and the bodies of the wicked shall be raised up in dishonor by him, as an offended judge.[d]

a Dan. 12:2; Acts 24:15 b Job 19:26; 1 Cor. 15:51–53; 1 Thess. 4:15–17; John 5:28–29; Rom. 8:11
c 1 Cor. 15:21–23, 42–44; Phil. 3:21 d John 5:27–29; Matt. 25:33

88. *What shall immediately follow after the resurrection?*

Immediately after the resurrection shall follow the general and final judgment of angels and men;[a] the day and hour whereof no man knoweth, that all may watch and pray, and be ever ready for the coming of the Lord.[b]

a Eccles. 12:14; 2 Pet. 2:4, 6–7, 14–15; Matt. 25:46; 2 Cor. 5:10; Rom. 14:10, 12 b Matt. 24:36, 42, 44; Mark 13:35–37

89. *What shall be done to the wicked at the day of judgment?*

At the day of judgment, the wicked shall be set on Christ's left hand,[a] and, upon clear evidence, and full conviction of their own consciences,[b] shall have the fearful but just sentence of condemnation pronounced against them;[c] and thereupon shall be cast out from the favorable presence of God, and the glorious fellowship with Christ, his saints, and all his holy angels, into hell, to be punished with unspeakable torments, both of body and soul, with the devil and his angels forever.[d]

a Matt. 25:33 b Rom. 2:15–16 c Matt. 25:41–43 d Luke 16:26; 2 Thess. 1:8–9

90. *What shall be done to the righteous at the day of judgment?*

At the day of judgment, the righteous, being caught up to Christ in the clouds,[a] shall be set on his right hand, and there openly acknowledged and acquitted,[b] shall join with him in the judging of reprobate angels and men,[c] and shall be received into heaven,[d] where they shall be fully and forever freed from all sin and misery;[e] filled with inconceivable joys,[f] made perfectly holy and happy both in body and soul, in the company of innumerable saints and holy angels,[g] but especially in the immediate vision and fruition of God the Father, of our Lord Jesus Christ, and of the Holy Spirit, to all eternity.[h] And this is the perfect and full communion, which the members of the invisible church shall enjoy with Christ in glory, at the resurrection and day of judgment.

a 1 Thess. 4:17; 1 Cor. 15:42–43 b Matt. 25:33; Matt. 10:32 c 1 Cor. 6:2–3 d Matt. 25:34, 46
e Eph. 5:27; Rev. 14:13 f Ps. 16:11 g Heb. 12:22–23 h 1 John 3:2; Rom. 8:29; 1 Cor. 13:12;
1 Thess. 4:17–18

Having Seen What the Scriptures Principally Teach Us
to Believe concerning God, It Follows to Consider
What They Require as the Duty of Man

91. *What is the duty which God requireth of man?*

The duty which God requireth of man, is obedience to his revealed will.[a]

a Deut. 29:29; Mic. 6:8; 1 John 5:2–3; Rom. 12:1–2; 1 Sam. 15:22

92. *What did God at first reveal unto man as the rule of his obedience?*

The rule of obedience revealed to Adam in the estate of innocence, and to all mankind in him, besides a special command not to eat of the fruit of the tree of the knowledge of good and evil, was the moral law.[a]

a Gen. 1:26–27; Rom. 2:14–15; Rom. 10:5; Gen. 2:17

93. *What is the moral law?*
The moral law is the declaration of the will of God to mankind, directing and binding everyone to personal, perfect, and perpetual conformity and obedience thereunto, in the frame and disposition of the whole man, soul and body,[a] and in performance of all those duties of holiness and righteousness which he oweth to God and man:[b] promising life upon the fulfilling, and threatening death upon the breach of it.[c]

a Deut. 5:1–3, 31, 33; Luke 10:26–27; 1 Thess. 5:23; Eph. 4:24 b Luke 1:75; Acts 24:16; 1 Pet. 1:15–16 c Rom. 10:5; Gal. 3:10, 12; Rom. 5:12

94. *Is there any use of the moral law to man since the fall?*
Although no man, since the fall, can attain to righteousness and life by the moral law;[a] yet there is great use thereof, as well common to all men, as peculiar either to the unregenerate, or the regenerate.[b]

a Rom. 8:3; Gal. 2:16 b 1 Tim. 1:8

95. *Of what use is the moral law to all men?*
The moral law is of use to all men, to inform them of the holy nature and will of God,[a] and of their duty, binding them to walk accordingly;[b] to convince them of their disability to keep it, and of the sinful pollution of their nature, hearts, and lives;[c] to humble them in the sense of their sin and misery,[d] and thereby help them to a clearer sight of the need they have of Christ,[e] and of the perfection of his obedience.[f]

a Rom. 1:20; Lev. 11:44–45; Lev. 20:7–8; Rom. 7:12 b Mic. 6:8; James 2:10–11; Rom. 1:32 c Ps. 19:11–12; Rom. 3:20; Rom. 7:7 d Rom. 3:9, 23 e Gal. 3:21–22, 24 f Rom. 10:4

96. *What particular use is there of the moral law to unregenerate men?*

The moral law is of use to unregenerate men, to awaken their consciences to flee from wrath to come,[a] and to drive them to Christ;[b] or, upon their continuance in the estate and way of sin, to leave them inexcusable,[c] and under the curse thereof.[d]

a Ps. 51:13; 1 Tim. 1:9–11 *b* Gal. 3:24 *c* Rom. 1:20; Rom. 2:15 *d* Gal. 3:10

97. *What special use is there of the moral law to the regenerate?*

Although they that are regenerate, and believe in Christ, be delivered from the moral law as a covenant of works,[a] so as thereby they are neither justified[b] nor condemned;[c] yet, besides the general uses thereof common to them with all men, it is of special use, to show them how much they are bound to Christ for his fulfilling it, and enduring the curse thereof in their stead, and for their good;[d] and thereby to provoke them to more thankfulness,[e] and to express the same in their greater care to conform themselves thereunto as the rule of their obedience.[f]

a Rom. 6:14; Rom. 7:4, 6; Gal. 4:4–5; Col. 2:13–14 *b* Rom. 3:20 *c* Gal. 5:23; Rom. 8:1
d Rom. 7:24–25; Gal. 3:13–14; Rom. 8:3–4; Acts 13:38–39 *e* Luke 1:68–69, 74–75; Col. 1:12–14;
Rom. 6:14 *f* Deut. 30:19–20; Rom. 7:22; Rom. 12:2; Titus 2:11–14; James 1:25

98. *Where is the moral law summarily comprehended?*

The moral law is summarily comprehended in the Ten Commandments, which were delivered by the voice of God upon Mount Sinai, and written by him in two tables of stone;[a] and are recorded in the twentieth chapter of Exodus: the four first commandments containing our duty to God, and the other six our duty to man.[b]

a Deut. 4:13; Deut. 10:4; Ex. 34:1–4; Rom. 13:8–10; James 2:8, 10–12 *b* Matt. 22:37–40;
Matt. 19:17–19

99. *What rules are to be observed for the right understanding of the Ten Commandments?*

For the right understanding of the Ten Commandments, these rules are to be observed:

1. That the law is perfect, and bindeth everyone to full conformity in the whole man unto the righteousness thereof, and unto entire obedience forever; so as to require the utmost perfection of every duty, and to forbid the least degree of every sin.[a]

2. That it is spiritual, and so reacheth the understanding, will, affections, and all other powers of the soul; as well as words, works, and gestures.[b]

3. That one and the same thing, in divers respects, is required or forbidden in several commandments.[c]

4. That as, where a duty is commanded, the contrary sin is forbidden;[d] and, where a sin is forbidden, the contrary duty is commanded:[e] so, where a promise is annexed, the contrary threatening is included;[f] and, where a threatening is annexed, the contrary promise is included.[g]

5. That what God forbids, is at no time to be done;[h] what he commands, is always our duty;[i] and yet every particular duty is not to be done at all times.[j]

6. That under one sin or duty, all of the same kind are forbidden or commanded; together with all the causes, means, occasions, and appearances thereof, and provocations thereunto.[k]

7. That what is forbidden or commanded to ourselves, we are bound, according to our places, to endeavor that it may be avoided or performed by others, according to the duty of their places.[l]

8. That in what is commanded to others, we are bound, according to our places and callings, to be helpful to them;[m] and to take heed of partaking with others in what is forbidden them.[n]

a Ps. 19:7; James 2:10; Matt. 5:21–22 *b* Rom. 7:14; Deut. 6:5; Matt. 22:37–39; Matt. 5:21–22, 27–28, 33–34, 37–39, 43–44 *c* Col. 3:5; Amos 8:5; Prov. 1:19; 1 Tim. 6:10 *d* Isa. 58:13; Deut. 6:13; Matt. 4:9–10; Matt. 15:4–6 *e* Matt. 5:21–25; Eph. 4:28 *f* Ex. 20:12; Prov. 30:17 *g* Jer. 18:7–8; Ex. 20:7; Ps. 15:1, 4–5; Ps. 24:4–5 *h* Job 13:7–8; Rom. 3:8; Job 36:21; Heb. 11:25 *i* Deut. 4:8–9; Luke 17:10 *j* Matt. 12:7 *k* Matt. 5:21–22, 27–28; Matt. 15:4–6; 1 Thess. 5:22; Jude 23; Gal. 5:26; Col. 3:21 *l* Ex. 20:10; Lev. 19:17; Gen. 18:19; Josh. 24:15; Deut. 6:6–7; Heb. 10:24–25 *m* 2 Cor. 1:24 *n* 1 Tim. 5:22; Eph. 5:11

100. *What special things are we to consider in the Ten Commandments?*

We are to consider, in the Ten Commandments, the preface, the substance of the commandments themselves, and several reasons annexed to some of them, the more to enforce them.[a]

a Eph. 6:1–3

101. *What is the preface to the Ten Commandments?*

The preface to the Ten Commandments is contained in these words, *I am the* LORD *thy God, which have brought thee out of the land of Egypt, out of the house of bondage.*[a] Wherein God manifesteth his sovereignty, as being JEHOVAH, the eternal, immutable, and almighty God;[b] having his being in and of himself,[c] and giving being to all his words[d] and works:[e] and that he is a God in covenant, as with Israel of old, so with all his people;[f] who, as he brought them out of their bondage in Egypt, so he delivereth us from our spiritual thraldom;[g] and that therefore we are bound to take him for our God alone, and to keep all his commandments.[h]

a Ex. 20:2; Deut. 5:6 *b* Isa. 44:6 *c* Ex. 3:14 *d* Ex. 6:3 *e* Acts 17:24, 28 *f* Gen. 17:7; Rom. 3:29 *g* Luke 1:74–75; Gal. 5:1 *h* 1 Pet. 1:15–19; Lev. 18:30; Lev. 19:37

102. *What is the sum of the four commandments which contain our duty to God?*

The sum of the four commandments containing our duty to God is, to love the Lord our God with all our heart, and with all our soul, and with all our strength, and with all our mind.[a]

a Luke 10:27; Matt. 22:37–40

103. *Which is the first commandment?*

The first commandment is, Thou shall have no other gods before me.[a]

a Ex. 20:3; Deut. 5:7

104. *What are the duties required in the first commandment?*

The duties required in the first commandment are, the knowing and acknowledging of God to be the only true God, and our God;[a] and to worship and glorify him accordingly,[b] by thinking,[c] meditating,[d] remembering,[e] highly esteeming,[f] honoring,[g] adoring,[h] choosing,[i] loving,[j] desiring,[k] fearing of him;[l] believing him;[m] trusting,[n] hoping,[o] delighting,[p] rejoicing in him;[q] being zealous for him;[r] calling upon him, giving all praise and thanks,[s] and yielding all obedience and submission to him with the whole man;[t] being careful in all things to please him,[u] and sorrowful when in anything he is offended;[v] and walking humbly with him.[w]

a 1 Chron. 28:9; Deut. 26:7; Isa. 43:10; Jer. 14:22 b Ps. 95:6–7; Matt. 4:10; Ps. 29:2 c Mal. 3:16 d Ps. 63:6 e Eccles. 12:1 f Ps. 71:19 g Mal. 1:6 h Isa. 45:23; Ps. 96:1–13 i Josh. 24:15, 22 j Deut. 6:5 k Ps. 73:25 l Isa. 8:13 m Ex. 14:31 n Isa. 26:4 o Ps. 130:7 p Ps. 37:4 q Ps. 32:11 r Rom. 12:11; Num. 25:11 s Phil. 4:6 t Jer. 7:23; James 4:7 u 1 John 3:22 v Ps. 119:136; Jer. 31:18 w Mic. 6:8

105. *What are the sins forbidden in the first commandment?*

The sins forbidden in the first commandment are, atheism, in denying or not having a God;[a] idolatry, in having or worshiping more gods than one, or any with or instead of the true God;[b] the not having and avouching him for God, and our God;[c] the omission or neglect of anything due to him, required in this commandment;[d] ignorance,[e] forgetfulness,[f] misapprehensions,[g] false opinions,[h] unworthy and wicked thoughts of him;[i] bold and curious searching into his secrets;[j] all profaneness,[k] hatred of God;[l] self-love,[m] self-seeking,[n] and all other inordinate and immoderate setting of our mind, will, or affections upon other things, and taking them off from him in whole or in part;[o] vain credulity,[p] unbelief,[q] heresy,[r] misbelief,[s] distrust,[t] despair,[u] incorrigibleness,[v] and insensibleness under judgments,[w] hardness of heart,[x] pride,[y] presumption,[z] carnal security,[a] tempting of God;[b] using unlawful means,[c] and trusting in lawful means;[d] carnal delights and joys;[e] corrupt, blind, and indiscreet zeal;[f] lukewarmness,[g] and deadness in the things of God;[h] estranging ourselves, and apostatizing from God;[i] praying, or giving any religious worship, to saints, angels, or any other creatures;[j] all compacts and consulting with the devil,[k] and hearkening to his suggestions;[l] making men the lords of our faith and conscience;[m] slighting and despising God and his commands;[n] resisting and grieving of his Spirit,[o] discontent and impatience at his dispensations, charging him foolishly for the evils he inflicts on us;[p] and ascribing the praise of any good we either are, have, or can do, to fortune,[q] idols,[r] ourselves,[s] or any other creature.[t]

a Ps. 14:1; Eph. 2:12 b Jer. 2:27–28; 1 Thess. 1:9 c Ps. 81:10–11; Rom. 1:21 d Isa. 43:22–24
e Jer. 4:22; Hos. 4:1, 6 f Jer. 2:32 g Acts 17:23, 29 h Isa. 40:18 i Ps. 50:21 j Deut. 29:29
k Titus 1:16; Heb. 12:16 l Rom. 1:30 m 2 Tim. 3:2 n Phil. 2:21 o 1 John 2:15–16; Col. 3:2, 5;
1 Sam. 2:29 p 1 John 4:1 q Heb. 3:12 r Gal. 5:20; Titus 3:10 s Acts 26:9 t Ps. 78:22 u Gen.
4:13 v Jer. 5:3 w Isa. 42:25 x Rom. 2:5 y Jer. 13:15 z Ps. 19:13 a Zeph. 1:12 b Matt. 4:7
c Rom. 3:8 d Jer. 17:5 e 2 Tim. 3:4 f Gal. 4:17; Rom. 10:2; John 16:2; Luke 9:54–55 g Rev.
3:16 h Rev. 3:1 i Ezek. 14:5; Isa. 1:4–5 j Hos. 4:12; Acts 10:25–26; Rev. 19:10; Matt. 4:10;
Col. 2:18; Rom. 1:25 k Lev. 20:6; 1 Sam. 28:7, 11; 1 Chron. 10:13–14 l Acts 5:3 m 2 Cor. 1:24;

Matt. 23:9 n Deut. 32:15; Prov. 13:13; 2 Sam. 12:9 o Acts 7:51; Eph. 4:30 p Job 1:22; Ps. 73:2–3, 13–15, 22 q 1 Sam. 6:7–9; Luke 12:19 r Dan. 5:23 s Deut. 8:17; Dan. 4:30 t Hab. 1:16

106. *What are we specially taught by these words before me in the first commandment?*

These words *before me* or before my face, in the first commandment, teach us, that God, who seeth all things, taketh special notice of, and is much displeased with, the sin of having any other God: that so it may be an argument to dissuade from it, and to aggravate it as a most impudent provocation:[a] as also to persuade us to do as in his sight, whatever we do in his service.[b]

a Ps. 44:20–21; Deut. 30:17–18; Ezek. 8:5–6, 12 b 1 Chron. 28:9

107. *Which is the second commandment?*

The second commandment is, *Thou shalt not make unto thee any graven image, or any likeness of anything that is in heaven above, or that is in the earth beneath, or that is in the water under the earth: thou shalt not bow down thyself to them, nor serve them: for I the LORD thy God am a jealous God, visiting the iniquity of the fathers upon the children unto the third and fourth generation of them that hate me; and shewing mercy unto thousands of them that love me, and keep my commandments.*[a]

a Ex. 20:4–6; Deut. 5:8–10

108. *What are the duties required in the second commandment?*

The duties required in the second commandment are, the receiving, observing, and keeping pure and entire, all such religious worship and ordinances as God hath instituted in his Word;[a] particularly prayer and thanksgiving in the name of Christ;[b] the reading, preaching, and hearing of the Word;[c] the administration and receiving of the sacraments;[d] church government and discipline;[e] the ministry and maintainance thereof;[f] religious fasting;[g] swearing by the name of God,[h] and vowing unto him:[i] as also the disapproving, detesting, opposing all false worship;[j] and, according to each one's place and calling, removing it, and all monuments of idolatry.[k]

a Deut. 12:32; Deut. 32:46–47; Matt. 28:20; 1 Tim. 6:13–14; Acts 2:42 b Phil. 4:6; Eph. 5:20 c Deut. 17:18–19; Acts 15:21; 2 Tim. 4:2; James 1:21–22; Acts 10:33 d Matt. 28:19; 1 Cor. 11:23–30 e Matt. 18:15–17; Matt. 16:19; 1 Cor. 12:28; 1 Cor. 5:1–13 f Eph. 4:11–12; 1 Tim. 5:17–18; 1 Cor. 9:7–15 g Joel 2:12–13; 1 Cor. 7:5 h Deut. 6:13 i Ps. 76:11; Isa. 19:21; Ps. 116:14, 18 j Acts 17:16–17; Ps. 16:4 k Deut. 7:5; Isa. 30:22

109. *What are the sins forbidden in the second commandment?*

The sins forbidden in the second commandment are, all devising,[a] counseling,[b] commanding,[c] using,[d] and anywise approving, any religious worship not instituted by God himself;[e][1] the making any representation of God, of all or of any of the three persons, either inwardly in our mind, or outwardly in any kind of image or likeness of any creature whatsoever;[f] all worshiping of it,[g] or God in it or by it;[h] the making of any representation of feigned deities,[i] and all worship of them, or service belonging to them;[j] all superstitious devices,[k] corrupting the worship of God,[l] adding to it, or taking from it,[m] whether invented and taken up of ourselves,[n] or received by tradition from others,[o] though under the title of antiquity,[p] custom,[q] devotion,[r] good intent, or any other pretense whatsoever;[s] simony;[t] sacrilege;[u] all neglect,[v] contempt,[w] hindering,[x] and opposing the worship and ordinances which God hath appointed.[y]

a Num. 15:39 b Deut. 13:6–8 c Hos. 5:11; Mic. 6:16 d 1 Kings 11:33; 1 Kings 12:33 e Deut. 12:30–32; Lev. 10:1–2; Jer. 19:5 f Deut. 4:15–19; Acts 17:29; Rom. 1:21–23, 25 g Gal. 4:8; Dan. 3:18 h Ex. 32:5 i Ex. 32:8 j 1 Kings 18:26, 28; Isa. 65:11 k Acts 17:22; Col. 2:21–23 l Mal. 1:7–8, 14 m Deut. 4:2 n Ps. 106:39 o Matt. 15:9 p 1 Pet. 1:18 q Jer. 44:17 r Isa. 65:3–5; Gal. 1:13–14 s 1 Sam. 13:11–12; 1 Sam. 15:21 t Acts 8:18–19 u Rom. 2:22; Mal. 3:8 v Ex. 4:24–26 w Matt. 22:5; Mal. 1:7, 13 x Matt. 23:13 y Acts 13:44–45; 1 Thess. 2:15–16

1 Original edition includes "tolerating a false religion" at this point.

110. *What are the reasons annexed to the second commandment, the more to enforce it?*

The reasons annexed to the second commandment, the more to enforce it, contained in these words, *For I the* L*ord* *thy God am a jealous God, visiting the iniquity of the fathers upon the children unto the third and fourth generation of them that hate me; and shewing mercy unto thousands of them that love me, and keep my commandments;*[a] are, besides God's sovereignty over us, and propriety in us,[b] his fervent zeal for his own worship,[c] and his revengeful indignation against all false worship, as being a spiritual whoredom;[d] accounting the breakers of this commandment such as hate him, and threatening to punish them unto divers generations;[e] and esteeming the observers of it such as love him and keep his commandments, and promising mercy to them unto many generations.[f]

a Ex. 20:5–6 *b* Ps. 45:11; Rev. 15:3–4; Ps. 95:2–3, 6–7; Ex. 19:5; Isa. 54:5 *c* Ex. 34:13–14
d 1 Cor. 10:20–22; Ezek. 16:26–27; Jer. 7:18–20; Deut. 32:16–20 *e* Hos. 2:2–4 *f* Deut. 5:29

111. *Which is the third commandment?*

The third commandment is, *Thou shalt not take the name of the* L*ord* *thy God in vain; for the Lord will not hold him guiltless that taketh his name in vain.*[a]

a Ex. 20:7; Deut. 5:11

112. *What is required in the third commandment?*

The third commandment requires, that the name of God, his titles, attributes,[a] ordinances,[b] the Word,[c] sacraments,[d] prayer,[e] oaths,[f] vows,[g] lots,[h] his works,[i] and whatsoever else there is whereby he makes himself known, be holily and reverently used in thought,[j] meditation,[k] word,[l] and writing;[m] by an holy profession,[n] and answerable conversation,[o] to the glory of God,[p] and the good of ourselves,[q] and others.[r]

a Matt. 6:9; Deut. 28:58; Ps. 68:4; Ps. 29:2; 1 Chron. 29:10–13; Rev. 15:3–4 b Eccles. 5:1; Luke 1:6; Mal. 1:11, 14 c Ps. 138:2 d 1 Cor. 11:24–25, 28–29 e 1 Tim. 2:8 f Jer. 4:2 g Eccles. 5:2, 4–6 h Acts 1:24, 26 i Job 36:24 j Mal. 3:16 k Ps. 8:1, 3–4 l Ps. 105:2, 5; Col. 3:17 m Ps. 102:18 n 1 Pet. 3:15; Mic. 4:5 o Phil. 1:27 p 1 Cor. 10:31 q Jer. 32:39 r 1 Pet. 2:12

113. *What are the sins forbidden in the third commandment?*

The sins forbidden in the third commandment are, the not using of God's name as is required;[a] and the abuse of it in an ignorant,[b] vain,[c] irreverent, profane,[d] superstitious,[e] or wicked mentioning or otherwise using his titles, attributes,[f] ordinances,[g] or works,[h] by blasphemy,[i] perjury;[j] all sinful cursings,[k] oaths,[l] vows,[m] and lots;[n] violating of our oaths and vows, if lawful,[o] and fulfilling them, if of things unlawful;[p] murmuring and quarreling at,[q] curious prying into,[r] and misapplying of God's decrees[s] and providences;[t] misinterpreting,[u] misapplying,[v] or anyway perverting the Word, or any part of it,[w] to profane jests,[x] curious or unprofitable questions, vain janglings, or the maintaining of false doctrines;[y] abusing it, the creatures, or anything contained under the name of God, to charms,[z] or sinful lusts and practices;[a] the maligning,[b] scorning,[c] reviling,[d] or anywise opposing of God's truth, grace, and ways;[e] making profession of religion in hypocrisy, or for sinister ends;[f] being ashamed of it,[g] or a shame to it, by unconformable,[h] unwise,[i] unfruitful,[j] and offensive walking,[k] or backsliding from it.[l]

a Mal. 2:2 b Acts 17:23 c Prov. 30:9 d Mal. 1:6–7, 12; Mal. 3:14 e 1 Sam. 4:3–5; Jer. 7:4, 9–10, 14, 31; Col. 2:20–22 f 2 Kings 18:30, 35; Ex. 5:2; Ps. 139:20 g Ps. 50:16–17 h Isa. 5:12 i 2 Kings 19:22; Lev. 24:11 j Zech. 5:4; Zech. 8:17 k 1 Sam. 17:43; 2 Sam. 16:5 l Jer. 5:7; Jer. 23:10 m Deut. 23:18; Acts 23:12, 14 n Est. 3:7; Est. 9:24; Ps. 22:18 o Ps. 24:4; Ezek. 17:16, 18–19 p Mark 6:26; 1 Sam. 25:22, 32–34 q Rom. 9:14, 19–20 r Deut. 29:29 s Rom. 3:5, 7; Rom. 6:1–2 t Eccles. 8:11; Eccles. 9:3; Ps. 39:1–13 u Matt. 5:21–22, 27–28, 31–35, 38–39, 43–44 v Ezek. 13:22 w 2 Pet. 3:16; Matt. 22:24–31 x Isa. 22:13; Jer. 23:34, 36, 38 y 1 Tim. 1:4, 6–7; 1 Tim. 6:4–5, 20; 2 Tim. 2:14; Titus 3:9 z Deut. 18:10–14; Acts 19:13 a 2 Tim. 4:3–4;

1 Kings 21:9–10; Jude 4; Rom. 13:13–14   b Acts 13:45; 1 John 3:12   c Ps. 1:1; 2 Pet. 3:3   d 1 Pet. 4:4   e Acts 13:45–46, 50; Acts 4:18; 1 Thess. 2:16; Heb. 10:29; Acts 19:9   f 2 Tim. 3:5; Matt. 23:14; Matt. 6:1–2, 5, 16   g Mark 8:38   h Ps. 73:14–15   i Eph. 5:15–17; 1 Cor. 6:5–6   j Isa. 5:4; 2 Pet. 1:8–9   k Rom. 2:23–24   l Gal. 3:1, 3; Heb. 6:6

114. *What reasons are annexed to the third commandment?*

The reasons annexed to the third commandment, in these words, *The* Lord *thy God,* and, *For the* Lord *will not hold him guiltless that taketh his name in vain,*[a] are, because he is the Lord and our God, therefore his name is not to be profaned, or anyway abused by us;[b] especially because he will be so far from acquitting and sparing the transgressors of this commandment, as that he will not suffer them to escape his righteous judgment,[c] albeit many such escape the censures and punishments of men.[d]

a Ex. 20:7   b Lev. 19:12   c Deut. 28:58–59; Ezek. 36:21–23   d 1 Sam. 2:29; 1 Sam. 3:13; 1 Sam. 2:12–17, 22–25

115. *Which is the fourth commandment?*

The fourth commandment is, *Remember the sabbath day, to keep it holy. Six days shalt thou labour, and do all thy work: but the seventh day is the sabbath of the* Lord *thy God: in it thou shalt not do any work, thou, nor thy son, nor thy daughter, thy manservant, nor thy maidservant, nor thy cattle, nor thy stranger that is within thy gates: for in six days the* Lord *made heaven and earth, the sea, and all that in them is, and rested the seventh day: wherefore the* Lord *blessed the sabbath day and hallowed it.*[a]

a Ex. 20:8–11; Deut. 5:12–15

116. *What is required in the fourth commandment?*

The fourth commandment requireth of all men the sanctifying or keeping holy to God such set times as he hath appointed in his Word, expressly one whole day in seven; which was the seventh from the beginning of the world to the resurrection of Christ, and the first day of the week ever since, and so to continue to the end of the world; which is the Christian sabbath,[a] and in the New Testament called the Lord's Day.[b]

a Deut. 5:12–14; Gen. 2:2–3; 1 Cor. 16:1–2; Acts 20:7; John 20:19, 26; Matt. 5:17–18; Isa. 56:2, 4, 6–7 b Rev. 1:10

117. *How is the Sabbath or the Lord's Day to be sanctified?*

The Sabbath or Lord's Day is to be sanctified by an holy resting all the day,[a] not only from such works as are at all times sinful, but even from such worldly employments and recreations as are on other days lawful;[b] and making it our delight to spend the whole time (except so much of it as is to be taken up in works of necessity and mercy[c]) in the public and private exercises of God's worship:[d] and, to that end, we are to prepare our hearts, and with such foresight, diligence, and moderation, to dispose and seasonably dispatch our worldly business, that we may be the more free and fit for the duties of that day.[e]

a Ex. 20:8, 10 b Ex. 16:25–28; Jer. 17:21–22; Neh. 13:15–22 c Matt. 12:1–13 d Isa. 58:13–14; Luke 4:16; Acts 20:7; 1 Cor. 16:1–2; Lev. 23:3; Ps. 92, title; Isa. 66:23 e Ex. 20:8; Luke 23:54, 56; Ex. 16:22, 25–26, 29; Neh. 13:19

118. *Why is the charge of keeping the Sabbath more specially directed to governors of families, and other superiors?*

The charge of keeping the Sabbath is more specially directed to governors of families, and other superiors, because they are bound not only to keep it themselves, but to see that it be observed by all those that are under their charge; and because they are prone ofttimes to hinder them by employments of their own.[a]

a Ex. 20:10; Ex. 23:12; Josh. 24:15; Neh. 13:15–17; Jer. 17:20–22

119. *What are the sins forbidden in the fourth commandment?*

The sins forbidden in the fourth commandment are, all omissions of the duties required,[a] all careless, negligent, and unprofitable performing of them, and being weary of them;[b] all profaning the day by idleness, and doing that which is in itself sinful;[c] and by all needless works, words, and thoughts, about our worldly employments and recreations.[d]

a Ezek. 22:26 *b* Amos 8:5; Acts 20:7, 9; Ezek. 33:30–32; Mal. 1:13 *c* Ezek. 23:38 *d* Jer. 17:24, 27; Isa. 58:13–14

120. *What are the reasons annexed to the fourth commandment, the more to enforce it?*

The reasons annexed to the fourth commandment, the more to enforce it, are taken from the equity of it, God allowing us six days of seven for our own affairs, and reserving but one for himself, in these words, *Six days shalt thou labour, and do all thy work:*[a] from God's challenging a special propriety in that day, *The seventh day is the sabbath of the* Lord *thy God:*[b] from the example of God, who *in six days . . . made heaven and earth, the sea, and all that in them is, and rested the seventh day:* and from that blessing which God put upon that day, not only in sanctifying it to be a day for his service, but in ordaining it to be a means of blessing to us in our sanctifying it; *Wherefore the* Lord *blessed the sabbath day, and hallowed it.*[c]

a Ex. 20:9 *b* Ex. 20:10 *c* Ex. 20:11

121. *Why is the word Remember set in the beginning of the fourth commandment?*

The word Remember is set in the beginning of the fourth commandment,[a] partly, because of the great benefit of remembering it, we being thereby helped in our preparation to keep it,[b] and, in keeping it, better to keep all the rest of the commandments,[c] and to continue a thankful remembrance of the two great benefits of creation and redemption, which contain a short abridgment of religion;[d] and partly, because we are very ready to forget it,[e] for that there is less light of nature for it,[f] and yet it restraineth our natural liberty in things at other times lawful;[g] that it cometh but once in seven days, and many worldly businesses come between, and too often take off our minds from thinking of it, either to prepare for it, or to sanctify it;[h] and that Satan with his instruments much labor to blot out the glory, and even the memory of it, to bring in all irreligion and impiety.[i]

a Ex. 20:8 b Ex. 16:23; Luke 23:54, 56; Mark 15:42; Neh. 13:19 c Ezek. 20:12, 19–20; Ps. 92:13–14; Ps. 92, title d Gen. 2:2–3; Ps. 118:22, 24; Rev. 1:10 e Ezek. 22:26 f Neh. 9:14 g Ex. 34:21 h Deut. 5:14–15; Amos 8:5 i Lam. 1:7; Jer. 17:21–23; Neh. 13:15–22

122.　What is the sum of the six commandments which contain our duty to man?

The sum of the six commandments which contain our duty to man is, to love our neighbor as ourselves,[a] and to do to others what we would have them to do to us.[b]

a Matt. 22:39 b Matt. 7:12

123.　Which is the fifth commandment?

The fifth commandment is, Honour thy father and thy mother: that thy days may be long upon the land which the Lord thy God giveth thee.[a]

a Ex. 20:12; Deut. 5:16

124.　Who are meant by father and mother in the fifth commandment?

By father and mother, in the fifth commandment, are meant, not only natural parents,[a] but all superiors in age[b] and gifts;[c] and especially such as, by God's ordinance, are over us in place of authority, whether in family,[d] church,[e] or commonwealth.[f]

a Prov. 23:22, 25; Eph. 6:1–2   b 1 Tim. 5:1–2   c Gen. 4:20–21; Gen. 45:8   d 2 Kings 5:13
e 2 Kings 2:12; Gal. 4:19; 2 Kings 13:14   f Isa. 49:23

125. *Why are superiors styled father and mother?*
Superiors are styled *father* and *mother,* both to teach them in all duties toward their inferiors, like natural parents, to express love and tenderness to them, according to their several relations;[a] and to work inferiors to a greater willingness and cheerfulness in performing their duties to their superiors, as to their parents.[b]

a Eph. 6:4; 2 Cor. 12:14; 1 Thess. 2:7–8, 11; Num. 11:11–12   b 1 Cor. 4:14–16; 2 Kings 5:13

126. *What is the general scope of the fifth commandment?*
The general scope of the fifth commandment is, the performance of those duties which we mutually owe in our several relations, as inferiors, superiors, or equals.[a]

a Eph. 5:21; 1 Pet. 2:17; Rom. 12:10; Rom. 13:1, 7; Eph. 5:22, 24; Eph. 6:1, 4–5, 9

127. *What is the honor that inferiors owe to their superiors?*
The honor which inferiors owe to their superiors is, all due reverence in heart,[a] word,[b] and behavior;[c] prayer and thanksgiving for them;[d] imitation of their virtues and graces;[e] willing obedience to their lawful commands and counsels;[f] due submission to their corrections;[g] fidelity to,[h] defense,[i] and maintenance of their persons and authority, according to their several ranks, and the nature of their places;[j] bearing with their infirmities, and covering them in love,[k] that so they may be an honor to them and to their government.[l]

a Mal. 1:6; Lev. 19:3   b Prov. 31:28; 1 Pet. 3:6   c Lev. 19:32; 1 Kings 2:19   d 1 Tim. 2:1–2
e Heb. 13:7; Phil. 3:17   f Eph. 6:1–2, 5–7; 1 Pet. 2:13–14; Heb. 13:17; Rom. 13:1–5; Prov. 4:3–4;

Prov. 23:22; Ex. 18:19, 24 g Heb. 12:9; 1 Pet. 2:18–20 h Titus 2:9–10 i 1 Sam. 26:15–16; 2 Sam. 18:3; Est. 6:2 j Matt. 22:21; Rom. 13:6–7; 1 Tim. 5:17–18; Gal. 6:6; Gen. 45:11; Gen. 47:12 k Gen. 9:23; 1 Pet. 2:18; Prov. 23:22 l Ps. 127:3–5; Prov. 31:23

128. **What are the sins of inferiors against their superiors?**

The sins of inferiors against their superiors are, all neglect of the duties required toward them;[a] envying at,[b] contempt of,[c] and rebellion[d] against, their persons[e] and places,[f] in their lawful counsels,[g] commands, and corrections;[h] cursing, mocking,[i] and all such refractory and scandalous carriage, as proves a shame and dishonor to them and their government.[j]

a Matt. 15:4–6; Rom. 13:8 b Num. 11:28–29 c 1 Sam. 8:7; Isa. 3:5 d 2 Sam. 15:1–12 e Ex. 21:15 f 1 Sam. 10:27 g 1 Sam. 2:25 h Deut. 21:18–21 i Prov. 30:11, 17 j Prov. 19:26

129. **What is required of superiors towards their inferiors?**

It is required of superiors, according to that power they receive from God, and that relation wherein they stand, to love,[a] pray for,[b] and bless their inferiors;[c] to instruct,[d] counsel, and admonish them;[e] countenancing,[f] commending,[g] and rewarding such as do well;[h] and discountenancing,[i] reproving, and chastising such as do ill;[j] protecting,[k] and providing for them all things necessary for soul[l] and body:[m] and by grave, wise, holy, and exemplary carriage, to procure glory to God,[n] honor to themselves,[o] and so to preserve that authority which God hath put upon them.[p]

a Col. 3:19; Titus 2:4 b 1 Sam. 12:23; Job 1:5 c 1 Kings 8:55–56; Heb. 7:7; Gen. 49:28 d Deut. 6:6–7 e Eph. 6:4 f 1 Pet. 3:7 g 1 Pet. 2:14; Rom. 13:3 h Est. 6:3 i Rom. 13:3–4 j Prov. 29:15; 1 Pet. 2:14 k Isa. 1:10, 17; Job 29:12–17 l Eph. 6:4 m 1 Tim. 5:8 n 1 Tim. 4:12; Titus 2:3–5 o 1 Kings 3:28 p Titus 2:15

130. **What are the sins of superiors?**

The sins of superiors are, besides the neglect of the duties required of them,[a] and inordinate seeking of themselves,[b] their own glory,[c] ease, profit, or pleasure;[d] commanding things unlawful,[e] or not in the power of inferiors to perform;[f] counseling,[g] encouraging,[h] or favoring them in that which is evil;[i] dissuading, discouraging, or discountenancing them in that which is good;[j] correcting them unduly;[k] careless exposing, or leaving them to wrong, temptation, and danger;[l] provoking them to wrath;[m] or anyway dishonoring themselves, or lessening their authority, by an unjust, indiscreet, rigorous, or remiss behavior.[n]

a Ezek. 34:2–4 b Phil. 2:21 c John 5:44; John 7:18 d Isa. 56:10–11; Deut. 17:17 e Acts 4:17–18; Dan. 3:4–6 f Ex. 5:10–19; Matt. 23:2, 4 g Matt. 14:8; Mark 6:24 h 2 Sam. 13:28 i Jer. 6:13–14; Judg. 20:1–48 j John 7:46–49; Col. 3:21; Ex. 5:17; John 9:28 k 1 Pet. 2:18–20; Deut. 25:3 l Gen. 38:11, 26; Acts 18:17; 1 Sam. 23:15–17; Lev. 19:29; Isa. 58:7 m Eph. 6:4 n Gen. 9:21; 1 Kings 12:13–16; 1 Kings 1:6; 1 Sam. 2:29–31; 1 Sam. 3:13

131. *What are the duties of equals?*

The duties of equals are, to regard the dignity and worth of each other,[a] in giving honor to go one before another;[b] and to rejoice in each other's gifts and advancement, as their own.[c]

a 1 Pet. 2:17 b Rom. 12:10; Phil. 2:3 c Rom. 12:15–16; Phil. 2:3

132. *What are the sins of equals?*

The sins of equals are, besides the neglect of the duties required,[a] the undervaluing of the worth,[b] envying the gifts,[c] grieving at the advancement of prosperity one of another;[d] and usurping preeminence one over another.[e]

a Rom. 13:8 b 2 Tim. 3:3; Prov. 14:21; Isa. 65:5 c Acts 7:9; Gal. 5:26 d Num. 12:2 e 3 John 9; Luke 22:24

133. *What is the reason annexed to the fifth commandment, the more to enforce it?*

The reason annexed to the fifth commandment, in these words, *That thy days may be long upon the land which the* Lord *thy God giveth thee,*[a] is an express promise of long life and prosperity, as far as it shall serve for God's glory and their own good, to all such as keep this commandment.[b]

a Ex. 20:12 b Eph. 6:2–3; Deut. 5:16; 1 Kings 8:25

134. Which is the sixth commandment?

The sixth commandment is, *Thou shalt not kill.*[a]

a Ex. 20:13; Deut. 5:17

135. What are the duties required in the sixth commandment?

The duties required in the sixth commandment are, all careful studies, and lawful endeavors, to preserve the life of ourselves[a] and others[b] by resisting all thoughts and purposes,[c] subduing all passions,[d] and avoiding all occasions,[e] temptations,[f] and practices, which tend to the unjust taking away the life of any;[g] by just defense thereof against violence,[h] patient bearing of the hand of God,[i] quietness of mind,[j] cheerfulness of spirit;[k] a sober use of meat,[l] drink,[m] physic,[n] sleep,[o] labor,[p] and recreations;[q] by charitable thoughts,[r] love,[s] compassion,[t] meekness, gentleness, kindness;[u] peaceable,[v] mild, and courteous speeches and behavior;[w] forbearance, readiness to be reconciled, patient bearing and forgiving of injuries, and requiting good for evil;[x] comforting and succoring the distressed, and protecting and defending the innocent.[y]

a Eph. 5:28–29 b 1 Kings 18:4 c Jer. 26:15–16; Acts 23:12, 16–17, 21, 27 d Eph. 4:26–27
e 2 Sam. 2:22–23; Deut. 22:8 f Matt. 4:6–7; Prov. 1:10–11, 15–16 g Gen. 37:21–22; 1 Sam.
24:12; 1 Sam. 26:9–11 h Ps. 82:4; Prov. 24:11–12; 1 Sam. 14:45; Jer. 38:7–13 i James 5:10–11;
Heb. 12:9; 2 Sam. 16:10–12 j 1 Thess. 4:11; 1 Pet. 3:3–4; Ps. 37:8, 11 k Prov. 17:22 l Prov.
23:20; Prov. 25:16, 27 m 1 Tim. 5:23 n Isa. 38:21 o Ps. 127:2 p 2 Thess. 3:12; Eccles. 5:12
q Eccles. 3:4, 11; Mark 6:31 r 1 Sam. 19:4–5; 1 Sam. 22:13–14 s Rom. 13:10 t Luke 10:33–34
u Col. 3:12–13 v James 3:17 w 1 Pet. 3:8–11; 1 Cor. 4:12–13; Prov. 15:1; Judg. 8:1–3 x Matt.
5:24; Eph. 4:2, 32; Rom. 12:17, 20–21 y 1 Thess. 5:14; Matt. 25:35–36; Prov. 31:8–9; Job
31:19–20; Isa. 58:7

136. *What are the sins forbidden in the sixth commandment?*

The sins forbidden in the sixth commandment are, all taking away the life of ourselves,[a] or of others,[b] except in case of public justice,[c] lawful war,[d] or necessary defense;[e] the neglecting or withdrawing the lawful and necessary means of preservation of life;[f] sinful anger,[g] hatred,[h] envy,[i] desire of revenge;[j] all excessive passions,[k] distracting cares;[l] immoderate use of meat, drink,[m] labor,[n] and recreations;[o] provoking words,[p] oppression,[q] quarreling,[r] striking, wounding,[s] and whatsoever else tends to the destruction of the life of any.[t]

a Acts 16:28 b Gen. 9:6 c Num. 35:31, 33; Rom. 13:4 d Deut. 20:1–20; Heb. 11:32–34 e Ex. 22:2 f Matt. 25:42–43; James 2:15–16 g Matt. 5:22 h 1 John 3:15; Lev. 19:17 i Prov. 14:30 j Rom. 12:19 k Eph. 4:31 l Matt. 6:31, 34 m Luke 21:34; Rom. 13:13 n Eccles. 12:12; Eccles. 2:22–23 o Isa. 5:12 p Prov. 15:1; Prov. 12:18 q Ex. 1:14; Isa. 3:15 r Gal. 5:15; Prov. 23:29 s Num. 35:16–21 t Ex. 21:18–36

137. *Which is the seventh commandment?*

The seventh commandment is, *Thou shalt not commit adultery.*[a]

a Ex. 20:14; Deut. 5:18

138. *What are the duties required in the seventh commandment?*

The duties required in the seventh commandment are, chastity in body, mind, affections,[a] words,[b] and behavior;[c] and the preservation of it in ourselves and others;[d] watchfulness over the eyes and all the senses;[e] temperance,[f] keeping of chaste company,[g] modesty in apparel;[h] marriage by those that have not the gift of continency,[i] conjugal love,[j] and cohabitation;[k] diligent labor in our callings;[l] shunning all occasions of uncleanness, and resisting temptations thereunto.[m]

a 1 Thess. 4:4–5; Job 31:1; 1 Cor. 7:34 b Eph. 4:29; Col. 4:6 c 1 Pet. 3:2 d 1 Cor. 7:2–5, 34–36 e Matt. 5:28; Job 31:1 f Acts 24:24–25 g Prov. 2:16–20 h 1 Tim. 2:9 i 1 Cor. 7:2, 9 j Prov. 5:19–20 k 1 Pet. 3:7; 1 Cor. 7:5 l Prov. 31:11, 27–28 m Prov. 5:8; Gen. 39:8–10

139. *What are the sins forbidden in the seventh commandment?*

The sins forbidden in the seventh commandment, besides the neglect of the duties required,[a] are, adultery, fornication,[b] rape, incest,[c] sodomy, and all unnatural lusts;[d] all unclean imaginations, thoughts, purposes, and affections;[e] all corrupt or filthy communications, or listening thereunto;[f] wanton looks,[g] impudent or light behavior, immodest apparel;[h] prohibiting of lawful,[i] and dispensing with unlawful marriages;[j] allowing, tolerating, keeping of stews, and resorting to them;[k] entangling vows of single life,[l] undue delay of marriage,[m] having more wives or husbands than one at the same time;[n] unjust divorce,[o] or desertion;[p] idleness, gluttony, drunkenness,[q] unchaste company;[r] lascivious songs, books, pictures, dancings, stage plays;[s] and all other provocations to, or acts of uncleanness, either in ourselves or others.[t]

a Prov. 5:7; Prov. 4:23, 27 b Heb. 13:4; Eph. 5:5; Gal. 5:19 c 2 Sam. 13:14; 1 Cor. 5:1; Mark 6:18 d Rom. 1:24, 26–27; Lev. 20:15–16 e Matt. 5:28; Matt. 15:19; Col. 3:5 f Eph. 5:3–4; Prov. 7:5, 21–22 g Isa. 3:16; 2 Pet. 2:14 h Prov. 7:10, 13 i 1 Tim. 4:3 j Mark 6:18; Mal. 2:11–12; Lev. 18:1–21 k 1 Kings 15:12; 2 Kings 23:7; Lev. 19:29; Jer. 5:7; Deut. 23:17–18; Prov. 7:24–27 l Matt. 19:10–11 m 1 Cor. 7:7–9; Gen. 38:26 n Mal. 2:14–15; Matt. 19:5 o Mal. 2:16; Matt. 5:32; Matt. 19:8–9 p 1 Cor. 7:12–13 q Ezek. 16:49; Prov. 23:30–33 r Gen. 39:19; Prov. 5:8 s Eph. 5:4; Rom. 13:13; 1 Pet. 4:3; Ezek. 23:14–16; Isa. 3:16; Isa. 23:15–17; Mark 6:22 t 2 Kings 9:30; Jer. 4:30; Ezek. 23:40

140. *Which is the eighth commandment?*

The eighth commandment is, *Thou shalt not steal.*[a]

a Ex. 20:15; Deut. 5:19

141. *What are the duties required in the eighth commandment?*

The duties required in the eighth commandment are, truth, faithfulness, and justice in contracts and commerce between man and man;[a] rendering to everyone his due;[b] restitution of goods unlawfully detained from the right owners thereof;[c] giving and lending freely, according to our abilities, and the necessities of others;[d] moderation of our judgments, wills, and affections concerning worldly goods;[e] a provident care and study to get,[f] keep, use, and dispose these things which are necessary and convenient for the sustentation of our nature, and suitable to our condition;[g] a lawful calling,[h] and diligence in it;[i] frugality;[j] avoiding unnecessary lawsuits,[k] and suretyship, or other like engagements;[l] and an endeavor, by all just and lawful means, to procure, preserve, and further the wealth and outward estate of others, as well as our own.[m]

a Ps. 15:2, 4; Mic. 6:8; Zech. 8:16–17; Zech. 7:4, 10   b Rom. 13:7   c Lev. 6:2–5; Luke 19:8
d Luke 6:30, 38; 1 John 3:17; Eph. 4:28; Gal. 6:10   e 1 Tim. 6:6–9; Gal. 6:14   f 1 Tim. 5:8
g Prov. 27:23–27; Eccles. 2:24; Eccles. 3:12–13; 1 Tim. 6:17–18; Isa. 38:1; Matt. 11:8   h 1 Cor.
7:20; Gen. 2:15; Gen. 3:19   i Eph. 4:28; Prov. 10:4; Rom. 12:11   j John 6:12; Prov. 21:20
k 1 Cor. 6:1–9   l Prov. 11:15; Prov. 6:1–6   m Lev. 25:35; Phil. 2:4; Deut. 22:1–4; Ex. 23:4–5; Gen.
47:14, 20; Matt. 22:39

142.   *What are the sins forbidden in the eighth commandment?*
The sins forbidden in the eighth commandment, besides the neglect of the duties required,[a] are, theft,[b] robbery,[c] manstealing,[d] and receiving anything that is stolen;[e] fraudulent dealing,[f] false weights and measures,[g] removing landmarks,[h] injustice and unfaithfulness in contracts between man and man,[i] or in matters of trust;[j] oppression,[k] extortion,[l] usury,[m] bribery,[n] vexatious lawsuits,[o] unjust enclosures and depredation;[p] [2] engrossing commodities to enhance the price;[q] unlawful callings,[r] and all other unjust or sinful ways of taking or withholding from our neighbor what belongs to him, or of enriching ourselves;[s] covetousness;[t] inordinate prizing and affecting worldly goods;[u] distrustful and distracting cares and studies in getting, keeping, and using them;[v] envying at the prosperity of others;[w] as

2   Original edition reads "depopulations" instead.

likewise idleness,[x] prodigality, wasteful gaming; and all other ways whereby we do unduly prejudice our own outward estate,[y] and defrauding ourselves of the due use and comfort of that estate which God hath given us.[z]

a James 2:15–16; 1 John 3:17 b Eph. 4:28 c Ps. 62:10 d 1 Tim. 1:10 e Prov. 29:24; Ps. 50:18
f 1 Thess. 4:6; Lev. 19:13 g Prov. 11:1; Prov. 20:10 h Deut. 19:14; Prov. 23:10 i Amos 8:5; Ps. 37:21 j Luke 16:10–12 k Ezek. 22:29; Lev. 25:17 l Matt. 23:25; Ezek. 22:12 m Ps. 15:5 n Job 15:34 o 1 Cor. 6:6–8; Prov. 3:29–30 p Isa. 5:8; Mic. 2:2 q Prov. 11:26 r Acts 19:19, 24–25 ˇ
s James 5:4; Prov. 21:6; Job 20:19 t Luke 12:15 u 1 Tim. 6:5; Col. 3:2; 1 John 2:15–16; Prov. 23:5; Ps. 62:10 v Matt. 6:25, 31, 34; Eccles. 5:12 w Ps. 73:3; Ps. 37:1, 7 x 2 Thess. 3:10–11; Prov. 18:9 y Prov. 21:17; Prov. 23:20–21; Prov. 28:19 z Eccles. 4:8; Eccles. 6:2; 1 Tim. 4:3–5; 1 Tim. 5:8

143. Which is the ninth commandment?

The ninth commandment is, *Thou shalt not bear false witness against thy neighbour.*[a]

a Ex. 20:16; Deut. 5:20

144. What are the duties required in the ninth commandment?

The duties required in the ninth commandment are, the preserving and promoting of truth between man and man,[a] and the good name of our neighbor, as well as our own;[b] appearing and standing for the truth;[c] and from the heart,[d] sincerely,[e] freely,[f] clearly,[g] and fully,[h] speaking the truth, and only the truth, in matters of judgment and justice,[i] and in all other things whatsoever;[j] a charitable esteem of our neighbors;[k] loving, desiring, and rejoicing in their good name;[l] sorrowing for,[m] and covering of their infirmities;[n] freely acknowledging of their gifts and graces,[o] defending their innocency;[p] a ready receiving of a good report,[q] and unwillingness to admit of an evil report,[r] concerning them; discouraging talebearers,[s] flatterers,[t] and slanderers;[u] love and care of our own good name, and defending it when need requireth;[v] keeping of lawful promises;[w]

studying and practicing of whatsoever things are true, honest, lovely, and of good report.[x]

a Zech. 8:16; Eph. 4:25 b 3 John 12 c Prov. 31:8–9 d Ps. 15:2 e 2 Chron. 19:9 f 1 Sam. 19:4–5 g Josh. 7:15–20 h 2 Sam. 14:18–20; Acts 20:27 i Lev. 19:15; Prov. 14:5, 25 j 2 Cor. 1:17–18; Eph. 4:25; Col. 3:9 k Heb. 6:9; 1 Cor. 13:7 l Rom. 1:8; 2 John 4; 3 John 3–4 m 2 Cor. 2:4; 2 Cor. 12:21; Ps. 119:158 n Prov. 17:9; 1 Pet. 4:8 o 1 Cor. 1:4–5, 7; 2 Tim. 1:4–5 p 1 Sam. 22:14 q 1 Cor. 13:6–7 r Ps. 15:3 s Prov. 25:23 t Prov. 26:24–25 u Ps. 101:5 v Prov. 22:1; John 8:49; 2 Cor. 11:1–12:13 w Ps. 15:4 x Phil. 4:8

145. *What are the sins forbidden in the ninth commandment?*

The sins forbidden in the ninth commandment are, all prejudicing the truth, and the good name of our neighbors, as well as our own,[a] especially in public judicature;[b] giving false evidence,[c] suborning false witnesses,[d] wittingly appearing and pleading for an evil cause, outfacing and overbearing the truth;[e] passing unjust sentence,[f] calling evil good, and good evil; rewarding the wicked according to the work of the righteous, and the righteous according to the work of the wicked;[g] forgery,[h] concealing the truth, undue silence in a just cause,[i] and holding our peace when iniquity calleth for either a reproof from ourselves,[j] or complaint to others;[k] speaking the truth unseasonably,[l] or maliciously to a wrong end,[m] or perverting it to a wrong meaning,[n] or in doubtful and equivocal expressions, to the prejudice of truth or justice;[o] speaking untruth,[p] lying,[q] slandering,[r] backbiting,[s] detracting,[t] talebearing,[u] whispering,[v] scoffing,[w] reviling,[x] rash,[y] harsh,[z] and partial censuring;[a] misconstructing intentions, words, and actions;[b] flattering,[c] vainglorious boasting;[d] thinking or speaking too highly or too meanly of ourselves or others;[e] denying the gifts and graces of God;[f] aggravating smaller faults;[g] hiding, excusing, or extenuating of sins, when called to a free confession;[h] unnecessary discovering of infirmities;[i] raising false rumors,[j] receiving and countenancing evil reports,[k] and stopping our ears against just defense;[l] evil suspicion;[m] envying or grieving at the deserved credit of any,[n] endeavoring or desiring to impair it,[o] rejoicing in their disgrace and infamy;[p] scornful contempt,[q] fond admiration;[r] breach of lawful promises;[s] neglecting such things as are of good report,[t] and practicing, or not avoiding ourselves, or not hindering what we can in others, such things as procure an ill name.[u]

a Luke 3:14; 1 Sam. 17:28; 2 Sam. 16:3; 2 Sam. 1:9–10, 15–16 b Lev. 19:15; Hab. 1:4 c Prov. 19:5; Prov. 6:16, 19 d Acts 6:13 e Jer. 9:3, 5; Ps. 12:3–4; Acts 24:2, 5; Ps. 52:1–4 f Prov. 17:15; 1 Kings 21:9–14 g Isa. 5:23 h 1 Kings 21:8 i Lev. 5:1; Acts 5:3, 8–9; Deut. 13:8; 2 Tim. 4:16 j 1 Kings 1:6; Lev. 19:17 k Isa. 59:4 l Prov. 29:11 m 1 Sam. 22:9–10; Ps. 52:1–5 n Ps. 56:5; Matt. 26:60–61; John 2:19 o Gen. 3:5; Gen. 26:7, 9 p Isa. 59:13 q Col. 3:9; Lev. 19:11 r Ps. 50:20 s Ps. 15:3 t James 4:11; Jer. 38:4 u Lev. 19:16 v Rom. 1:29–30 w Gen. 21:9; Gal. 4:29 x 1 Cor. 6:10 y Matt. 7:1 z Acts 28:4; James 2:13 a Gen. 38:24; Rom. 2:1 b Rom. 3:8; Ps. 69:10; Neh. 6:6–8; 1 Sam. 1:13–15; 2 Sam. 10:3 c Ps. 12:2–3 d 2 Tim. 3:2 e Luke 18:9, 11; Acts 12:22; Ex. 4:10–14; Rom. 12:16; Gal. 5:26; 1 Cor. 4:6 f Luke 9:49–50; 2 Cor. 10:10; Acts 2:13; Job 27:5–6; Job 4:6 g Matt. 7:3–5 h Prov. 28:13; Gen. 3:12–13; Prov. 30:20; Jer. 2:35; 2 Kings 5:25; Gen. 4:9 i Prov. 25:9–10; Gen. 9:22 j Ex. 23:1 k Prov. 29:12; Ps. 41:7–8 l Acts 7:56–57; Job 31:13–14 m 1 Cor. 13:5; 1 Tim. 6:4 n Matt. 21:15; Num. 11:29 o Ezra 4:12–13; Dan. 6:3–4 p Jer. 48:27 q Matt. 27:28–29; Ps. 35:15–16, 21 r Jude 16; Acts 12:22 s Rom. 1:31; 2 Tim. 3:3 t 1 Sam. 2:24 u 2 Sam. 13:12–13; Prov. 5:8–9; Prov. 6:33

146. Which is the tenth commandment?

The tenth commandment is, *Thou shalt not covet thy neighbour's house, thou shalt not covet thy neighbour's wife, nor his manservant, nor his maidservant, nor his ox, nor his ass, nor anything that is thy neighbour's.*[a]

a Ex. 20:17; Deut. 5:21

147. What are the duties required in the tenth commandment?

The duties required in the tenth commandment are, such a full contentment with our own condition,[a] and such a charitable frame of the whole soul toward our neighbor, as that all our inward motions and affections touching him, tend unto, and further all that good which is his.[b]

a Heb. 13:5; 1 Tim. 6:6; Phil. 4:11 b Job 31:29; Rom. 12:15; Ps. 122:7–9; 1 Tim. 1:5; Est. 10:3; 1 Cor. 13:4–7

148. *What are the sins forbidden in the tenth commandment?*

The sins forbidden in the tenth commandment are, discontent-ment with our own estate;[a] envying[b] and grieving at the good of our neighbor,[c] together with all inordinate motions and affections to anything that is his.[d]

a 1 Cor. 10:10; 1 Kings 21:4; Est. 5:13 *b* Gal. 5:26; James 3:14, 16 *c* Ps. 112:9–10; Neh. 2:10
d Rom. 7:7–8; Rom. 13:9; Col. 3:5; Deut. 5:21

149. *Is any man able perfectly to keep the commandments of God?*

No man is able, either of himself,[a] or by any grace received in this life, perfectly to keep the commandments of God;[b] but doth daily break them in thought,[c] word, and deed.[d]

a James 3:2; John 15:5; Rom. 8:3 *b* Eccles. 7:20; 1 John 1:8, 10; Gal. 5:17; Rom. 7:18–19 *c* Gen. 6:5; Gen. 8:21; James 1:14 *d* Rom. 3:9–19; James 3:2–13

150. *Are all transgressions of the law of God equally heinous in themselves, and in the sight of God?*

All transgressions of the law of God are not equally heinous; but some sins in themselves, and by reason of several aggravations, are more heinous in the sight of God than others.[a]

a John 19:11; 1 John 5:16; Heb. 2:2–3; Ps. 78:17, 32, 56; Ezek. 8:6, 13, 15

151. *What are those aggravations that make some sins more heinous than others?*

Sins receive their aggravations,

1. From the persons offending:[a] if they be of riper age,[b] greater experience or grace,[c] eminent for profession,[d] gifts,[e] place,[f] office,[g] guides to others,[h] and whose example is likely to be followed by others.[i]
2. From the parties offended:[j] if immediately against God,[k] his attributes,[l] and worship;[m] against Christ, and his grace;[n] the

Holy Spirit,[o] his witness,[p] and workings;[q] against superiors, men of eminency,[r] and such as we stand especially related and engaged unto;[s] against any of the saints,[t] particularly weak brethren,[u] the souls of them, or any other,[v] and the common good of all or many.[w]

3. From the nature and quality of the offense:[x] if it be against the express letter of the law,[y] break many commandments, contain in it many sins:[z] if not only conceived in the heart, but breaks forth in words and actions,[a] scandalize others,[b] and admit of no reparation:[c] if against means,[d] mercies,[e] judgments,[f] light of nature,[g] conviction of conscience,[h] public or private admonition,[i] censures of the church,[j] civil punishments;[k] and our prayers, purposes, promises,[l] vows,[m] covenants,[n] and engagements to God or men:[o] if done deliberately,[p] willfully,[q] presumptuously,[r] impudently,[s] boastingly,[t] maliciously,[u] frequently,[v] obstinately,[w] with delight,[x] continuance,[y] or re-lapsing after repentance.[z]

4. From circumstances of time[a] and place:[b] if on the Lord's Day,[c] or other times of divine worship;[d] or immediately before[e] or after these,[f] or other helps to prevent or remedy such miscarriages:[g] if in public, or in the presence of others, who are thereby likely to be provoked or defiled.[h]

a Jer. 2:8 b Job 32:7, 9; Eccles. 4:13 c 1 Kings 11:4, 9 d 2 Sam. 12:14; 1 Cor. 5:1 e James 4:17; Luke 12:47–48 f Jer. 5:4–5 g 2 Sam. 12:7–9; Ezek. 8:11–12 h Rom. 2:17–24 i Gal. 2:11–14 j Ps. 2:12; Matt. 21:38–39 k 1 Sam. 2:25; Acts 5:4; Ps. 5:4 l Rom. 2:4 m Mal. 1:8, 14 n Heb. 2:2–3; Heb. 12:25 o Heb. 10:28–29; Matt. 12:31–32 p Eph. 4:30 q Heb. 6:4–6 r Jude 8; Num. 12:8–9; Isa. 3:5 s Prov. 30:17; 2 Cor. 12:15; Ps. 55:12–15 t Zeph. 2:8, 10–11; Matt. 18:6; 1 Cor. 6:8; Rev. 17:6 u 1 Cor. 8:11–12; Rom. 14:13, 15, 21 v Ezek. 13:19; 1 Cor. 8:12; Rev. 18:12–13; Matt. 23:15 w 1 Thess. 2:15–16; Josh. 22:20 x Prov. 6:30–33 y Ezra 9:10–12; 1 Kings 11:9–10 z Col. 3:5; 1 Tim. 6:10; Prov. 5:8–12; Prov. 6:32–33; Josh. 7:21 a James 1:14–15; Matt. 5:22; Mic. 2:1 b Matt. 18:7; Rom. 2:23–24 c Deut. 22:22, 28–29; Prov. 6:32–35 d Matt. 11:21–24; John 15:22 e Isa. 1:3; Deut. 32:6 f Amos 4:8–11; Jer. 5:3 g Rom. 1:26–27 h Rom. 1:32; Dan. 5:22; Titus 3:10–11 i Prov. 29:1 j Titus 3:10; Matt. 18:17 k Prov. 27:22; Prov. 23:35 l Ps. 78:34–37; Jer. 2:20; Jer. 13:5–6, 20–21 m Eccles. 5:4–6; Prov. 20:25 n Lev. 26:25

o Prov. 2:17; Ezek. 7:18–19 p Ps. 36:4 q Jer. 6:16 r Num. 15:30; Ex. 21:14 s Jer. 3:3; Prov. 7:13 t Ps. 52:1 u 3 John 10 v Num. 14:22 w Zech. 7:11–12 x Prov. 2:14 y Isa. 57:17 z Jer. 34:8–11; 2 Pet. 2:20–22 a 2 Kings 5:26 b Jer. 7:10; Isa. 26:10 c Ezek. 23:37–39 d Isa. 58:3–5; Num. 25:6–7 e 1 Cor. 11:20–21; Jer. 7:8–10 f Prov. 7:14–15; John 13:27, 30 g Ezra 9:13–14 h 2 Sam. 16:22; 1 Sam. 2:22–24

152. *What doth every sin deserve at the hands of God?*

Every sin, even the least, being against the sovereignty,[a] goodness,[b] and holiness of God,[c] and against his righteous law,[d] deserveth his wrath and curse,[e] both in this life,[f] and that which is to come;[g] and cannot be expiated but by the blood of Christ.[h]

a James 2:10–11 b Ex. 20:1–2 c Hab. 1:13; Lev. 10:3; Lev. 11:44–45 d 1 John 3:4; Rom. 7:12 e Eph. 5:6; Gal. 3:10 f Lam. 3:39; Deut. 28:15–68 g Matt. 25:41 h Heb. 9:22; 1 Pet. 1:18–19

153. *What doth God require of us, that we may escape his wrath and curse due to us by reason of the transgression of the law?*

That we may escape the wrath and curse of God due to us by reason of the transgression of the law, he requireth of us repentance toward God, and faith toward our Lord Jesus Christ,[a] and the diligent use of the outward means whereby Christ communicates to us the benefits of his mediation.[b]

a Acts 20:21; Matt. 3:7–8; Luke 13:3, 5; Acts 16:30–31; John 3:16, 18 b Prov. 2:1–5; Prov. 8:33–36

154. *What are the outward means whereby Christ communicates to us the benefits of his mediation?*

The outward and ordinary means whereby Christ communicates to his church the benefits of his mediation, are all his ordinances; especially the Word, sacraments, and prayer; all which are made effectual to the elect for their salvation.[a]

a Matt. 28:19–20; Acts 2:42, 46–47

155. *How is the Word made effectual to salvation?*

The Spirit of God maketh the reading, but especially the preaching of the Word, an effectual means of enlightening,[a] convincing, and humbling sinners;[b] of driving them out of themselves, and drawing them unto Christ;[c] of conforming them to his image,[d] and subduing them to his will;[e] of strengthening them against temptations and corruptions;[f] of building them up in grace,[g] and establishing their hearts in holiness and comfort through faith unto salvation.[h]

a Neh. 8:8; Acts 26:18; Ps. 19:8 b 1 Cor. 14:24–25; 2 Chron. 34:18–19, 26–28 c Acts 2:37, 41; Acts 8:27–38 d 2 Cor. 3:18; Col. 1:27 e 2 Cor. 10:4–6; Rom. 6:17–18 f Eph. 6:16–17; Col. 1:28; Ps. 19:11; Matt. 4:4, 7, 10; 1 Cor. 10:11 g Eph. 4:11–12; Acts 20:32; 2 Tim. 3:15–17 h Rom. 16:25; 1 Thess. 3:2, 10–11, 13; Rom. 15:4; Rom. 10:13–17; Rom. 1:16

156. *Is the Word of God to be read by all?*

Although all are not to be permitted to read the Word publicly to the congregation,[a] yet all sorts of people are bound to read it apart by themselves,[b] and with their families:[c] to which end, the Holy Scriptures are to be translated out of the original into vulgar languages.[d]

a Deut. 31:9, 11–13; Neh. 8:2–3; Neh. 9:3–5 b Deut. 17:19; Rev. 1:3; John 5:39; Isa. 34:16 c Deut. 6:6–9; Gen. 18:17, 19; Ps. 78:5–7 d 1 Cor. 14:6, 9, 11–12, 15–16, 24, 27–28; Neh. 8:8

157. *How is the Word of God to be read?*

The Holy Scriptures are to be read with an high and reverent esteem of them;[a] with a firm persuasion that they are the very Word of God,[b] and that he only can enable us to understand them;[c] with desire to know, believe, and obey the will of God revealed in them;[d] with diligence,[e] and attention to the matter and scope of them;[f] with meditation,[g] application,[h] self-denial,[i] and prayer.[j]

a Ps. 119:97; Ps. 19:10; Ex. 24:7; 2 Chron. 34:27; Isa. 66:2; Neh. 8:3–10 b 2 Pet. 1:19–21; Matt. 4:4; 1 Thess. 2:13; Mark 7:13 c Luke 24:45; 2 Cor. 3:13–16 d Deut. 17:10, 20 e Acts 17:11

f Acts 8:30, 34; Luke 10:26–28 g Ps. 1:2; Ps. 119:97 h 2 Chron. 34:21 i Prov. 3:5; Deut. 33:3; Matt. 16:24; Luke 9:23; Gal. 1:15–16 j Prov. 2:1–6; Ps. 119:18; Neh. 8:6, 8

158. *By whom is the Word of God to be preached?*

The Word of God is to be preached only by such as are sufficiently gifted,[a] and also duly approved and called to that office.[b]

a 1 Tim. 3:2, 6; Eph. 4:8–11; Mal. 2:7; 2 Cor. 3:6; 2 Tim. 2:2 b Jer. 14:15; Rom. 10:15; Heb. 5:4; 1 Cor. 12:28–29; 1 Tim. 3:10; 1 Tim. 4:14; 1 Tim. 5:22

159. *How is the Word of God to be preached by those that are called thereunto?*

They that are called to labor in the ministry of the Word, are to preach sound doctrine,[a] diligently,[b] in season and out of season;[c] plainly,[d] not in the enticing words of man's wisdom, but in demonstration of the Spirit, and of power;[e] faithfully,[f] making known the whole counsel of God;[g] wisely,[h] applying themselves to the necessities and capacities of the hearers;[i] zealously,[j] with fervent love to God[k] and the souls of his people;[l] sincerely,[m] aiming at his glory,[n] and their conversion,[o] edification,[p] and salvation.[q]

a Titus 2:1, 8 b Acts 18:25 c 2 Tim. 4:2 d 1 Cor. 14:9–19 e 1 Cor. 2:4 f Jer. 23:28; 1 Cor. 4:1–2 g Acts 20:27 h Col. 1:28; 2 Tim. 2:15 i 1 Cor. 3:2; Heb. 5:12–14; Luke 12:42 j Acts 18:25; Ps. 119:139; 2 Tim. 4:5 k 2 Cor. 5:13–14; Phil. 1:15–17 l Col. 4:12; 2 Cor. 12:15 m 2 Cor. 2:17; 2 Cor. 4:2 n 1 Thess. 2:4–6; John 7:18 o 1 Cor. 9:19–22 p 2 Cor. 12:19; Eph. 4:12 q 1 Tim. 4:16; Acts 26:16–18

160. *What is required of those that hear the Word preached?*

It is required of those that hear the Word preached, that they attend upon it with diligence,[a] preparation,[b] and prayer;[c] examine what they hear by the Scriptures;[d] receive the truth with faith,[e] love,[f] meekness,[g] and readiness of mind,[h] as the Word of God;[i] meditate,[j] and confer of it;[k] hide it in their hearts,[l] and bring forth the fruit of it in their lives.[m]

a Prov. 8:34 b 1 Pet. 2:1–2; Luke 8:18 c Ps. 119:18; Eph. 6:18–19 d Acts 17:11 e Heb. 4:2 f 2 Thess. 2:10 g James 1:21 h Acts 17:11 i 1 Thess. 2:13 j Luke 9:44; Heb. 2:1 k Luke 24:14; Deut. 6:6–7 l Prov. 2:1; Ps. 119:11 m Luke 8:15; James 1:25

161. How do the sacraments become effectual means of salvation?

The sacraments become effectual means of salvation, not by any power in themselves, or any virtue derived from the piety or intention of him by whom they are administered, but only by the working of the Holy Ghost, and the blessing of Christ, by whom they are instituted.[a]

a 1 Pet. 3:21; Acts 8:13, 23; 1 Cor. 3:5–7; 1 Cor. 1:12–17; 1 Cor. 12:13; 1 Cor. 6:11

162. What is a sacrament?

A sacrament is an holy ordinance instituted by Christ in his church,[a] to signify, seal, and exhibit[b] unto those that are within the covenant of grace,[c] the benefits of his mediation;[d] to strengthen and increase their faith, and all other graces;[e] to oblige them to obedience;[f] to testify and cherish their love and communion one with another;[g] and to distinguish them from those that are without.[h]

a Gen. 17:7, 10; Ex. 12:1–51; Matt. 28:19; Matt. 26:26–28; Mark 14:22–25; Luke 22:19–20; 1 Cor. 11:22–26 b Rom. 4:11; 1 Cor. 11:24–25 c Rom. 15:8; Ex. 12:48; Rom. 9:8; Gal. 3:27, 29 d Acts 2:38; 1 Cor. 10:16 e Rom. 4:11; Gal. 3:27 f Rom. 6:3–4; 1 Cor. 10:21 g Eph. 4:2–5; 1 Cor. 12:13; 1 Cor. 10:16–17 h Eph. 2:11–12; Gen. 34:14

163. What are the parts of a sacrament?

The parts of a sacrament are two; the one an outward and sensible sign, used according to Christ's own appointment; the other an inward and spiritual grace thereby signified.[a]

a Matt. 3:11; 1 Pet. 3:21; Titus 3:5; Westminster Confession of Faith 27.2; Deut. 10:16; Deut. 30:6; Jer. 4:4

164. How many sacraments hath Christ instituted in his church under the new testament?

Under the new testament Christ hath instituted in his church only two sacraments, baptism and the Lord's Supper.[a]

a Matt. 28:19; 1 Cor. 11:20, 23; Matt. 26:26–28

165. *What is baptism?*

Baptism is a sacrament of the new testament, wherein Christ hath ordained the washing with water in the name of the Father, and of the Son, and of the Holy Ghost,[a] to be a sign and seal of ingrafting into himself,[b] of remission of sins by his blood,[c] and regeneration by his Spirit;[d] of adoption,[e] and resurrection unto everlasting life;[f] and whereby the parties baptized are solemnly admitted into the visible church,[g] and enter into an open and professed engagement to be wholly and only the Lord's.[h]

a Matt. 28:19 *b* Gal. 3:27; Rom. 6:3 *c* Mark 1:4; Rev. 1:5; Acts 2:38; Acts 22:16; 1 Pet. 3:21 *d* Titus 3:5; Eph. 5:26; Acts 2:38 *e* Gal. 3:26–27 *f* 1 Cor. 15:29; Rom. 6:5 *g* 1 Cor. 12:13; Acts 2:41 *h* Rom. 6:4; Acts 2:38–42

166. *Unto whom is baptism to be administered?*

Baptism is not to be administered to any that are out of the visible church, and so strangers from the covenant of promise, till they profess their faith in Christ, and obedience to him,[a] but infants descending from parents, either both, or but one of them, professing faith in Christ, and obedience to him, are in that respect within the covenant, and to be baptized.[b]

a Acts 2:38–39, 41; Acts 8:12, 36, 38; Acts 16:15 *b* Col. 2:11–12; Acts 2:38–39; Rom. 4:11–12; 1 Cor. 7:14; Luke 18:15–16; Gen. 17:7–9; Gal. 3:9–14; Rom. 11:16

167. *How is our baptism to be improved by us?*

The needful but much neglected duty of improving our baptism, is to be performed by us all our life long, especially in the time of temptation, and when we are present at the administration of it to others;[a] by serious and thankful consideration of the nature of it, and of the ends for which Christ instituted it, the privileges and benefits conferred and sealed thereby, and our solemn vow made therein;[b] by being humbled for our sinful defilement, our falling short of, and walking contrary to, the grace of baptism, and our engagements;[c] by growing up to assurance of pardon of sin, and of all other blessings sealed to us in that sacrament;[d] by drawing strength from the death and resurrection of Christ, into whom we are baptized, for the mortifying of sin, and quickening of grace;[e] and by endeavoring to live by faith,[f] to have our conversation in holiness and righteousness,[g] as those that have therein given up their names to Christ;[h] and to walk in brotherly love, as being baptized by the same Spirit into one body.[i]

a Col. 2:11–12; Rom. 6:4, 6, 11 b Rom. 6:3–5; 1 Pet. 3:21 c 1 Cor. 1:11–13; Rom. 6:2–3 d Rom. 6:4–7, 22; 1 Pet. 3:21; Rom. 5:1–2; Jer. 33:8 e Rom. 6:3–5 f Gal. 3:26–27 g Rom. 6:22 h Acts 2:38; Gal. 2:20; Rev. 2:17 i 1 Cor. 12:13, 25

168. *What is the Lord's Supper?*

The Lord's Supper is a sacrament of the new testament,[a] wherein, by giving and receiving bread and wine according to the appointment of Jesus Christ, his death is showed forth; and they that worthily communicate feed upon his body and blood, to their spiritual nourishment and growth in grace;[b] have their union and communion with him confirmed;[c] testify and renew their thankfulness,[d] and engagement to God,[e] and their mutual love and fellowship each with other, as members of the same mystical body.[f]

a Luke 22:20 b Matt. 26:26–28; 1 Cor. 11:23–26 c 1 Cor. 10:16 d 1 Cor. 11:24 e 1 Cor. 10:14–16, 21; Rom. 7:4 f 1 Cor. 10:17

169. *How hath Christ appointed bread and wine to be given and received in the sacrament of the Lord's Supper?*

Christ hath appointed the ministers of his Word, in the administration of this sacrament of the Lord's Supper, to set apart the bread and wine from common use, by the word of institution, thanksgiving, and prayer; to take and break the bread, and to give both the bread and the wine to the communicants: who are, by the same appointment, to take and eat the bread, and to drink the wine, in thankful remembrance that the body of Christ was broken and given, and his blood shed, for them.[a]

a 1 Cor. 11:23–24; Matt. 26:26–28; Mark 14:22–24; Luke 22:19–20

170. *How do they that worthily communicate in the Lord's Supper feed upon the body and blood of Christ therein?*

As the body and blood of Christ are not corporally or carnally present in, with, or under the bread and wine in the Lord's Supper,[a] and yet are spiritually present to the faith of the receiver, no less truly and really than the elements themselves are to their outward senses;[b] so they that worthily communicate in the sacrament of the Lord's Supper, do therein feed upon the body and blood of Christ, not after a corporal and carnal, but in a spiritual manner; yet truly and really,[c] while by faith they receive and apply unto themselves Christ crucified, and all the benefits of his death.[d]

a Acts 3:21 b Matt. 26:26, 28 c 1 Cor. 11:24–29; Westminster Confession of Faith 27.2; John 6:51, 53 d 1 Cor. 10:16

171. *How are they that receive the sacrament of the Lord's Supper to prepare themselves before they come unto it?*

They that receive the sacrament of the Lord's Supper are, before they come, to prepare themselves thereunto, by examining themselves[a] of their being in Christ,[b] of their sins and wants;[c] of the truth and measure of their knowledge,[d] faith,[e] repentance;[f] love to God and the brethren,[g] charity to all men,[h] forgiving those that have done them wrong;[i] of their desires after Christ,[j] and of their new obedience;[k] and by renewing the exercise of these graces,[l] by serious meditation,[m] and fervent prayer.[n]

a 1 Cor. 11:28 b 2 Cor. 13:5 c 1 Cor. 5:7; Ex. 12:15 d 1 Cor. 11:29 e 2 Cor. 13:5; Matt. 26:28
f Zech. 12:10; 1 Cor. 11:31 g 1 Cor. 10:16–17; Acts 2:46–47 h 1 Cor. 5:8; 1 Cor. 11:18, 20 i Matt.
5:23–24 j Isa. 55:1; John 7:37 k 1 Cor. 5:7–8 l 1 Cor. 11:25–26, 28; Heb. 10:21–22, 24; Ps. 26:6
m 1 Cor. 11:24–25 n 2 Chron. 30:18–19; Matt. 26:26

172. *May one who doubteth of his being in Christ, or of his due preparation, come to the Lord's Supper?*

One who doubteth of his being in Christ, or of his due preparation to the sacrament of the Lord's Supper, may have true interest in Christ, though he be not yet assured thereof;[a] and in God's account hath it, if he be duly affected with the apprehension of the want of it,[b] and unfeignedly desires to be found in Christ,[c] and to depart from iniquity:[d] in which case (because promises are made, and this sacrament is appointed, for the relief even of weak and doubting Christians[e]) he is to bewail his unbelief,[f] and labor to have his doubts resolved;[g] and, so doing, he may and ought to come to the Lord's Supper, that he may be further strengthened.[h]

a Isa. 50:10; 1 John 5:13; Ps. 88:1–18; Ps. 77:1–4, 7–10; Jonah 2:4 b Isa. 54:7–10; Matt. 5:3–4;
Ps. 31:22; Ps. 73:13, 22–23 c Phil. 3:8–9; Ps. 10:17; Ps. 42:1–2, 5, 11 d 2 Tim. 2:19; Isa. 50:10; Ps.
66:18–20 e Isa. 40:11, 29, 31; Matt. 11:28; Matt. 12:20; Matt. 26:28 f Mark 9:24 g Acts 2:37;
Acts 16:30 h Rom. 4:11; 1 Cor. 11:28

173. *May any who profess the faith, and desire to come to the Lord's Supper, be kept from it?*

Such as are found to be ignorant or scandalous, notwithstanding their profession of the faith, and desire to come to the Lord's Supper, may and ought to be kept from that sacrament, by the power which Christ hath left in his church,[a] until they receive instruction, and manifest their reformation.[b]

a 1 Cor. 11:27–34; Matt. 7:6; 1 Cor. 5:1–13; Jude 23; 1 Tim. 5:22 b 2 Cor. 2:7

174. *What is required of them that receive the sacrament of the Lord's Supper in the time of the administration of it?*

It is required of them that receive the sacrament of the Lord's Supper, that, during the time of the administration of it, with all holy reverence and attention they wait upon God in that ordinance,[a] diligently observe the sacramental elements and actions,[b] heedfully discern the Lord's body,[c] and affectionately meditate on his death and sufferings,[d] and thereby stir up themselves to a vigorous exercise of their graces;[e] in judging themselves,[f] and sorrowing for sin;[g] in earnest hungering and thirsting after Christ,[h] feeding on him by faith,[i] receiving of his fullness,[j] trusting in his merits,[k] rejoicing in his love,[l] giving thanks for his grace;[m] in renewing of their covenant with God,[n] and love to all the saints.[o]

a Lev. 10:3; Heb. 12:28; Ps. 5:7; 1 Cor. 11:17, 26–27 *b* Ex. 24:8; Matt. 26:28 *c* 1 Cor. 11:29 *d* Luke 22:19 *e* 1 Cor. 11:26; 1 Cor. 10:3–5, 11, 14 *f* 1 Cor. 11:31 *g* Zech. 12:10 *h* Rev. 22:17; Matt. 5:6 *i* John 6:35, 47–58 *j* John 1:16 *k* Phil. 3:9 *l* Ps. 63:4–5; 2 Chron. 30:21 *m* Ps. 22:26; 1 Cor. 10:16 *n* Jer. 50:5; Ps. 50:5 *o* Acts 2:42

175. *What is the duty of Christians, after they have received the sacrament of the Lord's Supper?*

The duty of Christians, after they have received the sacrament of the Lord's Supper, is seriously to consider how they have behaved themselves therein, and with what success;[a] if they find quickening and comfort, to bless God for it,[b] beg the continuance of it,[c] watch against relapses,[d] fulfill their vows,[e] and encourage themselves to a frequent attendance on that ordinance:[f] but if they find no present benefit, more exactly to review their preparation to, and carriage at, the sacrament;[g] in both which, if they can approve themselves to God and their own consciences, they are to wait for the fruit of it in due time:[h] but, if they see they have failed in either, they are to be humbled,[i] and to attend upon it afterwards with more care and diligence.[j]

a Ps. 28:7; Ps. 85:8; 1 Cor. 11:17, 30–31 *b* 2 Chron. 30:21–23, 25–26; Acts 2:42, 46–47 *c* Ps. 36:10; Song 3:4; 1 Chron. 29:18 *d* 1 Cor. 10:3–5, 12 *e* Ps. 50:14 *f* 1 Cor. 11:25–26; Acts 2:42, 46 *g* Eccles. 5:1–6; Ps. 139:23–24 *h* Ps. 123:1–2; Ps. 42:5, 8; Ps. 43:3–5 *i* 2 Chron. 30:18–19 *j* 2 Cor. 7:11; 1 Chron. 15:12–14

176. *Wherein do the sacraments of baptism and the Lord's Supper agree?*
The sacraments of baptism and the Lord's Supper agree, in that the author of both is God;[a] the spiritual part of both is Christ and his benefits;[b] both are seals of the same covenant,[c] are to be dispensed by ministers of the gospel, and by none other;[d] and to be continued in the church of Christ until his second coming.[e]

a Matt. 28:19; 1 Cor. 11:23 *b* Rom. 6:3–4; 1 Cor. 10:16 *c* Rom. 4:11; Col. 2:12; Matt. 26:27–28 *d* John 1:33; Matt. 28:19; 1 Cor. 11:23; 1 Cor. 4:1; Heb. 5:4 *e* Matt. 28:19–20; 1 Cor. 11:26

177. *Wherein do the sacraments of baptism and the Lord's Supper differ?*
The sacraments of baptism and the Lord's Supper differ, in that baptism is to be administered but once, with water, to be a sign and seal of our regeneration and ingrafting into Christ,[a] and that even to infants;[b] whereas the Lord's Supper is to be administered often, in the elements of bread and wine, to represent and exhibit Christ as spiritual nourishment to the soul,[c] and to confirm our continuance and growth in him,[d] and that only to such as are of years and ability to examine themselves.[e]

a Matt. 3:11; Titus 3:5; Gal. 3:27 *b* Gen. 17:7, 9; Acts 2:38–39; 1 Cor. 7:14 *c* 1 Cor. 11:23–26 *d* 1 Cor. 10:16 *e* 1 Cor. 11:28–29

178. *What is prayer?*

Prayer is an offering up of our desires unto God,[a] in the name of Christ,[b] by the help of his Spirit;[c] with confession of our sins,[d] and thankful acknowledgment of his mercies.[e]

a Ps. 10:17; Ps. 62:8; Matt. 7:7–8 *b* John 16:23 *c* Rom. 8:26 *d* Ps. 32:5–6; 1 John 1:9; Dan. 9:4–19 *e* Phil. 4:6; Ps. 103:1–5; Ps. 136:1–26

179. *Are we to pray unto God only?*

God only being able to search the hearts,[a] hear the requests,[b] pardon the sins,[c] and fulfill the desires of all;[d] and only to be believed in,[e] and worshiped with religious worship;[f] prayer, which is a special part thereof,[g] is to be made by all to him alone,[h] and to none other.[i]

a 1 Kings 8:39; Acts 1:24; Rom. 8:27 *b* Ps. 65:2 *c* Mic. 7:18 *d* Ps. 145:18 *e* Rom. 10:14 *f* Matt. 4:10 *g* 1 Cor. 1:2 *h* Isa. 45:22; Matt. 6:9; Ps. 50:15 *i* Isa. 43:11; Isa. 46:1–13

180. *What is it to pray in the name of Christ?*

To pray in the name of Christ is, in obedience to his command, and in confidence on his promises, to ask mercy for his sake;[a] not by bare mentioning of his name,[b] but by drawing our encouragement to pray, and our boldness, strength, and hope of acceptance in prayer, from Christ and his mediation.[c]

a John 14:13–14; John 16:24; Dan. 9:17 *b* Matt. 7:21 *c* Heb. 4:14–16; 1 John 5:13–15

181. *Why are we to pray in the name of Christ?*

The sinfulness of man, and his distance from God by reason thereof, being so great, as that we can have no access into his presence without a mediator;[a] and there being none in heaven or earth appointed to, or fit for, that glorious work but Christ alone,[b] we are to pray in no other name but his only.[c]

a John 14:6; Isa. 59:2; Eph. 3:12 *b* John 6:27; Heb. 7:25–27; 1 Tim. 2:5 *c* Col. 3:17; Heb. 13:15

182. *How doth the Spirit help us to pray?*

We not knowing what to pray for as we ought, the Spirit helpeth our infirmities, by enabling us to understand both for whom, and what, and how prayer is to be made; and by working and quickening in our hearts (although not in all persons, nor at all times, in the same measure) those apprehensions, affections, and graces which are requisite for the right performance of that duty.[a]

a Rom. 8:26–27; Ps. 10:17; Zech. 12:10

183. *For whom are we to pray?*

We are to pray for the whole church of Christ upon earth;[a] for magistrates,[b] and ministers;[c] for ourselves,[d] our brethren,[e] yea, our enemies;[f] and for all sorts of men living,[g] or that shall live hereafter;[h] but not for the dead,[i] nor for those that are known to have sinned the sin unto death.[j]

a Eph. 6:18; Ps. 28:9 b 1 Tim. 2:1–2 c Col. 4:3 d Gen. 32:11 e James 5:16 f Matt. 5:44
g 1 Tim. 2:1–2 h John 17:20; 2 Sam. 7:29 i 2 Sam. 12:21–23 j 1 John 5:16

184. *For what things are we to pray?*

We are to pray for all things tending to the glory of God,[a] the welfare of the church,[b] our own[c] or others' good;[d] but not for anything that is unlawful.[e]

a Matt. 6:9 b Ps. 51:18; Ps. 122:6 c Matt. 7:11 d Ps. 125:4 e 1 John 5:14

185. *How are we to pray?*

We are to pray with an awful apprehension of the majesty of God,[a] and deep sense of our own unworthiness,[b] necessities,[c] and sins;[d] with penitent,[e] thankful,[f] and enlarged hearts;[g] with understanding,[h] faith,[i] sincerity,[j] fervency,[k] love,[l] and perseverance,[m] waiting upon him,[n] with humble submission to his will.[o]

a Ps. 33:8; Ps. 95:6; Ps. 145:5 b Gen. 18:27; Gen. 32:10 c Luke 15:17–19 d Luke 18:13–14
e Ps. 51:17 f Phil. 4:6 g 1 Sam. 1:15; 1 Sam. 2:1 h 1 Cor. 14:15 i Mark 11:24; James 1:6
j Ps. 145:18; Ps. 17:1 k James 5:16 l Ps. 116:1–2; Rom. 15:30 m Eph. 6:18 n Mic. 7:7
o Matt. 26:39

186. *What rule hath God given for our direction in the duty of prayer?*
The whole Word of God is of use to direct us in the duty of prayer;[a] but the special rule of direction is that form of prayer which our Savior Christ taught his disciples, commonly called the Lord's Prayer.[b]

a 1 John 5:14 b Matt. 6:9–13; Luke 11:2–4

187. *How is the Lord's Prayer to be used?*
The Lord's Prayer is not only for direction, as a pattern, according to which we are to make other prayers; but may also be used as a prayer, so that it be done with understanding, faith, reverence, and other graces necessary to the right performance of the duty of prayer.[a]

a Matt. 6:9; Luke 11:2

188. *Of how many parts doth the Lord's Prayer consist?*
The Lord's Prayer consists of three parts; a preface, petitions, and a conclusion.

189. *What doth the preface of the Lord's Prayer teach us?*
The preface of the Lord's Prayer (contained in these words, *Our Father which art in heaven*[a]) teacheth us, when we pray, to draw near to God with confidence of his fatherly goodness, and our interest therein;[b] with reverence, and all other childlike dispositions,[c]

heavenly affections,[d] and due apprehensions of his sovereign power, majesty, and gracious condescension:[e] as also, to pray with and for others.[f]

a Matt. 6:9; Luke 11:2 b Ps. 103:13; Luke 11:13; Rom. 8:15 c Isa. 64:9 d Col. 3:1–2; Ps. 123:1; Lam. 3:41 e Isa. 63:15–16; Neh. 1:4–6; Ps. 113:4–6 f Acts 12:5; 1 Tim. 2:1–2; Eph. 6:18

190. *What do we pray for in the first petition?*

In the first petition (which is, Hallowed be thy name[a]), acknowledging the utter inability and indisposition that is in ourselves and all men to honor God aright,[b] we pray, that God would by his grace enable and incline us and others to know, to acknowledge, and highly to esteem him,[c] his titles,[d] attributes,[e] ordinances, Word,[f] works, and whatsoever he is pleased to make himself known by;[g] and to glorify him in thought, word,[h] and deed:[i] that he would prevent and remove atheism,[j] ignorance,[k] idolatry,[l] profaneness,[m] and whatsoever is dishonorable to him;[n] and, by his overruling providence, direct and dispose of all things to his own glory.[o]

a Matt. 6:9; Luke 11:2 b 2 Cor. 3:5; Ps. 51:15 c Ps. 67:2–3; Ps. 99:1–3 d Ps. 83:18 e Ps. 86:10–13, 15 f 2 Thess. 3:1; Ps. 147:19–20; Ps. 138:1–3; 2 Cor. 2:14–15 g Ps. 145:1–21; Ps. 8:1–9 h Ps. 103:1; Ps. 19:14 i Phil. 1:9, 11; Ps. 100:3–4 j Ps. 67:1–4 k Eph. 1:17–18 l Ps. 97:7 m Ps. 74:18, 22–23 n 2 Kings 19:15–16 o 2 Chron. 20:6, 10–12; Rom. 11:33–36; Rev. 4:11; Ps. 83:1–18; Ps. 140:4, 8

191. *What do we pray for in the second petition?*

In the second petition (which is, Thy kingdom come[a]), acknowledging ourselves and all mankind to be by nature under the dominion of sin and Satan,[b] we pray, that the kingdom of sin and Satan may be destroyed,[c] the gospel propagated throughout the world,[d] the Jews called,[e] the fullness of the Gentiles brought in;[f] the church furnished with all gospel officers and ordinances,[g] purged from corruption,[h] countenanced and maintained by the civil magistrate:[i] that the ordinances of Christ may be purely dispensed, and made effectual to the converting of those that are yet in their sins, and the confirming, comforting, and building up of those that are already converted:[j] that Christ would rule in our hearts here,[k] and hasten the time of his second coming, and our reigning with him forever:[l] and that he would be pleased so to exercise the kingdom of his power in all the world, as may best conduce to these ends.[m]

a Matt. 6:10; Luke 11:2 b Eph. 2:2–3 c Ps. 68:1, 18; Rev. 12:10–11 d Ps. 67:1–2; 2 Thess. 3:1 e Rom. 10:1 f John 17:9, 20; Rom. 11:25–26; Ps. 67:1–7 g Matt. 9:38; 2 Thess. 3:1 h Mal. 1:11; Zeph. 3:9 i 1 Tim. 2:1–2; Isa. 49:23 j Acts 4:29–30; Eph. 6:18–20; Rom. 15:29–30, 32; 2 Thess. 1:11; 2 Thess. 2:16–17 k Eph. 3:14–20; Col. 3:15 l Rev. 22:20; 2 Tim. 2:12; 2 Pet. 3:12 m Isa. 64:1–2; Rev. 4:8–11

192. *What do we pray for in the third petition?*

In the third petition (which is, *Thy will be done in earth, as it is in heaven*[a]), acknowledging, that by nature we and all men are not only utterly unable and unwilling to know and do the will of God,[b] but prone to rebel against his Word,[c] to repine and murmur against his providence,[d] and wholly inclined to do the will of the flesh, and of the devil:[e] we pray, that God would by his Spirit take away from ourselves and others all blindness,[f] weakness,[g] indisposedness,[h] and perverseness of heart;[i] and by his grace make us able and willing to know, do, and submit to his will in all things,[j] with the like humility,[k] cheerfulness,[l] faithfulness,[m] diligence,[n] zeal,[o] sincerity,[p] and constancy,[q] as the angels do in heaven.[r]

a Matt. 6:10; Luke 11:2 b Rom. 7:18; Job 21:14; 1 Cor. 2:14 c Rom. 8:7 d Ex. 17:7; Num. 14:2 e Eph. 2:2 f Eph. 1:17–18 g Eph. 3:16 h Matt. 26:40–41 i Jer. 31:18–19 j Ps. 19:14; Acts 21:14; Ps. 119:1–76; 1 Thess. 5:23; Heb. 13:20–21 k Mic. 6:8 l Ps. 100:2; Job 1:21; 2 Sam. 15:25–26 m Isa. 38:3 n Ps. 119:4–5 o Ps. 69:9; John 2:17; Rom. 12:11 p Josh. 24:14; Ps. 119:80; 1 Cor. 5:8; 2 Cor. 1:12 q Ps. 119:112 r Isa. 6:2–3; Ps. 103:20–21; Matt. 18:10

193. *What do we pray for in the fourth petition?*

In the fourth petition (which is, *Give us this day our daily bread*[a]), acknowledging, that in Adam, and by our own sin, we have forfeited our right to all the outward blessings of this life, and deserve to be wholly deprived of them by God, and to have them cursed to us in the use of them;[b] and that neither they of themselves are able to sustain us,[c] nor we to merit,[d] or by our own industry to procure them;[e] but prone to desire,[f] get,[g] and use them unlawfully:[h] we pray for ourselves and others, that both they and we, waiting upon the providence of God from day to day in the use of lawful means, may, of his free gift, and as to his fatherly wisdom shall seem best, enjoy a competent portion of them;[i] and have the same continued and blessed unto us in our holy and comfortable use of them,[j] and contentment in them;[k] and be kept from all things that are contrary to our temporal support and comfort.[l]

a Matt. 6:11; Luke 11:3 *b* Gen. 2:17; Gen. 3:17; Rom. 8:20–22; Jer. 5:25; Deut. 28:15–68
c Deut. 8:3 *d* Gen. 32:10 *e* Deut. 8:17–18 *f* Jer. 6:13; Mark 7:21–22 *g* Hos. 12:7 *h* James 4:3
i Gen. 43:12–14; Gen. 28:20; Eph. 4:28; 2 Thess. 3:11–12; Phil. 4:6 *j* 1 Tim. 4:3–5 *k* 1 Tim.
6:6–8 *l* Prov. 30:8–9

194. *What do we pray for in the fifth petition?*

In the fifth petition (which is, *Forgive us our debts, as we forgive our debtors*[a]), acknowledging, that we and all others are guilty both of original and actual sin, and thereby become debtors to the justice of God; and that neither we, nor any other creature, can make the least satisfaction for that debt:[b] we pray for ourselves and others, that God of his free grace would, through the obedience and satisfaction of Christ, apprehended and applied by faith, acquit us both from the guilt and punishment of sin,[c] accept us in his Beloved;[d] continue his favor and grace to us,[e] pardon our daily failings,[f] and fill us with peace and joy, in giving us daily more and more assurance of forgiveness;[g] which we are the rather emboldened to ask, and encouraged to expect, when we have this testimony in ourselves, that we from the heart forgive others their offenses.[h]

a Matt. 6:12; Luke 11:4 *b* Rom. 3:9–22; Matt. 18:24–25; Ps. 130:3–4 *c* Rom. 3:24–26; Heb. 9:22 *d* Eph. 1:6–7 *e* 2 Pet. 1:2 *f* Hos. 14:2; Jer. 14:7; 1 John 1:9; Dan. 9:17–19 *g* Rom. 15:13; Ps. 51:7–10, 12 *h* Luke 11:4; Matt. 6:14–15; Eph. 4:32; Col. 3:13; Matt. 18:21–35

195. *What do we pray for in the sixth petition?*

In the sixth petition (which is, *And lead us not into temptation, but deliver us from evil*[a]), acknowledging, that the most wise, righteous, and gracious God, for divers holy and just ends, may so order things, that we may be assaulted, foiled, and for a time led captive by temptations;[b] that Satan,[c] the world,[d] and the flesh, are ready powerfully to draw us aside, and ensnare us;[e] and that we, even after the pardon of our sins, by reason of our corruption,[f] weakness, and want of watchfulness,[g] are not only subject to be tempted, and forward to expose ourselves unto temptations,[h] but also of ourselves unable and unwilling to resist them, to recover out of them, and to improve them;[i] and worthy to be left under the power of them:[j] we pray, that God would so overrule the world and all in it,[k] subdue the flesh,[l] and restrain Satan,[m] order all things,[n] bestow and bless all means of grace,[o] and quicken us to watchfulness in the use of them, that we and all his people may by his providence be kept from being tempted to sin;[p] or, if tempted, that by his Spirit we may be powerfully supported and enabled to stand in the hour of temptation;[q] or when fallen, raised again and recovered out of it,[r] and have a sanctified use and improvement thereof:[s] that our sanctification and salvation may be perfected,[t] Satan trodden under our feet,[u] and we fully freed from sin, temptation, and all evil, forever.[v]

a Matt. 6:13; Luke 11:4 *b* 2 Chron. 32:31 *c* 1 Chron. 21:1 *d* Luke 21:34; Mark 4:19 *e* James 1:14 *f* Gal. 5:17 *g* Matt. 26:41 *h* Matt. 26:69–72; Gal. 2:11–14; 2 Chron. 18:3; 2 Chron. 19:2

196.   *What doth the conclusion of the Lord's Prayer teach us?*

The conclusion of the Lord's Prayer (which is, *For thine is the king-dom, and the power, and the glory, for ever. Amen*[a]), teacheth us to enforce our petitions with arguments,[b] which are to be taken, not from any worthiness in ourselves, or in any other creature, but from God;[c] and with our prayers to join praises,[d] ascribing to God alone eternal sovereignty, omnipotency, and glorious excellency;[e] in regard whereof, as he is able and willing to help us,[f] so we by faith are emboldened to plead with him that he would,[g] and quietly to rely upon him, that he will fulfill our requests.[h] And, to testify this our desire and assurance, we say, *Amen.*[i]

a Matt. 6:13   b Rom. 15:30   c Dan. 9:4, 7–9, 16–19   d Phil. 4:6   e 1 Chron. 29:10–13; 1 Tim. 1:17; Rev. 5:11–13   f Eph. 3:20–21; Luke 11:13   g 2 Chron. 20:6, 11   h 2 Chron. 14:11   i 1 Cor. 14:16; Rev. 22:20–21

The Westminster Shorter Catechism

INTRODUCTION

The Shorter Catechism is almost entirely a byproduct of the Larger but with a more personal focus, often considering the individual where the Larger Catechism considers the church. Christians using the Westminster Standards are best served when they use each of the documents as it was intended. The Westminster Confession serves as a quick-reference guide for careful statements of Christian doctrine. The Larger Catechism is intended as a teaching tool for churches and families, covering matters of faith and life. The Shorter Catechism is a tight summary of classic Christian doctrines, capable of being memorized even by a child.

One of the reasons the Westminster Catechisms have been so well received has to do with their suitability for memorization. Three features stand out. First, each question follows logically after the one preceding it. Second, and to an extent not previously seen in major catechisms, each question can be understood on its own terms without reference to a prior sequence of questions and answers. Finally, each answer offers an aphorism that can be understood independently from the question asked. For example, "There are three persons in the Godhead; the Father, the Son, and the Holy Ghost; and these three are one God, the same in substance, equal in power and glory" (WSC 6); "Justification is an act of God's free grace, wherein he pardoneth all our sins, and accepteth us as righteous in his sight, only for the righteousness of Christ imputed to us, and received by faith alone (WSC 33).

The Shorter Catechism is well known for its crisp statements of key Christian doctrines. But its claim to fame is found in the questions and answers that bookend the whole and encapsulate a vision for the Christian life. First, "What is the chief end of man? Man's chief end is to glorify God, and to enjoy him forever" (WSC 1). And, at the end, "What doth the conclusion of the Lord's prayer teach us? The conclusion of the Lord's Prayer, which is, *For thine is the kingdom, and the power, and the glory, for ever. Amen,* teacheth us to take our encouragement in prayer from God only, and in our prayers to praise him, ascribing kingdom, power, and glory to him; and, in testimony of our desire, and assurance to be heard, we say, *Amen.*" (WSC 107).

THE WESTMINSTER
SHORTER CATECHISM

1. *What is the chief end of man?*
   Man's chief end is to glorify God,[a] and to enjoy him forever.[b]

   a Ps. 86:9; Isa. 60:21; Rom. 11:36; 1 Cor. 6:20; 1 Cor. 10:31; Rev. 4:11 b Ps. 16:5–11; Ps. 144:15; Isa. 12:2; Luke 2:10; Phil. 4:4; Rev. 21:3–4

2. *What rule hath God given to direct us how we may glorify and enjoy him?*
   The Word of God, which is contained in the Scriptures of the Old and New Testaments,[a] is the only rule to direct us how we may glorify and enjoy him.[b]

   a Matt. 19:4–5; Gen. 2:24; Luke 24:27, 44; 1 Cor. 2:13; 1 Cor. 14:37; 2 Pet. 1:20–21; 2 Pet. 3:2, 15–16 b Deut. 4:2; Ps. 19:7–11; Isa. 8:20; John 15:11; John 20:30–31; Acts 17:11; 2 Tim. 3:15–17; 1 John 1:4

3. *What do the Scriptures principally teach?*
   The Scriptures principally teach, what man is to believe concerning God,[a] and what duty God requires of man.[b]

   a Gen. 1:1; John 5:39; John 20:31; Rom. 10:17; 2 Tim. 3:15 b Deut. 10:12–13; Josh. 1:8; Ps. 119:105; Mic. 6:8; 2 Tim. 3:16–17

4. *What is God?*
   God is a Spirit,[a] infinite, [b] eternal,[c] and unchangeable,[d] in his being,[e] wisdom,[f] power,[g] holiness,[h] justice,[i] goodness,[j] and truth.[k]

   a Deut. 4:15–19; Luke 24:39; John 1:18; John 4:24; Acts 17:29 b 1 Kings 8:27; Ps. 139:7–10; Ps. 145:3; Ps. 147:5; Jer. 23:24; Rom. 11:33–36 c Deut. 33:27; Ps. 90:2; Ps. 102:12, 24–27; Rev. 1:4, 8 d Ps. 33:11; Mal. 3:6; Heb. 1:12; Heb. 6:17–18; Heb. 13:8; James 1:17 e Ex. 3:14; Ps. 115:2–3;

1 Tim. 1:17; 1 Tim. 6:15–16 f Ps. 104:24; Rom. 11:33–34; Heb. 4:13; 1 John 3:20 g Gen. 17:1; Ps. 62:11; Jer. 32:17; Matt. 19:26; Rev. 1:8 h Hab. 1:13; 1 Pet. 1:15–16; 1 John 3:3, 5; Rev. 15:4 i Gen. 18:25; Ex. 34:6–7; Deut. 32:4; Ps. 96:13; Rom. 3:5, 26 j Ps. 103:5; Ps. 107:8; Matt. 19:17; Rom. 2:4 k Ex. 34:6; Deut. 32:4; Ps. 86:15; Ps. 117:2; Heb. 6:18

5.   Are there more Gods than one?
There is but one only,^{a} the living and true God.^{b}

a Deut. 6:4; Isa. 44:6; Isa. 45:21–22; 1 Cor. 8:4–6 b Jer. 10:10; John 17:3; 1 Thess. 1:9; 1 John 5:20

6.   How many persons are there in the Godhead?
There are three persons in the Godhead; the Father, the Son, and the Holy Ghost;^{a} and these three are one God, the same in substance, equal in power and glory.^{b}

a Matt. 3:16–17; Matt. 28:19; 2 Cor. 13:14; 1 Pet. 1:2 b Ps. 45:6; John 1:1; John 17:5; Acts 5:3–4; Rom. 9:5; Col. 2:9; Jude 24–25

7.   What are the decrees of God?
The decrees of God are, his eternal purpose, according to the counsel of his will, whereby, for his own glory, he hath foreordained whatsoever comes to pass.^{a}

a Ps. 33:11; Isa. 14:24; Acts 2:23; Eph. 1:11–12

8.   How doth God execute his decrees?
God executeth his decrees in the works of creation and providence.^{a}

a Ps. 148:8; Isa. 40:26; Dan. 4:35; Acts 4:24–28; Rev. 4:11

9.   What is the work of creation?
The work of creation is, God's making all things of nothing, by the word of his power,^{a} in the space of six days, and all very good.^{b}

a Gen. 1:1; Ps. 33:6, 9; Heb. 11:3 b Gen. 1:31

10. *How did God create man?*

God created man male and female, after his own image,[a] in knowledge,[b] righteousness, and holiness,[c] with dominion over the creatures.[d]

a Gen. 1:27 *b* Col. 3:10 *c* Eph. 4:24 *d* Gen. 1:28; Ps. 8:1–9

11. *What are God's works of providence?*

God's works of providence are, his most holy,[a] wise,[b] and powerful[c] preserving[d] and governing[e] all his creatures, and all their actions.[f]

a Ps. 145:17 *b* Ps. 104:24 *c* Heb. 1:3 *d* Neh. 9:6 *e* Eph. 1:19–22 *f* Ps. 36:6; Prov. 16:33; Matt. 10:30

12. *What special act of providence did God exercise towards man in the estate wherein he was created?*

When God had created man, he entered into a covenant of life with him, upon condition of perfect obedience; forbidding him to eat of the tree of the knowledge of good and evil, upon pain of death.[a]

a Gen. 2:16–17; James 2:10

13. *Did our first parents continue in the estate wherein they were created?*

Our first parents, being left to the freedom of their own will, fell from the estate wherein they were created, by sinning against God.[a]

a Gen. 3:6–8, 13; 2 Cor. 11:3

14. *What is sin?*

Sin is any want of conformity unto, or transgression of, the law of God.[a]

a Lev. 5:17; James 4:17; 1 John 3:4

15. *What was the sin whereby our first parents fell from the estate wherein they were created?*

    The sin whereby our first parents fell from the estate wherein they were created, was their eating the forbidden fruit.[a]

    a Gen. 3:6

16. *Did all mankind fall in Adam's first transgression?*

    The covenant being made with Adam,[a] not only for himself, but for his posterity; all mankind, descending from him by ordinary generation, sinned in him, and fell with him, in his first transgression.[b]

    a Gen. 2:16–17; James 2:10   b Rom. 5:12–21; 1 Cor. 15:22

17. *Into what estate did the fall bring mankind?*

    The fall brought mankind into an estate of sin and misery.[a]

    a Gen. 3:16–19, 23; Rom. 3:16; Rom. 5:12; Eph. 2:1

18. *Wherein consists the sinfulness of that estate whereinto man fell?*

    The sinfulness of that estate whereinto man fell, consists in the guilt of Adam's first sin,[a] the want of original righteousness,[b] and the corruption of his whole nature,[c] which is commonly called original sin; together with all actual transgressions which proceed from it.[d]

    a Rom. 5:12, 19   b Rom. 3:10; Col. 3:10; Eph. 4:24   c Ps. 51:5; John 3:6; Rom. 3:18; Rom. 8:7–8; Eph. 2:3   d Gen. 6:5; Ps. 53:1–3; Matt. 15:19; Rom. 3:10–18, 23; Gal. 5:19–21; James 1:14–15

19. *What is the misery of that estate whereinto man fell?*

    All mankind by their fall lost communion with God,[a] are under his wrath[b] and curse,[c] and so made liable to all the miseries of this life,[d] to death[e] itself, and to the pains of hell forever.[f]

a Gen. 3:8, 24; John 8:34, 42, 44; Eph. 2:12; Eph. 4:18 b John 3:36; Rom. 1:18; Eph. 2:3; Eph. 5:6 c Gal. 3:10; Rev. 22:3 d Gen. 3:16–19; Job 5:7; Eccles. 2:22–23; Rom. 8:18–23 e Ezek. 18:4; Rom. 5:12; Rom. 6:23 f Matt. 25:41, 46; 2 Thess. 1:9; Rev. 14:9–11

20. *Did God leave all mankind to perish in the estate of sin and misery?*

God, having out of his mere good pleasure, from all eternity, elected some to everlasting life,[a] did enter into a covenant of grace to deliver them out of the estate of sin and misery, and to bring them into an estate of salvation by a Redeemer.[b]

a Acts 13:48; Eph. 1:4–5; 2 Thess. 2:13–14 b Gen. 3:15; Gen. 17:7; Ex. 19:5–6; Jer. 31:31–34; Matt. 20:28; 1 Cor. 11:25; Heb. 9:15

21. *Who is the Redeemer of God's elect?*

The only Redeemer of God's elect is the Lord Jesus Christ,[a] who, being the eternal Son of God,[b] became man,[c] and so was, and continueth to be, God and man in two distinct natures, and one person, forever.[d]

a John 14:6; Acts 4:12; 1 Tim. 2:5–6 b Ps. 2:7; Matt. 3:17; Matt. 17:5; John 1:18 c Isa. 9:6; Matt. 1:23; John 1:14; Gal. 4:4 d Acts 1:11; Heb. 7:24–25

22. *How did Christ, being the Son of God, become man?*

Christ, the Son of God, became man, by taking to himself a true body, and a reasonable soul,[a] being conceived by the power of the Holy Ghost, in the womb of the Virgin Mary, and born of her,[b] yet without sin.[c]

a Phil. 2:7; Heb. 2:14, 17 b Luke 1:27, 31, 35 c 2 Cor. 5:21; Heb. 4:15; Heb. 7:26; 1 John 3:5

23. *What offices doth Christ execute as our Redeemer?*

Christ, as our Redeemer, executeth the offices of a prophet,[a] of a priest,[b] and of a king,[c] both in his estate of humiliation and exaltation.

a Deut. 18:18; Acts 2:33; Acts 3:22–23; Heb. 1:1–2 b Heb. 4:14–15; Heb. 5:5–6 c Isa. 9:6–7; Luke 1:32–33; John 18:37; 1 Cor. 15:25

24. *How doth Christ execute the office of a prophet?*

Christ executeth the office of a prophet, in revealing to us, by his Word[a] and Spirit,[b] the will of God for our salvation.[c]

a Luke 4:18–19, 21; Acts 1:1–2; Heb. 2:3 b John 15:26–27; Acts 1:8; 1 Pet. 1:11 c John 4:41–42; John 20:30–31

25. *How doth Christ execute the office of a priest?*

Christ executeth the office of a priest, in his once offering up of himself a sacrifice to satisfy divine justice,[a] and reconcile us to God,[b] and in making continual intercession for us.[c]

a Isa. 53:1–12; Acts 8:32–35; Heb. 9:26–28; Heb. 10:12 b Rom. 5:10–11; 2 Cor. 5:18; Col. 1:21–22 c Rom. 8:34; Heb. 7:25; Heb. 9:24

26. *How doth Christ execute the office of a king?*

Christ executeth the office of a king, in subduing us to himself, in ruling and defending us,[a] and in restraining and conquering all his and our enemies.[b]

a Ps. 110:3; Matt. 28:18–20; John 17:2; Col. 1:13 b Ps. 2:6–9; Ps. 110:1–2; Matt. 12:28; 1 Cor. 15:24–26; Col. 2:15

27. *Wherein did Christ's humiliation consist?*

Christ's humiliation consisted in his being born, and that in a low condition,[a] made under the law,[b] undergoing the miseries of this life,[c] the wrath of God,[d] and the cursed death of the cross;[e]

in being buried, and continuing under the power of death for
a time.[f]

a Luke 2:7; 2 Cor. 8:9; Gal. 4:4 b Gal. 4:4 c Isa. 53:3; Luke 9:58; John 4:6; John 11:35; Heb. 2:18
d Ps. 22:1; Matt. 27:46; Isa. 53:10; 1 John 2:2 e Gal. 3:13; Phil. 2:8 f Matt. 12:40; 1 Cor. 15:3–4

28. *Wherein consisteth Christ's exaltation?*

Christ's exaltation consisteth in his rising again from the dead
on the third day,[a] in ascending up into heaven,[b] in sitting at
the right hand of God the Father,[c] and in coming to judge the
world at the last day.[d]

a 1 Cor. 15:4 b Ps. 68:18; Acts 1:11; Eph. 4:8 c Ps. 110:1; Acts 2:33–34; Heb. 1:3 d Matt. 16:27;
Acts 17:31

29. *How are we made partakers of the redemption purchased by Christ?*

We are made partakers of the redemption purchased by Christ,
by the effectual application of it to us by his Holy Spirit.[a]

a Titus 3:4–7

30. *How doth the Spirit apply to us the redemption purchased by Christ?*

The Spirit applieth to us the redemption purchased by Christ,
by working faith in us,[a] and thereby uniting us to Christ in our
effectual calling.[b]

a Rom. 10:17; 1 Cor. 2:12–16; Eph. 2:8; Phil. 1:29 b John 15:5; 1 Cor. 1:9; Eph. 3:17

31. *What is effectual calling?*

Effectual calling is the work of God's Spirit, whereby, convincing
us of our sin and misery, enlightening our minds in the knowledge of Christ,[a] and renewing our wills,[b] he doth persuade and enable us to embrace Jesus Christ,[c] freely offered to us in the gospel.[d]

a Acts 26:18; 1 Cor. 2:10, 12; 2 Cor. 4:6; Eph. 1:17–18 b Deut. 30:6; Ezek. 36:26–27; John 3:5;
Titus 3:5 c John 6:44–45; Acts 16:14 d Isa. 45:22; Matt. 11:28–30; Rev. 22:17

32. *What benefits do they that are effectually called partake of in this life?*
They that are effectually called do in this life partake of justification, adoption, and sanctification, and the several benefits which in this life do either accompany or flow from them.[a]

a Rom. 8:30; 1 Cor. 1:30; 1 Cor. 6:11; Eph. 1:5

33. *What is justification?*
Justification is an act of God's free grace,[a] wherein he pardoneth all our sins,[b] and accepteth us as righteous in his sight,[c] only for the righteousness of Christ imputed to us,[d] and received by faith alone.[e]

a Rom. 3:24 b Rom. 4:6–8; 2 Cor. 5:19 c 2 Cor. 5:21 d Rom. 4:6, 11; Rom. 5:19 e Gal. 2:16; Phil. 3:9

34. *What is adoption?*
Adoption is an act of God's free grace,[a] whereby we are received into the number, and have a right to all the privileges, of the sons of God.[b]

a 1 John 3:1 b John 1:12; Rom. 8:17

35. *What is sanctification?*
Sanctification is the work of God's free grace,[a] whereby we are renewed in the whole man after the image of God,[b] and are enabled more and more to die unto sin, and live unto righteousness.[c]

a Ezek. 36:27; Phil. 2:13; 2 Thess. 2:13 b 2 Cor. 5:17; Eph. 4:23–24; 1 Thess. 5:23 c Ezek. 36:25–27; Rom. 6:4, 6, 12–14; 2 Cor. 7:1; 1 Pet. 2:24

36. *What are the benefits which in this life do accompany or flow from justification, adoption, and sanctification?*
The benefits which in this life do accompany or flow from justification, adoption, and sanctification, are, assurance of God's

love,[a] peace of conscience,[b] joy in the Holy Ghost,[c] increase of grace,[d] and perseverance therein to the end.[e]

a Rom. 5:5 b Rom. 5:1 c Rom. 14:17 d 2 Pet. 3:18 e Phil. 1:6; 1 Pet. 1:5

37. What benefits do believers receive from Christ at death?
The souls of believers are at their death made perfect in holiness,[a] and do immediately pass into glory;[b] and their bodies, being still united to Christ,[c] do rest in their graves, till the resurrection.[d]

a Heb. 12:23 b Luke 23:43; 2 Cor. 5:6, 8; Phil. 1:23 c 1 Thess. 4:14 d Dan. 12:2; John 5:28–29; Acts 24:15

38. What benefits do believers receive from Christ at the resurrection?
At the resurrection, believers, being raised up in glory,[a] shall be openly acknowledged and acquitted in the day of judgment,[b] and made perfectly blessed in the full enjoying of God[c] to all eternity.[d]

a 1 Cor. 15:42–43 b Matt. 25:33–34, 46 c Rom. 8:29; 1 John 3:2 d Ps. 16:11; 1 Thess. 4:17

39. What is the duty which God requireth of man?
The duty which God requireth of man, is obedience to his revealed will.[a]

a Deut. 29:29; Mic. 6:8; 1 John 5:2–3

40. What did God at first reveal to man for the rule of his obedience?
The rule which God at first revealed to man for his obedience, was the moral law.[a]

a Rom. 2:14–15; Rom. 10:5

41. *Wherein is the moral law summarily comprehended?*

The moral law is summarily comprehended in the Ten Commandments.[a]

a Deut. 4:13; Matt. 19:17–19

42. *What is the sum of the Ten Commandments?*

The sum of the Ten Commandments is, to love the Lord our God with all our heart, with all our soul, with all our strength, and with all our mind; and our neighbor as ourselves.[a]

a Matt. 22:37–40

43. *What is the preface to the Ten Commandments?*

The preface to the Ten Commandments is in these words, *I am the* Lord *thy God, which have brought thee out of the land of Egypt, out of the house of bondage.*[a]

a Ex. 20:2; Deut. 5:6

44. *What doth the preface to the Ten Commandments teach us?*

The preface to the Ten Commandments teacheth us, that because God is the Lord, and our God, and Redeemer, therefore we are bound to keep all his commandments.[a]

a Luke 1:74–75; 1 Pet. 1:14–19

45. *Which is the first commandment?*

The first commandment is, *Thou shalt have no other gods before me.*[a]

a Ex. 20:3; Deut. 5:7

46. *What is required in the first commandment?*
The first commandment requireth us to know and acknowledge God to be the only true God, and our God; and to worship and glorify him accordingly.[a]

a 1 Chron. 28:9; Isa. 45:20–25; Matt. 4:10

47. *What is forbidden in the first commandment?*
The first commandment forbiddeth the denying,[a] or not worshiping and glorifying, the true God as God,[b] and our God;[c] and the giving of that worship and glory to any other, which is due to him alone.[d]

a Ps. 14:1   b Rom. 1:20–21   c Ps. 81:10–11   d Ezek. 8:16–18; Rom. 1:25

48. *What are we specially taught by these words, before me, in the first commandment?*
These words, *before me,* in the first commandment teach us, that God, who seeth all things, taketh notice of, and is much displeased with, the sin of having any other God.[a]

a Deut. 30:17–18; Ps. 44:20–21; Ezek. 8:12

49. *Which is the second commandment?*
The second commandment is, *Thou shalt not make unto thee any graven image, or any likeness of anything that is in heaven above, or that is in the earth beneath, or that is in the water under the earth: thou shalt not bow down thyself to them, nor serve them: for I the* Lord *thy God am a jealous God, visiting the iniquity of the fathers upon the children unto the third and fourth generation of them that hate me; and shewing mercy unto thousands of them that love me, and keep my commandments.*[a]

a Ex. 20:4–6; Deut. 5:8–10

50.   *What is required in the second commandment?*
The second commandment requireth the receiving, observing, and keeping pure and entire, all such religious worship and ordinances as God hath appointed in his Word.[a]

a Deut. 12:32; Matt. 28:20

51.   *What is forbidden in the second commandment?*
The second commandment forbiddeth the worshiping of God by images,[a] or any other way not appointed in his Word.[b]

a Deut. 4:15–19; Rom. 1:22–23 b Lev. 10:1–2; Jer. 19:4–5; Col. 2:18–23

52.   *What are the reasons annexed to the second commandment?*
The reasons annexed to the second commandment are, God's sovereignty over us,[a] his propriety in us,[b] and the zeal he hath to his own worship.[c]

a Ps. 95:2–3, 6–7; Ps. 96:9–10 b Ex. 19:5; Ps. 45:11; Isa. 54:5 c Ex. 34:14; 1 Cor. 10:22

53.   *Which is the third commandment?*
The third commandment is, *Thou shalt not take the name of the* Lord *thy God in vain: for the* Lord *will not hold him guiltless that taketh his name in vain.*[a]

a Ex. 20:7; Deut. 5:11

54.   *What is required in the third commandment?*
The third commandment requireth the holy and reverent use of God's names, titles,[a] attributes,[b] ordinances,[c] Word,[d] and works.[e]

a Deut. 10:20; Ps. 29:2; Matt. 6:9 b 1 Chron. 29:10–13; Rev. 15:3–4 c Acts 2:42; 1 Cor. 11:27–28 d Ps. 138:2; Rev. 22:18–19 e Ps. 107:21–22; Rev. 4:11

55. *What is forbidden in the third commandment?*

The third commandment forbiddeth all profaning or abusing of anything whereby God maketh himself known.[a]

a Lev. 19:12; Matt. 5:33–37; James 5:12

56. *What is the reason annexed to the third commandment?*

The reason annexed to the third commandment is, that however the breakers of this commandment may escape punishment from men, yet the Lord our God will not suffer them to escape his righteous judgment.[a]

a Deut. 28:58–59; 1 Sam. 3:13; 1 Sam. 4:11

57. *Which is the fourth commandment?*

The fourth commandment is, *Remember the sabbath day, to keep it holy. Six days shalt thou labour, and do all thy work: but the seventh day is the sabbath of the LORD thy God: in it thou shalt not do any work, thou, nor thy son, nor thy daughter, thy manservant, nor thy maidservant, nor thy cattle, nor thy stranger that is within thy gates: for in six days the LORD made heaven and earth, the sea, and all that in them is, and rested the seventh day: wherefore the LORD blessed the sabbath day, and hallowed it.*[a]

a Ex. 20:8–11; Deut. 5:12–15

58. *What is required in the fourth commandment?*

The fourth commandment requireth the keeping holy to God such set times as he hath appointed in his Word; expressly one whole day in seven, to be a holy Sabbath to himself.[a]

a Ex. 31:13, 16–17

59. *Which day of the seven hath God appointed to be the weekly Sabbath?*

From the beginning of the world to the resurrection of Christ, God appointed the seventh day of the week to be the weekly

Sabbath;[a] and the first day of the week ever since, to continue to the end of the world, which is the Christian Sabbath.[b]

a Gen. 2:2–3; Ex. 20:11 *b* Mark 2:27–28; Acts 20:7; 1 Cor. 16:2; Rev. 1:10

60. *How is the Sabbath to be sanctified?*
The Sabbath is to be sanctified by a holy resting all that day, even from such worldly employments and recreations as are lawful on other days;[a] and spending the whole time in the public and private exercises of God's worship,[b] except so much as is to be taken up in the works of necessity and mercy.[c]

a Ex. 20:10; Neh. 13:15–22; Isa. 58:13–14 *b* Ex. 20:8; Lev. 23:3; Luke 4:16; Acts 20:7
c Matt. 12:1–13

61. *What is forbidden in the fourth commandment?*
The fourth commandment forbiddeth the omission, or careless performance, of the duties required, and the profaning the day by idleness, or doing that which is in itself sinful, or by unnecessary thoughts, words, or works, about our worldly employments or recreations.[a]

a Neh. 13:15–22; Isa. 58:13–14; Amos 8:4–6

62. *What are the reasons annexed to the fourth commandment?*
The reasons annexed to the fourth commandment are, God's allowing us six days of the week for our own employments,[a] his challenging a special propriety in the seventh, his own example, and his blessing the Sabbath day.[b]

a Ex. 20:9; Ex. 31:15; Lev. 23:3 *b* Gen. 2:2–3; Ex. 20:11; Ex. 31:17

63. Which is the fifth commandment?

The fifth commandment is, *Honour thy father and thy mother: that thy days may be long upon the land which the* LORD *thy God giveth thee.*[a]

a Ex. 20:12; Deut. 5:16

64. What is required in the fifth commandment?

The fifth commandment requireth the preserving the honor, and performing the duties, belonging to everyone in their several places and relations, as superiors, inferiors, or equals.[a]

a Rom. 13:1, 7; Eph. 5:21–22, 24; Eph. 6:1, 4–5, 9; 1 Pet. 2:17

65. What is forbidden in the fifth commandment?

The fifth commandment forbiddeth the neglecting of, or doing anything against, the honor and duty which belongeth to everyone in their several places and relations.[a]

a Matt. 15:4–6; Rom. 13:8

66. What is the reason annexed to the fifth commandment?

The reason annexed to the fifth commandment is, a promise of long life and prosperity (as far as it shall serve for God's glory and their own good) to all such as keep this commandment.[a]

a Ex. 20:12; Deut. 5:16; Eph. 6:2–3

67. Which is the sixth commandment?

The sixth commandment is, *Thou shalt not kill.*[a]

a Ex. 20:13; Deut. 5:17

68. What is required in the sixth commandment?

The sixth commandment requireth all lawful endeavors to preserve our own life, and the life of others.[a]

a Eph. 5:28–29

69. *What is forbidden in the sixth commandment?*

The sixth commandment forbiddeth the taking away of our own life, or the life of our neighbor unjustly, or whatsoever tendeth thereunto.[a]

a Gen. 9:6; Matt. 5:22; 1 John 3:15

70. *Which is the seventh commandment?*

The seventh commandment is, *Thou shalt not commit adultery.*[a]

a Ex. 20:14; Deut. 5:18

71. *What is required in the seventh commandment?*

The seventh commandment requireth the preservation of our own and our neighbor's chastity, in heart, speech, and behavior.[a]

a 1 Cor. 7:2–3, 5; 1 Thess. 4:3–5

72. *What is forbidden in the seventh commandment?*

The seventh commandment forbiddeth all unchaste thoughts, words, and actions.[a]

a Matt. 5:28; Eph. 5:3–4

73. *Which is the eighth commandment?*

The eighth commandment is, *Thou shalt not steal.*[a]

a Ex. 20:15; Deut. 5:19

74. *What is required in the eighth commandment?*

The eighth commandment requireth the lawful procuring and furthering the wealth and outward estate of ourselves and others.[a]

a Lev. 25:35; Eph. 4:28b; Phil. 2:4

75. *What is forbidden in the eighth commandment?*
The eighth commandment forbiddeth whatsoever doth, or may, unjustly hinder our own, or our neighbor's, wealth or outward estate.[a]

a Prov. 28:19–20, 22, 24; Eph. 4:28a; 2 Thess. 3:10; 1 Tim. 5:8

76. *Which is the ninth commandment?*
The ninth commandment is, *Thou shalt not bear false witness against thy neighbour.*[a]

a Ex. 20:16; Deut. 5:20

77. *What is required in the ninth commandment?*
The ninth commandment requireth the maintaining and promoting of truth between man and man, and of our own and our neighbor's good name,[a] especially in witness bearing.[b]

a Zech. 8:16; Acts 25:10; 3 John 12 b Prov. 14:5, 25

78. *What is forbidden in the ninth commandment?*
The ninth commandment forbiddeth whatsoever is prejudicial to truth, or injurious to our own, or our neighbor's, good name.[a]

a Lev. 19:16; Ps. 15:3; Prov. 6:16–19; Luke 3:14

79. *Which is the tenth commandment?*
The tenth commandment is, *Thou shalt not covet thy neighbour's house, thou shalt not covet thy neighbour's wife, nor his manservant, nor his maidservant, nor his ox, nor his ass, nor anything that is thy neighbour's.*[a]

a Ex. 20:17; Deut. 5:21

80. *What is required in the tenth commandment?*

The tenth commandment requireth full contentment with our own condition,[a] with a right and charitable frame of spirit toward our neighbor, and all that is his.[b]

a Ps. 34:1; Phil. 4:11; I Tim. 6:6; Heb. 13:5 *b* Luke 15:6, 9, 11–32; Rom. 12:15; Phil. 2:4

81. *What is forbidden in the tenth commandment?*

The tenth commandment forbiddeth all discontentment with our own estate,[a] envying or grieving at the good of our neighbor, and all inordinate motions and affections to anything that is his.[b]

a I Cor. 10:10; James 3:14–16 *b* Gal. 5:26; Col. 3:5

82. *Is any man able perfectly to keep the commandments of God?*

No mere man, since the fall, is able in this life perfectly to keep the commandments of God, but doth daily break them in thought, word, and deed.[a]

a Gen. 8:21; Rom. 3:9–11, 23

83. *Are all transgressions of the law equally heinous?*

Some sins in themselves, and by reason of several aggravations, are more heinous in the sight of God than others.[a]

a Ezek. 8:6, 13, 15; Matt. 11:20–24; John 19:11

84. *What doth every sin deserve?*

Every sin deserveth God's wrath and curse, both in this life, and that which is to come.[a]

a Matt. 25:41; Gal. 3:10; Eph. 5:6; James 2:10

85. *What doth God require of us, that we may escape his wrath and curse,*
due to us for sin?

To escape the wrath and curse of God, due to us for sin, God requireth of us faith in Jesus Christ, repentance unto life,[a] with the diligent use of all the outward means whereby Christ communicateth to us the benefits of redemption.[b]

a Mark 1:15; Acts 20:21 b Acts 2:38; 1 Cor. 11:24–25; Col. 3:16

86. *What is faith in Jesus Christ?*

Faith in Jesus Christ is a saving grace,[a] whereby we receive and rest upon him alone for salvation, as he is offered to us in the gospel.[b]

a Eph. 2:8–9; Rom. 4:16 b John 20:30–31; Gal. 2:15–16; Phil. 3:3–11

87. *What is repentance unto life?*

Repentance unto life is a saving grace,[a] whereby a sinner, out of a true sense of his sin, and apprehension of the mercy of God in Christ,[b] doth, with grief and hatred of his sin, turn from it unto God,[c] with full purpose of, and endeavor after, new obedience.[d]

a Acts 11:18; 2 Tim. 2:25 b Ps. 51:1–4; Joel 2:13; Luke 15:7, 10; Acts 2:37 c Jer. 31:18–19; Luke 1:16–17; 1 Thess. 1:9 d 2 Chron. 7:14; Ps. 119:57–64; Matt. 3:8; 2 Cor. 7:10

88. *What are the outward and ordinary means whereby Christ communicateth*
to us the benefits of redemption?

The outward and ordinary means whereby Christ communicateth to us the benefits of redemption are, his ordinances, especially the Word, sacraments, and prayer; all which are made effectual to the elect for salvation.[a]

a Matt. 28:18–20; Acts 2:41–42

89. *How is the Word made effectual to salvation?*

The Spirit of God maketh the reading, but especially the preaching, of the Word, an effectual means of convincing and converting sinners, and of building them up in holiness and comfort, through faith, unto salvation.[a]

a Neh. 8:8–9; Acts 20:32; Rom. 10:14–17; 2 Tim. 3:15–17

90. *How is the Word to be read and heard, that it may become effectual to salvation?*

That the Word may become effectual to salvation, we must attend thereunto with diligence, preparation, and prayer;[a] receive it with faith and love, lay it up in our hearts, and practice it in our lives.[b]

a Deut. 6:16–18; Ps. 119:18; 1 Pet. 2:1–2 b Ps. 119:11; 2 Thess. 2:10; Heb. 4:2; James 1:22–25

91. *How do the sacraments become effectual means of salvation?*

The sacraments become effectual means of salvation, not from any virtue in them, or in him that doth administer them; but only by the blessing of Christ, and the working of his Spirit in them that by faith receive them.[a]

a 1 Cor. 3:7; 1 Cor. 1:12–17

92. *What is a sacrament?*

A sacrament is a holy ordinance instituted by Christ;[a] wherein, by sensible signs, Christ, and the benefits of the new covenant, are represented, sealed, and applied to believers.[b]

a Matt. 28:19; Matt. 26:26–28; Mark 14:22–25; Luke 22:19–20; 1 Cor. 1:22–26 b Gal. 3:27; 1 Cor. 10:16–17

93. *Which are the sacraments of the New Testament?*

The sacraments of the New Testament are, baptism,[a] and the Lord's Supper.[b]

a Matt. 28:19 b 1 Cor. 11:23–26

94. *What is baptism?*

Baptism is a sacrament, wherein the washing with water in the name of the Father, and of the Son, and of the Holy Ghost,[a] doth signify and seal our ingrafting into Christ, and partaking of the benefits of the covenant of grace, and our engagement to be the Lord's.[b]

a Matt. 28:19 b Acts 2:38–42; Acts 22:16; Rom. 6:3–4; Gal. 3:26–27; 1 Pet. 3:21

95. *To whom is baptism to be administered?*

Baptism is not to be administered to any that are out of the visible church, till they profess their faith in Christ, and obedience to him;[a] but the infants of such as are members of the visible church are to be baptized.[b]

a Acts 2:41; Acts 8:12, 36, 38; Acts 18:8 b Gen. 17:7, 9–11; Acts 2:38–39; Acts 16:32–33; Col. 2:11–12

96. *What is the Lord's Supper?*

The Lord's Supper is a sacrament, wherein, by giving and receiving bread and wine, according to Christ's appointment, his death is showed forth;[a] and the worthy receivers are, not after a corporal and carnal manner, but by faith, made partakers of his body and blood, with all his benefits, to their spiritual nourishment, and growth in grace.[b]

a Luke 22:19–20; 1 Cor. 11:23–26 b 1 Cor. 10:16–17

97. *What is required for the worthy receiving of the Lord's Supper?*

It is required of them that would worthily partake of the Lord's Supper, that they examine themselves of their knowledge to discern the Lord's body, of their faith to feed upon him, of their repentance, love, and new obedience; lest, coming unworthily, they eat and drink judgment to themselves.[a]

a 1 Cor. 11:27–32

98. *What is prayer?*

Prayer is an offering up of our desires unto God,[a] for things agreeable to his will,[b] in the name of Christ,[c] with confession of our sins,[d] and thankful acknowledgment of his mercies.[e]

a Ps. 10:17; Ps. 62:8; Matt. 7:7–8 b 1 John 5:14 c John 16:23–24 d Ps. 32:5–6; Dan. 9:4–19; 1 John 1:9 e Ps. 103:1–5; Ps. 136:1–26; Phil. 4:6

99. *What rule hath God given for our direction in prayer?*

The whole Word of God is of use to direct us in prayer;[a] but the special rule of direction is that form of prayer which Christ taught his disciples, commonly called the Lord's Prayer.[b]

a 1 John 5:14 b Matt. 6:9–13

100. *What doth the preface of the Lord's Prayer teach us?*

The preface of the Lord's Prayer, which is, *Our Father which art in heaven,* teacheth us to draw near to God with all holy reverence[a] and confidence,[b] as children to a father,[c] able and ready to help us;[d] and that we should pray with and for others.[e]

a Ps. 95:6 b Eph. 3:12 c Matt. 7:9–11; Luke 11:11–13; Rom. 8:15 d Eph. 3:20 e Eph. 6:18; 1 Tim. 2:1–2

101. *What do we pray for in the first petition?*

In the first petition, which is, *Hallowed be thy name,* we pray that God would enable us, and others, to glorify him in all that whereby he maketh himself known;[a] and that he would dispose all things to his own glory.[b]

a Ps. 67:1–3; Ps. 99:3; Ps. 100:3–4 b Rom. 11:33–36; Rev. 4:11

102. *What do we pray for in the second petition?*

In the second petition, which is, *Thy kingdom come,* we pray that Satan's kingdom may be destroyed;[a] and that the kingdom of grace may be advanced,[b] ourselves and others brought into it, and kept in it;[c] and that the kingdom of glory may be hastened.[d]

a Matt. 12:25–28; Rom. 16:20; 1 John 3:8 b Ps. 72:8–11; Matt. 24:14; 1 Cor. 15:24–25 c Ps. 119:5; Luke 22:32; 2 Thess. 3:1–5 d Rev. 22:20

103. *What do we pray for in the third petition?*

In the third petition, which is, *Thy will be done in earth, as it is in heaven,* we pray that God, by his grace, would make us able and willing to know, obey, and submit to his will in all things,[a] as the angels do in heaven.[b]

a Ps. 19:14; Ps. 119:1–176; 1 Thess. 5:23; Heb. 13:20–21 b Ps. 103:20–21; Heb. 1:14

104. *What do we pray for in the fourth petition?*

In the fourth petition, which is, *Give us this day our daily bread,* we pray that of God's free gift we may receive a competent portion of the good things of this life, and enjoy his blessing with them.[a]

a Prov. 30:8–9; Matt. 6:31–34; Phil. 4:11, 19; 1 Tim. 6:6–8

105. *What do we pray for in the fifth petition?*

In the fifth petition, which is, *And forgive us our debts, as we forgive our debtors*, we pray that God, for Christ's sake, would freely pardon all our sins;[a] which we are the rather encouraged to ask, because by his grace we are enabled from the heart to forgive others.[b]

a Ps. 51:1–2, 7, 9; Dan. 9:17–19; 1 John 1:7 b Matt. 18:21–35; Eph. 4:32; Col. 3:13

106. *What do we pray for in the sixth petition?*

In the sixth petition, which is, *And lead us not into temptation, but deliver us from evil*, we pray that God would either keep us from being tempted to sin,[a] or support and deliver us when we are tempted.[b]

a Ps. 19:13; Matt. 26:41; John 17:15 b Luke 22:31–32; 1 Cor. 10:13; 2 Cor. 12:7–9; Heb. 2:18

107. *What doth the conclusion of the Lord's Prayer teach us?*

The conclusion of the Lord's Prayer, which is, *For thine is the kingdom, and the power, and the glory, for ever. Amen*, teacheth us to take our encouragement in prayer from God only,[a] and in our prayers to praise him, ascribing kingdom, power, and glory to him;[b] and, in testimony of our desire, and assurance to be heard, we say, *Amen*.[c]

a Dan. 9:4, 7–9, 16–19; Luke 18:1, 7–8 b 1 Chron. 29:10–13; 1 Tim. 1:17; Rev. 5:11–13 c 1 Cor. 14:16; Rev. 22:20

GENERAL INDEX

church
  authority of, 41, 68–75, 123
  discipline of, 102, 104, 162, 232–33,
    317
  government of, 103
  marks of, 38, 102–3
  members of, 101, 281–82
  officers of, 103–4
  visibleness of, 123, 224–25, 278–82
Church of England, 113
circumcision, 105, 106–7, 196, 312, 346
civil government, 29, 41–42, 68–70,
    109–10, 131, 182, 221–25, 233n6,
    276–77, 404–5
comfort, 291, 430
common grace, 164, 261. *See also* nature, light of
communion, 356, 361, 362
communion of saints, 226–27, 282–83,
    306
confession, 39, 56–57
Confirmation, 125
Congregationalists, 181, 237–38
conscience, 40, 41, 59, 71–73, 215–16,
    234, 267, 271–72
consecration, 130–31
contentment, 388–89, 428
contingency, 188, 189, 192, 244, 247
conversion, 158–59, 165, 200, 318
Coptic churches, 25
corruption, 54, 90, 155, 193, 195, 205,
    250, 260, 293
Council of Chalcedon, 25
Council of Ephesus, 25
Council of Nicaea, 15
Council of Trent, 113
councils, 123–24, 233–34
covenant, 143, 195–97, 250–51
covenant of grace, 196–97, 206, 261,
    262, 345–46, 353, 394
covenant of works, 196, 213–14, 268,
    269–70, 344
Cranmer, Thomas, 113
creation, 87–88, 191–92, 246–47, 270,
    298, 340–41, 412–13

Creator-creature distinction, 195,
    243–44
credo, 7
Cusanus, Nicolaus, 50
Cyprian, 52

deacons, 56, 103, 280
death, 234–35, 287, 362, 419
descent into hell, 13, 22, 36, 116, 297,
    303, 350
devils, 87–88
Diet of Spires, 33
divorce, 223–24, 384
Donatists, 38
doubts, 171, 398
Dutch Reformed, 9

Eastern Orthodox Church, 25, 62, 114
ecclesiastical power, 41, 68–75
ecumenicity, 9, 86
effectual calling, 201–2, 256–57, 355–56,
    417–18
eighth commandment, 320, 325–26,
    384–86, 426–27
elders, 103–4, 280
election, 91, 121–22, 133–34, 137–41,
    201–2, 210, 266, 415
Elizabeth I (Queen), 113, 181
employments, 219, 275, 344, 376, 377,
    424
equals, 381, 425
essence, 15, 35, 86, 87, 149, 238, 244
eternal life, 261, 307
Eucharist, 53–54
Eunomians, 35
exaltation, 11, 348, 351, 416, 417
excommunication, 68, 76, 104, 128, 233
Extreme Unction, 125

faith
  as gift, 150, 160, 429
  as justifying, 203, 258, 357–58
  righteousness of, 44–45, 95–96, 308
  as saving, 205–6, 260–61, 391

sources of, 136–37, 309
as trust, 46, 296
fall, 89–90, 155, 163, 194–95, 249–50, 255, 293, 342–43, 414
false accusations, 177–79
false testimony, 326, 386–88, 427
fasting, 218, 371–72
fifth commandment, 320, 324, 378–82, 425
first commandment, 319, 321, 369–71, 420–21
First Council of Constantinople, 15
"five points of Calvinism," 133
foreseen faith, 134, 139, 146
forgiveness, 307, 331–32, 406, 434
fornication, 224, 384
fourth commandment, 319–20, 323, 375–78, 423–24
free will, 42–43, 89–90, 119, 163–64, 167, 200–201, 255–56
fruit, 37, 120, 147, 208, 263. *See also* good works
fulfillment, 98, 151

Gelasius I (Pope), 50
Gerson, Jean, 59, 67
God
    attributes of, 411
    eternal decree of, 137, 151, 188–91, 203, 244–46, 339–40, 412
    as Father, 329
    glory of, 188–89
    good pleasure of, 139, 148
    knowledge of, 79
    love of, 136
    name of, 322–23, 373–75, 404, 422
    sovereignty of, 408, 422
    as unchangeable, 140
    whole counsel of, 241
Godhead, 115, 189, 197, 227, 338, 339, 409, 412
godliness, 62, 128, 171, 176, 177
golden chain of salvation, 144–45
good works, 37–38, 40, 44–47, 66, 97–98, 120, 207–9, 263–65, 308–9, 317, 318

gospel
    call of, 157–58
    grace of, 214, 270–71
    preaching of, 102, 136, 150, 172, 316
    revelation of, 295–96
    saving power of, 157, 353–54
grace, 45, 161, 167, 214
Greek language, 25, 119, 187, 242
Gregory I (Pope), 55, 62

hardening of heart, 193, 248–49
Hebrew language, 187, 242
Heidelberg Catechism, 134, 289–333
hell
    descent into, 13, 22, 36, 116, 297, 303, 350
    punishment of, 235, 287, 344, 362, 363, 415
heresy, 48, 85–86, 223
holiness, 139, 146, 163, 191, 204, 308
holy days, 41, 44, 58, 61, 62, 70, 71, 73, 74
Holy Spirit
    conception by, 301
    and conversion, 159
    divinity of, 87, 116, 306
    illumination of, 186, 187, 241
    and prayer, 402
    procession of, 189
    sin against, 121, 169, 175, 207, 210
homilies, 129–30
human nature, 36, 47, 92, 93, 155, 198, 252, 295, 301, 304, 347
human responsibility, 150, 158
humiliation, 11, 214, 269, 274, 348, 349, 350, 416
humility, 66, 88, 109, 142
hypocrites, 38, 102, 111, 173, 177, 211, 315, 316, 374

idleness, 130, 377, 384, 386, 424
idolatry, 321, 369–70, 404
image of God, 84–85, 163, 191, 292
images, 321–22, 372–73, 422
immersion, 284
implicit faith, 215, 272
incarnation, 19, 22, 92, 199, 253, 347, 415

indwelling sin, 168
inferiors, 379–80, 425
intercession, 352
invisible church, 224, 278, 355, 356, 361, 362, 364
Irenaeus, 62
Irish Articles, 182
Islam, 30, 31, 35, 48, 85, 177

Jerome, 50
Jesus Christ
  ascension of, 304, 351–52
  blood of, 108, 310–11, 331, 397
  death of, 55, 134, 149, 150–51, 154, 203, 302–3, 350
  deity of, 19, 36, 86
  exaltation of, 348, 351, 416, 417
  as head of the church, 279
  holiness of, 308
  humiliation of, 348, 349–50, 416–17
  as mediator, 98–100, 197–200, 251–55, 295, 346
  merit of, 57, 58, 71, 95, 98, 119, 145, 152, 153, 170, 210, 266
  obedience of, 198–99, 253, 257–58
  resurrection of, 303–4, 351
  return of, 42, 110–12, 305, 353
  sacrifice of, 128, 230
  salvation in, 122–23, 299
  satisfaction of, 149
  two natures of, 93, 198–99, 254, 304, 347–48
  as without sin, 121
  as Word of God, 115
John Chrysostom, 56, 57
Judaism, 55, 85, 404
Judas Iscariot, 109
judgment, 42, 110–12, 209, 210, 235–36, 238, 287–88, 305, 363–64
judicial laws, 213, 269
justice, 94, 148–49, 191, 294, 357
justification, 8–9, 37, 55, 96, 119, 174, 202–4, 257–59, 261, 356–58, 359, 418

keys of the kingdom, 316–17
kingdom of God, 330, 404–5, 433, 434

kingly office, 100, 197, 221, 232, 251, 254, 255, 260, 276, 332, 348, 349, 416

language, 187, 242
last judgment, 110–12, 235–36, 287–88, 363–64
Latin, 7, 19, 32, 53, 114
law
  fulfillment of, 98
  inadequacy of, 156
  of nature, 218, 274, 281
  as moral, 118, 212–14, 268–70, 365–66, 419
  requirements of, 292, 293
  in Ten Commandments, 319–27, 420
Libertinism, 177
London Baptist Confession, 237–88
Lord's Prayer, 328–33, 336, 403–8, 432–34
Lord's Supper, 39, 49–50, 107–9, 125, 126–27, 230–32, 260–61, 274, 283, 284–86, 312–16, 396–400, 431–32
Lutherans, 8, 9, 29
Luther, Martin, 29

magistrate. See civil government
Mani, 86
Manichaeans, 35, 88, 177
manstealing, 385
Marcion, 86
marriage, 50–52, 63–64, 67, 125, 128, 223–24, 277–78, 383–84
Mass, 53–56, 128, 231, 285, 315
meats, distinction of, 58–62
Melanchthon, Philip, 29
memorization, 409
mercy, 94, 294
merit, 97, 145, 153, 208, 264
Methodists, 181
ministers, 124, 125–26, 130–31, 280–81
monastic vows, 46, 62–67, 221, 276
moral law, 212–14, 279, 365–66, 419–20
murder, 43, 320, 324–25

schism, 62, 75

Scripture
  authority of, 81–82, 185, 240–41
  interpretation of, 187, 242
  reading of, 218, 392, 430
  revelation of, 183, 239
  sufficiency of, 82–83, 116, 186, 241–42
  teaching of, 411
  as Word of God, 80, 337–38

second causes, 189, 192, 247

second commandment, 319, 321–22, 371–73, 421–22

Second Helvetic Confession, 182

self-assurance, 177–78

seventh commandment, 320, 325, 383–84, 426

Simon the Sorcerer, 109

sin
  author of, 43–44, 88, 142, 177, 189, 193
  definition of, 413–14
  forgiveness of, 307, 331–32, 434
  imputation of, 194–95, 249–50
  as indwelling, 168, 205
  punishment of, 428–29
  as serious, 168–69, 389–91
  state of, 343
  as unpardonable, 207
  of weakness, 167–68

sixth commandment, 320, 324–25, 382–83, 425–26

stealing, 384–86

Stoicism, 177

substance, 15, 17, 115, 116, 189, 197, 231, 286, 346, 409, 412

superiors, 376, 378–82, 425

superstition, 127, 131, 221, 231, 276, 286, 321, 372, 374

synods, 110n1, 182, 222n3, 233–34

temptations, 193, 210, 248–49, 342, 360, 407, 434

Ten Commandments, 156, 268, 319–27, 336, 366–89, 420–28

tenth commandment, 320, 327, 388–89, 427–28

theft, 325–26, 385

third commandment, 319, 322–23, 373–75, 422–23

Thirty-Nine Articles, 113–32, 182

Three Forms of Unity, 133

total depravity, 36, 90, 109, 164

total inability, 155–56, 255, 404

tradition, 60–61, 71–73, 129

transubstantiation, 231, 286, 314

Trinity, 21, 83–86, 115, 188–89, 243–44, 252, 297, 339

unbelief, 99, 136–37, 150

union with Christ, 266, 355, 356, 360, 396

unity, 9, 19, 21, 22, 32, 38, 101, 104, 115, 128, 189, 222n3

universal church, 13n1, 100–101, 278, 306

unregenerate, 164, 209, 211, 265, 266, 365, 366

Ursinus, Zacharias, 289

Valentinians, 35

visible church, 123, 125, 225, 228, 354, 395, 431

vows, 218, 219–21, 275–76, 371–72, 374

wars, 41, 48, 68, 131, 181, 221, 277, 383

Westminster Confession of Faith, 181–236, 237, 355

Westminster Larger Catechism, 355–408

Westminster Shorter Catechism, 409–34

Word of God, 80, 115, 162, 337, 392. *See also* Scripture

works of supererogation, 120

worship, 8, 216–19, 225, 226, 273–75, 372–73, 376, 422

SCRIPTURE INDEX